Other Books by Adriana Bardolino

Confessions of a Hippie, Always Searching for Love

Love and Redemption in the Tropics, Missing Gauguin

LOVE AND LOATHING IN THE ISLANDS

Searching for Gauguin

ADRIANA BARDOLINO

LOVE AND LOATHING IN THE ISLANDS
SEARCHING FOR GAUGUIN

iUniverse books may be ordered through booksellers or by contacting:

iUniverse
1663 Liberty Drive
Bloomington, IN 47403
www.iuniverse.com
844-349-9409

Because of the dynamic nature of the Internet, any web addresses or links contained in this book may have changed since publication and may no longer be valid. The views expressed in this work are solely those of the author and do not necessarily reflect the views of the publisher, and the publisher hereby disclaims any responsibility for them.

Any people depicted in stock imagery provided by Getty Images are models, and such images are being used for illustrative purposes only. Certain stock imagery © Getty Images.

ISBN: 978-1-6632-2824-6 (sc)
ISBN: 978-1-6632-2823-9 (e)

Library of Congress Control Number: 2022908810

Print information available on the last page.

iUniverse rev. date: 01/18/2024

Some people fall in love with a person forever
I fell in love with a place.

CONTENTS

Preface.. ix

Chapter 1   I Left My Heart on Maui 1
Chapter 2   Bois Froid 19
Chapter 3   Alice in Wonderland...38
Chapter 4   Escape from Babylon 58
Chapter 5   Not an Ordinary Life 75
Chapter 6   Stormy Weather...96
Chapter 7   Birds of a Feather 116
Chapter 8   Monkey Business... 134
Chapter 9   Mango Breath 150
Chapter 10   Girl on Fire.. 169
Chapter 11   Barking Dogs 185
Chapter 12   Hooked on You.. 204
Chapter 13   Poor Butterfly 226
Chapter 14   Two Peas in a Pod 246
Chapter 15   Hot Blooded.. 266
Chapter 16   Bad Case of Loving You... 284
Chapter 17   Blush like You Mean It... 303
Chapter 18   Hair Makes the Man 324
Chapter 19   The Madland.. 341
Chapter 20   Aloha Oe 360

PREFACE

never had a dream of being a starving artist in a tiny apartment in New York City. I was twenty-eight, and my goal was to make my art and work synonymous. I was also maneuvering my way through the second decade of the sexual revolution, which began in the sixties and continued into the seventies. After a few failed love affairs, I was looking for true love, hoping that such a thing really existed. I was seeking a relationship where my sense of "self" did not disappear into the mundane of everyday life. Along the way I realize I am addicted to romantic love, which I need like a drug to feel alive. I also discovered that even paradise has a loathsome underbelly.

A break in the harmony of my communal family, whom I had lived with during the late sixties and early seventies, forced me to search for a new home. We'd spent eight years traveling between New York and California until politics split our commune apart.

I experience renewed artistic inspiration in Hawaii and see a possible future path open before me. Romance is sparked when I meet a young artist, a New York transplant, who lives on the island. I fall in love with the island of Maui. I want to leave everything I know and everyone I love behind to pursue a life in Gauguin (in other words, art). Upon returning to the mainland after my vacation, I decide that Maui is where I want to live and vow to return to the island, until a tragic event thwarts my plan. When everything goes up in flames and turns to ashes, I seek therapy to release myself from a self-imposed bondage. My life begins to spin out of control like a roulette wheel, and I want to get off.

Upon leaving one's friends and family there is always apprehension, but for some, the need for a change in one's life, and well-being, supersedes everything else. We tend to romanticize our friends while apart, but when we are with them again, we are stuck in the character they see us as. My communal brothers and sisters, mentioned in my first book, *Confessions of a Hippie: Always Searching for Love*, remain an integral part of my story. Although I leave my hippie days behind, I maintain many of the spiritual beliefs, as well as the concept of free love (well, when it suits me).

I meet some crazy characters along my tropical journey, each one adding richness and beauty to my life. I almost miss the disco era completely, having been a hippie during its peak craze, but I catch the tail end when I meet a tall intriguing stranger. My life in paradise becomes a novel, and explodes in beauty and passion. What could possibly go wrong?

There are a series of journals I kept during the late sixties and seventies that my memoir is largely based on. They include so much detail of my life and experiences. I entered my thoughts and feelings in those notebooks in an effort to unravel the mysteries of life. My thoughts and emotions flow out in poems, drawings, and watercolors on the pages. I describe in detail the carnival ride that becomes my journey. I find that life is indeed complicated and sometimes poses difficult choices. I recorded excerpts from books I'd read in an attempt to define an experience that paralleled my own, perhaps in a way I couldn't express myself. I jotted down lyrics of songs to explain my feelings at a specific moment in time. Isn't that the wonder of music? How it prompts us to remember, with graphic detail, a certain person or event in our lives.

My memoir is written in the language and expressions my friends and I used at that time. I describe people the way I saw them and events the way I experienced them, which may not have been theirs. The names of the characters are all fictitious, as well as some of the places we inhabited. There are explicit sex scenes that were part of my story—well, they are part of life and love. Irish poet and playwright Oscar Wilde said, "Everything in the world is about sex, except sex. Sex is about power."

Writing my memoir has tossed me back into my past, reacquainting me with people I loved and memories, as well as times of great loss. I've always found people I'd loved hard to put aside. I think that once we love someone and share our lives, there is no forgetting. Even after their physical presence is gone from us, they remain part of our being. I hope you will enjoy my story and even have a few laughs along the way. Perhaps you will find something of yourself in me. It was a crazy but wonderful time.

As the plane was circling the airport I stared out the window at a large mountain. I could see fires burning below as we descended through the clouds. The airport was much less constructed than I expected, with an open-air terminal surrounded by fields of sugar cane as far as the eye could see. For a moment I felt uncertainty. Walking onto the runway the trade winds were so strong they almost knocked me over. The palm trees were swaying wildly, and I could see a rainbow in the distance. Then the sweet smell of the air enveloped me with an intoxicating sense of freedom, and I felt a thrill. It was like entering heaven.

ONE

I LEFT MY HEART ON MAUI

Millions upon millions of years ago, when the continents were already formed
and the principal feature of the earth had been decided, there existed, then
as now, one aspect of the world that dwarfed all others. It was a mighty
ocean, resting uneasily to the east of the largest continent, a restless, ever-
changing, gigantic body of water that would later be described as pacific.

—*James A. Michener,* **Hawaii**.

There I was on a tiny island in the middle of the Pacific Ocean. The
island was Maui, part of the Hawaiian chain, one of the remotest
places on earth. It was a beautiful spring day in 1975, and I was
looking forward to a month's vacation.

I walked up a dirt driveway to a small cottage in Haiku. It looked scanty compared to the Garden of Eden I had just left. I assumed someone was home because there were two cars in the driveway. I nervously knocked, wondering if I should have let my new friends leave me and drive away, but when I looked back, their jeep was already far down the road.

After a few minutes, a guy opened the door. I knew right away it was Loretta's ex-boyfriend, because he was just as she'd described him. He looked like a Greek Adonis with dark, curly hair and dark skin and eyes.

He said, "Yeah. What can I do for you?"

"You're Sammy, right? Samuel Cooper?"

"Yeah, that's me."

"I'm Adriana, Adriana Bardolino. I'm Loretta Perino's friend. Didn't she tell you I was coming?"

He glanced down at my backpack a little dumbfounded, maybe even a bit annoyed. "No, I haven't talked to her in months."

I was at a loss for words and stood there pondering my options.

"I guess you'd better come inside," he said, taking my backpack and tossing it on the floor.

His place was a one-room cottage, and I wondered where I would sleep. I noticed a woman standing in the kitchen area. She looked eerily like Loretta. She was cutting up avocados and tomatoes.

She looked up and asked, "Are you hungry? I was just preparing lunch."

"I haven't eaten since breakfast, so lunch sounds good to me," I replied.

Sammy said, "That's my girlfriend, Rain." He walked over to her, squeezed her around the waist, and gave her a peck on the cheek.

"So Loretta sent you here to find me, huh?" He shook his head, laughing. "How the hell is Loretta doing these days back in Brooklyn?"

"I came here directly from San Francisco, but I spoke to her a few weeks ago. She's fine. Look, I really feel uncomfortable and don't want to put you guys out."

"No worries. You're already here, so we'll make it work. As you can see there's not much room, but you can sleep over there," he said, pointing to a space on the floor in a corner of the cottage.

Rain rolled her eyes.

"So how'd you ever find me?" Sammy asked.

"Well, it's a crazy story, but I met a young couple on the plane who live in Haiku, and they took me home with them last night. We went to the

Haiku post office this morning and found out where you live. Loretta had given me your post office box number."

"You mean to tell me you got on a plane blindly and headed to the islands? Wow, that's brave."

Samuel Cooper was a good-looking guy with a heavy Brooklyn accent. He reminded me of Tony Curtis, who played a slave in the movie *Spartacus*. As he talked to Rain, I pictured Tony Curtis in that Roman bath washing the emperor. None of us said much during lunch, and I was hoping something would break the ice to make me feel less like an intruder.

The next day was another beautiful day, and I thought, *I could get used to this*. I woke early and sneaked out of the cottage to give Sammy and Rain privacy. There was a rainbow in the distance, so I figured it was raining somewhere on the horizon.

Sammy opened the door, walked over to me, and said, "I'm taking you to work with me today because Rain has some things she wants to do on her own."

"Where's work?"

"Lahaina. It's a small town, used to be the capitol of Hawaii when this was a monarchy. There are quaint shops, so you can roam around town while I'm working."

It was about an hour and a quarter drive, and we chatted all the way. Sammy asked if I'd heard about Bill Gates and Paul Allen, who owned a company called Microsoft. He said they invented something called a computer. It all sounded Greek to me.

The ocean glistened as I gazed out the window along a narrow two-lane road that wound its way over a mountain pass.

"We just drove over the Pali," Sammy said as we descended to sea level again.

I told him I had been living in San Francisco for the past year, but I needed a change. I explained the roller-coaster ride I was on between New York and California over the past eight years or so and was looking for a new place to break that pattern.

"Do you think you'll ever go back to New York?"

"I don't know, Sammy. I just don't know."

When we arrived in Lahaina, he drove down a side street on the back side of town and parked. We walked just a little way to an outside restaurant in a banana grove. It was really just a hut with some outside wooden picnic tables right on the dirt.

"So this is the place I manage," he said. "I started this place from scratch. There was nothing in the way of fresh, natural, organic food restaurants when I landed on the island. We serve mostly Mexican food, all fresh ingredients, and we make our own tortilla chips."

I looked up at the sign, which read La Tortilla Natural. He put me to work in the kitchen for a while, I guess to earn my keep. When I was done in the kitchen, I sat outside at one of the tables. Sammy brought me a burrito, and I tried the chips with fresh-made salsa. I sat there for a while watching people come and go, mostly young people with unkempt sun-bleached hair, wearing shorts and T-shirts, many barefoot.

Sammy was going to be busy all day, so I told him I would cruise around town for a few hours and would return before he closed the restaurant. I wandered through the sleepy side streets. I noticed quite a few mango trees, which I recognized from the summer I spent in Colombia, South America. The fruits were small and still green. There was a laid-back atmosphere, and I felt easy and serene. The peace and tranquility of the island gave me a feeling of safety.

When I reached the main drag, Front Street, it reminded me a lot of Provincetown in Cape Cod, Massachusetts. At the time I was not aware there was a direct link between Cape Cod and Lahaina from the old whaling days. I learned that in the early 1800s, King Kamehameha sent his son to school in Boston and visited there often.

I walked along the sidewalk parallel to the ocean. I smelled the sea air and felt the gentle trade winds. A couple of surfer dudes ran past me with their boards in tow. I stopped and leaned against the seawall to watch them for a while. They walked onto the beach and jumped in the water, paddled out a ways, and sat on their surfboards waiting for waves. I stayed there for quite a while watching them on their quest to ride the perfect wave.

Walking back to La Tortilla Natural, I passed an old, abandoned, walled-in prison. The gates in the high stone wall were open, so I wandered inside. There were crude holding cells, and I wondered what sort of offenses people were imprisoned for in those early days. I imagined Lahaina was a wild place a hundred years in the past, with all those whaling ships in the harbor. I figured there was a constant battle between the missionaries and the sailors who settled in the islands to bring Christianity to the native peoples, only to kill a large portion of the population with imported diseases.

On the ride back to the cottage, Sammy directed my attention to the kiawe bushes along the roadway. He informed me that the missionaries planted the thorny bushes so the islanders would learn to wear shoes. That gave me an unpleasant chill. *What a loathsome thing to do,* I thought.

At the cottage, I got the vibe that Rain wasn't happy with my presence, which made me uncomfortable. I felt foolish for showing up on Sammy's doorstep and wanted to wring Loretta's neck for telling me it was a great idea. This uncomfortable situation went on for days. I spent each day going into Lahaina with Sammy, wandering around town while he worked in the restaurant.

Sometimes I'd find a spot on the beach and lie in the sun watching the surfers. Hawaiian men were big and strong with cocoa skin, rough island features, and light eyes. Women surfed as well, and the Hawaiian *wahine* (women) were big girls, yet they were as graceful as a Gauguin painting. I got friendly with some local girls, and we talked for a while. They took me on a walk to the harbor to show me the sacred birthing stone used by ancient royalty to have their babies. It's called the Hauola Stone and is partially underwater. They also told me that Hawaiian queens were fat because it was considered a mark of wealth and beauty, and that they could have more than one husband. I laughed, thinking that my mother, being a big woman, would feel at home in the islands.

Some days I'd just wander in and out of the many shops along Front Street. Everyone was super friendly. One of the shop owners told me that most of the storefronts were around for more than a hundred years. The buildings were once all grog shops that served liquor and beer to the sailors who passed through town back then. She told me it got pretty wild during the winter whaling season. These seafaring men spent their days out on the ocean hunting whales and their nights in the grog shops looking for drink and women. I was thankful to hear that the Hawaiian Islands eventually became a whale sanctuary. Knowing it was whale season, I was hoping to catch sight of some.

~~~~~~

When I woke the next morning, Rain was doing yoga on the floor of the cottage. I watched her silently for a while. Then she sat up, closed her eyes, folded her legs, and began to meditate.

I thought, *Well that's a good sign!* I lay in my sleeping bag for quite a while, not wanting to disturb her. Afterward, she got up and walked into the kitchen area and made breakfast. It was nothing I wanted to eat, and by now I realized she was a vegetarian.

I went outside, and Sammy was already out there picking fruit off a papaya tree in their yard. That I could eat. I'd developed a liking for them in Colombia, South America.

"I'm going into Lahaina alone today. I have a lot to do in the restaurant and will probably be there late into the night. Besides, Rain wants to take you to a happening."

This surprised me since she didn't seem to have much use for me. It was the fourth day of my vacation. I was getting bored with the daily routine and was ready for something different.

Rain said, "There's a festival up on the crater today, and I thought you'd enjoy it."

"What kind of festival?" I asked, gazing at her eyebrows, which were not plucked.

"It's a Krishna festival. A holy man is visiting Maui, who will be speaking. There will be lots of music and food. It will be fun. Or you can hang out here at the cottage if you prefer."

"No, I'd love to go with you."

I thought, *Maybe she's warming up to me.*

After breakfast, Rain and I headed out driving up a winding road, way up on Haleakala Crater. As we ascended the volcano, the weather became cooler and less humid. I noticed an odor in the air I was familiar with, eucalyptus. These trees looked a little different than the ones I'd seen in California. Their bark was multicolored, but upon closer inspection, I noticed their branches had the same tiny blue acorns. Rain told me they were called rainbow eucalyptus and that perhaps their colors were due to the volcanic soil.

As we drove along, Rain continued talking about this and that, but I was fascinated with her natural eyebrows. Mexican artist Frida Kahlo came to mind.

About four thousand feet up the volcano, we began to see people walking along the road, mostly hippie types. We drove down a bumpy dirt road and parked. As we got closer to the festival I heard music: drums, sitars, guitars, and flutes. Women wore saris, men wore white turbans, and some had white symbols painted on their faces. It was a chaotic scene yet seemed peaceful in contrast. There were exotic foods, some of which I didn't care to sample, and everything reeked of curry.

Rain grabbed my hand and dragged me into a circle where women were dancing. Some were adorned with beautiful, flowing garments and large, intricate jewelry. I began dancing in the circle with the other women, and a feeling of joy and unity came over me. When we'd had enough, the men got up and replaced us dancing together, some holding their children in the air. When the drums and symbols got faster, the men were almost running. Then all became silent. The dancing stopped, and everyone hugged and chanted.

I sat at the foot of a large tree and rested my head against the bark. A woman sat near me nursing her baby. All became silent when the yogi began to speak. He was seated on a large Persian carpet with a few of his close followers. He didn't have a loud voice, but it had become so quiet that it was easy to hear his words. I listened intently to his sermon and understood his message. Occasionally, people clapped or asked him questions. This culminated in a group chant with music. People sang joyfully: "Hare Krishna, Hare Krishna, Krishna Krishna, Hare Hare … Hare Rama, Hare Rama, Rama, Rama, Hare, Hare …"

It was late afternoon when Rain said, "Let's go before the crowds start leaving."

"Okay. Whenever you want to leave is fine with me."

On the drive back down the mountain, Rain asked, "Have you met Hank yet?"

I stared at her blankly.

"Sammy's brother, Harvey. Everyone calls him Hank," she said.

"I didn't even know Sammy had a brother."

"He doesn't hang out with us much, likes to do his own thing. I think you'll like him. He's an artist and a musician. He lives in Kahului."

I smiled and said, "I look forward to meeting him."

That evening we were sitting at the counter in the kitchen area of the cottage.

Sammy said, "My brother is playing at a café in Wailuku with some friends tonight. We're going, and you're coming with us."

Since that would get me out of the cottage for a change of scenery, I was all for it. Besides, it sounded as if I had no choice in the matter.

When we arrived at the café, people sat around drinking coffee and talking. I didn't notice a bar. We sat at a table and ordered coffee and desserts to share. I wondered which of the musicians was Hank. We got to talking and laughing and I didn't even notice that the music had stopped.

A guy walked to our table, looked straight at me, and held out his hand. "I'm Harvey Cooper, Sammy's brother, but everyone calls me Hank. My brother told me all about you."

I thought, *That doesn't sound good,* and wondered what Sammy told him. I accepted his hand, smiled, and said, "I'm Adriana Bardolino"

"My brother asked me to show you around the island since he's busy with the restaurant."

"I'd really like that, Hank."

"Why don't I pick you up at Sammy's tomorrow, and we'll make a day of it."

"Sounds good. I'll be waiting for you to come by."

"I have a late set tonight, but we'll talk more tomorrow." With that remark he walked away.

Harvey Cooper, aka Hank, was nothing like Sammy, except for the Brooklyn accent. He had wavy dirty blond hair and soft blue eyes.

On the drive back to the cottage, I got the feeling Sammy and Rain had had enough of me and were pawning me off on Hank. I felt uneasy and had no idea what was in store for me.

~~~~~

The next morning, when Sammy went to work, Rain and I lay out on the grass in our bathing suits taking in the sun. As I listened to the myna birds chattering, my mind drifted off to a pleasant place. I was just about to say something when I heard a motor coming up the driveway. It was Hank Cooper in an old Jeep Wrangler.

He got out and walked over to us. "You ready to experience Maui?"

"It'll just take me a few minutes to throw some shorts on over my bathing suit," I answered.

He shot me a big smile as I ran inside.

Driving away from the cottage, the breeze scrambled my hair. I felt not a care in the world as I was living in the moment once again.

"Where are we going?"

"I'm taking you on the road to Hana."

"What's Hana?"

"It's what the real Hawaii is all about. You'll see," he said.

We drove for a long time on a narrow road filled with switchbacks that went over bridges and past waterfalls. In some places the road was only one lane and it was necessary to pull over to let oncoming vehicles pass. We stopped and walked through a bamboo forest with filtered light, jungle plants, and exotic flowers. Once in a while the road came out along the ocean. I made Hank stop the jeep quite a few times to take photographs. He was really laid-back and patient with me. He told me that he moved to Maui because of his brother, that they had a really tight bond. I mentioned that Loretta told me to look Sammy up, that he'd take care of me and show me around the island.

Hank laughed like hell at that remark. "How do you know Loretta?"

"She dated a good friend of mine for a while, Ross Grant."

"I know Ross; he's a funny guy. How's Loretta doing these days?"

"Honestly, I haven't seen her recently. We talk on the phone once in a while."

When we finally arrived in Hana, we parked and walked down to Black Sands Beach.

Hank said, "Let's see if we can find some puka shells."

He described them to me as being tiny white bead-like shells with a hole in the center. We strolled along the beach for a while and then sat in the sand.

"Maui's cool, but sometimes I miss New York," he said, his blue eyes squinting in the bright sun.

"Oh, believe me, I know that feeling really well. I've tried to live in California a few times over the past eight years, but as much as I like it, I just don't feel at home there."

"Still," he said, "I've been thinking about going back to New York."

I didn't answer. I knew exactly how he felt, and I didn't want to persuade him either way.

"Let's go. I want to take you to the Sacred Pools," he said.

Walking back to the jeep, Hank grabbed my hand and helped me over some rocks. I felt something when his hand touched mine. Our eyes met, and I felt a warm calm feeling wash over me. He let go of my hand, but the feeling lingered.

Oheo Gulch, also known as the Seven Sacred Pools, was a sight to behold. Waterfalls cascaded down the mountains from one rocky pool to another, eventually emptying into the ocean. The water rushed down with such force that the sound was deafening. The backdrop was tall mountains behind us, and the vast ocean was in front of us. People climbed all over the rocks and swam at each level. It was crowded, but we found an empty pool, stripped down to our bathing suits, and jumped in. The water was cool and refreshing, caressing me as I bobbed around enjoying the scenery. Someone dived off a bridge over one of the pools with a thunderous splash. I thought, *This is a place I could get used to.* I was hoping my vacation would never end, and I dreaded the thought of going back to California.

On the drive back from Hana, Hank and I talked easily with each other. Maybe it had something to do with his Brooklyn accent and my Bronx accent. We clicked and understood each other. Besides, sharing New York accents, we seemed to share similar life philosophies. I felt comfortable with Harvey Cooper and didn't want the day to end.

When we reached Sammy's cottage in Haiku, he said, "I'm just gonna drop you off and not come in. A friend is meeting me at my house in an hour."

I got out of the jeep a little disappointed and was walking away when Hank shouted after me, "I was wondering if you might want to come with me later to a friend's house. They're really nice people. Besides, I think you'd be much better off hanging out with me than here with Tweedledum and Tweedledee."

I laughed and said, "That sounds like fun."

We waved at each other as he drove off.

I yelled after him, "Thanks for today!"

Hank turned and smiled back at me.

Later that evening Hank came by to pick me up, only briefly chatting with Sammy and Rain. I sensed a strained dialogue between the brothers and wondered what that was about.

We drove to Wailuku along the Iao River and stopped at a small wooden house. A bunch of people were drinking Primo beer, a brand I'd never heard of, and eating strange snacks that resembled dry seaweed. We all sat around a table in the kitchen. I remember the kitchen windows were right on the river, and the sound of the rushing water drowned out our voices. People sang and played guitars, and one guy played a ukulele.

It was such a windy night, and for a moment, listening to the rushing water and the howling wind, I fantasized being on a ship out at sea. I felt at home among these people, even though they were Hank's friends. Hank told me I was connecting to the "aloha spirit."

When it was time to leave, we said our goodbyes and headed out the door. We climbed in the jeep, and Hank sat there motionless for a while looking up at the stars.

"Adriana, why don't you stay with me tonight?" he said, staring straight ahead. "You don't really want to drive all the way back to Haiku, do you?"

I didn't answer but tilted my head sideways.

"I live in Kahului, only a few minutes away. So what do you say?"

"Okay," I answered, tilting my head back and smiling.

Hank smiled, still staring straight ahead. He turned the key in the ignition, and we drove off.

Hank's house was in a row of old plantation-style houses, which he told me were filled in the old days with families who worked the sugarcane and pineapple fields. The rooms were large, and there was a yard in the back off the kitchen. I loved the simplicity of the house and the fact that artists lived there.

Two other people lived in the house, Verity and Milo. Verity DeVoe was an artist. She was petite, very fair, with freckles and flowing strawberry-blonde hair. Milo Wilson was a friend of Hank's from Brooklyn. He was short with dark curly hair, always smiling, but sparse with words.

We walked through a long hallway into the kitchen where Milo and Verity were sitting at a large table, passing a joint back and forth. We sat down and exchanged names. I overheard Hank tell Milo that I knew Loretta, which put a big smile on Milo's face.

"You know Loretta?" Milo asked, after taking a long drag off the joint.

"Yeah, me and Loretta are friends. Why?"

"I haven't seen or talked to her in ages. We used to be pretty tight," he said, passing the joint to me.

I wasn't sure what he meant, but I figured I'd ask Loretta what the deal with Milo was the next time I spoke to her.

Verity rifled the joint from my fingers, saying, "Don't forget me while you guys are reminiscing about people you all know."

Hank laughed and said, "*Bois froid*" (pronounced bwa fwa), in a very nasal New York tone. Three years of French in high school told me *bois froid* meant cold wood.

"How about passing that Thai stick in my direction?" Milo said.

We sat around the table trading stories and snide comments for a long time. Well, there were three stoned New Yorkers sitting at the table.

Verity, who probably felt a little left out by our New York banter, looked directly at me and asked, "So what's your story?"

"I'm here on vacation," I replied.

"From where and for how long?"

"I'm here for a month, then back to San Francisco, maybe even New York in the summer."

Upon hearing that, Hank glanced at me but said nothing. He grabbed my hand and led me down the hallway. There were bedrooms scattered here and there, like in a railroad apartment.

He stopped in front of his room and motioned me to walk in ahead of him. It was neat with a double bed next to a window. A guitar stood against the wall, as well as an easel with a painting on it.

"Did you paint this?" I asked.

"Yeah, I did. You like it?"

"It's interesting. Not tropical though, considering this paradise you live in."

"I paint a lot of different subjects. This is just one piece."

"Either way, I like it. I paint too. Mostly watercolors, and I like to sketch in charcoal."

"I'd love to see your work," Hank said.

"Yeah, well it's a few thousand miles from here."

Hank snickered. He pulled me to him and gave me a long kiss on the lips. I liked him a lot, but my better judgement was not to get romantically involved. That decision should have been made back at his friend's house in Wailuku, not in his bedroom. We fell on the bed in a tangled mess of tearing off our clothes. There was no talking, a bit of sighing, and it was over pretty quickly.

He laughed and said, "Sorry, it's been a while."

"It's okay," I said. "Anyway, it was just the first time."

Hank sat up in bed and lit a cigarette. "Are you saying there will be more times?"

"I guess I am."

"Good to know I still have a chance," he said, grinning. His blue eyes disarmed me.

The next morning I woke up alone in an empty room. The myna birds were arguing outside the window. Hearing voices coming from the kitchen, I quickly got dressed and walked down the hallway.

Hank and Milo were sitting at the kitchen table talking and drinking coffee. Hank pointed to a space next to him on a bench along the window and motioned for me to sit. He gave me a quick kiss.

"Coffee?" he asked. I nodded, then watched him pour me a cup.

"Smells so good. Is it Kona?" I asked.

"What else?"

"Where's Verity?"

Milo stood up. He wore a pair of OPI shorts, a popular Hawaiian logo. He wore those same shorts every day during the weeks I was there. Sometimes with a shirt, sometimes without.

"Verity went to the Dairy Queen to get us something for breakfast."

It was nice being in a small town and able to walk to various places without the use of a car, but Dairy Queen wasn't my idea of breakfast, maybe dessert.

Hank said, "I thought we'd just hang out here at the house today, but tonight I was invited to a big party at a beachfront house in Lahaina. Maybe you'd like to come with me?"

"That sounds really cool, but at some point today I have to get back to your brother's place. All my clothes are there."

"No worries; I'll take you this afternoon. Meanwhile ..." With that, Hank took my hand and walked me down the hallway to his bedroom, leaving Milo sitting at the kitchen table.

I heard the screen door and figured Verity was back from Dairy Queen. Hank threw me on the bed and began kissing and touching me all over. We had sex amid the sounds of talking and laughter coming from the kitchen. Afterward, we walked into the kitchen holding hands. Hank made me bacon and eggs while I sat at the table talking to Verity and Milo.

"I really need to wash up, and I didn't notice a shower in the bathroom," I said.

Hank smiled and said, "I guess I'd better heat some water."

Hank walked out the back door of the kitchen into the yard, and I followed him, a little befuddled. I watched him get some wood and place it under a large water tank and light a fire. His actions were precise and seemed like a strange ritual to me.

"You're going to love this, Adriana. I'll let you experience this alone, even though I want nothing more than to take a shower with you."

He handed me a towel and led me into a medium-sized shed. He smiled at me and then turned and walked back to the house.

I got undressed and stood there nude, looking around for the knob to turn the water on. I finally found it and flipped the lever. A torrent of warm water flowed from the ceiling and covered a large portion of the interior of the shed. It was a glorious experience, and I was happy to enjoy it all by myself (at least that first time). Afterward, I dried myself off, got dressed, and walked back into the house to join the others.

Hank and I drove to his brother's cottage to collect my belongings. It was a short visit, and I had the feeling Sammy and Rain were happy to get rid of me. I guess I was right in thinking Sammy's aim all along was to pawn me off on his brother. For me, it turned out to be a wonderful thing.

Later that day we stopped in the town of Wailuku, filled with antique shops, secondhand stores, small cafes, and the historic Iao Theater. We decided to see the movie *Shampoo*. We walked up to the ticket booth, and I noticed that the guy selling tickets was wearing a white turban. Inside the theater, the people selling candy behind the counter also wore white turbans, as did the guy who walked us to our seats. I'd even noticed the turbans pumping gas at the local station when we drove into town. It was all so surreal!

I whispered in the darkness of the theater, "Hank, what's with all the turbans?"

Hank breathed out slowly and said, "The swamis have taken over!"

That night we went to a party at a house in Lahaina that sat right on the beach. It was a rather large house, but people were encouraged to not walk through the rooms. I talked to one of the women inside and told her I had to use the bathroom. She ushered me down a hallway where there was a bathroom inside her bedroom. Music was playing on the stereo in the living room.

I said, "I've always loved Jefferson Airplane."

She said, "They're called Jefferson Starship now."

While sitting on the toilet, I noticed a whale painted on the tile inside the shower stall. It was impressive. The whole house was beautiful. We had arrived late, so midnight came quickly. The moon was large and hypnotic.

Hank and I sat on the beach staring at the moon while the waves washed up on the shore. Little sand crabs danced around our feet. Hank put his arm around me and pulled me toward him. I rested my head on his shoulder. He rubbed his hand along my arm and I shivered a little.

"Cold?" he asked.

"A little."

He took his jeans jacket off and placed it around my shoulders. We French kissed for a while. It was warm and tender yet thrilling.

"Maybe we should sleep here on the beach tonight," he said.

"Yeah, let's do that. We're both pretty drunk, and I don't think we should drive back over that mountain pass to the other side of the island in the dark."

"Driving over the Pali can be dangerous at night; not many lights," he said.

We slept on the beach that night. When I woke up the next morning, the sun was just rising. Hank was still asleep. I could see the Island of Lanai off in the distance across the channel. Hank had pointed the island out to me when we arrived the evening before. Fishing boats were setting out from Lahaina Harbor for a day out on the ocean.

I sat up. ALL of a sudden, two huge whales jumped out of the ocean and crossed over each other in an awesome breach that formed a heart.

Hank sat up, rubbing his eyes.

I said, "You have no idea what you just missed!"

I felt content with Hank. He was an artist like me, and we spent some wonderful days just hanging out drawing and painting. I enjoyed watching Milo and Hank fish for our evening meals, while I bobbed around in the ocean. Of course there were torrid nights of sex, and hints of love. I knew I'd have a hard time forgetting us taking showers together in the shed in the yard at the back of their house. Hawaii had a down-to-earth, laid-back way of living, and I liked it. Maui was definitely a place I wanted more of, perhaps a place I wanted to live.

~~~~~~

A flashlight shining in our faces woke us in the middle of the night. My eyes focused on a guy standing beside the bed. I was groggy as I sat up, trying to wrap my head around the invasion, and shielding my eyes from the flashlight. He seemed drugged, desperate, and was threatening Hank with a large kitchen knife.

"Hey man, you owe me money. I got some guys outside with a gun, so you either give me the money or some pot until you get it," the guy said.

I'd say I was afraid of this loathsome character, but Hank's calm demeanor kept the guy at bay, and he was able to defuse the situation. After a few harrowing minutes, the guy set the knife down on the nightstand and sat on the bed next to Hank. I covered my naked body with a sheet that was at the foot of the bed. They were able to talk things out, which was a big relief. Hank gave him a bag of weed and assured him that he'd have money for him in the next few days.

We were both shaken a bit, even after the guy left. Hank sat up against the wall behind the bed and reached for his pack of Lucky Strikes.

"What the hell was that all about, Hank?"

"Some jerk I owe money to," he said, taking a drag off the cigarette.

"Why haven't you paid him? I mean, for him to come here in the middle of the night threatening you with a knife!"

"I'm short on cash. I haven't played a gig since that night I met you."

"Why don't you ask Sammy if you can work in the restaurant for a while?"

"Bois froid," he said in that nasal voice he liked to use. "I guess I'm gonna have to do that." He took another thoughtful drag.

Hank took my advice and spent a couple of weeks working at La Tortilla Natural. I helped out as well, and it was actually a fun part of my vacation. We'd walk to the ocean each day after the restaurant closed and sit on the beach to watch the sunset. I thought, *God, I'm going to miss this.* As the month wore on, I felt uneasy and sad about leaving the island.

I was moping around the kitchen table at Hank's house.

"What's with the long face?"

"I have to leave soon," I said.

"I know, I've been thinking about that too. What if we move this party to California?"

"Hank, where would you get the money for a plane ticket?"

"My brother will lend me the money."

"That would make me so happy, but can you leave just like that?"

"Actually, I've been thinking about it for a while. Meeting you just clinched it for me."

That night we sat up in bed and talked most of the night about what we were going to do when we got to San Francisco. I assured him that Star Green lived in a great neighborhood, and that I had my own room. I explained that she and I were like sisters, that we'd lived on a commune together.

Hank got out of bed and reached for a small, velvet, maroon pouch on the dresser. He sat next to me and handed me the pouch, waiting for a response.

"What's this?"

"Remember the day we walked along Black Sands Beach in Hana collecting puka shells?"

"Yeah," I said, opening the pouch.

"Verity sewed the pouch together for me. There weren't enough shells to make a necklace, but I made you an anklet."

I opened the pouch, and out dropped a puka shell anklet with a Hawaiian charm dangling from the center.

"Hank, I love it. It's beautiful." I threw my arms around his neck. "When did you have the time to do this?"

"You belong to me now," he said, taking it out of my hand and placing it around my left ankle.

I looked into those dreamy blue eyes and kissed him softly on the lips. He had such an innocent look on his face, and a little pride as well. We lay on his bed and made love.

Since I hardly used any of the vacation money I'd brought with me, I rented a room at a resort in Lahaina for a few days. I figured we could play tourist, and we'd have time alone to be romantic. We saw incredible sunsets from the lanai of our hotel room, and it was an intense few days.

Hank took me to Kaanapali Beach. We lay on the sand for hours watching the ocean and people frolicking in the waves. An old Hawaiian guy was pushing a grocery shopping cart, dragging the wheels though the sand with difficulty. He was laughing, talking loudly, and had a white towel wrapped around his neck and shoulders.

"Here comes Captain Kenny," Hank said.

"Who's that?"

"Kenneth Roland Neizman is a well-known local artist on Maui, the Picasso of the Pacific."

The man stopped in front of us, unfurling a long painting that went on and on like a scroll. It was filled with abstract images of fish and other ocean creatures. His work was fascinating. He wiped the sweat off his face with the white towel but never stopped talking.

He rolled up the scroll and asked, "You wan' I paint som'ting special fa you?"

Hank said, "Paint us something, Cap."

He fished through a bunch of fiberglass chunks in his shopping cart and pulled out a small oblong one, not stopping his pidgin chatter for a moment. He painted abstract sharks and turtles on it.

When he was done, Hank took it, gave Captain Kenny some money, and handed it to me. "This is a piece of Maui to take home with you," Hank said.

~~~~~~

There was the better part of a week to go before my flight out of Maui, and I wondered if this new development was a good idea—I mean Hank coming back to the mainland with me. Was one month enough time to know if our relationship was a lasting one? Was I in love with Hank or with Maui? Only time would tell.

As my last week drew to a close, I felt comfort in the fact that Hank was coming with me. Maybe in an odd way I was taking a piece of Maui with me. I called Star Green, back in San Francisco, to let her know I was on my way back and bringing someone with me.

From my journal:

This is the first time I've written in my journal for a month. No need to, as I'm living in the *now*, my life being so full. No dreams, hopes, or visions because it's all just happening in the moment. Days filled with art and nature's beauty. Watched the sunrise over the clouds of Haleakala Crater, the sky shades of yellow and orange. It was a spiritual experience. I feel so free here among Thai sticks, palm trees, and trade winds. Can't remember what I was feeling a month ago. Oh yes, I was walking alone on the streets of San Francisco feeling numb and weird. How it has all changed, meeting a fellow artist.

TWO

BOIS FROID

From my journal:

Is this take five or six, forever, or never? It's always different, yet always the same, going home. Thoughts filled with apple orchards at sunrise, and sunsets along the Hudson River. Dirty city streets in winter with hot, salted pretzels, chocolate egg creams, pizza by the slice, and the Staten Island Ferry. Packed subway cars with so many Kojak look-alikes in the flesh. Millions of people rushing everywhere and nowhere. Memories of running through the snow in the Catskill Mountains. Will I get lost again, or be found? God knows I've been both. Once again I will leave some plants behind with friends and kiss another California sunset goodbye!

San Francisco was chilly and foggy as we hailed a taxi from the airport. Through the open window there was the sound of traffic and the occasional clang of a streetcar. Even though Hank was holding my hand and smiling at me, a mounting sadness came over me as we drove away from San Francisco International Airport. In my heart and mind, I was still on Maui.

We dragged our bags up the flight of stairs to Star Green's apartment and I found the door unlocked. Star was sitting at the kitchen table when we walked in. I delighted in her mass of kinky brown hair, heart-shaped face, and expressive blue eyes.

"Hi honey, I'm home," I said.

She didn't look at me directly but said, "Hey," as she scrutinized Hank.

I immediately felt uncomfortable, though Hank seemed oblivious. I realized I was bringing someone into the mix, and unlike my last boyfriend, Blake Middleton, Hank would be living with us.

"Star, this is Harvey Cooper."

"You can call me Hank; everyone else does."

"I heard all about you," she said, looking him up and down.

"You've got a nice place here, Star," he said.

"So how was Maui?" she asked, not taking her eyes off him.

"I had a great time. I loved the island and can't wait to go back," I answered.

"Hawaii's a cool place," Hank said.

"I'm going to take Hank back to my room. We've had a long day and we're tired."

"Yeah, we'll catch up with you later," Hank said.

We gathered our bags and walked down the hallway to my bedroom.

Hank liked the mattress on the floor and commented "That's different." He walked around the room looking at everything, picking items up and carefully putting them back. I had an old-fashioned dresser with a large round mirror.

Hank said, "Take your clothes off. I want to take a photograph of you in front of that mirror."

I did as he asked and stood nude in front of the mirror.

He narrowed his eyes and picked up the camera, saying, "Oooooo, yeah, stand just like that."

I heard the shutter click. Hank set the camera down on the dresser. He took off his clothes, starting with his jeans jacket and then his jeans. He walked over to me at the dresser and put his arms around me. We embraced and kissed.

"I'm so glad you're here with me," I said.

"That was a chilly reception. What the hell's with her?"

"I don't know. Sometimes Star gets weird when I'm involved with someone. You know how friends can be jealous of your attention. They don't mean to be, but it oozes out. I didn't realize you picked up on it. Try not to take it to heart."

"I don't get my feathers ruffled that easy," he said in his Brooklyn accent.

We stood nude for a while, gazing into that big round mirror. Hank fondled my breasts, still looking at our image. He picked me up and lay me on the mattress. I liked looking at his eyes while we did it. They were a soft shade of blue with specks of brown and green, often changing color with his mood. The corners slanted down slightly, which gave the appearance of sensuality. We made love, and everything around us seemed to disappear. For a while I was back on Maui.

When we woke, it was getting dark. I put on my Oriental kimono robe, which I'd purchased in Manhattan's Chinatown the last time I was in New York.

I sauntered into the kitchen. Star wasn't around, so I put a flame under the tea kettle.

Hank came into the kitchen, luckily with his jeans on. I didn't want him to be too laid-back, because Star could walk in at any moment. He came up behind me, put his arms around me, and bent his face against my cheek. He was hard against my behind.

He said, "Forget the tea, I want to do it again."

After we made love, we fell asleep and didn't wake up until the next morning. Star was in the kitchen making breakfast when we walked in. She was a vegetarian, but everything she made was something I wanted to eat. I just wondered if Hank would like it.

She turned and looked at us. "Well, you two are finally back from the dead."

Hank laughed and said, "Bois froid."

Star looked at him with a glazed-over expression, but I chose not to interpret.

"So what are you two planning to do today?"

"I thought I'd show Hank around the city, maybe give him a tour of the art school I attended. Hank's an artist too," I said.

Star looked at Hank for a moment and then returned her attention to the skillet.

"I'm making us omelets with avocado and sour cream," she said.

"Sounds awesome," Hank said, and Star smiled.

Hank and I roamed around San Francisco for the better part of that first day. We stopped in Tower Records to check out new music. He told me he was into that song "Takin' Care of Business" by Bachman-Turner Overdrive. He made the guy behind the counter play the song a few times as he bobbed to the lyrics. I took him to see the art school I'd attended for a semester. Well, that's the story I told Hank. I didn't want to get into that saga of how I quit midsemester.

Matthew Romeola, aka Romeo, my boyfriend from the commune, popped into my head, and that whole sad time on Huntington Road in Sonoma came back to me. I guess I didn't want Hank to know too many details about the commune, and how I left Romeo and California a broken woman.

I just told him a snippet of that time, and he remarked, "Yeah, well, you know, in life there's a slap in the face around every corner!"

I couldn't argue with that.

Hank loved everything about the art school. He hung out in the doorway of one of the studios to watch an artist paint. After a while I tugged on his arm and told him I had more of San Francisco to show him. The truth was that just walking through the school brought back troubling memories.

As soon as we walked out of the building, my spirits lifted. I dragged Hank to my favorite thrift shop. He loved rummaging around the secondhand stores almost as much as I did. We had fun combing through the bins. Hank found a black beret and immediately put it on his head.

"Oh, that looks so good on you, so French!" I said, smiling.

Hank tilted his head, grinned, and said, "Bois froid."

~~~~~

That night I had the strangest dream about Romeo. I recorded it in my journal:

> I walked into the lobby of a hotel, or maybe it was a university. There were couches everywhere, and I was with a male friend, although I don't know who he was. I glanced around the room and saw Romeo sitting on one of the couches. I hadn't seen him in so long. I'd heard through the grapevine he'd been in jail.
>
> I was walking in his direction when I noticed Bella McTavish, his last girlfriend, walk his way and sit next to him on the couch. I sat somewhere else with my friend but couldn't take my eyes off Romeo. He wasn't responding to Bella, and she seemed annoyed. She got up and walked away with a frown.

I left my friend and walked toward Romeo. He smiled up at me but didn't say anything, so I sat next to him.

"I haven't seen you for a long time," I said.

"Well, I've been gone for a while, but now I'm back," he answered.

There was a silence, but I felt warmth coming from him. He took my hand and stood up, so I stood up as well.

"I want to talk to you, Adriana, so let's go somewhere where we can catch up."

We walked to a private area of the lobby and Romeo faced me. "I've been thinking about you," he said.

I put my arms around his neck and said, "Romeo, I've missed you. I never stopped loving you." I held him tight and began to cry. I didn't want to let him go.

He said, "Don't cry, Chica, don't cry. I'll always love you. We'll always have our summer of love." Then, with a blank expression, he said, "I'm going on a trip to Alaska, and you should come with me."

I hesitated. Then I said, "I want to, but—"

He interrupted. "I'm driving."

My heart sank a bit. "You're not delivering drugs, are you?"

"Well yeah. I need the money," he said.

"I can fly there and meet you in Anchorage."

He stared at me with a puzzled expression and said, "Let's go to my place."

We exited the lobby holding hands and walked through the streets.

I said, "I love this city" (it was New York City).

Romeo didn't answer. When we arrived at his place, it was an apartment in a rundown area. There were people sitting around the living room shooting up drugs, and I felt uncomfortable.

I woke up when Hank turned to spoon me and rested his arm on my waist.

For that whole day the dream about Romeo plagued my thoughts. Whatever Hank and I did, wherever we went, flashes of the dream ran across my brain. I thought that staying in California wasn't a good thing for me. San Francisco was a far cry from Maui. I missed the island and reminisced about every detail I treasured about life there. I had gotten used to falling asleep to the sound of the soft rustle of palm trees, and being woken in the morning by the chatter of myna birds. There, I became like the trees swaying in the trade winds. When Hank touched me, I felt total joy and unity. Well, that was on the island. I wasn't sure about it on the mainland.

~~~~~

In May, my mind drifted toward New York City, my family, and East Coast friends. Hank was of a similar mind-set, although we both missed Maui. We made plans to move back east. I heard from Loretta Perino that Milo Wilson was back in Brooklyn. Hank mentioned that Milo had an apartment in a nice area near the water. It was a positive clue into our future. We'd have a place to land and figure out what our lives would look like going forward.

Star thought I was making a big mistake leaving California again, but knew it was useless to try to dissuade me. When a thought occupied my head, I had to follow through. Blake Middleton, my last boyfriend, called me from Marin. I thought of all the nights and days I spent in that old wooden house in the country north of San Francisco. I suppose the last time he called, Star must have told him I was on my way back from Hawaii. I said nothing about bringing a guy back with me from Maui or that we were planning to go back to New York together.

Blake was full of piss and vinegar, probably from his stint behind bars for a DUI. We had a nice chat, but I kept the conversation light and airy. He told me all about Reverend Ike, the new rage in the spiritual realm. Blake told me the reverend referred to himself and his wife as Mr. and Mrs. Big Money! Blake went on about how he always appears in public dripping in diamonds, touts the greatness of wealth, and asks for big donations during his ministries. We laughed up a storm on the phone, and for a moment I missed Blake's good humor.

When he asked to see me, I ended the conversation abruptly, saying I was late and had to meet a friend. I felt adrift in California, never seemed to settle in, always felt like a visitor. Besides, I had Hank now, and we were of like mind, heart, and spirit, and I wasn't letting go of that.

~~~~~

It was June 1975, the beginning of summer, when Hank and I landed at LaGuardia Airport in New York. It was after midnight, so we didn't want to inconvenience anyone. I hailed a cab while Hank waited inside with the rest of our luggage. I left one of my bags and my guitar with the cabbie and ran back inside the terminal where Hank was standing with our suitcases, my large art portfolio, and his guitar.

"I got a cab," I yelled at Hank.

We rushed through the exit doors. As I approached the sidewalk, I saw the cab driving away with my suitcase and guitar.

"What the fuck?" I shouted.

Hank asked, "What just happened?"

"The cab just drove away with my stuff."

Hives immediately broke out all over my face and neck, I suppose from nerves, helplessness, and frustration. Hank hailed another cab, and we got in with what was left of our baggage and headed to Brooklyn. *Well this is a lousy start,* I thought. I hoped it wasn't a bad omen.

~~~~~~

The apartment Milo Wilson and Harvey Cooper shared in Brooklyn was large, with a number of bedrooms, so we had privacy. There was a guy living there while they were in Hawaii. I never got to meet him. After Maui, Brooklyn felt like "paradise lost"!

We were sitting on the couch in the living room when Loretta Perino drifted in with a six pack of beer. She had cut her long, beautiful, brown hair into a short bob. It looked cute on her and accentuated her dark, almond-shaped eyes. Loretta was tall, slim, and as beautiful as an Italian actress. She sat on the couch next to me.

Hank said, "I'm gonna put these beers in the freezer so they get really cold."

She and I hugged. I couldn't wait to catch up with all the gossip. When Hank didn't return from the kitchen, I told her all about how I met him on my Maui vacation, and how it all went down. She listened with interest and had a smile on her face but didn't say anything. I thought, *That's not like Loretta, to not have something to say!*

That night, we all went to the theater to see the premier of the movie *Jaws*. It reminded me that I had a fear of the ocean.

~~~~~~

Two weeks later, after we were settled, my mother called from the Bronx to tell me that she received a call from St. Luke's Hospital in Manhattan. Apparently they had my guitar and my other suitcase. Luckily my medical card from St. Luke's was inside my suitcase. The hospital told her the cabbie picked up another girl at the airport who looked like me and felt terrible about the mix-up. The cab driver called St. Luke's, and they in turn asked him to bring my items to the hospital, telling him they would contact me directly, not wanting to give out my personal information. The cabbie made an honest mistake, and my trust in humanity was restored.

My parents were overjoyed to have me back on the East Coast. I took Hank to the Bronx to meet them. It was a long train ride. It took about an hour and a half with the use of three separate train lines to navigate from Brooklyn, through Manhattan, to the Bronx. After dinner we watched television. The news was about Jimmy Hoffa, the ex-teamster boss who had mysteriously disappeared. It was a nice visit with my parents but a long train ride back to Brooklyn.

~~~~~~

Old neighborhoods, bagels for breakfast, pizza for lunch, and whatever was around for dinner, it didn't take long for this routine to become monotonous. Sometimes we'd spend days on end in the apartment, and I began to wonder why we came back to New York, when I felt we should be in Hawaii. I didn't say anything to Hank about how I was feeling, since he seemed happy with the situation. I was happy with him, but our relationship was drifting into a blasé space. I knew how I was, and when I didn't feel excitement, I feared a change of heart coming. My mind often drifted to that shed in the yard at the back of Hank's house on Maui. In Brooklyn we didn't do much showering together. Women need romance to keep love going. I began to wonder if New York was my home, or just the place I was born. I didn't know anymore. Could the next stop be the old country (Italy), or were those grapes already wine?

~~~~~~

My twenty-ninth birthday came and went without fanfare.

"I wish I had the money to buy you something really nice, but I'm broke!" Hank said.

I felt let down but didn't make a big deal out of the slight.

"I promise things will get better. Maybe we should think about going back to Maui."

That comment lifted my spirits, and as he walked toward the door with Milo I thought we were back on the same page.

Not long after they left I heard the front door.

Loretta walked in with pizza and a six pack of beer, shouting, "Where is everyone?"

"Hank and Milo went to the avenue a little while ago," I yelled out.

"Good. I want to talk to you about something." She walked into the kitchen and opened the freezer to unload the beer. "What the hell is this hockey puck doing in the freezer again?"

"I don't know, Loretta. These guys are like children sometimes with their silly games."

Loretta walked into the living room, set the pizza down, and sat on the couch next to me. "Look, I know that you and Hank are in love, but Harvey Cooper is a funny sort."

"What do you mean? Is there something I should know?"

"Well, Hank and his brother, Sammy? Let's just say they have an unnatural relationship."

I reached for a slice of pizza waiting for Loretta to explain herself, because I didn't quite know what she was getting at.

"How so?"

"The Cooper boys are a team. Hank will do whatever his older brother, Sammy, tells him to do. And they share everything, and I mean everything. Hank has gone out with a number of Sammy's old girlfriends. He even hit on me once," she said, taking a giant bite out of her slice.

I was a little shocked, but knew I had to hear her out.

"I was concerned when you said you got involved with Hank. I've known all these guys for a long time, and I've never known Hank to have a real job. He just coasts along in life and relies on his brother to look out for him. I know you're in love, but think about how that can quickly fade with money problems. I'm just talking from one woman to another."

I needed time to think about what Loretta was saying. Yes, I was in love with Hank, and he was in love with me. Love was easy on Maui with all the beauty around us, and a fairytale of a vacation. But I knew love could fly right out the window when things got tough. My birthday sparked doubt and confusion inside me. It wasn't the absence of a gift but the thoughtlessness of it all. I gazed down at the puka shell anklet Hank had given me and played with it.

I heard the front door, and in walked Hank and Milo.

Loretta and I glanced at each other. "We saved some pizza for you, and there's beer in the freezer," she yelled out. "And for God's sake, get rid of that hockey puck!"

Later that night, I told Hank I wanted to talk to him.

"Sounds serious," he said.

"Lately I've been feeling suspended in time without a plan. I've been thinking of getting a job in Manhattan for a while. I need to save some money. Especially if we want to go back to Hawaii. You do want to go back to Maui, don't you, Hank?"

Hank had a troubled look on his face. "Yeah, but we haven't made definite plans yet."

"We have to start somewhere though, and money is what can make it happen."

He seemed disturbed, as if he didn't want to deal with any of what I was saying. He lay on the bed and didn't answer me. I curled up next to him, but he didn't respond. I pulled my hand back, and we fell asleep without talking or kissing for the first time since we'd met.

～～～～

On the Fourth of July we watched the fireworks from the boardwalk, which had a great view of Manhattan and the Statue of Liberty in the harbor. That night I felt the spark back between us. But after that weekend, I felt Hank drifting off into Never-Never Land—or maybe it was me. Was I willing to turn my back on love to prove a point? I had to question myself, because I knew it was my pattern. I began that dialogue and now I felt I had to follow through.

WATERCOLOR OF CITY SCENE

Hank walked into the bedroom while I was painting a watercolor in my journal. Right outside the bedroom window was a great view of the building across the street with a large tree in front.

"That's the first time I saw you paint anything since we left Maui. I really like it," he said.

I set my journal down and held my hand out. Hank took it and sat on the bed next to me.

"I dreamt of Maui last night. We had a house by the ocean with fruit trees in the yard," I said.

He smiled but didn't say anything. He took my journal, set it on the nightstand, and kissed me softly on the lips. "Don't worry; we'll get back there."

He lay me on the bed and we made love. It was warm and loving, yet hot and exciting. I climaxed before he did, my pleasure going on and on in waves radiating through my body. Afterward, we lay in bed silently, Hank caressing my arm.

~~~~~

I answered a newspaper ad looking for a sportswear designer. I took my art portfolio and hopped the train to Manhattan for an interview. I was able to secure a great job working for a sportswear company. I had my own office, and all I did all day was sketch stick figures of models in sportswear, bathing suits, and cruise wear. The owners were two brothers, religious Orthodox Jews. They often invited me into the conference room for lunch. They ate special kosher foods that their wives prepared for them. I didn't care for the food, so I brought my own lunch, and we always ate together.

SPORTSWEAR DESIGN ILLUSTRATION

Life was rolling along, though Hank didn't seem to relish the idea of work. He did odd jobs for friends in the neighborhood and made a little cash off pot transactions with people he trusted. I often wondered if Hank's brother, Sammy, sent him money once in a while. The day Loretta and I talked changed my outlook on our relationship. I wanted Hank to show me that he wanted our union as much as I wanted it. A plan for the future wasn't looking promising, and I became disillusioned. I was orbiting in space, which was how I liked to described my status in limbo.

I spent a couple of weeknights with my parents in the Bronx after work, which grounded me.

My mother knew something was bothering me. "Adriana, you're my daughter. You can't fool me. What's wrong?"

I told her how I was feeling about my relationship with Hank. I let her know that emotionally it was good, but practically, I didn't see a future.

She silently mulled over my words. "Remember when we had that talk after you left Romeo in California and moved back to the commune in New York?"

"Yeah, Ma, I remember. What are you getting at?"

"Love is a beautiful thing, but just because we love someone, or they love us, doesn't mean they're right for us. Love is not always a forever thing."

"I know, but it's hard to walk away from someone when you're in love with him."

"I never told you this, but when your father and I were first married, we went through a rough time, especially when I went into business with my brother Victor. It was before you were born. Your father was resentful. He didn't care about money like I did. We grew apart for a while."

I knew all about the affair my mother had had with the Italian importer/exporter, Dario, but that was when I was a child of eight or nine years old. It was an affair that went on for many years. She even dragged me on a few dates with them. Once she took me to Dario's apartment in Manhattan. His wife and daughter where there, and I wondered if his wife had any idea about the relationship between her husband and my mother. No one in that house spoke English, only Italian. We drank espresso and ate cannoli, and for a few hours I was in the old country. I remember his daughter showing me a photograph of a good-looking young man.

Dario said in English, "That's the man my daughter is going to marry. He's back in Sicily. I picked him out for her the last time I was there."

My mother and I glanced at each other but held back comments. I thought, *This is crazy. Have I gone back in time?*

Dario had been dead for years. My mother told me the awful story. The basement of his import store in Manhattan flooded after a rainstorm. He went into the basement to check the freezers for damage, and as soon as he stepped in the water, he was electrocuted.

My mother went on. "There was a young fella I met through my business, much younger than me. His name was Johnny. He paid a lot of attention to me and made me feel special, showering me with gifts. I was going to leave your father for him. I was to meet him at Penn Station in Manhattan. We were going away together."

I looked at my mother's face and listened with my mouth hung open as she continued.

"I did go to the train station that day to meet Johnny, but he saw that I arrived without a suitcase. When he realized I wasn't going away with him, he took the bouquet of flowers he'd brought for me and threw them on the train tracks. I began to cry. He turned away and boarded the train without me. I never forgot him."

I took her hand in mine and kissed it. "Ma, I'm sorry you were so unhappy."

"We all were young once. We all had dreams of what we thought love and marriage would be like. It's not always what we imagine."

There was so much about my mother I didn't know. She reminded me that in so many ways, she was just a woman like me.

I left their apartment remembering something my friend Casey Cutler used to say, "You can't put an ace bandage around a broken heart!"

When I got back to the apartment in Brooklyn, Hank was fumbling with wires. Milo was sitting on the couch reading instructions to him.

"What's going on?" I asked.

"It's a VCR. I got some new speakers, and we're trying to hook everything up," Hank said.

I sat down thinking, *he had money for a VCR, but not for a birthday gift for me.* Soon drowsiness overtook me. I lay on the couch and drifted off into a pleasant sleep.

~~~~~~

I settled into a daily routine of taking the train into Manhattan and coming home to Hank. It was nice, and it kept me happy for a while. But toward the end of the summer, I felt the need to get away. I told Hank I wanted to go upstate and visit my friends. I wanted him to come with me, but he said he had things to do. I got the feeling he was just making an excuse, though I wasn't sure why. Perhaps he felt me wanting more than him in my life.

Once I was upstate in the country, it was all déjà vu. Same people, different houses. Deer Creek, where I'd lived, had been sold. God, I missed that place. I was sitting on Kelly Cooke's porch in her new house when I noticed my plants hanging from hooks all along the eaves. We reminisced about our happy days living at Deer Creek in the Hudson River Valley. She told me that one of our friends opened a health-food store, so I drove to the store in town expecting to see her. A very young girl was working behind the counter, and my friend wasn't there. I noticed my framed woodcut ink print hanging on the wall near the register. I had given it to her as a gift. I was sorry I missed her, but I was told she was out of town on vacation.

Later that day, Kelly and I picked raspberries in the woods behind her house. She made fresh raspberry muffins for breakfast the next morning, and it felt like old times at Deer Creek.

On another weekend, I borrowed my parents' car and drove to Cape Cod to spend time with my cousin Angela. She was my cousins Cody and Arlo's younger sister. She was just a little girl when I spent my summers in Connecticut at their mini-farm. She was too little to actually get involved with the crazy escapades that Arlo, Cody, and I got into back then. She'd turned into a beautiful young woman and had a boyfriend, Asher, Ash for short. They had just moved to Truro, right outside Provincetown. We spent days at the ocean playing on the sand dunes and nights by their fireplace telling family stories. When Cody and his wife, Becky, came to Truro for the weekend, we all went to a secluded area of the beach and lay naked in the sun. Cody and Becky were in the Peace Corps together. They lived on the island of Palau for two years and got married there. They had a little boy.

We were having fun until a policeman appeared and interrupted our nude fest.

I thought we were going to get a citation, until Cody's little boy said, "You born naked!"

The cop laughed and said, "I won't give you a ticket, but you have to put your bathing suits on."

The next day, walking along Commonwealth, the main drag in Provincetown, I ran into a guy from Ireland that I knew from California. He was selling his jewelry in one of the shops. He closed the shop for lunch, and we sat in one of the outside cafes and drank piña coladas. All this without Hank!

Back in Brooklyn, Hank talked about Maui and how we should go back soon, and my heart began to fly. We were so good together. We had so much in common. Our love was warm, beautiful, and serene, like a misty afternoon in the country. Sometimes hot and throbbing, like when we had sex. How could things get any better?

Hank said he would go back to Maui first and set things up. I would stay with my parents in the Bronx until he sent for me. We finally had a plan.

I made the mistake of mentioning Maui and my future plans to my bosses at the sportswear company, and they fired me. I couldn't blame them, but geez, it was such a great job. Eventually, I went back to coding at the same market research company I'd worked for in the past. None of my friends worked there anymore, so I had to get used to a whole new crew. The manager was a very attractive young woman who had her favorites, and I wasn't one of them.

～～～～～

It was September 8, 1975, when Harvey Cooper left for Maui. I lived on the couch in my parents' apartment in the Bronx and continued working in Manhattan. Their apartment was actually in a nice area, at the northeastern tip of the Bronx, near a body of water called the Bronx Lagoon. On Sundays I enjoyed watching the old Italian men play cards and bocce ball in the park.

Whenever the subject of my moving to Hawaii came up at the dinner table, my mother visibly tensed up. I think her heart was sinking at the thought of my living so far away. My mother, Vita, had sold her dress factory and was working as a dress operator in Manhattan's garment district. Perhaps it was a time in her own life when she was unhappy and floundering. I didn't see her smile much anymore. She was the type whose face exhibited every emotion she felt.

～～～～～

I was at work when there was a telephone call for me. The manager called me into her office, closed the door, and handed me the phone.

It was my father's voice. "Adriana, sit down."

As soon as he said that I knew something terrible had happened. "Your mother is in the hospital. She had a heart attack."

I stood there numb, and I remember the manager putting her arm around my shoulder. My eyes filled with tears. I blurted out, "I have to go," and ran out of her office.

I ran to the subway station and boarded the train in a fog. I don't remember walking to the hospital, but I remember that when I got to my mother's room, she caught sight of me and we both began crying.

Her doctor stopped me and said, "Stay out of there; you're upsetting her."

I ran to my father. He held me, and we both cried.

My mother was in intensive care for more than a week. It was touch and go for a while, and we were afraid we'd lose her. Her doctor told me that she'd had a massive heart attack, and that only half of her heart was working. She'd need plenty of rest, love, and care for a while, and that she definitely couldn't work anymore. My father and I spent a lot of time alone at home, taking turns cooking, and going to the hospital. I suppose we mostly felt sorry for ourselves.

In the course of one day, everything had changed! My life with Hank, my Maui dream, everything went up in flames and turned to ashes.

When she was out of intensive care, my mother remained in the hospital for two weeks hooked up to machines and tubes pumping various treatments into her body, while the doctors and nurses played tic-tac-toe on her arms with all sorts of medications.

I was sitting on a chair next to her bed when she woke up.

"Adriana, I had a dream about Dario."

"What are you saying, Ma?"

"Dario, he came to me in a dream, or maybe I was dead for a while. He was pulling me toward him, and I was telling him that I wasn't ready yet, that I wanted to live. I was fighting his grip on me."

I took her hand and caressed it. "No, Ma. We need you here."

She smiled and said, "Do you think I'll see him again someday?"

"I think so, Ma. I think you will, but not now."

~~~~~~

I received a letter form Adam Hirschfeld, one of my oldest friends from the commune, and a former lover. The letter was written on watercolor paper. He had painted a border of a sunset across the top. I clipped the watercolor from the letter and glued it into the pages of my journal. I felt sad after reading his letter. He seemed so creative, and I realized I had absolutely no inspiration to paint or draw. I was in limbo once again. I was tired and worn out from the nightly routine of going to the hospital after work and then going home and conjuring something up for dinner for me and my father.

~~~~~~

I took the train to the neighborhood where my mother's old dress factory was. The building was still a dress factory, and I could hear the hum of the sewing machines as I walked past. I spent more time in that neighborhood growing up than where we lived. The junior high school I attended was only a few blocks away. I started out there as a journalism major, but art won out, and I zeroed in on painting and drawing.

My favorite art teacher, Mr. Hobson, was black and gay. The boys in art class teased him a lot. Their comments rolled off him like water off a duck's back. When he heard them snickering as he swished toward the blackboard, he'd turn around, glare at them, and say, "What's the matter? Is my slip showing?"

The school had a strict dress code. Girls were not allowed to wear pants, and skirts had to be below the knee. Students were lined up outside the building every morning for inspection. The principal was a gestapo. If she saw you with a short skirt or a pair of earrings, you were pulled out of the line and sent home.

After my little trip down memory lane, I walked back to the Circle Train Station and headed home. I vowed to say nothing to my mother about her old dress factory, knowing how much she missed it.

~~~~~

When my mother came home from the hospital, she needed help and care. I was in a prison of sorts, a prison of circumstance, doing time. What crimes had I committed to warrant this turn of events? I felt dead in a way, an empty space in my head. Of course, looking back, I was the selfish type. I always thought it was all about me. I wondered what would come out of all this. I made my mother a cup of tea and sat on the corner of her bed while she drank it.

After a time she gazed at me. "Now you can't go to Hawaii," she said.

I was a little shocked, and for a moment I didn't know what to say. I chose my words carefully before answering. "Mom, I'll stay here and take care of you for however long it takes for you to get well, but whenever that day comes, I will be moving to Hawaii."

She stared at me, expressionless, perhaps disappointed. I wanted to make sure she knew the situation was only temporary, and that at some point I would go on with my life's plan.

What about Harvey Cooper? Well, sadly, I had to inform Hank that I wouldn't be coming to Maui anytime soon. There was a long silence on the other end of the phone line. I didn't expect him to fly back to New York. I expected he'd go on with his life. He had his brother there in Hawaii and was already back in the island groove.

"Everyone here misses you," he said.

I held back tears.

Hank called me on a regular basis, but over time his calls were less frequent, until eventually they stopped. I never did see Hank again. Loretta Perino moved to Maui that winter as well. I was left all alone in the twilight zone. Years later, Loretta told me she'd heard that Hank met a rich girl and married her. I guess it was meant to be that way.

Love is a funny thing. It could be as beautiful as a rose in a French garden—but be careful. It has thorns.

THREE

ALICE IN WONDERLAND

The psychologist as a spectator, both of Greek tragedies and of present-day human tragedy, learns or should learn, human beings are deeply affected by and submissive to the will of the specific divinities of their household. Their parents—whose injunctions they are impotent against as they blindly follow them through life, sometimes to their self-destruction.

—Claude M. Steiner, **Scripts People Live**

It was late fall 1975, and the holidays were right around the corner, but I felt there wasn't much to celebrate. I left the office for an hour lunch and walked to Fifth Avenue and Fifty-Ninth Street. I passed the famous Plaza Hotel and thought of my cousin Giovanna Ferrari's wedding reception in one of the suites. It was a small event with just immediate family after their civil ceremony at city hall. Still, it was emotional and I cried. Gia chose me to be her witness. I had a suspicion that an event such as this wasn't ever going to happen for me.

I walked into Central Park and observed all the leaves turning beautiful reds, yellows, oranges, and endless shades of brown. A cool wind whipped up the fallen leaves as I strolled along aimlessly. I found a park bench and unwrapped the liverwurst and Swiss cheese sandwich on Italian bread my mother had made for me. A woman was playing a concertina and singing English folk ballads. Then she played German oompah music as a young girl danced alongside her. I stared at the quick step of her black patent-leather tap shoes. I watched for a while with great interest and then stood up, tossed the empty brown paper bag in the trash, dropped some change in their tip jar, and walked out of the park.

Back in the office, my mind played the last phone call I'd had with Hank. I wanted to say, "I love you so much, I miss you every day, and I can't stop thinking about you." But I said none of those things. I didn't want him to feel guilty about moving on with his life on Maui. He was still talking about me coming there and telling me he couldn't wait to see me. It was the same day I received a letter from Verity DeVoe, letting me know she'd gone back to Maui.

From my journal:

I remember the way you looked up at me from the yard behind your house in Kahului. You were making a fire to heat the water tank so we could take a shower in the shed. Life there was so basic and motions were instinctive. I smiled at you from the window. A thrill went through me just to look at you. I can still feel it now. You're in such a beautiful place, and I'm trapped here in this concrete limbo. There's simply no formula for love. It's not science, it's an affair of the heart—a silver heart taken from its chain. A thousand steps taken out of a dream. A pink flamingo for the sweet bird of youth.

Boredom and general malaise settled into that winter for me. I hung around brooding about my situation, and doing watercolors, and charcoal sketches with Hawaiian themes and landscapes. I watched a new detective TV series called *Kojak* with my parents and their three cats. Life seemed mundane and meaningless.

CHARCOAL SKETCH OF HAWAIIAN GIRL WITH UKULELE

I thought of a fantasy I'd had as a child. Whenever I passed a large tree, I searched for a secret door in the trunk, imagining a passageway. I'd picture myself falling down a rabbit hole. The reality that I was no longer free to leave anytime soon depressed me. Keep in mind that the game of rescue of another, even if it's your own mother, holds inevitable resentment. I felt deterioration of the "self." I figured what I needed was a weekend in the country, conversation with friends, and a good screw. The latter of which was not a possibility. I set my mind on spending a weekend in upstate New York in the near future.

I enrolled in a night class called Art and Civilization. It filled a few evenings a week with interesting facts about how each era in time displayed art, architecture, clothing, and furniture following the same lines of design. For instance, when women wore those huge hoop skirts, furniture also had that same curved and puffed out design, as did the architecture of buildings.

I got friendly with a guy who always took the seat next to mine. He was the dark, swarthy type, with long, dark, curly hair and dark, mysterious eyes. I found him attractive. I could tell by his accent he was foreign, though I didn't know from where. His name was Djelko Bogdanic (the D was silent).

One night after class, Djelko asked me to go for coffee. We found a coffee shop near the university and settled into a booth.

He said with a Slavic accent, "I am here from Yugoslavia. My father is an ambassador for Yugoslavia to the UN."

I thought, *That sounds intriguing.*

As the weeks passed, we spent time together, and not just after class. He was quite handsome, dark, and dashing, with a serious air. He had a Serbian intensity about him. He reeked of money and prestige and seemed to take very good care of himself. He took me to his family's compound in Brooklyn, which was so vast that it took up half a city block. I never saw any women there, only his father and brother. We always had sex in his room. Sometimes just the close physical contact helped me feel I wasn't forgotten and was still part of the human race. We enjoyed sitting in Central Park, watching the squirrels gather and hide nuts for the coming winter, when everything would be covered with snow. He played guitar, and he knew I was an artist.

One night, as he watched me scribble and paint in my journal, he said in a serious tone, "An artist is like a flower. A flower needs air. Without air it will die." Djelko was always dramatic with his profound quotes.

"Where's your mother?"

"Back in Yugoslavia with the rest of my family," he said.

"My mother's family is from Bari, Italy," I said.

"Bari is right across the Adriatic Sea from Yugoslavia, so there must be some Serbian in you."

He picked up his guitar and sang a few folk ballads from his native country. The songs were touching, but I found them sad, like Russian folk songs. I told him they were beautiful.

I enjoyed my weekends at the compound, although I had occasional flashes of them being spies. I loved to watch Djelko build things and work in their yard. He did his own cooking and cleaning. There was never a dull moment around Djelko Bogdanic. I thought of how most American men impressed me as perpetual boys, and even though Djelko was young, he was a man in every way.

~~~~~

On a sunny but chilly afternoon in the Bronx, I took a walk to Crosby Avenue with my mother. Her Italian neighborhood had a pasta factory on the corner, import stores with delicacies from Italy, numerous pizza joints, and a restaurant where all the famous mob bosses ate. We had to stop and rest on a bench between stores, because she would get out of breath with only half her heart working.

She seemed to have a comment about every person that passed by. "I know that man. He thinks he's Astor's pet horse," she said, with a smug expression.

When she was rested enough to walk further, we ran into a friend of hers from our old neighborhood. He was a jeweler who designed many beautiful rings and necklaces for my mother (which I still have). We were shocked that he was being led around by his wife. She told us he had Alzheimer's and didn't know where he was or who anyone was. He held on to his wife's arm as if he were a little child hiding behind his mother's skirts.

His wife said, "You remember Vita and Adriana, don't you? Say hello to them."

He simply asked, "Why?"

My mother and I walked back to the avenue and went into a discount store. We both cried a little to think of such a brilliant and talented man reduced to nothing.

I hadn't seen Djelko Bogdanic for a while. The art history class was over, and I guess so was our connection.

I wrote in my journal:

I haven't picked up my guitar in so long. I played Djelko's guitar at his compound, but that was weeks ago, and anyway we're not lovers anymore. The class we attended is over, and so is our romance. It was a short lived fantasy. Only a clandestine pastime of sandwiches in a steamy bar room on a cold winter's day. I didn't even finish my beer when his brother kept filling me with plum wine they brought from Yugoslavia, while they traded stories about the old country. I haven't picked up a paintbrush lately either. It all fits together, steady work and artistic stagnation. No time to do the things that keep one's spirit alive. When will this change?

I amused myself with a new guy at the office named Jordan. He liked to wear leather chaps over his jeans, which accentuated his great ass. He wore his brown hair in a modern short chopped cut, and had a tiny ring in his left ear. I assumed he was gay. He was very attractive, smart and sexy. He weaseled his way to the top of the heap in the office, and became the Manager's favorite. I figured he was just another free spirit floating around in the movie that had become my life. I sensed he liked me. He'd lean over my shoulder to give me coding instructions on a consumer response sheet, and he'd let his hair brush my cheek. I'd catch him gazing at me over a stack of papers with a suggestive smile. At other times he'd completely ignore me. I couldn't figure him out.

I watched Jordan approach my desk with great interest. I could hear the swish of his leather chaps as he walked my way. He said, "Let's grab lunch?" Before I could respond he coaxed me out of my chair, and nearly dragged me out of the office. He was an interesting character, and I looked forward to getting to know more about him. We rode down in the elevator together, out of the lobby, and strolled through the streets looking for a place to eat. We found a small storefront eatery and Jordan reached over me to open the door. We walked in and settled in a booth and ordered iced teas and burgers. We were having a nice chat and laughing about the craziness that went on at the office.

He suddenly blurted out, "You know about me, don't you?"

I shook my head, searching his eyes for meaning.

He swept his short straight brown hair aside, saying, "I'm asexual!"

"What the hell does that mean?" I asked.

"I'm not into sex at all, not with men, not with women," he answered.

I was taken aback and didn't know what to say. "And you're telling me this because …" I wondered, *Why did he even bother to make himself attractive?*

"Look, I really like you, but I get the feeling you want more than friendship, and that's just not going to happen," he said. "I wouldn't want to lead you on."

"If I'm being perfectly honest, I am attracted to you. God only knows why!"

He chuckled at my remark. "I do feel the need for love and warmth, but I can't give it back."

"I can handle that. I'll be your friend if you want me to."

"I do really want that, Adriana." He took my hand, patted it, and seemed relieved.

On the subway ride back to the Bronx after work that day, I tossed around Jordan's words. He'd convinced himself that he couldn't give love or warmth. It was a difficult concept for someone like me to understand. I gave away my feelings so easily.

~~~~~~~

It was yet another Christmas Eve, and I was celebrating with my parents and their three cats. It was like old times, only I wasn't a child anymore waiting for Santa Claus. It all seemed different at twenty-nine years old. It was more solemn and spiritual, less joyful and frivolous.

I wrote in my journal:

Last Christmas I missed my parents, and this Christmas I miss my friends. It's a time of year we reflect on what's gone by. The star of Bethlehem brings to mind olden days of splendor (or was it really prayers of the poor?). "Behold, a child is born of wondrous joy and love." That's the true meaning of Christmas. Not trees with lights and cranberries strung. Not hams trimmed with pineapple glaze. It's also a cabbie hustling a buck on a snowy night so his kids can eat a nice holiday dinner, or a man parking cars for extra cash to buy his kids gifts. Isn't that also Christmas? Or is it just Christmas cards wishing you a Merry Xmas, toots, or postcards from faraway places saying, "Wish you were here." Office holiday parties, where straight-laced business suits get wrinkled before going home to their wives. I guess Christmas is all these things and more.

It was January 1976, and winter was in full swing with three feet of snow on the city streets. Cumbersome layers of boots, hats, gloves, and scarves were a must to venture outside. I gazed out the window of my parents' bedroom and noticed a man walking his dog along the snowy street. The dog was hobbling along on three legs through a narrow path made by a shovel. Then I noticed the man was also hobbling; he was missing a leg as well. I watched them for a while with interest. I had a pleasant flashback of sitting on this very floor as a teenager talking to my boyfriend, Zack Darcy. We'd talk for hours, much to my parents' chagrin.

Every time I told him about something I did or found out, he'd reply, "Is that a fact?" I still think of him when I hear that expression. It is true that I had no immediate troubles to worry about, but my heart was empty, and my patience was wearing thin. The Concord took its first passenger flight, but I was going nowhere.

Is it always beyond the horizon, our dreams and fantasies? If we only had the courage to live them out. To go to the places we hunger for, because to stay is to die, slowly and cruelly. What did Frank Sinatra once say? "I'd rather go one year that way than a hundred years this way!" We all have an inner spirit that can guide us if we let it. If we refuse to listen to it, we would be out of harmony with the universe. That is the way my mind was working. I also recalled my mother telling me once that she wouldn't sleep with Sinatra if his dick was painted with gold. I guess he wasn't her type.

～～～～

Being it was a new year, I wanted to reboot my life. I needed to get out of the situation I was in and gain some hope for my future. It was a dilemma, because I didn't want to hurt my family. I had to admit that I was unhappy and depressed most of the time. I decided some sort of therapy was in order. I fooled around with group therapy for a short while but got very little out of it. I found the group to be a bunch of miserable people bitching about their lives just for the hell of it. A coworker told me about something called transactional analysis, and gave me the name of a therapist who helped him through a rough time in his life.

"I know Joan can help you," he said, handing me her card.

I made an appointment with Joan, even though he warned me that she was expensive. I thought of a verse from the bible, "When a man seeks the prize of his heart, he does not count horses!" I went for an interview with Joan, who put me at ease right away.

"What method do you use to unlock plaguing patterns?" I asked.

Joan said, "Life events are recorded in our brains from childhood. Strokes are given as attention. There are good strokes and bad strokes. For some people, bad strokes are better than no strokes at all. In our childhoods, we write our life script. Throughout our lives we live out that script, like a play, sometimes over and over again with different people. The script can be changed, but it's very difficult. Adriana, together we can try to change yours, if you're willing."

Joan had me give her a quick synopsis of what was going on in my life, what my goals were, and my hopes and dreams. She also gave me a questionnaire to fill out. "Truthfully!" she insisted.

"Well, I want to feel free to do my artwork and surround myself with creative energy. I want to live in Hawaii. The islands inspire me to paint and draw. I want to find true love, or at least a lasting, meaningful relationship. I want to keep my mind on track to pursue my goals."

"Those are all good intentions. What do you think is holding you back?"

"I guess that's what I'm here to find out."

She picked up the paperwork I'd filled out and said, "On this questionnaire, you mentioned that your favorite story as a child was *Alice in Wonderland*." She paused for a moment. "I have to ask: Did you do a lot of drugs?"

"I did," I answered reluctantly, not wanting to let on that I still enjoyed them from time to time.

"After we have a few sessions, I want you to jot down bullet points of things that become clear to you. It would also be a good idea to record any dreams that you remember upon waking."

"Well, I already have a journal. I've been writing and drawing in it for years."

"That's good. It shows that you've been sorting things out in your mind."

The next day after work, I stopped in a cathedral I passed every day on my route to and from the office. I hadn't been to Mass for many years. I walked in and down the center nave, kneeled, and crossed myself. I sat in a pew for a while looking at all the saints. I thought of how religious I was as a child, and a memory popped into my head.

> I must have been about nine years old and I'd just had my first holy communion. My mother bought me a pair of earrings as a gift. I had to get my ears pierced in order to wear them. They had a gold flower with a small diamond in the center, and a tiny pearl drop. I wore the earrings to church on Easter Sunday. On our way out of church, I reached my fingers to my earlobes to play with the earrings, and one was missing. I took the other earring out and slipped it in my pocket so my mother wouldn't notice.

Outside after Mass, I told her I'd left something in church and had to go back. My parents waited outside. I looked under the pew where we were sitting and then went up to the alter railing where I'd received the holy host and scanned the marble floor. I looked everywhere, but the earring was gone.

I told my mother my earlobes hurt and I wasn't wearing the earrings for a while.

She said, "The hole will close up if you leave the earrings out for too long."

I didn't have the heart to tell her that I'd lost one of the earrings. I wondered why God would do such a thing to me.

During that next week, I walked back to the church on my own. The doors were unlocked, so I went inside and sat in a pew. I said a prayer to St. Anthony, the patron saint of lost things. I was upset and crying.

On my way out, I went up to the altar, knelt, and crossed myself before leaving. My eyes drifted down to the marble floor, and there was my other earring. My prayers had been answered. Even though I considered it a miracle, I never told my mother.

Even at twenty-nine that memory was forever imprinted on my brain. I still believed in miracles. I said a prayer, lit a candle, dipped my fingers in holy water, crossed myself, genuflected, and left the church. I walked through the city streets oblivious to the sounds of car horns blowing, music streaming from bars, and made my way to the train station. I felt peaceful, as if somehow, my future plans would eventually work out. Although in reality, I was afraid that would require an actual miracle.

It was painful to admit I was living in my parents' world, and no longer in mine. Their fears became my fears in exchange for a protected emotional environment. I felt strangled by my mother's love. She had the kind of love that grabs you and doesn't let go. I became a victim of it, and it wouldn't let me live my own life. I thought of what made her happy and not enough about what made me happy. I felt that she was disappointed in me, in the decisions I'd made, and in the path I'd chosen for my life. She always had a miserable look on her face, as if I'd failed her in some way. I felt guilty writing letters to friends, as if I was betraying my parents.

Star Green called me from San Francisco, and we had a long chat on the phone. My father asked, "What the hell did she want?"

Even my friends became perpetual threats to them. I thought, *What else could a friend want but to connect with you and hear your voice?* It was time for a weekend in the country, away from the mad tea party that was my current existence!

I spent a weekend upstate in the Catskills with my friend Daisy Holmes. We took a long walk in the mountains. The weather was windy and cold with snow flurries, but typical for February. We visited her friend Lucas Garzetti, who I'd been romantically involved with a few years back. He was living alone in the house he built. It gave me a warm feeling to see one of my charcoal sketches framed and hanging by the fireplace over the wood bin.

I picked up his guitar and played a little. His house was filled with artwork, dry swamp grass in barrels, pottery, and exotic wall hangings. It was masculine but homey. As I watched him speaking to Daisy, I flashed on us making love on a blanket in front of that fireplace the winter we were together. I remembered the bleakness of that winter, the snow blowing like a tempest past the windows outside. Yet looking at him as they were talking, I felt nothing. The three of us walked up on the hill near his house, and I was glad I wore my rabbit fur jacket. There is such a thing as a winter sky over the Catskill Mountains. A spectacular thing you don't see anywhere else. Low rolling clouds with shocks of pink on the horizon. We watched it through bare black trees lining the distant hills. There was a final blast of colored light before the darkness couldn't wait any longer. I felt normal and alive in the country.

I remembered a romantic passage in a book I'd read during that time, **The Blithedale Romance** by Nathaniel Hawthorne, published in 1852:

> Paradise, indeed! Nobody else in the world, in our bleak little world of New England, had dreamed of paradise that day. We made a summer of it in spite of the wild drifts. Toward noon there had come snow, driven along the streets by a northeasterly blast whitening the roofs and sidewalks that did credit to our January tempest. We rode on, however, with still unflagging spirits, and made such good companionship with the tempest, that at our journey's end we professed ourselves both to bid the bluster goodbye. Then we sat by the fire, with snow

melting out of our hair and beards, and our faces all ablaze.

I was having a great weekend until I got into a political argument with a friend of Daisy's who was spouting the Communist rap. I was familiar with that spiel. I guess I saw in her myself at twenty-one. She had all that idealism and enthusiasm as she spoke about the future liberation of workers.

"Soon it will all come down to the line, and you'll have to take a stand," she said.

I thought, *Where have I heard that before?* A new struggle that will lead nowhere, with promises of a chicken in every pot.

"So the common people are fighting among themselves, while the heads of state of both parties are meeting at an elite private club for dinner and drinks," I said.

She stared at me, annoyed. "It's a revolution."

"The way I see it, money talks and bullshit walks!"

"There's a real platform, one that's worth laying your body down for," she said.

"I'm interested in my art and have no desire to change the world. Many have tried," I said.

She blew out her breath to express her exasperation with me, and gave me a dirty look to show what she thought of me.

I didn't care and figured I'd let her have her youthful delusions. I never thought violence resulted in solving any of the world's problems, although people continue to try.

"Let's revisit this conversation in about ten years," I said, walking out of the room.

It was Sunday afternoon, and I had to get back to the city. Daisy drove me to the Hudson train station. We had a flat in the town of Cairo and missed the train. Luckily, two guys in a pickup truck stopped to help us.

I heard Daisy say, "Shit, all we really needed was a lug wrench!"

I shot her a nasty look and swiped my fingers across my lips, urging her to shut up. Daisy was a petite young blonde from England who'd lived in America for a long time but maintained her accent. She looked soft and needy at times, but she was a tough cookie who built her own cabin. The Hudson train station was usually deserted, but on that day there were sleazy types everywhere. They were hanging around the platform, in the phone booth, inside in the waiting area, and sitting on benches outside. Even the ticket agent was a creep. The next train to New York City wouldn't be along for another hour. We drove around looking for a place to eat and found a greasy spoon in Catskill. We ate tuna fish sandwiches and drank chocolate egg creams. *God,* I thought, *I'll miss chocolate egg creams, and Daisy too, when I move to Hawaii.*

Back in the Bronx, I received a phone call from my longtime friend/ commune brother Ross Grant in California. He was thinking of starting a business and wanted me to be involved. I figured he was lonely and wanted familiar companionship, and we were definitely family. Although I planned on spending a few months in California before heading to Hawaii, I did not want to bog myself down with anything permanent in that state. I told him we'd discuss it when I got to California, that I was not ready to leave New York, and that everything was presently up in the air!

From my journal after sessions with Joan:

- I've taken on a task to make my parents happy, but you can't make others happy.
- I am waiting for my parents' approval that it's okay to be the way I am. That will never come.
- My mother has power over me—not because she has it, but because I lend her the power.
- Though my parents were overly protective and openly affectionate, I never got the message that I was okay, that I was a good daughter, and that they'd love me no matter what.

The months rolled in and out, and I continued to feel trapped, but eventually that turned into resentment. I was not aware at the time that resentment is the beginning of inner strength. The truth was my parents were not happy with each other, and I was a catalyst. I was reliving my childhood in some way, listening to them argue and being powerless to escape the situation. Of course I wasn't a child anymore, and in reality I could just walk away. I was aware that they didn't see any of this and didn't even realize that they were using guilt as a weapon. I observed my mother revisiting old bad health habits: over salting her food, smoking cigarettes, drinking too much scotch, and expecting the shoebox full of medications she took every day to cancel all that out. I could just hear Grace Slick singing, "One pill makes you larger, and one pill makes you small." I began to challenge her actions, asking why I was even there helping her when she refused to help herself.

〜〜〜〜〜

It was the beginning of April, and I decided to spend another weekend upstate in the country. Even though it was spring, patches of snow remained on the ground. Daisy and I sat around the fireplace in the evening talking and reminiscing about Deer Creek. Daisy had left Jerimiah Murphy, her longtime boyfriend. He was much older than her. She was currently hooked up with a really nice young guy from Alaska. Hanging out in the country kept me aware of how much I enjoyed simplicity in life, although I did want to live in a more temperate climate. I didn't like being cold anymore, or the bleakness of winter which lasted so long. Maybe having been born in the summer, I seemed to blossom in warm weather. Daisy mentioned that she wanted to move to Alaska with her new beau.

"He's from Anchorage," she said. "He tells me Alaska is the last American frontier."

"I'm planning on moving to Hawaii. I hate being cold."

"I'll be selling my car when I leave. Are you interested in buying it?"

"Yes," I said with excitement.

"I guess we both have a plan," Daisy said, grinning.

When I returned to the city, Joan and I worked out a revised payment plan. I'm glad she suggested it, because I was getting to the point of not being financially able to continue. I would make her jewelry in exchange for half the cost of my therapy sessions. I had been making glass beaded necklaces for a while. She happened to admire a couple I wore and suggested the barter going forward.

Joan had a way of asking questions that made me delve deeper and deeper into my subconscious. During a session, she asked me to tell her why I didn't feel close to my mother. I told her that my mother had owned a dress factory and was always busy, and that at six months old she gave me to a woman who took care of me every day throughout my childhood.

"That woman, Filomena Genoa, was more like a mother to me," I said. I recalled an incident during one of the few times my mother took me to the park. I described how proud I was to have my mother there with me while I played with my friends under the sprinklers on a hot summer afternoon.

Joan listened to my story and asked, "How do you feel right now?"

Suddenly I burst into tears and couldn't stop, as if I were that little girl again.

She handed me some tissues and said, "All those times you and your mother missed can never be made up."

From my journal after sessions with Joan:

—If I leave New York, my mother might die. It wouldn't be my fault. My guilt is invalid, useless to her and to me. If she's made up her mind to die, there's nothing I can do.
—My playful child says, "Go and be happy," while my nurturing parent says, "It's unfeeling and irresponsible to think of myself."
—I resent that now that I want distance, my mother wants closeness.
—My parents are also victims of their childhoods and their lives. There is no blame.
—My parents will accept my decisions and lifestyle more easily if I fully accept it.
—My father looked to me for love and affection he didn't receive from my mother.

I had a loosely strung-together plan going forward. I would continue to work and save as much money as I could. I'd sell stock my mother coaxed me into buying a few years back and buy Daisy's car when she moved to Alaska. I'd drive across the country to California and have the car shipped to Hawaii. I didn't know if that was exactly how it all would unfold, but it was a plan. I realized how wrong the whole scheme of putting my life on hold was, but at the time, I didn't see any other way.

~~~~~~

I received a phone call from Dean, a guy I'd had a short romance with in the late sixties when I was a hippie in Berkeley. When he went back to school in upstate New York, we exchanged phone numbers, but I only visited him once on his campus. I was surprised to hear from him after so many years. He said he had been thinking about me, that he never forgot me, and wanted us to get together for a reunion. I figured he recently got dumped and was looking up old girlfriends. For me, this was just another excuse to have a weekend away from the situation I was in.

He lived far north in New York State, almost to Canada. I took a commuter bus, which was a six-hour ride. Dean picked me up at the bus depot. He was glad to see me, and we talked on the way to his apartment. We spent the better part of the evening reminiscing about our affair in Berkeley. After a few glasses of wine, the truth came out. His wife had left him, and he felt lost. He reiterated how much he thought of me over the years and that he'd made some major mistakes in his life.

"Dean, we've all made mistakes, and have regrets, but we can't go back."

We were having a nice weekend together, and I felt strangely comfortable with him. Dean mentioned that he had some LSD. I stared at him.

"Dean, that was six years ago."

"Come on, remember how much fun we had?"

Against my better judgement, I popped a capsule with him. Perhaps I thought it would be a religious experience, or open up some clogged brain vessels that were stopping me from being free. We floated around the rabbit hole for a while in his living room. We laughed at everything.

I decided a bath was in order, so Dean ran me one. He lit candles all around the room and watched me in the tub for a while. Later that night we had sex, which wasn't emotional or satisfying, but was interesting on LSD.

The second day he showed me around his neighborhood and we stopped in a small coffee house, like we used to do on Telegraph Avenue in Berkeley. We sat there for quite a while talking about our lives. He reached across the table and took my hand. I let him but didn't respond as he stroked it, so he pulled his hand back.

He dropped me off at the bus depot on Sunday afternoon, and I headed back to the city. A month later Dean called me from a phone booth in New York City. He insisted he was still in love with me. I refused to see him. In reality, our connection was long gone.

~~~~~

It was the end of May, and with summer approaching, I seemed to be gaining strength in the "self" department. We had a new manager at work, Reggie Paulsen. I could tell by the way he moved, by his mannerisms and tone of speech, that he was gay. We hit it off immediately and became good friends in the months to come. We hung out together after work and sometimes got together on weekends. I drove him crazy with talk of Hawaii and how I wanted to move there. He told me I was "island possessed!" He lived with his boyfriend, a ginger named Leo Thomas. They were getting bored with my talk of the islands and often changed the subject whenever I brought it up.

That summer I turned thirty. My friend Daisy Holmes moved to Alaska with her boyfriend. I bought her car, a gray Datsun 510, which I nicknamed the Gray Mouse. It afforded me a new sense of freedom and mobility. Getting it from upstate New York to the Bronx was an ordeal in itself. It had a flat tire and something wrong with the emergency brake. But a couple of my friends in the country, who knew about cars, helped me with everything. I rolled my way back to the Bronx in the Gray Mouse with a new lease on life. I felt like Nadia Comaneci, who had just won seven perfect scores in gymnastics at the summer Olympics in Montreal, Canada. Suddenly, my life was looking up!

July 4, 1976, was a huge event in New York City, the country's bicentennial. There were tall ships from all over the world sailing down the Hudson River to the Statue of Liberty in the harbor. I rushed downtown alone to lower Manhattan to be part of the two hundredth anniversary of American independence. Millions of people teemed through the streets, like something in a scene out of a Godzilla movie. People were shoulder to shoulder, everyone joyous and celebrating. I did not feel alone at all. I worked my way down to Battery Park at the bottom tip of Manhattan. People were perched on monuments, lamp posts, anyplace where they could have an unobstructed view of the harbor. Once it was dark, you felt the energy in the air, everyone anticipating the fireworks. Suddenly there was a loud boom, and it all began. The fireworks were spectacular and gave me goose bumps. The culmination was a final set of fireworks that formed the American flag, which dropped from the sky over the Statue of Liberty. Everyone around me locked arms, strangers but together. All you could hear were a million voices singing the "Star Spangled Banner," and then "America the Beautiful." It was all so emotional, people were actually crying. When it was over, that huge mass of people rushed to the subway entrances, quietly and orderly, stunned by what they'd experienced. It was a day I will never forget.

On my way home from work that next week, I passed the cathedral I'd gone into a few months back. There must have been a high Mass being celebrated, because music streamed from the entrance. The interior of the church reeked of frankincense. Thirty choir boys of varying sizes and ages sang choral hymns. Soon these same boys slowly walked down the center nave of the church carrying candles and a large jeweled cross, reciting prayers as they approached the altar. It was quite a ritual, like a spectacle in an Italian Fellini movie. For a moment I imagined I was at the Vatican in Rome. The sudden, loud, organ music forced my gaze upward to the towering stained-glass windows. At that moment, all I could think of was that old movie *The Hunchback of Notre Dame*. And like the movie, the organ music, stained-glass windows, and bells ringing were awe-inspiring, beautiful, and holy yet somewhat frightening. I sat there for a while remembering the neighborhood church I attended growing up. I pictured the white towers on the altar, and the priest in the pulpit describing what heaven was like, as if he had already been there.

It was late, and I was lying on the couch trying to fall asleep, but a summer thunderstorm brought back a thousand memories. Earlier in the evening we watched a TV special on a search for a remote tribe of Indians along the Amazon River in Brazil. Of course the program sparked memories of my summer in Colombia, South America. I flashed on Lucas Antonio Castanera, my traveling companion and lover. I still felt the thrill of him and the wildness of the country. The smell of the rain brought back the smell of the jungle. I pictured a murky river filled with alligators, and wild parrots flying and screeching overhead. I longed for that feeling of total abandon and the freedom I felt there. Memories kept my senses alive in this bleak place of hibernation.

From my journal:

Just to stand in an Incan temple in the Peruvian Andes with you. The shadow of a stone sculpture where kings were painted with gold dust. A civilization so ancient, induced by cocaine fantasies no doubt. My lips are numb, but I can still feel yours on mine, a kiss now cold upon my mouth. Memories of random unexpected experiences under a powerful moon, and stars that watched it all happen.

During my next session with Joan, I talked about my plans, dreams, and wishes.

"You do know it was no coincidence that you walked into my office when you were approaching your thirtieth birthday, don't you?"

I turned my head to the side questioningly.

"Perhaps you're at a crossroads in your life," she said.

That revelation became clear once she verbalized it.

She asked me to tell her a story from my teenage years that I remembered vividly.

I began. "I started dating at age thirteen." I noticed Joan wince, but I continued. "Well, I was thirteen going on eighteen, and it was the Bronx after all. I met a guy in the neighborhood where my mother's dress factory was. He was a little older than me, maybe sixteen. His name was Ethan Edwards, but everyone called him Whitey, because he had really blonde hair, I mean, almost white. He wore it in a flattop, short and spikey on the top, slicked back on the sides. He had a funny way of talking. He would stretch out his sentences, and the words would roll out of his mouth in a singsong fashion, while twirling a toothpick around at the same time. He liked to say, 'Oh, yeah,' a lot, in that stretched-out, singsong way."

Joan laughed. "You have an intricate way of recalling your memories and describing people."

I continued. "Whitey was a popular guy, and I guess I thought he was cool. In the summer, Bronx Beach & Pool was the place we all went to cool off from the sweltering city streets. I knew Whitey liked me, a girl can just tell when a guy likes her. We were horsing around in the pool. Elvis's song "It's Now or Never" was playing on the transistor radio. I still think of him when I hear that song.

I rested my arms on the pool deck and dangled my legs in the water. Whitey came up behind me and put his hands under the water and around my waist. He spooned me from behind, and I could feel everything, I mean everything. I was filled with curiosity, excitement, and fear, all at the same time. He didn't kiss me, but later on that day, and in subsequent days to come, we did a lot of kissing."

Joan asked, "And this was okay with your parents?"

I hesitated. "I would let Whitey come over when my parents weren't home. We'd watch TV and make out on the couch. He'd always try to touch me all over, and even though I wanted him to, I was hesitant. One night I let him put his hands under my blouse, take off my bra, and touch my breasts. Afterward, I felt bad, as if I had done something really dirty. When my parents came home later that night, he had already gone home.

My mother could tell by my expression that something wasn't right and asked me what was wrong."

"What did you tell your mother?"

I wondered why Joan was so interested in such a silly story from my teen years.

I went on. "I told my mother Whitey had been over that night. She asked me if he hurt me in any way. I was ashamed, and a little scared to tell her. I pointed to my cute little perky breasts, and told her he touched me there. My mother's expression changed, and she roared with laughter. She said, "'Oh Adriana, it's all right; don't worry. After all, he didn't take a piece out of you, now did he?'"

Joan didn't take her eyes off mine. "And what did you think of your mother's response?"

I thought about it for a while and said, "I was shocked that she took my admission so lightly. It was as if she was only concerned about my virginity, and nothing else. I was twelve years old when I got my period, and I remember my mother saying, "'Now you can't let boys touch you down there anymore.'" I thought that was a weird thing for a mother to say to her daughter. I wondered what she thought I'd been doing all those years in my childhood."

"How did that make you feel?"

"Confused. I didn't know what was important. I felt misunderstood, and that she was making light of my experience."

Joan summed up by saying, "Maybe your mother was just making an effort to ease your fears. Perhaps she was letting you know that what had happened wasn't all that bad. I think you're too hard on your mother. You refuse to accept any of the good strokes she gives you. Do you think maybe you're punishing her? At some point, Adriana, you have to stop punishing your mother for the past."

FOUR

ESCAPE FROM BABYLON

Illusions are to the soul what atmosphere is to the earth. Roll up
that tender air and the planet dies, the color fades. The earth we
walk on is a parched cinder. It is marl we tread and fiery cobbles
scorch our feet. By truth we are undone. Life is a dream. 'Tis waking
that kills us. He who robs us of our dreams robs us of our life.

— *Virginia Woolf,* **Orlando**: *A Biography*

I knew the longer I stayed, the more difficult it would be to leave and
continue with my own life. But I had a plan and walked around singing
songs of freedom. I longed to be in a creative environment again. I saw
myself tying up loose ends and solidifying my goal: moving to Maui.

It was August 1976. I drove to Cape Cod to spend two weeks with my cousin
Angela and her boyfriend Ash. I had to drive through a virtual rainstorm
to get there. Muddy water covered the wheels of the Gray Mouse, and for
a while it seemed as if the ocean was reclaiming the Cape. Once I reached
Buzzard's Bay the weather cleared, and I was passing quaint old houses
with lots of history. Shades of the movie *Grey Gardens* came to mind. I was
looking forward to ending my summer there. I arrived wet and hungry
at my cousin's house. They had a fire going, and I immediately sat in a
comfortable chair.

"The weather tomorrow is expected to be nice," Ash said.

I looked up "Right now I'm just happy to be sitting here by the fire."

"I went to the fish market today and got everything for the makings of a real cioppino."

"Oh, Ash, that sounds wonderful. I should have brought some Italian bread from the Bronx."

"I stopped at the market for a decent bread while I was in town. We can make garlic toast."

TROPICAL GOUACHE

The next day was cloudy as well, so I sat around doing watercolors of tropical scenes in the pages of my journal. We recounted family stories and did a lot of laughing. It was so good to be with my cousins again. I spent a few summers at the Cape, and it always recharged my batteries. Angela and I reminisced about me and Gia spending weeks at her parents' mini farm in Connecticut. My aunt Mari would send me into the chicken coop in the morning to collect eggs for breakfast. Walking out the kitchen door, she'd yell after me, "Keep an eye on that rooster, he's a mean one." Angela laughed.

"Angela, you were just a baby, so you probably don't remember a lot of our antics. One time your brother, Cody, and I went hunting for blueberries. Your mother wanted to make muffins. The farmer who owned the land came running after us with a shotgun. I'm sure he never intended to shoot us, just scare us off."

"No, I don't remember any of that. But I do remember when you and Gia were teenagers. I loved watching the two of you tease up your hair into beehives, and put all that black eye makeup on. I was fascinated."

"Yeah, the city girls visiting the country. You can take the girls out of the Bronx, but you can't take the Bronx out of the girls."

"Adriana, what ever happened to that boyfriend you had, Jamie?"

"Jamie Fitzpatrick? You were so little, I can't believe you remember him."

Angela said, "My mother always spoke of him as such a nice guy, and my father said he was a real gentlemen. He even wrote a letter to my parents thanking them for letting you stay at our house over the summer. Weren't you guys together for a few years?"

"Yeah, well, I was only seventeen when we got engaged. My mother always said, "What sort of a union could this be? You're going to be a dress designer, and he's going to be a garbage man?"

"What happened?" Angela asked.

"When Jamie went into the National Guard, I went to fashion college. My life changed rapidly, and he had only been gone a few weeks when I met someone else. Jamie had been going to night classes to study aeronautics, I suppose to appease my parents, and impress me. I had all his notebooks, so I called his parents and told them we needed to talk. I showed up at their apartment and handed Jamie's notebooks to his father. I confessed that I was having second thoughts about our engagement. Of course, I didn't mention that I was already dating someone else. His mother looked me over from head to foot and said, "You've lost a lot of weight." His father held the books with a bewildered expression, and told me that Jamie never went to Aeronautics classes. He made up the whole story."

"You're kidding!" Angela said.

"No, and the worst thing was that even after I sent him a dear John letter, when he was at Fort Dix, he showed up at a family wedding in his uniform. I suppose he thought springing a visit on me was a great idea. Instead I was having a good time dancing with one of the groomsmen in the wedding party, while he was sitting on a chair in the lobby crying. It was a horrible scene. My aunts were comforting him while I was gliding around the dance floor, riddled with guilt."

"Oh brother, what a scene that must have been," she said, shaking her head.

I told Angela and Ash about my plans to move to Hawaii. They remarked that we all should follow our dreams, although they knew that it meant we probably wouldn't see much of each other in the years to come. I admitted that I fell in love with Maui, and felt artistically inspired there. I told them that I had fantasies about Hawaii since I was a child. My parents had an old LP that they played often. It was all Hawaiian music, and I would listen to it and drift off into a tropical fantasy. I recalled a guy I dated, a football player from the Czech Republic, taking me to the Hawaii Kai Night Club in New York City when I was eighteen, and the excitement I felt in the island atmosphere. Even then, I think, Hawaii was a dormant volcano in my subconscious.

After two weeks of fun and sun on the sand dunes in Cape Cod, I drove back to the Bronx. My summer vacation at work was over as well, and the drudgery of the daily commute into Manhattan began again. The quality of air in the city was unbearable. It was a struggle for every breadth. But I saw light at the end of the long dark tunnel I was in.

~~~~~~

During my first session back with Joan, she prompted me to delve into my love for and relationship with Filomena Genoa, the woman who took care of me during my formative years.

"Tell me what you remember about growing up around Filomena and her family."

"God, I remember her apartment vividly. Filomena was from a different part of Italy than my parents. She spoke English with a heavy Italian accent. Her apartment building was right across the street from my mother's dress factory. It was on the top floor of the building, and had an expansive view of the neighborhood. The furnishings were very austere compared to my parents' opulent apartment. Hell, we even had a fake fireplace in our living room, and cut glass candelabras. All the furniture in Filomena's apartment was of dark wood, very plain, and there was a red velvet couch with white doilies where your head should rest. I have photos of me as a baby on that couch. There were two bedrooms, similarly decorated. Filomena slept with her daughter Anna Maria, a secretary, in one bedroom. Her son Nico, a cop, had the other bedroom. They were much older than me, but were like siblings. My mother's youngest sister, Camille, was actually friends with

Nico and Anna Maria. That's how much of an age difference there was between us.

"The kitchen had a pale green wooden cabinet with glass doors which took up a whole wall. It was a small kitchen, so all the dishes, pots and pans, everything was in that cabinet. A large table sat against the wall with four chairs that barely fit into the space. She cooked different foods than my mother did. I distinctly remember the potato balls. I loved to watch her mix mashed potatoes with garlic, parsley, Italian cheese and an egg. She'd roll them in breadcrumb and fry them in olive oil. When I became an adult, she'd make them for me whenever I visited."

"Adriana, how did you feel there?"

"Like it was my real home. Like she was my real mother. She took me to school every day and picked me up after class. She performed most of the motherly duties my mother didn't. As a small child, I imagined Filomena gave me to my mother because she was poor, and felt I'd have a better life. It was really screwed up, but I was a very confused kid."

"When your mother became aware of your feelings, you told me she distanced you from Filomena. You, in turn, felt that love snatched away from you. You suppressed your love for Filomena so as not to hurt your mother. But inside you went on loving her for a very long time. Didn't you?"

"Yes, yes, it's true," I said, sobbing uncontrollably.

~~~~~~

At work that week, my manager, Reggie Paulson, approached me with excitement. He pulled me aside and said, "Guess where Leo and I are moving? Maui," he blurted out before I even had a chance to ask where.

I stood there dumbfounded. After all the months I drove them crazy with talk of the islands, and their telling me I was island obsessed.

"How did this come about?"

"We started looking into Maui after you spoke so positively about your experience there."

"Wow. I'm a little surprised, but I'm happy for you both."

"Don't give me that sad look. You can stay with us until you find a place there."

"Really?"

"Of course, so we will stay in close touch."

Excitement filled my being as I left the office that day, knowing the universe was kicking in.

As soon as I got home, I took out Jimmie Cliff's album *The Harder They Come,* and played it over and over again. The song "By the Rivers of Babylon" stuck in my head for days. My parents were aware of my plans, and my father suggested I leave my car with his brother Rosario in San Lorenzo, California. He told me my car would be safe there and not to ship it until I was sure I was staying on Maui.

At another session with Joan, she asked me about my last relationship. I told her about Harvey Cooper, aka Hank, and how we'd had an artistic connection, which I liked. We had similar backgrounds, and I felt at peace with him. Prior to Hank, I had chosen men who were attractive but had no affinity for the arts. True, I connected with them in other ways but always got the feeling that my art was a threat to the relationship in some way, so I stifled my artistic side.

From my journal after sessions with Joan:

—I am on the path to seeking men I have more things in common with.

—My boyfriend from the commune, Romeo, was not artistic and rejected the artistic part of me. I hung on to his memory because it was a time in my life when I was happy, and I felt protected and safe with him and the group I lived with on the commune.

—Relationships and art seem to be in conflict. I neglect my art when I am in a relationship.

—I have an "alone script" that says I can never be happy with someone for a long time.

—I get romantically involved before I question if the relationship is good for me. I don't protect myself. If I am disappointed and feel vulnerable, I get angry and want to end the relationship.

—My childhood was emotionally unstable.

—In relationships with men, I fear love and happiness will be snatched away from me.

—I'm attracted to men who are affectionate and nurturing but unmotivated, like my father. Or I am attracted to men like my mother who are not nurturing but are aloof and independent. Somehow I got the message that men cannot be both.

—I was instrumental in bringing about the ends of my relationships.

Joan summed up by reflecting on a few things we had discussed. "I know you think your issue is with your mother, but I think the issue is with your father. You told me that your father left you and your mother a few times when she was having the affair with Dario. He even had his own apartment. I think you have abandonment issues with men in relationships. You fear they will leave you like your father did. Perhaps you yourself initiate things to make the relationship end, feeling the end is inevitable anyway."

~~~~~

I took a weekend trip upstate to visit my friends, Kelly Cooke and Johnny Doyle. As soon as I drove out of the city, I noticed the difference in the air, and I could breathe again. Their infant was a toddler now. I picked her up and held her in my arms.

"Kelly, remember when she was just born and I held her in my lap? You and Johnny were living in that cottage in Fort Bragg in Northern California."

"They grow so fast," Kelly answered. "So what are your plans now?"

"Drive cross country, stay with my friends in California for a while, and then fly to Maui."

"You're not planning on driving across the country alone, are you?"

"No, but I haven't worked out all the details yet. Have you heard anything from Daisy Holmes since she moved to Alaska?"

"Yeah, they're living about two hundred miles outside Anchorage in a really remote area! She told me they had to travel inland through the wilderness via dog sled, then a few days further by canoe along a river. They're in a fishing camp for now. She told me she'd write to you when they get settled somewhere permanent."

"Wow, that wouldn't be for me, but I'm sure Daisy is loving the Alaskan backcountry."

When I left Kelly's place and drove back to the Bronx, I wondered if I'd ever see her again, if I'd ever see upstate New York again. I thought of our long snowy winter living at Deer Creek. Kelly was a substitute teacher, and the phone would ring at five in the morning, calling her to cover a class. She'd be called in on the worst days of the year, when the regular teachers called in sick. We'd run out to her car through the cold snowy air in the dark with a flashlight. She'd lift up the hood and insert an electric dipstick into the oil to heat it enough to start the engine. I'd scrape the snow and ice off the windows and then watch her drive away along a treacherous road.

As I drove over the George Washington Bridge into the Bronx, I thought of how I loved being around lots of people on the commune. Perhaps it was because I'm an only child and saw the members of the commune as the brothers and sisters I never had. They filled the empty spaces in myself. Now I relished being on my own. I am not sure how that evolved—perhaps living on my parents' couch in the living room and not having a personal space.

~~~~~~

The fall is opera season in New York City, and I decided to treat my parents to a performance at the Metropolitan Opera House at Lincoln Center. My mother told me that her father used to walk around their house singing Italian arias, but they never actually went to an opera. My parents and I dressed up and took a cab into Manhattan. We arrived at the Met very excited. We had great seats, and soon the chatter faded as the crystal globes lifted to the ceiling and the theater darkened. It was Giuseppe Verdi's *Rigoletto*, my favorite opera. I closed my eyes when the tenor sang "La Donna è Mobile," my favorite aria, and I drifted off to somewhere magical. The richness of voices, sets of tapestry, costumes from the sixteenth century in velvets and brocades. My parents loved it.

At the end, my father stood up and yelled, "Bravo!" as people threw roses and bouquets of flowers on the stage. The fullness of life at that moment was sublime.

My parents seemed to calm down about my leaving soon, and we settled into a stride over the next few weeks. I assured them that I would come back to visit every year over the holidays.

My mother said, "Your father won't ever get on a plane, but I will come to Hawaii for a visit when you are settled."

Joan, my therapist, was right. If I accepted my life decisions, so would my family. I regarded the past year and a half as a test of endurance and inner reflection. We began to enjoy each other again. I wanted to leave on a high note. I knew all about leaving people I loved, and leaving my family was even more difficult than I had anticipated.

As my mother and father talked away over supper, a memory popped into my head. It was the very first house we lived in when I was a child. Saturday was cleaning day, and there was no going out with friends.

My mother would say, "Adriana, put the Italian records on."

Then we spent the whole day cleaning the apartment. There were steep alleyways between the buildings, and occasionally an old man would appear below the kitchen window. He played the accordion and had a monkey on his shoulder. My mother would tell me to give him some change, and I'd run to the window and throw some coins into the alley. The monkey would retrieve them, and they would both smile up at me. Out in the street, I heard a man yelling in Italian about what he was selling. He drove a large wagon drawn by two horses. On one side were stacked fresh fruits in boxes, and on the other side, vegetables. My mother would send me out in the street with a list of what to buy.

I became emotional at this memory and my eyes teared up.

"What's wrong, Adriana?"

"Nothing, ma. Just a precious memory."

From my journal:

We laughed a lot, just the three of us. We played Italian music, and I danced with my father. In English, the words of the song are, "Just say I need her like roses need the rain." It felt so good to get really down with my folks. I love them so much. It's difficult for me to understand loving yet having to leave. That you have to live all the same, like proving to yourself you can make it without them. They will continue to live inside me. I think they understand me now, or perhaps it was me who didn't understand myself.

During a session with Joan, she reflected on some of the issues she saw in my life. She was summing everything up in ways I could understand, hoping I would react differently in the future. "You may not be successful in changing your 'alone script,' but at least you will understand what is behind some of your actions and life choices. That can be a consolation if nothing else."

I told her I was envious of the bond my mother had with her three sisters. "I always thought they were more important to her than me or my father. I knew it by the way she reacted if we spent a holiday without them. She didn't feel it was a holiday unless they were all together. My uncles referred to the four sisters as the *eight hundreds*," I added, and I snickered.

Joan looked at me with a blank expression.

"Well ... my mother and her sisters were all big women. I guess it was a snide comment my uncles made about their weight in retaliation to their feeling left out, when the sisters were all together! Perhaps they felt the same way I did."

Joan nodded. "I think you're afraid to show your mother too much affection. Somewhere along the line, you got the message that showing love is a sign of weakness. You want to show her love, but she has a lot of power over you, and you don't want to be consumed by it. I think you must hold back love from men for the same reason. You want to appear strong and independent. But from the description of your last relationship, you seem to be overcoming that. From what you've told me, it sounds like, because you were an only child, your parents told you that you were alone in the world. They reiterated that enough times so that you believed that your place in the world was to be alone."

I listened intently to Joan's observations.

She said, "Adriana, you have to make a contract with yourself to stop running and to let someone love you."

From my journal after sessions with Joan:

—My parents think of me as an extension of themselves. I see myself as a separate being.
—I try to measure up to my mother because she was a successful, independent woman.
—Joan remarked that from what I'd described, my father has a lot of "nurturing parent," and my mother, "playful child," according to the transactional parenting model.
—I've attempted to push my methods for happiness on my parents, concerts, traveling, new places, and people. But that is my enjoyment and may not be theirs

Leaving Joan's office, I was walking to the train station when I ran into Jordan, the guy with the leather chaps I worked with at the market research company.

He said, "I want to take you to dinner."

"It's late," I said. "I hate riding these trains at night."

"That's easy. I'll give you money for a taxi."

"Really? You'd do that? Are you sure?"

"Of course. I'm making good money now," he said.

We walked to a restaurant a few blocks away and had a nice dinner. It was great catching up with him. As promised, he gave me $20 for a taxi. Cabs sped past us going uptown, and he finally snagged one.

"So good to see you again, Adriana." He helped me into the backseat.

"Where are you going to?" the driver asked.

"To the northeastern tip of the Bronx," I answered, surprised at how young he was.

We rode in silence for a while as I checked out his name and number on the license hanging on the sun visor.

He took out a bag of weed. "Do you mind rolling me a joint? By the way, my name is Elliot."

"Elliot, I have to confess, I can't roll a joint to save my life."

"Damn, it's Colombian," he said.

Somehow he managed to roll himself a joint while driving. He lit it up and took a hit, then passed the joint to me. We proceeded to get stoned. It turned out to be a crazy and chaotic ride back to the Bronx. He was chatty the whole way, and I barely got a word in edgewise.

When we reached my parents' apartment house, he said, "We should stay in touch," as I handed him the money for the total fare flashing on the meter.

"Sure, Elliot," I said as he wrote down his phone number. I smiled, waved, and got out of the cab. I had no intention of ever calling him. I was just happy to make it home in one piece.

~~~~~~

At the next session with Joan, she asked me to delve into my relationship with my artwork. "Tell me something about art in your life. What inspires you? How did your parents relate to that part of you when you were a child?"

"I would say I'm most inspired by color. When I see a particular color or fabric, it sets off all sorts of design combinations and forms in my head. Also, looking at the work of other artists, I see endless possibilities. Gauguin is my favorite artist, and a big influence on my own artwork. I love the way he incorporates color, nudes, and tropical scenes. I've experimented in so many different forms of artistic expression: painting, drawing, pottery, stained glass, wood cuts, poetry, writing, photography, fashion design, and illustration. And one you're familiar with right now, glass bead jewelry. You know, I designed a coatdress for a fashion show in college, which was on the front page of the *Herald Tribune*."

Joan lifted her eyebrows. "Really?"

"I was so proud. I still have the newspaper clipping in a drawer somewhere. Of course, I gave the coatdress to the model who wore it in the fashion show. That was the customary thing to do."

Joan smiled.

SKETCH OF TWEED COATDRESS IN FASHION SHOW

"I do understand that art is my life's work, but it wasn't easy to come to that conclusion. As a child, whenever I was drawing or painting, my mother would find something else for me to do. She'd say, 'Adriana, that's something you do when you have nothing else to do!' As if it were just a hobby, a meaningless pastime. But anyone who has a creative nature knows it's a need. You have to paint, draw, write, play music, take photographs, whatever your artistic gift is. That is the life of a creative person."

Joan said, "I believe what you are saying is correct."

That day, after we discussed art in my life, I left her office wanting more, so I roamed around a few of the art stores in Manhattan. There was a definite knowledge that I would not have such a selection of supplies, paints, brushes, and various mediums where I was going. I would have to deal with that aspect of life on a remote island. In New York you have constant access to your wish list. I knew the lack of it would take getting used to.

From my journal after sessions with Joan:

—My concept of work is a job, usually one that I don't relate to at all.

—I am intimidated by a large white canvas, as to how I will use the total space.

—I need a supportive environment and the energy and feedback of other artists.

—In art school I was just another artist, not The Artist, and had to compete for strokes.

—Negative criticism from instructors caused me to withdraw from my work at times.

—I saw painting and drawing as "real art," and often overlooked photography and writing as valid forms of art and creativity.

—As a child, I received mixed signals about being both an artist and a success in life.

Joan closed that session by telling me I was a talented, creative, and beautiful person. She said, "I think you're finally seeking friends and partners who reinforce, admire, and encourage your artistic traits. Adriana, don't forget that art is your work, and you do not have to feel guilty about wanting to paint and draw."

I put a newspaper ad in the *Village Voice* stating I was driving to California and was looking for people to share the driving and expenses. Days went by without a response. Then one day I received a phone call from a woman who said she and her sister were planning to go to California, and that they were more than willing to share the driving and expenses. I took the train to Greenwich Village and met the sisters in a café for lunch. Sophie and Fiona O'Brien seemed really cool. We discussed what route we wanted to take. They mentioned having an aunt who lived in Georgia and wanted to visit and stay with her for a few days. I was agreeable to doing that, and we set a date to leave.

Since I was already in the Village, I arranged to meet my friend Adam Hirschfeld at the Ninth Circle for a beer. He had called to tell me he was staying in Manhattan for a few days.

I arrived early and got a table. I looked around the bar and thought of how it was when I went there with my first lover, Zackery Darcy. At that time there were peanut shells all over the floor, and barrels of peanuts randomly placed between tables. You would eat the peanuts and toss the shells on the floor, which were never swept up. It was such a cool place back then.

Adam walked in and I got up to hug him. We ordered beers and caught up on gossip. I told him I was driving to California with two sisters.

"I'm sure I'll stay with Suki and Star in California for a while, but my goal is to move to Maui."

"You know I'll come visit you for sure. I've always wanted to visit a tropical island."

"Yes, Adam, for sure. I will write to you when I get settled."

We walked out of the Ninth Circle together. We hugged again, kissed, and said our goodbyes. Adam headed toward the lower East Village, and I headed to the Eighth Street subway station. I was glad we'd remained friends through the years. Before walking down the steps to the train platform, I turned to take one last look at Greenwich Village, knowing I probably wouldn't see it for quite a while. Then I turned back around and walked down the steps into the darkness of the subway tunnel.

~~~~~~

On my last session with Joan, I walked in smiling.

"You seem uplifted today."

"I had the craziest dream last night," I said and began to laugh.

"Tell me about it."

"I dreamt I had an apartment, but I don't know what city it was in. I told a guy I met casually that he could stay with me, but I didn't know who he was. I gave him sheets for the sofa bed in the living room. I had a small baby monkey that someone had given me to take care of. It was so tiny that I put it in a box, and fed it formula.

"There was a knock on the door and it was my cousin Gia's husband, Stu. He walked in as if he lived near me, which he did not. He looked around my apartment with a puzzled expression. I asked him where Gia was, and he said she was on her way up the stairs. The apartment was a mess, with things all over the kitchen counter, and my new roommate's stuff strewn on the furniture. Gia walked in the front door examining every inch of my apartment. As her eyes circled the room, she seemed displeased but didn't comment. Then she said, 'let's go somewhere for lunch.' The three of us left the apartment and looked for a place to eat.

"We were having fun and were gone for a long time. I'd forgotten about the monkey. Suddenly I remembered that I had left it closed up in a small box. I jumped up from the table and told them I had to go. I rushed home as fast as I could. As soon as I arrived at my apartment, I ran to the box and opened it up, fearing the little monkey might be dead. It was alive, so I took it out and hugged it. I carried the monkey over to show Gia and Stu, who had just walked in the front door. They looked at the monkey and then at me as if I was crazy. After they left, my new roommate asked me what I was going to do with the monkey. I shrugged.

"Suddenly, the monkey was the size of a child. Then it turned into an adult male midget speaking for himself. I told him I'd make a small futon that he could sleep on. He noticed the Castro convertible chair bed, which was where I slept. I kept pointing to the little futon, but he kept shaking his head and pointing to the chair bed. I succumbed and began looking for single-sized sheets for the chair bed. When I found them, I woke up."

"So what do you think that dream symbolized?"

"The only thing that made sense was that I had a cat for a while who I affectionately called Monkey. Monkey is what my mother always called her three cats when they were mischievous. She always said it in a loving way. Now, I do the same thing," I answered.

"That was a crazy dream, but I think there's more there than the affectionate term Monkey!"

I sat there for a while pondering the dream. "Well, I know my mother spent a lot of time comparing me to my cousin Gia—how she was married, how she had a child and a traditional, secure life, and that I had none of those things. Perhaps I was feeling 'less than' in their presence, feeling ashamed of my living situation. Perhaps I felt as though I had to measure up to Gia in some way."

"That's good. You're beginning to figure things out. Even though you chose a different path in life than your family and friends, that doesn't mean you'd be happy living their lives."

I continued. "I have to give more thought to the monkey. Maybe it started off as if I was nurturing it, then I felt guilty that I forgot about it, that it could die. Then the innocent little monkey turned into a demanding midget that I had no control over. Maybe that was my relationship with my mother—how I thought I was taking care of her, nurturing her back to health. I felt guilty every time I was out having fun with friends, as if I was neglecting her. That she might die as a result."

"You've made some huge strides during these sessions. You're able to decipher the meaning behind many of the things that occur in your life, even your dreams."

Joan told me she hoped she'd helped me to recognize and understand my patterns, and how my "alone script" colored everything. Of course I felt she helped me immensely. The sessions revealed the secrets and the root of why I did what I did, and how I reacted to the people around me. I told her that knowledge was priceless.

She wore one of the glass bead necklaces I'd made for her. She touched it and said, "I'll think of you whenever I wear it."

I teared up a little.

She said, "Don't cry. I was happy I could help you see that you alone have the power to set yourself free and live the life you want to live. If you do that, everything else will fall into place. You know that now, don't you, Adriana?"

"Yes, I felt the 'self' slowly coming back to me with each session. I know now what triggers me to do things, and to react in certain ways, ways that are not always in my own best interest."

Joan and I hugged. I left her office feeling light as a feather as I strolled down the street to the subway station. Walking along the streets of Manhattan, my mind kept playing Jimmie Cliff's song "By the Rivers of Babylon."

From my journal after my last session with Joan:

—I am definitely part of the clinging relationship with my parents for emotional support.
—I am not responsible for my parents' or anyone else's happiness.
—I am discovering my self-worth and not feeling defensive any longer.
—I will love and miss my family a lot, but that is normal.

From my journal on November 4, 1976:

Sounds of faraway places call with exotic music, wonder, and fantasy. A driving force since the beginning of time. The unknown, which holds all the promise of tomorrow, and answers the questions of today. Now that it's time to leave, I can only pray for everything to fall into its proper place in the universe. I feel as if I've been a captive in a world that I had left behind a long time ago. I can feel the universe carrying me away from captivity. Once, my nuclear family and communal family were everything to me; they completed me. Now I must toss myself into the unknown again, searching for Gauguin.

FIVE

NOT AN ORDINARY LIFE

"Never love anyone who treats you ordinary"

Oscar Wilde

W e began our long cross-country journey in the first week of November 1976. Three women in the Gray Mouse rolling south on I-95. We did a lot of driving on that first day, but it gave us time to get acquainted. I wasn't sure how old these sisters were, but I knew they were younger than me, because they spoke about college a lot. Sophie and Fiona O'Brien were two blonde bubbleheaded sisters, basically out for fun, and I was willing to go right along with them. The open road gives one a license to chuck inhibitions out the window, and we did just that.

We stayed in a motel that first night. I walked up to the desk to secure a room, and they sneaked in. Luckily the room had a sofa bed. We were wiped out, so after supper at a diner we'd stumbled across, we went straight to sleep.

When we hit Virginia, someone told us about Luray Caverns, a popular tourist attraction, so we decided to spend some time exploring the caves. It was all we expected and more. Strange cathedral-high formations of limestone in varying colors and sizes lined the cavern's underground walls. Clear pale green water exposed what looked like crystals at the bottom.

I expected a phantom to appear around every corner of the cavern. It's amazing what goes on underground that we rarely see.

That night we stayed overnight at a women's college as guests. We were given our own rooms with TVs, and I felt lucky to be traveling with college students. The O'Brien sisters seemed to know how to take advantage of perks like these wherever we went. The food was nice in the cafeteria, and we had a comfortable night off the road.

～～～～

When we reached Georgia, Fiona called her aunt for directions to her house. I wasn't prepared for such a stately home. We drove down a very long drive lined with weeping willow trees, which opened to a large plantation-style house. I thought I was driving onto the set of *Gone with the Wind*.

Her aunt was waiting on the porch steps. "Come on in, girls," she said in a southern drawl.

The house was beautiful inside. Large rooms with wood floors, and tall windows. It seemed crazy that this old woman lived all alone in that huge house. There was a wide staircase that led to the bedrooms upstairs.

She walked us up the stairs and opened the door to a room, looked at me, and said, "This is your room, luv," in her drawl.

It was plush and comfortable, with a fireplace. I felt like a ruffian in my Air Force parka with the fur-trimmed hood in such opulent surroundings. I threw myself on the bed, stared at the frescoed ceiling, and smiled. There were peach trees on the property, but it was November.

Pecans were in season, and her aunt made pecan pies, which we consumed with lots of whipped cream. We ate and drank like aristocrats. I found out that down south, happy hour is any hour. At night I would take a mint julep up to my bedroom and sit on a chair by the fireplace with my legs slung over the side, and sip it slowly. I felt cozy and safe. We spent a few days at their aunt's house in Georgia, and I was almost sad when it was time to continue on our journey. Auntie waved goodbye from the front porch as we drove away.

～～～～

Our next stop was New Orleans, Louisiana. The girls knew some guys attending college there and decided to stay in the men's dorm. I checked it out but decided to get a hotel room instead. Actually, it felt good to be on my own for a night. Sophie and Fiona wanted to go to a college game with their friends, and I had no interest in football.

I found a restaurant in town for lunch. I walked around the French Quarter while it was still daylight. I took note of all the Spanish wrought-iron balconies and wondered who lived in those apartments. There were palm trees everywhere, and most of the court yards had bananas. I hung out on Jackson Square for a bit, observing street artists drawing and painting. I sat on a park bench and pictured riverboats chugging down the Mississippi River.

After I freshened up, I went back to Bourbon Street. It was a whole different scene at night. I passed by Preservation Hall, which at the time I did not know the historical significance of. I heard Dixieland Jazz and saw people sitting at tables shouting, "Yeah!" I asked who was playing the piano.

"That's Sweet Emma," I heard a voice say.

Someone else called out, "That's Tuba Joe."

Voices in the crowd rattled off the names of various people playing different instruments. They knew each musician by name. The music was soulful and invigorating. I strolled along the sidewalks teeming with people, enjoying life in the French Quarter.

From my journal:

Old men and women of jazz out of the past—Tuba Joe, blaring horns, and Sweet Emma tickling the ivories on a cold night. People standing outside on the street peering into foggy windows, with musical notes streaming out. Satin ladies and red crystal beads. Bourbon Street, blazing with jazz and flesh clubs. Seedy men hustling tourists off the sidewalks into hot, steamy clubs, with the promise of heaven.

It was November 19, and we were on the Arizona-New Mexico border, Native American country, the Navajo and Zuni tribes. There were quite a few street markets, and we had fun roaming among the pottery and jewelry. I bought a turquoise necklace and two silver rings. We planned on driving to Santa Fe, New Mexico, to spend a day or two there. Sophie and Fiona O'Brien had friends they wanted to spend time with, and I planned to get a room somewhere and enjoy the local flavors. California was quite a few days away at the rate we were traveling.

From Albuquerque we drove into Santa Fe. The weather was sunny, but there was a chill in the air. I was happy I had my Air Force parka in the trunk. I knew I'd need it when the sun went down. Sophie and Fiona couldn't wait to see their friends, who were attending a university in the area. We parked the car outside a marketplace, and while Fiona and I cruised around, Sophie went looking for a public phone. We spied an outside café and sat down to have lunch.

When the waitress walked to our table, Fiona said, "We have a third joining us." The waitress soon returned with another menu.

"Fiona, are you enjoying the trip?" I asked.

"You know, I think this is one of the best trips I've been on."

I was happy about that, but wondered, *How many trips could this girl have possibly been on if she's still in college?*

When Sophie joined us, she was excited after talking to their friends. "They're picking us up here in an hour, so we have time to look around the markets."

"You don't mind if we leave you for a day or so, do you?" Fiona asked.

"No, not at all," I answered.

"You're welcome to come stay in the dorm with us if you want," Sophie said.

"No, I think I'll find a place to stay in Santa Fe and look around town. Maybe even catch some music." In reality, I was looking forward to some time alone.

~~~~~~

After we had lunch, the girls left. I got back in the car and drove around looking for a place to stay. There was nothing affordable in town, so I drove back out onto the main road. I passed by a place that looked decent, The Desert Inn. I parked near the office and walked in.

"I'd like a room for the night," I said.

"Well, we have some of those," said the older lady behind the desk.

"Yes, I'd like a room for tonight, maybe a few nights."

"Will you be wanting a window?" she asked.

"Aaah, that would be nice."

"That'll be an extra ten dollars a night."

"That's fine," I said.

She handed me the key to room number ten, and I walked around a corner, up a staircase, and down a corridor until I came to room ten. I unlocked the door and went inside. It was a typical motel room with a bed, desk, chair, a dresser with a TV on top, and an ice bucket. The bathroom was clean, and that was a plus.

I went back to the car and got my suitcase and a bottle of tequila out of the trunk. Once I brought my suitcase into the room and hung a few things up, I was set for the night. I took a long shower and gathered my thoughts. I walked down the hall to the ice machine I'd passed on my way to the room, filled the ice bucket, and put it in the mini fridge. I watched a couple hours of TV and was bored, so I got dressed and ventured out.

NATIVE AMERICAN CAPE

I walked around Santa Fe, wandering in and out of all the stores in town. I came across a Native American museum. It was so fascinating, all the handmade leather clothes decorated with beads, and the long, feathered headdresses. I especially loved the moccasins, and was so captivated by a cape that I whipped out my journal and sketched it. I walked a little further down the street and found a café with a bar. It was dark inside, and for a moment I was blinded after being in the bright sun. Soon everything came into focus. I sat at the bar and ordered a top-shelf margarita on the rocks.

The bartender made small talk as he mixed the drink and set it in front of me. "Where are you from? I can tell you're not from around here."

"I'm from New York, on my way to California."

There was a guy playing guitar on a small stage. No one paid attention to him, but the music added atmosphere. The bartender was really chatty, until a guy walked through the front door and sat on the barstool next to mine. The bartender apparently knew him, because he put a drink in front of him without any conversation.

"I haven't seen you around Santa Fe," the guy said without looking at me.

"I don't live here. I'm just passing through." I stared at him through the mirror behind the bar.

"Well, I've been living here for quite a while. It's a really neat place with a lot of history."

"Yes, I could tell by just walking around town."

"I'm Tommy, by the way."

I gave him my hand, smiled, and said, "I'm Adriana."

He seemed really young. I guessed somewhere between nineteen and twenty-two. Tommy and I got into a conversation, and I found him to be friendly and sweet. The guy on the stage stopped playing guitar, and the silence was deafening.

Tommy got up and walked to the jukebox to play some tunes. He wore a jeans jacket over his jeans, and a green plaid shirt underneath. I stared at his nice cowboy boots as he walked back toward me at the bar. He had straight brown hair in a traditional cut. He wasn't handsome but had a pleasant face and a great smile with dimples. I found him very attractive—well, in a young and innocent way.

"Well, Adriana, I know of a lot of cool places around here. Do you have a car?"

"I do, and I'm down with that, if you have some time to show me around."

I fished through my purse for money, but Tommy patted my arm to stop me. "I'll take care of that."

He threw some money on the bar and then helped me off the barstool. I noticed the bartender had a smirk on his face as we were leaving. We walked out of the bar and into the bright sun.

"Have you been to the museum?" he asked.

"Yeah, I was there earlier today."

He took me to another market that was off the main drag, and we roamed among the tables looking at more jewelry. The squash blossom necklaces were heavy and ornate, some with large turquoise stones. They were beautiful, and quite expensive.

"They're all so unique and beautiful," I said.

"Like you," Tommy said.

At first his attention was uncomfortable, but then I began to like it. He made me feel confident about my looks at thirty.

"I want to take you to the San Ildefonso Pueblo in the mountains north of here," he said.

"That sounds really interesting."

"You'll love the place; it's full of history."

"Tommy, I know I will. I love all that stuff."

With that, he smiled at me and said, "Let's get going while the sun is still high in the sky."

~~~~~~~~

We got in the Gray Mouse and drove into the mountains north of Santa Fe. The air was cool and dry and the surrounding scenery was arid and displayed various forms of cactus. Each new hill offered a new *buena vista*. When we reached the pueblo, it was a small village, and I saw smoke bellowing out of adobe chimneys. As we got out of the car, children and barking dogs followed us. Native American women sat on the ground with colorful blankets hanging behind them, and mounds of pottery ready to be fired. Tommy told me they were the Tewa Tribe.

Tommy didn't take his eyes off me for a second. He followed every move I made and hung on every word and gesture. He seemed really into me, and I liked it. I thought perhaps he had a thing for older women, some young guys do. I wanted to buy pottery but thought, *Where would I keep it?* I bought a colorful blanket, which I knew would travel well, and I could always use it as a wall hanging.

We drove away from the village through the mountains as the sun was setting. It was spectacular, with the sky turning shades of yellow, red, and purple. There were glistening rivers below in the valleys.

Tommy began playing with my hair. I felt strangely on fire, and was happy Tommy was sitting next to me. He lightly ran his hand along my arm.

"Your skin is so warm and soft."

I shuddered a little. "I'm probably warm from the sun."

He gazed at me. "But still," he said, his caress giving me thrills all over. "I want you real bad," he whispered, his breath tickling my ear.

"I think I want you too, Tommy."

I was shocked at my forwardness, not really knowing anything about him. He could have been an axe murderer for all I knew. Woman's intuition told me he wasn't.

"I'll take you to my place," he said.

I turned my face in his direction and smiled.

"They're probably cooking supper right about now."

I wondered who "they" were.

~~~~~~

We approached a freestanding house in the middle of vacant land. I noticed a group of men lurking outside, some younger and some older. We got out of the car, and I immediately felt uneasy. There was a breezy chill in the air, so I fetched my Air force parka out of the trunk.

Tommy reassuringly took my hand and led me inside. We went straight into the kitchen, where a few older Indian and Mexican men were sitting at the table. Another man stood at the stove. Indeed, the food smelled wonderful.

Tommy slipped my parka off and hung it on the back of a chair. I tried to act as if I was okay with the situation, but I wasn't. I was freaked out and felt I'd made a grave mistake.

Tommy noticed a change in my demeanor and asked what was wrong. I admitted I felt uneasy with all the men standing around.

Tommy took my hand and laughed. "Don't worry, they're harmless. And besides, I'll kill anyone who comes near you!"

I snickered at the youthful yet macho comment. Tommy left me standing in the kitchen alone while he went to the bathroom to wash up. I took the opportunity to disappear. I ran out to my car, started the engine, and drove away.

~~~~~~

After smelling the Mexican food in Tommy's kitchen, I looked for a place along Cerillos Road to eat. I came across an old storefront eatery, parked out front, and went inside. It looked a little sleazy, but the food smelled authentic. A few people sat at the counter eating, and a large Mexican woman was cooking in the kitchen. I sat down and ordered a traditional meal. I got lost watching her make the enchilada from scratch, but I couldn't get Tommy out of my mind. She set the plate down in front of me and stood there until I began eating. I was so hungry, I wolfed the beans and rice down quickly.

One of the men sitting at the counter suggested I try the sopapilla for dessert. "You'll love it."

I nodded in affirmation.

"A sopapilla for the young lady," he yelled at the woman in the kitchen.

She soon returned with a small bowl of honey and a few pieces of fried dough on a plate.

"Dip them," the same man said.

I ate again with gusto and thanked the man profusely. As I was dipping the last piece of fried dough into the honey, the whole day passed before me. I thought of Tommy, and how I'd split without a word or an explanation. I felt ashamed of myself, of my thoughtlessness. How sweet he was to me, showing me around Santa Fe. After all, wasn't that what the day was about? Suddenly I knew that Tommy was the whole point of the day, and I was going back to get him.

I jumped up, threw some money on the counter, and said, "Muchas gracias," as I ran out.

Driving toward Tommy's house, I wondered what I would say to him when I got there. I parked the car, and as I walked toward the house I noticed there were no men lurking around. I walked into the kitchen and saw Tommy sitting alone at the table.

He smiled when he saw me. "Adriana, where the hell did you disappear to?" Before I had a chance to answer, he added, "I knew you were coming back, because your parka was on the back of this chair."

He smiled at me as he ran his hand along the fur trim of the hood. In my madness, I forgot my Air Force parka.

I laughed and said, "Well, I had a momentary lapse of judgement."

"You don't have to feel afraid when you're with me."

"How old are you anyway, Tommy?"

"Does it really matter? I don't give a damn how old you are." He grabbed me and kissed me.

I blurted out, "I'm staying at the Desert Inn. Wanna talk about it there?"

"Even better," he said. "Then I can show you how I really feel about you."

I grabbed my Airforce parka with the fur-trimmed hood, raced for the front door, and we drove to the Desert Inn.

As we approached the motel, I told Tommy to wait for me in front of room ten. He grinned, gave me a kiss on the cheek, and got out of the car. I watched him walk toward the Desert Inn in his cowboy boots with a large stride, his green plaid shirt blowing in the breeze, and I felt a thrill. I waved at the woman behind the desk and headed around the corner and up the stairs. Tommy was leaning against the door at the end of the hallway waiting for me.

As soon as I reached him, he grabbed me and kissed me on the lips. "Ooooh, I can't wait to get you inside."

"Down boy." I laughed. Tommy snickered.

Once inside, he said, "This ain't so bad."

I became a little nervous, but he took my hand and sat on the bed. I stood in front of him. He began undressing me slowly, looking at every part of my body. He let out a few "mmms," as if he was pleased with what he saw.

"Come on, lie down," he said.

I lay on the bed watching him get undressed, happy I was still on birth control pills.

He took his boots off. When he took his shirt off, I noticed he had no hair on his chest. He slipped off his jeans and wasn't wearing any underwear. He was already hard, and I waited for him to get on top of me.

After we had sex, I got up and rifled through my suitcase for my Chinese robe.

Tommy sat up in bed and covered the lower half of his body with the sheet. I sat on the bed next to him and gave him a soft kiss on the lips. He put his arm around me, and I ran my hand along his bare chest.

"You don't have any hair on your chest. I like that," I said.

"Well, I have some Navajo in me," Tommy said with pride.

It wasn't long before he slid his hands under my robe, reached for my breasts, and began fondling them.

"I could tell you didn't get off. I'll make sure you do this time," he said, pushing me down.

He opened my robe, pushed my legs apart, and went down on me.

"That feels so good," I whispered.

He stayed down there for a while, until he knew by my breathing that I was ready for him. He moved on top of me, and we did it again. I couldn't hold back any longer and began to groan and whimper uncontrollably.

"That's better," Tommy said when we were finished.

"I know you're pleased with yourself, but take that grin off your face," I said teasingly.

"I can't help smiling, I just fucked the most beautiful woman."

"If you say so," I said, running my finger affectionately across his lips.

"You're the most beautiful thing I've seen around these parts in a long time."

"See that bottle of tequila on the dresser? Why don't you make us a drink?"

"They always leave glasses on the sink in the bathroom," he said, getting up.

"There's a bucket of ice in the mini fridge," I called after him.

Tommy put his jeans on and walked to the bathroom. I watched him set two glasses on the dresser, toss the ice in, and then the tequila. He walked back and handed me a glass. His thick, dark hair was all messed up, and he looked sexy. He sat on the bed, and we clanked our glasses together.

"How come there were all those guys hanging around your house?" I asked.

"Well, I sort of make sure they have at least one good meal every day. I buy the food, and they cook it. These guys live on the streets, and they look forward to that each day."

"Really? How did you get into doing that?"

"I grew up here in New Mexico, but my family moved to Colorado when I was young. I hated it there, missed my friends, and wanted to come back here. I ran away from home when I was fifteen. I lived here on the streets for a time. I know how it feels to be hungry and not know where your next meal is coming from."

"That's a really good thing you're doing. I admire that," I said, gently rubbing his shoulder.

"What's this?" Tommy asked, picking up my journal from the nightstand.

"I like to write in a journal. Been doing it for years."

Tommy picked it up and began drawing something on a blank page. "You don't mind if I do this, do you?"

"You're not the first person to sketch or write in my journals."

"I'm drawing a Navajo squash blossom necklace, so you won't ever forget me."

"Tommy, how in the world could I ever forget you?"

"Hey, you're not leaving tomorrow, are you? I have more of New Mexico to show you."

"No, I'm not leaving tomorrow. I'm traveling with two other women. They're having fun with their friends, and we've decided to stay here a few days."

"Good." He leaned in and parted my lips, kissing me. He stopped and smiled. "And we can do more of this too. At some point though, we need to pick up my truck. I left it in town."

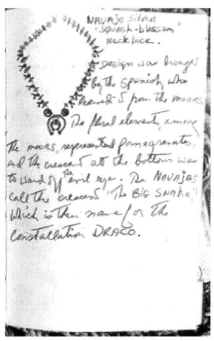

NAVAJO SQUASH BLOSSOM NECKLACE

Tommy put down my journal, reached over me, and turned on the radio. He pulled me close and put his arm around me. I remember the Rolling Stones singing "You Got the Silver." I took another sip of tequila and thought, *This is anything but an ordinary life.*

It certainly was a memorable few days in New Mexico, and I loved Santa Fe. I felt lucky to have met Tommy, who took me to some really neat places, places I would have missed if not for him. I thought, *If only I were a little younger, or he was a little older!*

I dropped him off at his house before meeting the girls in town.

"I won't ever forget you, Adriana," he said as he kissed me goodbye. I waved and blew a kiss at him as I drove off.

～～～～～

I met Sophie and Fiona at that same café in town we started out in. They told me all about the exciting few days they spent with their friends, but I said nothing about Tommy. I didn't think they'd understand. After lunch, we set out on the last leg of our journey. While driving, I felt little twinges of desire—you know where—every time I thought of Navajo Tommy.

Within two days, the Gray Mouse rolled into California.

After I dropped Sophie and Fiona O'Brien off in San Diego, I drove up the coast to San Francisco. The scenery along the coastal highway was as spectacular as I remembered it. It had been about two years since I'd been in California. I tried to keep in mind what Daisy Holmes and Kelly Cooke had said on my last visit with them in upstate New York: "Don't get bogged down in California. Remember, you weren't happy there! Keep Maui as the destination in your mind's eye."

I hoped I would be able to do that once I was with my communal family again.

～～～～～

San Francisco was the same as I had left it. My friend Suki Rosmond had a really cool apartment in Pacific Heights. She lived in a white Victorian with green and purple trim. I stayed with her for a while and enjoyed roaming around the city. She was into real estate and dragged me to parties to meet all her coworkers and friends.

One of her realtor friends, Kenny, tickled my fancy. He was younger than us but was very successful in his real estate endeavors. He was tall, good looking, with slicked-back, straight, dark hair and a baby face. He wore mirrored Aviator sunglasses, and reeked of ego. He drove a hot sports car, a silver Pontiac Firebird he called "the Silver Bullet."

One night, Suki and I attended a party in a posh section of San Francisco, and Kenny was there.

"Hey, wanna take a ride in my new sports car?" he asked.

His comment struck me as immature, but I figured what the hell. We ended up having a great time. That is after I got past his constant radio station searching with one hand, and slurping his drink with the other. When we arrived back at the party, Suki asked where we'd disappeared to.

"I took Adriana for a ride in the Silver Bullet."

She smiled at me and then at him.

"You know she'll be wanting to ride that silver bullet again!" Kenny said.

I got the feeling he was implying something else had happened.

I saw a lot of Kenny in the days to come. He took me to a new restaurant where there was a hibachi right on the table. You were given raw meat or fish so you could cook your own meal. All I could think was, *Why the hell would I want to pay good money at a nice restaurant and have to cook my own food?* But Kenny was paying. He was an attractive guy, and I liked him, but I felt nothing deeper below the surface.

After drinks at a bar a few days later, we got into the Silver Bullet, and as we drove away, he said, "I'm taking you someplace really cool."

He stopped at a liquor store to buy a bottle of red wine and some plastic glasses. I wondered what he had up his sleeve. He parked the car in a downtown area on Market Street. I looked up, and the sign on the building read Grand Central Sauna.

He got out of the car, walked around to my side, and opened the door. He handed me the plastic glasses, took my hand, and said, "Let's go, baby."

He grabbed the bottle of wine and led me inside the building. I didn't quite know what to expect. It was a bathhouse in downtown San Francisco. We stood at the front desk, and the clerk handed Kenny the key to a private room. The room was small, just a large compartment with a deep wooden Japanese-style hot tub. I wasn't expecting this, but we were there already, and I didn't feel I could turn back.

We stripped down nude and got into the warm water. It was actually very pleasant at first. He opened the bottle of wine and poured it in the plastic glasses. I wondered where he got the corkscrew and figured he had it all planned. Pretty soon he was all over me like ham and Swiss on rye bread.

Everything was going great until he began fucking me to the beat of the song playing over the sound system. I had to divorce my brain from my body, listening to Steve Miller Band's "Rock'n Me" while he was pumping away. It was tacky, and I couldn't wait for it to be over.

After we left the baths, Kenny took me to a party given by his real estate firm. Of course, by the time we arrived, the crowd had thinned out, and only a few stragglers weaved around corners of the townhouse. The boss's daughter ran over to us, ignoring me, and made a fuss over Kenny. I could tell she had a crush on him.

"Kenny, your hair is all wet," she said.

"We spent a couple of hours at the Grand Central Sauna," he boasted.

She shot me a jealous look, since my hair was also wet. "Kenny, I want you to promise to take me next time," she said in a pouty voice.

He blushed like a little boy. I didn't bother to give her the details about the experience. I figured I'd let her find out for herself.

I thought of a passage in a book I'd read, from *The Golden Notebook* by Doris Lessing:

> "Maryrose smiled good-humoredly, and remained in the circle of his arms, but as if she detached herself from him and every other man. Very many as it were professionally pretty girls have this gift of allowing themselves to be touched, kissed, held, as if this were a fee they have to pay to providence for being born beautiful. There is a tolerant smile which goes with a submission to the hands of men, like a yawn or a patient sigh."

It was December, and a bunch of us from the old commune went to hang out at Romeo's place (Romeo being Matthew Romeola, my boyfriend from the commune days). He was still with Bella McTavish at her apartment in the Sunset district. We sat around the fireplace. Cocaine was being passed around, which I did partake of. Ross and Romeo were suggesting I go into some sort of business venture they cooked up. I hated the idea and didn't want to get tied up in California for too long. In my mind I was just there for a few months, keeping the friendly fires burning before heading to Maui. The familiarity of everyone and the cocaine bamboozled me, and I wanted out. I loved all these people very much, but the distance between me and Romeo was daunting. I knew the situation wasn't good for me. I shut my eyes and imagined myself drifting out the window, up over the hills of San Francisco, toward the ocean.

From my journal:

Cocaine visions. Wild seekers of the city. *Dante's Inferno* and this rap definitely have something in common. The loss of inner beauty and spirituality. I saw it so clearly, or was it the power of the powder? The hunger for money, and the tallying up of one-night stands. As I sip this Absinthe, I still want you. I don't care if you belong to another woman now. I feel a current still there between us, yet we are like strangers. There is a difference between a peaceful fire and the fires of hell. Sitting here with so many I love, somehow, I am able to drift out of these bounds and over the hills. I can smell the mountain flowers as I make my way to the sea.

Star Green was renting a house in a eucalyptus forest up on Mount Tamalpais in Marin. She mentioned that her roommate was moving out, and I could move in. Star was trying to convince me that California, not Maui, was the place for me. The house was impressive, with an outside porch suspended in the trees. The smell of the eucalyptus hypnotized me. I loved it up there on the mountain, so I moved into the empty room. I hung the Native American blanket on the wall behind my bed, a mattress on the floor. I thought of Navajo Tommy and Santa Fe every time I looked at it. I'd wake up in the mornings, put on my Chinese robe, and drink my coffee on the porch inhaling the fragrance of the eucalyptus. *I could get used to this place,* I thought.

I called Jackie, the manager of the market research company I'd worked for before, hoping to get some temporary work. I wanted to see how I felt this time in California, if it could be different. She was happy to hear from me and hired me right away. I knew I was forgetting my goal and throwing myself into Never-Never Land, but somehow I couldn't stop myself. Star had a string of friends she introduced me to, and soon I was on a wheel of fortune, trying to land on the right square.

Star took me to a local café in town called The Bus Stop. They had great lunches, and I tried their Bus Stop Chili. It was so good that I took one of their postcards, which had the recipe on the back, and tucked it into my journal for safe keeping.

~~~~~~~

Adriana Bardolino

I began the daily grind of driving down the mountain to work in San Francisco's Embarcadero. At the time I rationalized it by telling myself that I was just saving more money for the move to Maui. I pushed to the back of my mind my therapist, Joan's, words, that taking a permanent job in New York was a mistake. That it was a way to put off my life's goal. I suspected I was repeating that same mistake in California. It also crossed my mind that I was getting cold feet about leaving everyone I knew and loved.

That night we went to a local pub to hear live music. It was Christmas week, and I felt nostalgic. When the piano player sang The Eagles' "Tequila Sunrise," my heart skipped a beat.

Star said, "I'm ordering us a new drink called a dark and stormy."

I glanced at her for a moment and then stared off into space.

"Are you thinking of Tubs?" she asked. "Didn't you affectionately call each other Stormy?"

"How could I not help thinking of him, being in his home town?" I said, still in a sort of trance.

She rested her hand on top of mine. "Sorry, I didn't mean to open up old wounds."

"It's the song, the name of the drink, Christmas, memories, all of that," I said.

All the signs around me pointed to Peyton Parker, aka Tubs, aka Stormy. I thought of our steamy love affair that winter in the Catskill Mountains. Thoughts of snow flying through the Hudson River Valley, and crazy tequila nights at Stormy's Pub in Forestville. The two of us were inseparable. We connected again when I moved to California that spring, and we both had fantasies about Hawaii. I had to hear through the grapevine that he went on a camping trip to Hawaii without me. We remained in touch, but only in phone conversations. That was three years past, and the thorn still pinched. I didn't like being reminded of my failed love affairs. The music and signs around me were anything but coincidental and ordinary.

From my journal:

As he played the piano, my mind drifted to a dream that never came true. I pictured sitting on a beach with you in Hawaii. I believed the spirit could still be conjured up within me. I fell asleep in the ray of a star. I wondered if love could come alive again for two souls whose love was spiritual, floating somewhere timelessly through the cosmos.

As the weeks passed, I continued riding a Ferris wheel with men who meant nothing to me. Star introduced me to a guy named Leif, who she privately referred to as The Flying Dutchman. He was older than me, maybe late thirties or early forties, and classically handsome. She raised her eyebrows when she mentioned he was a record producer. I sort of liked him and thought of the Viking explorer Leif Erikson every time I looked at him. He had a nice house overlooking the bay in Sausalito.

As we walked up the steps to his house, he told me about himself. "I was born in Indonesia but grew up in Holland. My family moved there when I was ten. I hated it there."

"How could it ever be possible to hate a place like Holland?"

Leif shrugged

Entering his house, he pulled aside a colorful Nordic blanket, which hung over the inside of the front door, I guessed to keep out the winter draft. I noticed a set of skis standing against the wall. I remember there were no curtains on the windows. He told me he was a sculptor. I glanced at a floral arrangement on top of the refrigerator. I didn't know any men who paid attention to details like that.

The first time I was there I flipped through his drawings and paintings.

"I plan to get some of those framed," he said, I imagined to impress me. He showed me his art studio and uncovered a clay sculpture he was working on. After I examined it, he quickly covered it back up with the wet cloth. I loved that he was an artist.

One night Leif called me and said, "Let's get some wood, a bottle of nice wine, go to my place and make a fire."

When he came to pick me up at Star's house in his BMW, I noticed wood was already stacked in the backseat. On the way to his house, we stopped to get a bottle of wine. That night, we had sex on the couch in front of his fireplace. It was a very nice thing. I wasn't feeling love, but I liked Leif and was comfortable with him. I wanted to get to know him more. After that night though, he never called me again. I was disappointed and let down.

A few weeks later, Star and I were at a bar in Fairfax and ran into him. He walked over to us, smiling. I was flustered and embarrassed. I left them talking at the bar and drove back up the mountain by myself.

An excerpt from a book I'd read, **Fear and Loathing in Las Vegas** by Hunter S. Thompson, came to mind:

The name rings a bell but I couldn't concentrate. Terrible things were happening all around us. Right next to me a huge reptile was gnawing on a woman's neck, the carpet was a blood-soaked sponge—impossible to walk on it, no footing at all. "Order some golf shoes," I whispered. "Otherwise we'll never get out of this place alive. You notice these lizards don't have any trouble moving around in this muck—that's because they have claws on their feet."

It was February 1977, and my life was at a standstill. I knew I was stuck on a roulette wheel like that little ball that goes around and around, and I needed it to stop. After going through transactional analysis with Joan, I realized my relationship with Star Green had similarities to my relationship with my mother. Star had a way of making me feel guilty for having a good time with other people. My reaction was always to appease her and compromise myself. I was hungry and living in her world! I felt the need to measure up in some way. It wasn't as easy as I'd hoped to break old patterns with friends, and I found myself in the same ruts and traps.

I called my mother in the Bronx to hear her voice.

"I thought you'd be in Hawaii by now. When are you going?"

"Soon, Ma. In the spring for sure."

"Did you hear Jimmie Carter's inaugural speech? The peanut farmer!" she said.

"Yeah, Ma. I'm not in New York but I still watch the news."

"I'm handing the phone to your father. He wants to talk to you."

"Did you call your uncle yet?" my father asked.

"No, Dad, but I'll call him soon. I plan on making my move in a month or so."

"My brother will keep your car safe until you're ready to have it shipped to Hawaii."

I hung up feeling a little lost, and apprehensive about the future.

From my Journal:

My thirtieth year on the planet saw a string of silly crushes,
and sometime and now-again lovers. I had a crush on
an untouchable guy from England who kept telling me
his marriage was only one of arrangement. Kenny, the
youth with the hot car, seemed to be at every party I
attended. Couldn't fuck to save his life, although he was
willing to learn. The Flying Dutchman was a man of class,
with spring blossoms atop his refrigerator, and skis at
the ready in his doorway. There was Nikko, who came
by with a bottle of white wine and a ripe pineapple. He
played guitar. We had sex, and he took me to a vineyard
in Napa. Then there was that weird thing with Stevie, who
hung around me for weeks telling me about his fantasy of
fucking me. I ran into him at Land of a Thousand Items in
the city the day after we finally had sex, and he gave me
the cold shoulder. Bear was my favorite. He was a young
guy with a lot of blond hair in cornrows, who shot a good
game of pool. He'd traveled to many different countries,
wore African trade beads, and had crooked teeth, which
I found very sexy.

Things were a little different at the market research company in
the Embarcadero. Jackie, the manager, was having her wooden legs
reconditioned and would be out of the office for a while. The office wasn't
the same without her. I spent the next few weeks getting ready for my move.

I finally called my father's brother in San Lorenzo, who assured me that
my car would be safe with him.

I also called my friend Reggie Paulson, who had already been living on
Maui for six months. He was ecstatic to hear I was taking the plunge. He
told me they had an apartment in Wailuku, with a great view of Haleakala
Crater. I was to call them when my plane landed in Honolulu, and that by
the time my connecting flight landed on Maui, they'd be there to meet
me. They insisted I stay with them until I got settled on the island. After
speaking with them, my spirits took flight.

~~~~~~~

There is a fear when plunging oneself into one's dream. I had my doubts. What if it was all a big pipe dream, like some people say about Our Lady of Fatima? But I decided it was time to just dive in! Upon leaving one's friends, there is always apprehension. My friends and I had a bond, but my draw to the islands was much stronger than even I imagined at the time. I would always cherish my communal family, but after five months in California again, with no good reason to stay, it was time to go.

From my Journal:

Upon leaving one's friends, there are always questions. Why am I leaving them again? Upon rejoining them, there is uncertainty. Why am I here again? Do friendships fade with the passage of time, the absence of experiences shared, or with one's own life changes? Is it shared memories that keep us together? When apart we romanticize our friendships. When together again we are trapped in the character they see us as.

It was March 1977 when I drove the Gray Mouse to my Uncle Rosario's house in San Lorenzo. I had packed three large boxes of personal items, which I left in the backseat of the car. Suki Rosmond followed me in her red '74 Fiat Station Wagon she called Bernardo, the Italian Stallion. I wanted her to meet my uncle Rosario and his wife, Lavinia. Suki would be shipping my car from the port of Oakland, if I decided to stay on Maui.

Uncle Rosario showed me a photograph of him with a Hawaiian *wahine* (woman). He told me he lived in Honolulu on the island of Oahu for five years, when he was in the army. He was there when the Japanese bombed Pearl Harbor in 1941. I remember my father telling me that the family didn't hear from him for a long time and didn't know if he was dead or alive.

~~~~~~~

Suki drove me to San Francisco International Airport, and as the plane took off for Hawaii, I hoped I would survive too. I was thirty years old, and my dream was finally coming true. I closed my eyes as I flew into a new life, hopefully a life in Gauguin.

SIX

STORMY WEATHER

From my journal:

Rustling palm trees, fragrant orchids, and the deep blue sea, Hawaii. I've had this dream for a long time, and I am ready for destiny to unfold. I never had a dream of being a starving artist struggling in a tiny apartment in New York City. True, at times I was inspired to paint from ugliness and strife, but I prefer being inspired by beauty and peace. Earth won out over concrete.

A s the plane landed in Honolulu, I became excited knowing my final destination, the island of Maui, was only a short connecting flight away. It was spring 1977, and my dream was coming true.

When I stepped off the plane, the smell of the air hit me, enveloping me with intoxicating freedom. I felt a thrill, as if I were returning to a lover after a long separation. I knew Reggie Paulson and Leo Thomas were waiting for my call, so I looked for a public phone.

"Reggie, I'm waiting for my flight to Maui."

"We'll be at Kahului Airport to pick you up," he said.

As the plane descended through the clouds, I had a great view of the island of Maui. I could see Haleakala Crater as the plane circled toward the airport.

In those days, Kahului Airport was an open-air terminal surrounded by fields of sugarcane. The trade winds were strong that day, and my hair blew wildly as I walked down the steps to the runway. As I approached the building, I saw Reggie and Leo behind the window at the gate, jumping up and down waving at me. They put pikake and plumeria leis around my neck, and the fragrance overwhelmed me. We all hugged, and I cried. It was a release from two years of dormancy.

After we got my suitcase at baggage claim, we jumped into their old blue Pontiac and headed for Wailuku. The car had a tiny squeak, but it ran really well. There was enough room in that old car for all three of us to sit in the front seat. They were so excited to tell me everything that I couldn't get a word in edgewise.

We drove down an old road dodging potholes, then under a bridge and past a graveyard. They'd created a futon in their living room for me, and I was able to see Haleakala Crater from the large picture window.

After dinner, we walked around the neighborhood. They wanted to show me how close we were to Main Street, close enough to walk to the café's, stores, and Ooka's Supermarket, where you could find anything and everything. It was more like a general store and even had a hardware section in the back.

On our way back to their apartment, we walked through the graveyard, which was spooky at night. The gravestones were from the seventeen and eighteen hundreds, most with Japanese names and inscriptions in character writing.

~~~~~~

The very next day I wanted to go to a beach, any beach, and just walk in the sand for a while. I wanted to be alone with my thoughts. We drove to a secluded part of the coastline, and the guys put a blanket down and set a cooler with cold drinks at the ready.

Reggie said, "Go walk if you want to; we'll be waiting here for you."

I got up and walked along the sand. It was still winter in Hawaii, so it was a perfect day, breezy and not too hot. Every care, tension, and concern drained from my body, like each footprint in the wet sand that disappeared as the waves washed them away. I felt completely at peace.

When I returned from my walk, the guys had a glass of chilled white wine waiting for me. The three of us sat there and talked for a long time watching the sunset, and strangely, I felt at home.

I wrote this poem:

Tranquil is my body at the mercy of the cool evening breeze.
Calm are the soft purple sands, and enchanting is the red sunset.
Walking alone on the beach I am free; I can be myself again.
Gone are the noises of the city and the troublesome daily routines.
Just the deep blue ocean as far as I can see.
I need not put on airs, nor play any roles, for nature completes me.
I feel no love, no hate, no passion, no sadness, and no fear—
Just complete peace as the waves break around my feet.

That night, after Reggie and Leo went to bed, I lay on the futon staring at Haleakala Crater. It had some sort of power over me. Even though it's a dormant volcano, I felt a force waiting to emerge. No one knows when, but an eruption could happen at any time. It could be in a hundred years, or it could be tomorrow. Madame Pele, the goddess of volcanoes and fire and the creator of the Hawaiian Islands, is alive in these volcanos, waiting to set herself free. I fell asleep with the beauty of the day on my mind. I dreamt of Peyton Parker that night, but couldn't remember details upon waking.

After a relaxing weekend, the daily grind began. Reggie and Leo worked on the west side of the island, which involved driving over the *pali* (mountain pass) each day to get to Lahaina. They would drop me off in Lahaina town, and I would busy myself for the day.

I wanted to search for a job, but on my first day back in town I hung out at the harbor and watched the fishing boats motor out on the ocean. I walked to the public library and sat there reading for a while. Some days I'd go to the beach for a swim. I always tried a different place in town to have lunch each day. One day I found myself walking down a side street to La Tortilla Natural. It had been almost two years to the day! It was still there, but I didn't see Sammy.

I asked the guys working in the kitchen, "Is Samuel Cooper still the manager here?"

A guy with dreadlocks answered, "Sammy went back to New York."

I ordered chips and salsa and sat at one of the picnic tables. In a way, I was glad he wasn't there. I didn't want to hear anything about his brother, Hank.

The routine of driving to and from Lahaina each day, and waiting for Reggie and Leo to finish work, went on for the better part of that first week.

Then one day I walked into a marketplace, and there were plenty of those in Lahaina. I saw jewelry carts, a frozen yogurt shop, an art gallery, clothing stores, a restaurant, and the studio of a local artist.

I came across an interesting shop. The sign over the entrance read the Crafty Mermaid. I walked in and looked around. There were two very slim and beautiful women standing at the counter chatting. They were so involved in conversation that they didn't notice me. I fished through the racks of mostly handcrafted clothing. There were some beautiful hand-painted silk and cotton sarongs.

As I approached the counter, they stopped talking and asked if I needed help.

"Do you make all the clothing here?" I asked.

"Yes," the blonde behind the counter said.

"I'm impressed. Everything seems so well constructed and beautiful."

The Hawaiian girl said, "We have sewing machines upstairs."

"Really," I said. "I was a fashion designer in New York City for years. I can sew really well."

"We're always looking for new talent," the Hawaiian girl said. "Why don't you try us out?"

"Oh, that would be just what I'm looking for," I answered.

The blonde said, "You can work a couple of days next week, and we'll see how you do."

"It's a deal," I said.

"I'm Hannah Klein," said the blonde, and this is my partner, Haku Neilson. We'll see how you work out, and if you're a good fit for our shop."

"I'm Adriana Bardolino, and I promise I won't disappoint you."

Haku and Hannah smiled at me.

I walked out of the shop and couldn't believe I'd been on Maui for less than a week and already found a job. I had a good feeling about it and couldn't wait to tell the guys.

I walked to the seawall and climbed over and onto the beach. I walked along the sand breathing in the fresh sea air, and thanked God for my good fortune. The waves were big that day, and I saw a bunch of surfers sitting on their boards waiting for a good set of waves. It was like a religion to them. All the darkness and uncertainty from the past two years dissolved in the air and blew away on the trades.

~~~~~

That weekend, Reggie took me on a hike in Iao Valley. We walked along the rocks alongside the Iao River until he found a familiar path. We walked way up into the mountains. Occasionally we came across a banana grove or a group of fruit trees.

"It seems possible to live off the land here in the islands," I said.

"Indeed, but there are parts of these mountains you don't want to wander into by mistake."

"What do you mean?"

"You've heard of Maui wowie, right? Well, there are marijuana farms up in these mountains, and they don't take kindly to trespassers. They patrol with dogs and could have weapons. You could easily disappear."

"Oh, I didn't even think of that," I said.

"Besides, there are wild pigs up here, and you never know when you'll run into one."

"Geez, Reggie, should we even be up here?"

"Well, this area is a state park, so we're safe. Leo and I have hiked up here plenty of times."

That night we went to Iao Theater in Wailuku to see the premier of the new movie *Star Wars*. I was happy to see the white turbans were still running the theater and the local gas station.

~~~~~~

On Monday I walked into the Crafty Mermaid, and the girls were happy to see me.

"We're swamped with orders and alterations. Maybe you could start with that," Hannah said, as she walked me up the stairs with a stack of trousers to be hemmed. There were two industrial Bernina sewing machines, and a decent-sized cutting table with rolls of fabric stacked underneath. It was hotter that hell up there, and I soon realized why the girls worked in little more than bathing suits, with a sarong wrapped around. A cool ocean breeze occasionally drifted in through the windows. Hannah Klein gave off a California vibe, and was very businesslike. She was tall, blonde, and slim, with fine facial features.

"We take in alterations from the clothing stores on Front Street. You can keep the cash from that today," she said.

I did as I was told, and my first day went smoothly.

When I was finished, Hannah handed me the cash, "Come back on Friday. We'll go from there."

I shoved the cash in my jeans pocket and walked out. I was hoping for fulltime work, but two days was a start. I walked to Front Street and sat on the seawall. I gazed out over the ocean to the island of Lanai in the distance. I wondered what it was like on that island, if it was different from Maui.

As I went over the day in my head, I thought of my mother, Vita's, dress factory. I'd spent a lot of time there as a child. Of course, her place was much bigger than the Crafty Mermaid. Twenty-four sewing machines constantly whirred, and the clipping sounds from all the scissors was endless. Most of the operators were from Italy. In those days, you needed a sponsor and a job waiting if you planned on coming to America. My mother sponsored these women, and in turn they loved and idolized her. We were always going through our kitchen cabinets, searching for items to help these families get started.

Vita's shop had four pressers, men who pressed all the finished garments. Their irons were suspended from springs attached to the ceiling. All day long you heard the hiss of the steam and the thud of the heavy irons coming down on the ironing boards. There were three finishers whose job it was to clip stray threads, sew buttons and snaps on by hand, and attach size tags. I remember getting my finger caught in the pinking machine as a child and being rushed to a doctor. I wondered what my mother would think of the Crafty Mermaid. Suddenly I felt a pang of missing her. I called her that night to tell her about my day and about the shop.

<hr>

That Friday I showed up at the Crafty Mermaid, and Hannah wasn't there. Haku took me upstairs and showed me the various patterns they used for sarongs, shorts, and tops. They made bathing suits as well.

"Do you want to be paid by the hour or by the piece?" she asked.

"I prefer to be paid by the piece, if that's all right with you."

Haku seemed surprised but said, "It's your choice."

Of course, she had no idea how fast I was on the sewing machine. She rolled some tropical fabric out on the cutting table, set the pattern on top, and cut a few layers out with large scissors.

"Here, start hemming these sarongs," she said, handing me a bunch of the fabric wraps.

I whipped those out in no time.

Haku looked at me and laughed. "I can see why you want to be paid by the piece."

Haku Neilson was an island girl from head to toe. She was very thin, pretty, with dark skin and eyes. Her thick brown hair was so long, it cascaded down her back past her waist. Still, she had fine features. Her mother was Hawaiian and her father was of German decent. Hawaiians call any mixed ancestry *hapa*.

~~~~~~

By the end of April I was working three days a week. I had a few free days, and even though I wasn't working that day, I drove into Lahaina with Reggie and Leo on what some might call a whim. They dropped me off at the harbor, and I walked into the Pioneer Inn for breakfast. I sat at a table by the window watching the goings on outside.

There were a couple of guys sitting at the bar drinking beer, and I wondered what the place was like at night. There was whaling memorabilia, harpoons, and busts of mermaids hanging on the walls. I ordered a bloody Mary and macadamia nut pancakes, their specialty. I was enjoying the pancakes with lots of butter and syrup, looking out at the ocean through the open window. I watched boats going out and coming into the harbor, and people shuffling along the docks.

Suddenly, a familiar form took shape as it got closer to the inn. "Of all the fucking gin joints on the planet," I said.

There was Peyton Parker walking down the dock toward the Pioneer Inn. He caught sight of me through the open window as he got closer. I took another sip of my bloody Mary to calm down. *What the hell?* I thought.

"Hi, Stormy," he said, peering through the window with a big grin. Then he walked inside.

We often called each other Stormy while we were entangled in a love affair. We met at a place called Stormy's Pub in a small town in upstate New York.

"What are you doing here?" I asked.

"I sailed over as part of a crew from California. It took about thirteen days. I'm staying here, at the Pioneer Inn. I have a pretty nice room upstairs."

I was in a state of shock, half wishing I hadn't run into him, half elated that I did. My stomach was a tempest in a teapot, and I couldn't finish the pancakes. I needed another bloody Mary.

He said, "I'm going to grab a beer, want another Mary?"

I nodded. He walked up to the bar and soon returned with a mug of beer and my second bloody Mary. It had been a long time since I'd seen him, and I'd forgotten how damn sexy he was. He set the drinks down on the table and sat across from me.

"We should hang out while I'm here on the island. You here on vacation too, Stormy?"

"No, I live here now," I said.

"Really, you live here on Maui? That's cool. When did that happen?"

"I just moved here about a month ago. I'm having my car shipped over soon."

"When you finish your drink, I'll show you my room, and we can catch up," he said.

Looking at the grin on his face, I knew exactly what he meant, and I wondered what the hell I was doing. I guess I was caught up in the moment, or maybe in the memory of the way we once were. I stared at him as he jabbered away between sips of beer. Every time he laughed, his long, brown, wavy hair shook. I flashed on the first time I saw him at Stormy's Pub in a gold brocade jacket and a tie-dyed bandana around his wild hair, looking like an eighteenth-century king.

We finished our drinks, and I followed him up the stairs. I didn't mention having a dream about him, although I thought that was uncanny. He was right. It was a decent room with a balcony. While Peyton took a shower, I walked out on the balcony, sat in one of the chairs, and stared at the ocean. I was nervous and felt distant from him for some reason. I thought of Tommy, the guy I met in Santa Fe. He was a virtual stranger, yet in a way I felt more at ease and natural with him.

I heard the water in the shower stop. Peyton called out, "Hey, Stormy, come in here."

I rose from the chair and walked inside. He grabbed and kissed me. He took my hand and caressed it.

"Tubs," I whispered, and he moaned a little. Why his friends called him Tubs I never understood. He was tall with a solid form, but not fat. He liked when I called him that.

We got undressed and lay on the bed. It was a little awkward at first, so I closed my eyes and made believe we were in his bedroom in Forestville. I knew it wouldn't be like the winter we spent together in the Catskill Mountains, but it was good. Afterward, my heart fluttered a little, and I knew I was vulnerable. My emotions were like a feather drifting up and down on the breeze. "Stormy weather, and my heart's like a feather." I could hear Etta James singing that old torch song from the 1930s, "Stormy Weather," as I lay there enjoying the moment.

We fell asleep soon after. Hours later I woke up with a start. I had to meet Reggie and Leo that afternoon, so I got up and began getting dressed.

Peyton woke up. "What's going on? I was hoping we could hang out. I want to take you sailing."

I didn't answer right away.

"You have a boyfriend now, Stormy?" he asked with a frown.

"Would I be here with you if I did? I'm living on the other side of the island in Wailuku with a couple of guys."

"So one of them is your guy?"

I laughed. "No, they're gay. They're a couple, friends of mine from New York City."

His expression lightened. "Just call them and say you're hanging with me for a while."

"Yeah, I'll call them from the lobby and let them know I'm staying in Lahaina tonight."

I spent that night with Peyton Parker. In the morning, he ran downstairs and got the Maui newspaper. I lay in bed watching him cut open a papaya and scoop out the seeds with a spoon. He ate it with such gusto as he read the paper. All I could think of was bacon and eggs but wouldn't eat it in front of him, knowing he was a vegetarian. I followed his lead and ate the other papaya on the table.

"I need coffee," I said, standing up.

"You still hooked on that stuff?" he asked, sighing.

I chuckled a little.

I went downstairs and got coffee from the restaurant and drank it upstairs on the balcony.

"What are we doing today, Tubs?"

He set the newspaper down and gazed at me. "You look so good sitting there. I've been on a boat for two weeks," he said teasingly.

I got up and stood in front of him. He lifted my T-shirt and unhooked my bra. He rubbed his face between my breasts and sucked on the nipples, looking up at me. His eyes were a clear soft green with brown specks, and there were sun freckles across his nose and cheeks. I was overcome with desire for him, and for the old us. I bent down and kissed his lips. Then I grabbed his hair and kissed him harder.

He stood up and walked me over to the bed, our legs together like those guys who tie dummies to their bodies and do a dance routine. We lay down and began touching each other all over. I couldn't believe I was with him.

I whispered, "Stormy, is it really you?"

"It's me," he said.

Soon I lost all concept of time—present, past, future, none of it mattered. We made love, and in my head our song "Tequila Sunrise" was playing, and I felt that old thrill.

When we finished, I lay there in a daze enjoying the afterglow, but Peyton jumped up and said, "We're going sailing today. I can't wait for you to meet the guys."

It was a perfect day out on the ocean. The sailboat was beautiful. Even though it was nearing the end of whale season, we were lucky enough to see a few pods. There were no girls on the boat, and there was plenty of wine. I had to admit I could still go for him, but I didn't know what he was feeling. I wasn't even sure what I was feeling. Just being around him appeased me for a while, but I knew he was leaving soon, and whatever this was, it wasn't going to be enough for me. I watched him working on the deck with his hair all wet in brown ringlets from the saltwater spray. He looked glorious as the sun was setting, lighting up his face. I thought maybe this was destiny, but sometimes the universe plays cruel tricks for laughs. I knew when he left, I would feel loss all over again.

WHALE'S TAIL

Peyton and I hung around together for more than a week, and it was all so good. For me, anyway. I never could figure out what went on in his head.

He eventually sailed away, leaving me on the dock. I watched him get smaller and smaller as the sailboat got farther and farther away. It was like the day we kissed goodbye on that turnpike in upstate New York, watching him disappear through the rear window of the car. It was hard, but I was happy we reconnected, even if it was for a short while. He mentioned that he might be back on Maui in the fall, but I wasn't going to hang on that. I felt like a girl in love with a sailor who comes home once in a while to rekindle something that gets less intense each time. That's the way nature works, and you can't fight nature.

I worked my three days at the Crafty Mermaid that week. Reggie and Leo picked me up after work on Friday. On the drive back to Wailuku I told them the whole Stormy saga, about how we met at Stormy's Pub in upstate New York, and about our winter romance.

I wrote in my journal:

I had a dream about you; perhaps it was a premonition, and then you appeared. I could still go for you, but how far? When you leave I know I will miss you. Whenever I hear that song I will think of you and Stormy's Pub, wanting to be next to you, the way we were. I could have drifted out to sea with you in a dream come true. You had your arm around me as we stood on the deck of the sailboat, and you said you didn't want to be anywhere else in the world. But it's only one day in a lifetime. Alas, the sweet smell of orchids must float out to sea, and my heart along with them

I walked into the Crafty Mermaid, and Hannah and Haku were there.

Haku said, "Hannah will run the shop alone today. I'm taking you to my house to paint sarongs and pareos."

"What's a pareo?" I asked.

"It's similar to a sarong, only longer." She showed me one. "See, it has ties that go around your neck, and it can be worn as a dress."

This was beyond my wildest dream job, and I was stoked as we left the shop and walked to her house. Haku Neilson lived in a large house on a corner in Lahaina with her boyfriend and a couple of other people. I didn't see much of her boyfriend in the weeks to come, except for the times he'd show up at the Crafty Mermaid wanting money from her, or to hassle her about something. She told me they'd been together for a few years.

Haku had a room with a skylight set aside on the top floor for painting. There were windows all around, and it was bright and airy. There were jars of water, paintbrushes, and tubes of acrylic paint.

"Just paint Hawaiian flowers, palm trees, fish, anything tropical. Go wild," she said.

I got myself set up with some silk and cotton sarongs. I was aware that each fabric needed a different painting technique, and that the paint would spread quicker on the silk. Sure enough, as I barely touched the paintbrush to the silk, it spread and absorbed immediately. Haku walked back into the room holding a small mirror with lines of cocaine. I took the short straw, snorted up two lines, and passed it back to her. My creative energy surged, and beautiful images were set on fabric.

"When you start working full time, we can do this every Friday. These hand-painted sarongs are popular with the tourists. We never have enough of them in the store."

TIE-DYED COTTON SARONG

I felt confident about my job and knew I wanted to live on Maui. I called Suki Rosmond in California and told her to ship my car. She was happy to hear from me, not so happy to know that I was staying in the islands. I called my Uncle Rosario in San Lorenzo and told him that Suki would be picking up my car and driving it to the port in Oakland. I reminded him to make sure that my three boxes were in the backseat, that I would need them when I got settled in my own place.

~~~~~

Knowing fulltime work was coming, I figured I'd better take advantage of the free time I had left. I began having Leo drop me off at Airport Beach in Kaanapali in the mornings, where he worked in one of the hotels. It was a secluded beach away from the tourists, and actually there were only a few hotels on Kaanapali Beach back then. It was next to a small airfield, which is how it got its name. Royal Hawaiian six-seater commuter prop planes flew between the islands from that airport. There was a famous bar on the site called the Windsock. High School Harry ran the bar up at the top of a spiral staircase. I'd heard Harry and the Windsock Bar were local icons.

I was getting very tan hanging out all day on the beach watching people frolic in the ocean, and occasionally I'd take a dip myself. Just about every time I was there, I'd see the same gorgeous guy walk the beach. He never actually went in the water, just walked along the sand. He'd stop and talk to sunbathers once in a while, and one day he stopped at my blanket. He was tall, blond, handsome, bronzed, and very buff. His name was Bjorn, but the girls called him Gorgeous George, after the famous wrestler. He'd stop and talk to me for a while, then move on to another blanket, like a bumblebee buzzing around different flowers. In the weeks to come, he began spending more time at my blanket, and we became good friends.

One afternoon he invited me to hang out at his house, saying it was only a little north of Lahaina on the ocean. It was a really cool place with an island feel, decorated with Hawaiian memorabilia. I passed a large tiki in the yard as we entered the front door. He wasn't a surfer, yet there were two surfboards standing against a wall. Walking into the living room I caught sight of an adequate bar set up in the corner with four bar stools. There was a large selection of liquor along the shelves. A lava lamp sat at the very end of the bar,. The bedroom had two hula girl statues as lamps with fancy shades, which sat on each night stand. A large picture window opened to the ocean, so you could watch the sunset from the bed. I wondered how he managed to put such a cleverly themed place together. I thought maybe he was an ex-model and had made a lot of money. I sat at the bar staring at the lava lamp.

"What do you like to drink?" Bjorn asked.

"I guess my drink is Tanqueray and tonic."

"That's so British," he said.

"A British guy I dated, Bobby Becker, turned me on to gin."

He touched my shoulder as he walked behind the bar. "Well, Adriana I'm making us mai tais."

"I'll try one," I said (although I wasn't keen on rum).

I watched him mix the drinks and was amazed at how he was able to float the dark rum on the very top, like a layer of frosting on a cupcake. He finished them off with a cherry in each tall glass. Bjorn handed me one, and we toasted each other. He was actually a really nice guy after all.

"What do you think of my place?" he asked.

"I really like it. I mean, the way you stuck to a Hawaiian theme. My decorating is always eclectic, whatever I pick up at garage sales, or at Sally Ann's."

Bjorn laughed. "Well, I had help. An old girlfriend. She had a flare for this sort of thing."

"You have surfboards, but I've never seen you out riding the waves."

"I did surf once, but I hurt my back really bad. I'm lucky to be alive. I leave them there as a reminder of the awesome power of the ocean."

We finished our drinks, and Bjorn made us two more. I was feeling tipsy as he pointed to the bedroom with his mai tai and said, "Let's watch the sunset."

The sky was on fire with one of those epic island sunsets. We sat on the bed and stared out the window. I was overcome with the beauty of it all. The place, Bjorn, the sunset, the mai tais, and my life on Maui. Bjorn put his drink down and set my glass on the nightstand next to his. He kissed me cautiously, maybe expecting me to pull away, but I didn't. I didn't want sex to change our friendship, but who the hell would say no to Gorgeous George? We had sex while I stared at the hula girl lamp only a few inches from my head. It was nothing spectacular, but we liked each other.

When it was over, we sat up. I felt a little awkward and didn't know what to say. He had the greatest smile and perfect teeth. I didn't know what made me think of that.

"Well, we got that over with," he said.

I laughed and said, "Yeah we did."

~~~~~~~

The summer was passing quickly. Then again, I was living in the land of the endless summer. It was the middle of August when I heard that Elvis Presley had died. He had just played a concert in Honolulu. If I would've known it would be his last, I would have flown to Honolulu to see him. He was the first big crush in my life as a young teenager, and I loved his music. Especially when he sang the blues on acoustic guitar, or when he got into a spiritual mood and sang gospel songs. His album, *Elvis*, was the first LP I purchased. I was eleven years old. I cut his photo out of a teen magazine and put it in my wallet, pretending he was my boyfriend. I was just a silly kid! After his death, the magazines talked about his drug use, and how fat he'd gotten, but sources close to him said that he had a close relationship with his mother, and after her death, he never was the same. I choked up when I read one of the newspaper headlines: The King Has Left the Building.

~~~~~~~

My friend Loretta Perino moved to Maui from Brooklyn that summer. We picked our friendship up exactly where it left off. At that time, however, we lived on opposite ends of the island and often met in Kaanapali for a day at the beach. I had already established a group of friends, and she had her own. One of the friends she made when she first arrived was Ann Craddock.

Loretta called me at work in a state of worry, verging on panic, because her friend Ann was missing. Ann's roommate told Loretta that she never came home the previous night, and it wasn't like her. Ann had broken up with her boyfriend, and he told Ann he wanted to talk to her. Just talk! They filed a missing person's police report, and the next day her car was found abandoned on the side of the road next to a cane field.

"We told her not to meet him, and I know something terrible has happened to her. I can feel it," Loretta said.

Days went by with no sign of her. Ann Craddock's parents flew to Maui from the mainland and paid for helicopters to search for their daughter, to no avail. Weeks went by, and weeks turned into months. Meanwhile, her boyfriend moved off island to the mainland. Two years later Ann's body was found in a swamp. Her head had been bashed in. Her boyfriend was extradited back to Hawaii and charged with her murder, but it took years. It was a loathsome, horrible event. It formed a cloud over Maui for a long time and gave pause to many of us girls who often hitched rides around the island.

My car finally arrived. Reggie and Leo went with me to pick it up on the dock at Kahului Harbor. My car had been stuck in Honolulu for more than a week because when it arrived from California, the barge to Maui had already left.

After filling out the paperwork in the office, we walked to the dock, looking for it. There were so many cars, it took us a while to find it.

"I think that's it!" I yelled. The Gray Mouse was covered in salt. I imagined it made the trip from Honolulu to Maui outside on the deck of the barge.

"You'll have to wash that salt off right away," Reggie said.

I was so excited. I unlocked the door and jumped into the driver's seat. I turned the ignition and nothing happened. The car was dead.

"Lolo [crazy], you mean you didn't disconnect the battery?" Leo asked.

"How the hell would I know to do something like that? Besides, I wasn't even there," I said.

"The guys who loaded the car in California should have done that," Reggie said with a frown.

"Now what the hell am I going to do?" I asked.

"Do you have Triple A?" Leo asked.

"I think I do. I hope I have the card in my wallet." I found the card and handed it to Leo.

The guys walked back to the office, complaining enough to the attendant sitting behind the window for him to come out and help me. He called AAA for me, and they brought a new battery. The attendant admitted that it happened all the time. I hadn't even driven the car yet, and I already had a bill. Anyway, after the slight setback, we agreed to meet back at their apartment in Wailuku. I opened the glove compartment to shove all the papers in, and something silver caught my eye. I reached inside, and it was Daisy Holmes's turquoise and silver ring. I was a little stunned that she would forget something like that when she sold me the car and wondered why I hadn't noticed it before. I slipped the ring on my finger. Little did I know how much that ring would come to mean to me. I turned the radio on, and "Shining Star" by Earth, Wind & Fire was playing. I cranked the volume way up, rolled down the windows, and drove away from the dock.

~~~~~

Walking toward the Crafty Mermaid the next morning, I parked on a side street. Lahaina was crowded with tourists. I gazed at the ocean, which seemed really rough. The waves were choppy, and the boats out on the water swayed from side to side. Dark clouds had formed over the island of Lanai across the channel.

When I walked into the shop, the girls were already there.

"We might have to close the shop. Looks like a storm is moving over the islands," Haku said.

"You should have seen the boats tossed around out there in the ocean," I said.

I headed upstairs and began sewing the shorts that I had started the last time I was there. The girls were busy downstairs talking to customers, and the day progressed like it always did. Toward the middle of the afternoon, the wind kicked up, and things flew around in the street. A gust of wind blew in through the window and tossed some patterns on the floor. Suddenly, the electricity went out, and everything got really quiet.

I went downstairs, and the girls were scurrying around the shop boarding up the front of the store. "We're closing up for the day. Want to come out drinking with us?" Hannah asked.

There were a few stragglers looking at clothing on the racks. She hurried them out of the store and locked the front door. Everything was wooden, so boarding up was as easy as shutting all the doors. The three of us walked to a bar across the street, which sat right on the ocean, to watch the storm roll in. It was quite a thrill as the system approached and began dumping torrential rain. We drank the rest of the afternoon away. There was no driving back to Wailuku in the storm, so I stayed at Haku's house that night.

~~~~~

It was a warm day in October. We were listening to the new Meatloaf LP, *Bat out of Hell,* at the shop. After work I walked down to Lahaina Harbor. The fishing tournament was going on and there was a weigh-in station right at the dock. I think the marlin that won top prize that year was 728 pounds. Well, at least, that was the talk among the harbor rats (the guys who lived on boats and hung out at the harbor). I walked into the Pioneer Inn, past the harpoons hanging on the wall, and through a crowd of people at the bar. I ordered a Tanqueray and tonic with lime and heard someone yell, "Hey, Stormy!" It was Peyton Parker. He was in jovial spirits standing at the other end of the bar with a group of rowdy guys. I noticed he'd chopped off his long, wavy hair.

"Stormy, come help me celebrate," he shouted.

I grabbed my drink and sauntered down to his end of the bar.

"Back so soon?" I asked, staring at his tightly wound brown ringlets.

"Well, I did say I might be back in the fall."

"Oh yeah, that's right," I said, not wanting him to know I still thought of him. "You cut your beautiful hair off!"

"Yeah, well, it was time for a change. We rented a fishing boat for the tournament. We caught a big mahi today."

"That's great, Tubs," I said, purposely not using the term Stormy, which was affectionate.

"You will stick around with me tonight, won't you?" he asked, his face softening.

"I guess so," I answered.

"I was able to get the same room," he said. He stared at me through the mirror behind the bar as he drank his beer.

I smiled at him, and saw a big grin break out on his face. Soon I was lost in the jovial atmosphere of the bar.

We spent the night together, and it was really nice.

The next morning he rented a car and took me to Hana for the day. I told the girls at the Crafty Mermaid that a friend was in town and I needed a few days off. They were totally okay with it.

One of Peyton's friends did the driving. He was the stoic, quiet type. No one said much on the long ride along that winding road to Hana. We stopped a few times to look at waterfalls and took photos at every vista. The scenery was incredible, and when the road opened to the ocean, we saw a whale really close to shore. The last time I was on that road was with Hank

Cooper. Funny how things can be the same, yet different. Peyton Parker seemed aloof, not upbeat like he was that first night at the bar.

That evening the three of us went to a restaurant in Lahaina for dinner, and I felt suspended in a strange space. I didn't feel the familiarity or the special connection we once had. It was a love lost situation, one that just couldn't be reenacted. I tried to turn my conscious mind off to it.

My friend Ross Grant was in Lahaina for Halloween. He had a woman with him I'd never met before. Halloween was still a few days away, and Peyton Parker was still in town. Ross was familiar with Peyton. He visited me when I lived with Ross and Suki in their house on the Russian River in California.

We all went out on a fishing boat the next day. The guys were making believe they were fishing, while we girls sat around looking cute in our bathing suits. Peyton was telling Ross about his trip to Hawaii from California on the sailboat.

They were talking and laughing, when I overheard Peyton say, "Yeah, the captain had his girlfriend with him on the trip, and they were doing the love thing, rubbing butts and all." He made a face as if it was a silly thing, being in love. I realized that whatever we had in the past had no chance of being resurrected. Perhaps I kept that Stormy fantasy alive for too long. I hung out with Peyton Parker for a few more days, but when he left, I knew our cosmic connection was gone. We were two planets orbiting light-years apart in the universe. Somehow I knew I'd never see him again.

~~~~~~

Halloween in Lahaina is also known as the Mardi Gras of the pacific! People come from everywhere around the globe to walk down Front Street in costume. That first Halloween, Reggie, Leo, and I dressed as tourists. The guys wore matching aloha shirts and straw hats and carried sunscreen. I wore a wraparound sarong that matched their shirts, and flowers in my hair. I had my camera slung over my shoulder, and the guys carried a cooler to add to the effect. We cruised up and down Front Street among the crowds. Some of the costumes were crazy. There were torsos without heads, and a family dressed up as a box of crayons in different colors. I saw many people practically nude with very little covering their private parts. Traffic along Front Street went slowly, with the occasional pickup truck filled with masked revelers in clown costumes, throwing candy at people walking on the sidewalks. It was a crazy scene. You couldn't get a drink at any of the bars, with people packed tightly together like sardines in a can. Some of the restaurants had costume contests. It was a magical night. I was celebrating my good luck at finding the perfect job, exploring art in Gauguin, and feeling very much in the "aloha spirit."

SEVEN

BIRDS OF A FEATHER

From my journal:

I hear, streaming in an open window, a bird's song, past fragrant tropical flowers and the hot sun. Is it just my imagination, or is there a completeness without and within? All the elements need each other in the circle of survival. A beautiful blossom in the sun lives forever and breeds sweetness in every thought. It's the memory of this that kept my heart ticking on cold days and through trying times. I think I will be happy here, a child of the elements.

E ven though I was living on a tropical island, Christmas was still a magical time of year. The heat of the afternoon was oppressive upstairs at the Crafty Mermaid, and I was still wearing my blue jeans. The girls had a bet going as to when I'd ditch my jeans for a bathing suit and sarong.

I needed a break. I walked across the street and wandered into the pawn shop that had recently opened. A buzzer went off as I entered the front door, but there was no response from the woman—a rather large, round woman with long gray hair wearing a Santa hat—sitting behind the counter reading a book. Her glasses dangled at the edge of her nose. I thought, *It's Mrs. Claus!*

She finally looked up at me with an annoyed expression, as if I'd interrupted her story. "Are you looking for something special?"

"No, I'm just looking around to see what you have."

"Another lookie-loo," she said. I figured she worked on commission. "I work across the street at the Crafty Mermaid."

It's a free country, and you can look all you want."

"You sound like you're from New York."

"I'm from Brooklyn," she said, and began to soften up.

"I'm Adriana Bardolino from the Bronx."

She eased herself off the chair and waddled around the corner of the counter. "I'm Annie Hughes. It's nice to meet someone who talks like me."

"Well, Annie, I have to get back to work, but I'm sure I'll drop in again."

"I have a feeling we'll be fast friends, Riana," she said.

I meant to correct her and say that my name was Adriana, but I just smiled and walked out. The buzzer went off again as I left the store. I had a good feeling about Mrs. Claus.

~~~~~~

When I walked back across the street into the Crafty Mermaid, all hell was breaking loose. Haku and Hanna were sliding the wooden doors shut.

"What's going on?" I asked.

"Stevie Nicks and the girls from Fleetwood Mac are on their way," Hannah said.

"Someone who shops here all the time recommended us to the band. They have a benefit concert coming up next week in Kaanapali, and they want us to make their outfits," Haku said.

Hanna said, "Run upstairs and take out some rolls of fabric for them to look through."

"I'm on it," I said, running up the stairs, the plumeria behind my ear falling to the floor.

My hands shook as I pulled bolts of fabric out from under the cutting table. I heard voices downstairs, so knew the women were in the shop. They were all about our age, very pretty and down-to-earth. I led them up the stairs into that little space we worked in, and we all stood around the cutting table while they flipped through the fabrics. They seemed attracted to the fancy silks and crushed velvets.

Stevie Nicks picked out a beautiful red-netted fabric with raised embroidery. I remained in a foggy whirlwind until they left. They told us exactly what they wanted, and Hannah took their measurements. Haku assured them we'd have it all ready for them in time for the concert. I knew Hannah and Haku would be making their garments, and though disappointed, I understood the importance of the task. We closed the store again for their fittings, and the whole experience with these women was a delight. We all went to their concert and felt proud, knowing we dressed them.

~~~~~

My friend Loretta Perino found an apartment in a semi-tourist condo complex in Honokowai on the west side, and I planned to move in with her. Reggie and Leo were also looking for a place on the west side, to be closer to work. We were all tired of the daily commute over the Pali.

They finally found a great high-rise apartment on Airport Beach in Kaanapali. Their apartment was on an upper floor, with an incredible view of the ocean and neighboring islands across the channel.

Loretta's apartment was a one-bedroom condo right on the ocean, with a sofa bed in the living room. I was looking forward to being close to work, especially now that I was working full time.

A week before I was scheduled to move in, there was a double homicide in an apartment on the same floor as Loretta's.

She called me. "I don't know what to say. Do you still want to live here?"

"Loretta, I'm from the Bronx. Do you think a loathsome double murder would scare me off?"

"I was afraid you'd have second thoughts. You know, they killed the wrong people."

"What are you talking about?"

"It was a drug hit, and they killed two innocent people."

"God, Loretta, that's horrible. Either way, I'm moving in with you next week."

"That's a relief. We're going to have so much fun," she said, her voice lifting.

I moved in with Loretta Perino that following week. We sat on the couch in our bathing suits, sipping happy hour cocktails, and planning all the things we would do in the coming months. She marveled at the lavender Lycra bathing suit I'd made, and told me I looked great in it.

~~~~~

Loretta and I spent that New Year's Eve with Reggie and Leo. We sat out on their lanai and watched the sun set over the ocean. It was a calm and peaceful way to ring in 1978. That night the sun put on a real show as it disappeared behind the clouds, and we were treated to that little green flash before it dipped into the ocean. The panoramic view from their apartment, of the vast ocean and the islands of Molokai and Lanai across the channel, afforded us the best sunset. That night the four of us got twisted drunk and laughed at everything.

~~~~~~

At the Crafty Mermaid, one day rolled into another. Haku followed through on her promise to spend Fridays at her house painting. On one particular Friday, though, she seemed really down. She opened a bottle of chilled white wine, and I could tell she was working up to something.

"Haku, you seem troubled, or unhappy in some way."

"Well, it's my boyfriend. We've been together for years, and now he wants to get married. I'm comfortable, but in my head I'm not sure I want to marry him."

"What about in your heart?"

"I do love him, and he's my best friend, but I don't feel happy. Shouldn't I be happy?"

"Look, maybe you're just getting cold feet because he's getting serious."

"No, Adriana, it's more than that. Something just doesn't feel right. Something's missing."

"Haku, picture yourself five years from now. Do you want to feel the way you do right now?"

She hesitated. "No, I don't, but I feel like I'm in too deep to turn back."

"Well, that's not a good sign. You really need to make a decision, not just for you, but for him as well. He deserves to be really loved too. No one wants someone to settle for them."

"I'm confused, but I'm glad we had this talk," Haku said.

We went on drinking and painting, and the afternoon slipped away. When her boyfriend came home, he walked straight upstairs to the art room, took her around the waist, and gave her a kiss. She glanced at me, and I prayed I'd said the right things to her. No one wants to be responsible for someone making the wrong decision because of something you said. I wondered if I should have kept my mouth shut.

~~~~~~

I left Haku's house around sunset and walked back to Front Street. I happened to pass the pawn shop and saw Annie Hughes locking up.

She caught sight of me. "Hey, Riana, I'm on my way to the Waterworks. Why don't you come with me, we'll make a night of it."

I was a caught off guard, but she grabbed my arm and said, "Come on, it'll be fun."

I walked with her around the corner and along Front Street until we came to a building at the end of town. I was familiar with Longhi's Restaurant, but I wasn't aware that there was a bar in the building. I followed Annie through a corridor to a hidden doorway.

As soon as we walked in the entrance, everyone shouted, "It's Fat Annie."

She sat on a barstool, and I sat next to her. It was pretty dark in there, but I could make out a jukebox against a wall. She ordered a vodka and soda and asked me what I wanted.

A guy sitting at the bar said, "I'm buying, so what do you want to drink, sweetie?"

"I'll have a gin and tonic with a lime," I said. Before I knew it I had a drink sitting in front of me.

"What's your name, sweetie?" the guy asked.

"Adriana," I shouted. Everyone was talking so loudly, you could barely hear anything.

"I didn't catch that," the guy said.

"What the hell's the matter, Bully, you deaf?" Annie shouted. "Her name's Riana."

I figured I'd better leave it at that.

During the course of the evening, people came and went, but a few patrons never moved from their barstools. I figured they were regulars.

Later on, a guy walked in and put his arms around Annie.

"Riana, this is my friend Tim Kork. We know each other from Vegas," she said.

Tim smiled at me and bought me another gin and tonic. By now I was definitely feeling it, and I wondered what the hell I'd gotten myself into. I wasn't used to drinking like that.

As the night progressed I realized that Annie was a well-known, and much loved, personality in town. I ended up getting so drunk that I slept on the floor of her apartment. There was no way I was driving my car to Honokowai.

~~~~~~~

Annie lived in a second floor studio apartment on Front Street. It had a New Orleans feel to it, with a balcony facing the street. I was sure you could see the ocean if it wasn't dark. As I lay there on her floor, I thought, *This would be a great place on Halloween.*

Annie went straight to the refrigerator and drank milk right out of the carton. Then she stood at the stove, and as drunk as she was, she made herself fried eggs. Turned my stomach, but I got the impression she did this on a regular basis. When she was finished eating, she threw the dish in the sink, stripped down nude, threw on a nightgown, and lay on her bed. Soon after that I heard snoring. I fell asleep listening to the drunk revelers on the street below. Despite it all, I had to admit I had fun.

~~~~~~~

A garbage truck woke me the next morning. Annie was already up and sitting on her porch, looking out at the goings on in the street below.

"Riana, I made coffee," she shouted.

"Great, thanks," I said. I poured myself a cup and joined her on the porch.

Front Street was already bustling with people opening up shops. The smell of the sea air flew into my nostrils. The ocean wasn't far from the apartment, and I saw surfers already out in the water.

"You look like the shit I took yesterday," Annie said, roaring with laughter.

"Well, that's exactly how I feel," I said.

"Let's go to the Broiler for breakfast."

"I've never eaten there."

"All the locals go there for breakfast," Annie said.

We walked into the Lahaina Broiler, which was already packed, to the loud clanking of silverware. Annie seemed to know all the waitresses, so we got a great table on the water. I was hungry and ordered the works: two eggs, bacon, Portuguese sausage, home fries, and wheat toast. I was sipping my orange juice when a bird flew on my plate and stole my last bite of toast.

"Those little bastards," Annie snarled.

Then I saw a line of birds on the railing waiting to dive my plate. They stared me down, but I finished what was left in defiance, so they turned their attention to Annie's leftovers. She had the traditional Hawaiian breakfast: fish and eggs over rice.

"I have to get to work," I said, watching the birds pick at her rice.

"I'm going to hang out here for a while, maybe have a bloody Mary. Tim Kork is meeting me."

I put some money on the table and got up.

"Well, thanks for last night, Annie, I really had a good time."

Annie was already involved in a conversation with one of the waitresses.

"We'll do it again, Riana," Annie shouted after me as I walked out of the restaurant.

~~~~~~

I drove into Lahaina and parked in front of the post office. The bank was right next door. I needed to cash a check from the Crafty Mermaid I'd been carrying around in my purse for a few days. I didn't need money at the Waterworks because everyone bought me drinks.

A guy watched me get out of my car and approached with a surprised look on his face. "How the hell did you get here all the way from New York?"

I was puzzled as to how this guy knew where I was from.

"Your license plate. You'd better get it registered in Hawaii or the cops will give you a ticket."

"Thanks for the tip," I said, smiling as I entered the bank.

Haku was in a good mood when I walked into the shop. We stood at the counter chatting for a while. I told her about the night I had at the Waterworks with Annie Hughes.

"So you finally met Fat Annie. We've been trying to get her to work for us in the store. That woman can sell anything," Haku said, laughing. "I met this cool guy who works on a boat in the harbor. They take tourists out for sunset cruises, and he's studying to get his captain's license."

I stared at her and smiled but didn't say anything. I figured she was probably in the process of ending her relationship with her longtime boyfriend. It was obvious she really liked this new guy, and I sensed a change coming in her life. I was glad we had that talk in her art room.

That afternoon, Annie Hughes walked into the shop looking for me. I heard someone yell, "Riana," as I was sitting at the sewing machine upstairs. I knew that voice. I looked over the railing.

"I'm going up to the hotels tonight to hear some jazz. My friend George is meeting me there, and I want you to meet him. He's a really cool guy," she shouted up at me.

"Okay," I yelled down. I wondered if this would be a repeat of the night at the Waterworks.

After Annie left, I went downstairs and asked Haku if she thought I should go. "Well, Annie sings at the hotels sometimes. She's sort of a torch singer. I think she was even in a big 'old-time' music review in one of the hotels."

I thought about it and figured if nothing else, it would be an experience. It wasn't my scene—I mean hanging out at the hotels in Kaanapali.

~~~~~

That night I wore a dress I'd made at the Crafty Mermaid, put flowers in my hair, and met Annie at the Waterworks. We usually went to the Missionaries Hotel after we'd had a drink at the Waterworks. The Hotel had a piano bar in the back room where a lot of locals and tourists hung out. But tonight she wanted to do something different, and I was going along for the ride. We walked to her place so she could freshen up. She took all but a few minutes in front of a mirror, putting rouge and lipstick on, then furiously waved a can of hair spray, creating a cloud around her head. You could tell she was once a very beautiful woman.

We got into her old beat-up station wagon and drove to Kaanapali.

One of the banquet rooms of the hotel was converted into a nightclub, and we found a table near the stage. We ordered drinks, and I was relaxed and ready to hear some jazz. I kept waiting for her friend to join us, but the music had already started. Annie pointed to the guy walking in, saying it was her friend George. I watched in disbelief as legendary musician George Benson took the microphone at center stage. He began playing "Breezin'" in that smooth style he had, and I was mesmerized.

"Annie, that's George Benson."

"I don't know his last name, I just like him," she said.

It occurred to me that she didn't know he was a big star. After his first set, he walked straight to our table, sat down, and hung out with us.

"Annie, I'm so glad you showed up," he said, taking her hand and kissing it. "I don't know anyone in town, so it's nice to see a familiar face in the audience."

We sat there talking and drinking until his break was over. He returned to the stage, and we left before the end of his second set. Over the months that followed, Annie never ceased to amaze me.

~~~~~~

It was uncanny the way I had a group of friends on the island who were from the East Coast. We kept our New York accents going and saw life through a similar lens. I guess that old saying is true, Birds of a feather flock together!

On the days when we had a day off together, Annie and I would take our sunscreen, visors, and her scrabble set and sit by the pool at El Crab Catcher Restaurant in Kaanapali. A restaurant called Hula Grill sits on that location now, and the swimming pool has been filled with sand. In those early days, we'd sit by the pool all day sipping tropical drinks, and switching off between the pool and the ocean to cool off. These were lazy, hazy days, and it became our routine for quite a while. Annie's girlfriend, who was in town from Los Angeles, came along with us one afternoon. We were frolicking in the waves when a big set rolled in. They were bobbing in the ocean way past where the waves were breaking, but I got stuck in a set. I struggled to stay above water, and my old fear of the ocean came alive. They thought I was swimming and were laughing, while I was tumbling, and swallowing water. A powerful wave tossed me back on the shore and I got dragged through the sand. I emerged from the water in front of the restaurant, coughing up sea water with the top of my bathing suit hanging around my neck by the ties, my breasts exposed. People stopped eating their lunch for a moment to gape at me. I soon regained my composure and put my bathing suit top back on, and everyone continued with their lunch.

~~~~~~

It was a balmy evening in Lahaina, and as had become my habit, I looked for Annie in the pawn shop across the street after work.

"Let's go to the Mission for a few drinks. I'm not in the mood for the Waterworks tonight."

"Yeah, I really like that place. Let's go there," I said.

There were a ton of gin joints and piano bars in town, but we liked the private club atmosphere of the Mission Bar. Annie closed the pawn shop, and we walked down a few back streets until we came to the Missionaries Hotel. It was a bed and breakfast, but the piano bar was a popular hangout with the locals. We walked up the steps, through the lobby, to the back room bar, the sound of the honky-tonk piano getting louder with each step. I saw Bully and some of the other usual suspects sitting at the bar. These people circulated around a number of clubs in Lahaina and could be seen at any bar, at any time of the day or night.

We got a table and ordered drinks.

"I've wanted you to meet my friend Demo for a long time. He keeps asking me about you."

"Who's that?" I asked.

The music stopped, and a guy walked over to our table. It was the piano player. "Riana, this is my dear friend Demo."

He smiled at me and extended his hand, and I noticed a string of musical notes tattooed up his right arm.

"Hi, I'm Dominick French, but you can call me Demo."

I felt an intense current pass from his hand to mine as we stared at each other.

"Hi, I'm Adriana Bardolino," I said with a big smile.

He wouldn't let go of my hand, and I felt something wonderful was going to happen.

"I'm on a break. Let me get a drink at the bar and I'll join you ladies," he said, reluctantly taking his eyes off me.

All the times we sat in the Mission Bar drinking and listening to the music, I never once noticed the piano player. Demo returned with a drink and sat between us. I felt an immediate attraction to him, something inexplicable. I listened to the two of them talk for a while. I was drawing his picture in my mind's eye: tall, solid, light-brown curly hair, boyish face, blue eyes. I scribbled it all down in my head. He had a great sense of humor and a gravelly voice. I thought, *Oh, he's my type all right.* I was smitten immediately. I did a lot of that in those days, I mean, diving right in. I guess all those months of transactional analysis flew right out the window when I saw his face!

When his break was over he asked me, "What song do you want to hear?"

"'Exactly like You,'" I said.

"Ahh, Nina Simone," he said, smiling.

He walked back to the piano and played my request.

~~~~~

Dominick French, aka Demo, was Italian and French. Annie told me his family was wealthy, and the house they built back east was featured in *House Beautiful* magazine. I was impressed, but none of that made a difference to me. I already had a crush on him.

Whenever Annie and I walked into the Mission Bar, Demo would switch whatever he was playing to my song, "Exactly like You." It was his way of saying hello when he was in the middle of a set.

One night he finished a set and walked to our table. He wore a pumpkin-colored suit and a ridiculous straw hat. I thought of the character actor Sydney Greenstreet. Oh, Dominick French was a character all right, in every way. He sat at our table and set his hat on an empty chair. He was a really funny guy with a great sense of humor. Funny is always good! He was getting friendly, and I liked it.

Annie did everything in her power to encourage us.

"Annie, why don't you sing a couple of songs with me during my next set?" Demo asked.

"I'll think about it," she answered.

When his break was over, he went back to the piano and announced over the microphone that Annie Hughes was going to sing a few tunes. The place erupted in applause and shouts, leaving Annie no choice. She stood up and walked to the piano, took the mike, and belted out a few classic torch songs. Watching them together, I soon realized I was "in with the in-crowd."

On other occasions, I'd walk into the Mission Bar, and Demo completely ignored me. I'd leave feeling rejected and confused. He seemed to enjoy playing a cat and mouse game with me. He liked to tease me, and he could be cruel at times. I thought maybe there was some tourist in town he was fooling around with and didn't want me gumming up the works.

~~~~~

One night I walked into the Mission Bar alone. I heard my song as I searched for a seat near the piano. He sat with me during his breaks, and at one point leaned over and said, "Cleopatra, when I'm finished tonight, I want you to come home with me." We hadn't been intimate, and I was lit up like a box of fireworks.

At the end of the night, he took my hand and walked me outside to his sports car parked In front of the Missionaries Hotel. It was a Chevy Corvette convertible. We drove along the side streets of Lahaina until we reached the back of a building.

He turned the engine off and got out. "Wait here," he said.

Watching him walk toward the building, I knew I wanted him bad. He stopped at a window in the middle of a brick wall. He came back with a pizza box and handed it to me.

"Hold this," he said as we sped away.

The box sat hot in my lap, and that wasn't the only thing that was hot.

He pulled into the driveway of a small wooden house right on the ocean under a grove of palm trees. It was old and funky with a front porch, and hibiscus bushes all around. Inside, the place was in disarray, but it had an eclectic feel. It definitely wasn't *House Beautiful* material, but I felt at home as soon as I walked through the screen door. An old upright piano sat against the wall in the living room, and there were LPs lying all over the floor.

We sat on the couch and didn't say much while eating pizza. He turned to look at me, and I found his blue eyes so hypnotic, I couldn't pull mine away.

"I love your bangs. You remind me of Cleopatra," he said.

He sat on the floor and played his favorite albums for me. I had other things on my mind. I didn't want to seem forward, so I patiently went along with his disk jockey routine.

He put one of the records away and said, "Cleopatra, the girl of my dreams."

He turned and smiled at me, took my hand and walked me to his bedroom. The first thing I noticed were two windows that opened to the ocean and the loud roar of the waves. I got undressed and lay in bed waiting for him. I couldn't see much in the dark but was full of anticipation. He got on top of me and kissed me. The kiss was affectionate, but not ardent. We made love, and afterward, I fell asleep to the sound of the waves breaking on the shore.

The next day was a Sunday.

When Demo woke up, he said, "I thought we'd go to my parents' place up north for breakfast."

Things were turning out better than I could have ever imagined. His parents lived in a condo complex on the ocean about twenty minutes north of Lahaina. Buddy and Betty French were a couple of characters. His mother was tiny, so I guessed Demo took after his father. Buddy made us mimosas while Betty cooked breakfast. I splashed around in the pool while Demo watched me with a satisfied grin on his face. His parents seemed pleased with our union, and I couldn't be happier. Breakfast with Buddy and Betty French became a Sunday routine.

~~~~~~~

One night after the Mission Bar closed, we drove our cars to Demo's house and parked.

"Demo, let's stay at my place tonight," I said.

"Whatever you want, Cleopatra."

I left the Gray Mouse in his driveway, and we drove to Honokowai in his Corvette. The night sky was full of stars. I gazed at them from the passenger seat of his convertible. Demo drove with one hand and held my hand with the other. I was a little tipsy as I unlocked the front door.

"Where do you sleep, Adriana?"

I opened the sofa bed and said, "Here."

He tossed me on the bed, and we began fooling around and laughing hysterically. On the fourth floor of the building, the loud roar of the waves drowned out our voices. We had to yell at each other to hear what we were saying.

Loretta stumbled out of her bedroom, rubbing her eyes. "What the hell?"

"It's just me," I said, slurring. "Oh, and this is my friend Demo."

"Have fun you guys," she said, walking back to her bedroom, shaking her head.

~~~~~~~

A friend told me about a studio apartment for rent further north in Napili, and I thought this was a good time to take the leap, never having lived alone. Besides, my mother was coming to stay with me in the summer, and I wanted to be ready with my own place. Loretta and I knew that our history would continue, so there was no sadness upon my moving out.

The studio was in a large complex of low-rise buildings called Napili Hui. It was a corner condo on the ground floor at the edge of a gulch, very private. I heard goats bleating in the gulch every once in a while, but I never saw them.

Napili Hui was one of the few affordable complexes to live in on the west side of the island. *Hui* means family in Hawaiian, but everyone referred to it as the hood! The complex was filled with young people, and at times it was like living in a college dorm. I liked walking to a neighbor's condo to borrow something, or to share a sunset drink. I loved the comradery between everyone, and when I wanted to be alone, all I had to do was shut my front door. It was the perfect set up for me. The resident manager was an old Japanese man. He often gave me discarded orchids to take care of. Plants were easy to tend to on the first floor. There was a large grassy lawn, and a hose right outside the sliding-glass door on my lanai. I remember listening to Earth, Wind & Fire a lot, and I still think of my first year living on Maui whenever I hear them.

From my journal:

He calls me Cleopatra, the girl of his dreams. Sitting at my table this morning with a cup of coffee, I stare at the oleander bushes outside the glass wall. The mild breeze is delightful against my skin as it drifts in through the sliding screen. I'm mad about the guy—the way he told me how he felt about me before we ever made love. His craziness and quirkiness allow me to be myself. I think about him all the time. It's truly been a long time, but I must be in love to be putting words together like this.

When spring arrived, Buddy and Betty French organized a trip to Honolulu for the four of us. I'd been to Honolulu on shopping trips with Annie Hughes. I knew it was a big city and that we were going to have a great time. We had adjoining rooms with his parents that were separated by Japanese shoji screens, so not very private. Demo and I did a lot of talking and laughing in bed, but there was no hanky-panky. It was a fun trip, and I was feeling like part of their family.

That's when he told me he was going to Europe in June for three months over the summer. I immediately felt downhearted and began to pout.

"Adriana, the summer will pass quickly, and before you know it I'll be back. You can stay at my house any time you want; bring your mom there. Annie will be cleaning and looking after my house for me while I'm gone. It would make me feel warm inside knowing you were spending time there."

I didn't understand his reasoning and gave him a smirky smile.

"Now, Riana," he said teasingly, knowing that's what Annie called me, and we both laughed.

He kissed me on the lips, as if that would appease me. *If he really loved me, he'd want to take me with him,* I thought.

———

The Crafty Mermaid filled my days, and Annie Hughes always came up with something interesting and crazy to fill my nights. I had just arrived home at my studio in Napili after spending the night at Demo's when the phone rang.

It was Annie. "There's a midnight pajama party at Nimble's tonight, and we're going. Wear a sexy slip or a nightgown. You can sleep in town at my place tonight."

I knew Demo would be working late at the Mission Bar, so I was up for anything.

We arrived at Nimble's all dolled up in our slips. We got a table, and it wasn't long before guys were buying us drinks. I began to realize that I was a hook for attention in Annie Hughes's world, but I really didn't care. She'd taken me under her wing and became my Maui mom. I wondered what my real mom was going to think of her. Annie was a little over-the-top and had a mouth like a sailor.

I crashed on Annie's floor that night. I was still miffed about Demo going to Europe for the whole summer without me, but soon fell asleep to the sound of Annie snoring and voices in the street.

When I hadn't shown up at the Mission that night, Demo called me a few times. I didn't even know that until I listened to my phone messages the next morning when I got home. I didn't call him back. Maybe I was playing a game, but I figured it was my only recourse.

———

The next day at the Crafty Mermaid, Hannah yelled up at me from the desk downstairs that someone was there to see me. I peered over the railing, and it was Demo.

"What are you doing here?" I yelled down.

"I thought I'd take you to Kimo's for lunch."

Hannah nodded at me. "Go ahead and take a break."

I grabbed my purse and we strolled along Front Street, Demo with his arm entwined in mine, talking away. I didn't say much. When we got to the restaurant, a waitress walked us to a table right on the water. She shot a flattering glance at Demo as she handed us menus. I was used to seeing women all over him. I'd actually witnessed Annie pulling women off his back a few times at the piano in the Mission Bar. They would become enamored with his funky blues style.

The waitress returned to take our order, flashing Demo a sexy smile.

"I'll have the crab salad in papaya," Demo said.

"I'll have the same, and bring us two iced teas, please."

"You're very quiet today. Are you still mad at me about Europe?"

"I'm not angry, just disappointed," I answered

"Look, it's not easy traveling all over Europe looking for gigs to play. Besides, I have to schmooze people, and I know you'd feel ignored."

He made sense, but inwardly I felt there was more to it. I figured he wanted his freedom to play around, and I didn't like it.

"Adriana, your mother will keep you busy. You can show her around the island."

"I suppose so," I said.

Demo walked me back to work. I told him I'd stop by the Mission in the next few nights. He seemed relieved, sensing I was still miffed about Europe. I let go of his arm and left him on the street.

~~~~~~~

I let a few days pass before going to the Mission Bar, so as not to seem eager. I walked in and the place was jumping. People were banging on tables as Dominick French was banging on the piano keys. It was a totally wild scene. He didn't play my song, but I figured he was taking requests from the crowd.

When he took a break, he walked right past me and went to the bar. He got another drink and sat at the rowdy table, ignoring me. My face flushed, and I felt numb. One of the girls, a regular, was all over him. Demo didn't respond to her at all, but still, he wouldn't even glance in my direction. I wanted to leap out of my chair, throw my drink in his face, and walk out, but I refused to react.

I remembered Annie telling me that it was his job, and when he was playing he belonged to everyone. She told me not to pay attention to his fans, that it was all a show. I sat there tossing her words around in my head to calm myself down. The place began to empty out, and I was one of the few people left for his last set.

He finally looked at me and smiled, but I wasn't having it. I finished my drink, smiled, and left without a word. This was the game we played.

From my journal:

Last night I just wanted to be close to you. You didn't look at me or talk to me all night. I sat there, set after set, waiting for you. God, I felt a fool. I would have left, but I was numb, frozen in my chair. When everyone left you went back to the piano, played my favorite song, turned, and winked at me. I was fuming inside. I stood up to leave and you shook your head no, as if I shouldn't go. You took your house key out of your pocket and placed it on top of the piano. That was my cue to take the key, go to your house, and wait for you. I finished my drink and sat there until the end of your set, stood up, ignoring you, and left without a word.

The next time Annie and I had a day off together, we drove to the other side of the island. We spent the day rummaging around the secondhand stores in Wailuku. She drove at a snail's pace in her old station wagon, cars passing us as the road took its twists and turns along the coast. Surfers' cars and trucks were parked all along the shore. The waves were up, and everyone was out in the water.

"When did you move to Maui, Annie?"

"I was living in Las Vegas for a few years. My husband was dying of cancer. He decided to sell our house in Brooklyn and sink all our money into a house in Vegas."

"No, Annie, really? So you left him?"

"No, he finally died."

"Oh, I'm sorry."

"Don't be," she said. "I'm glad the bastard's dead!"

I had the feeling I'd be hearing more about that story the next time she was drunk.

We spent a really fun day buying treasures at the secondhand shops. We had lunch at Hamburger Mary's in Wailuku and then headed back to Lahaina. On the ride back to the west side, the ocean was as flat as a sheet of glass. The beaches along the coastline were empty. No waves and no surfers in sight.

Annie pulled the station wagon off the road and parked on the beach. We got out, stripped down to our bathing suits, and headed straight to the ocean and dived in. The water was cool and refreshing as we bobbed around for a while. We laughed and talked about our day and discussed our plans for the evening. It was all so glorious.

"I think it's time to ditch my blue jeans for a bathing suit and sarong," I said.

"It's about fucking time," Annie squawked, signaling me that a wave was coming.

"It's just so damn hot under that roof upstairs at the Crafty Mermaid."

"Ha, I guess I won that bet!" Annie screeched, slapping the water.

I turned and floated on my back, closed my eyes, and enjoyed the moment.

CLEOPATRA WALKING ON FRONT STREET

EIGHT

MONKEY BUSINESS

How many more nights and weird mornings can this terrible shit go on?
How long can the body and the brain tolerate this doom-struck craziness?

—*Hunter S Thompson,* ***Fear and Loathing in Las Vegas***

A cat hung around outside my studio apartment in the hood. He'd stare at me through the glass door every day until I finally let him in. He was gray with white patches and had a friendly disposition. I wondered if he was someone's cat, or if someone had moved away and left him behind. I couldn't resist picking him up and making a fuss over him. Pretty soon I was buying cat food, treats, and toys. I named him Ono, which means the best, or number one, in Hawaiian. He became my companion, and I delighted in watching him chase the green geckos that ran up and down the walls inside my condo.

Dominick French went to Europe in June, and Annie went on a campaign to redecorate his house. I wanted no part of it. Who the hell changes someone's house around while they're away on vacation? I was driving past his house after work and saw Annie's station wagon parked in the driveway. I figured I'd hang out while she was cleaning. True, Demo's place was a total mess and could use a little TLC, but Annie was taking a sledgehammer to it. I noticed she had hung layers of Arabian fabric in the living room, and dragged the coin-operated carnival camel that was in a shed behind the house, and set it up in a prominent corner of the living room. His bedroom seemed a little more orderly, and I liked how she was organizing the kitchen. Demo liked to cook, so I figured he'd appreciate that.

While I was there Buddy and Betty French stopped in, I guess noticing our cars in their son's driveway. Betty stood there with her mouth agape, staring at the camel in the corner of the living room, with the Arabian curtains flapping in the afternoon breeze.

"That's interesting," Betty said.

"Demo left Annie in charge," I said. "I had nothing to do with it!"

Buddy seemed dumbfounded and was simply at a loss for words.

After they left, I hung around watching Annie clean and move stuff from room to room. I went around picking up Demo's personal items, turning them over in my hands, and putting them back down. It was a way of feeling him around me, even though he was thousands of miles away.

"Let's go see that new movie, *Grease,* tonight," Annie shouted from the kitchen.

"Yeah, that sounds like a plan."

She walked into the living room and saw me moping on the couch.

"What the hell is wrong with you?"

"I just miss him," I said, pouting.

"He does this every summer. The time will fly by; you'll see."

"If he really loved me, he wouldn't want to be without me."

"Absence makes the heart grow fonder. Don't you know that?"

"Maybe so, but we were just getting close, and I feel like he was pumping the brakes."

"I can tell he's crazy about you," she said, walking back into the kitchen with a dishrag.

"Really?"

"I've never seen him make such a fuss over a girl until you came along."

"I'm going home. It's been a long day. Call me later, and we'll meet at the movie theater."

"Okay," she said, hugging me.

I walked out, the screen door slamming behind me.

When I got home, Ono was waiting behind the glass door of my lanai. I opened it and let him in. He was so appreciative and nuzzled his face against my leg. I noticed two new potted orchids on my lanai and figured the resident manager left them there for me.

There was a knock on the door. It was one of the guys from the condo across the way. "Adriana, come on by our place, we're out on the lanai for sunset drinks."

I took a shower, threw on shorts and a T-shirt, and walked across the lawn to their condo. I was brought back to a happy place in no time. These were funny guys who kept me laughing that whole summer, despite missing Demo.

The sun had gone down and I'd lost track of time. I told the guys I had to meet a friend for a movie, and left. As I approached my front door I heard the telephone ringing. I ran to the phone, hoping it was Demo. He promised he would call me from Europe.

It was Annie. "Where the hell have you been?"

"I was across the way at a neighbor's house."

"Forget the movies tonight, the fleet is in," she said.

"What fleet? What are you talking about?"

"There's a navy ship docked in Lahaina Harbor, and it's going to be wild in town tonight."

"What is it we're supposed to do?"

"We're going down to the Pioneer Inn at the harbor and rip the place up."

"What should I wear?"

"As little as possible," she said. "I can guarantee tonight we'll be drinking for free!"

~~~~~

It was dark as I drove along the coastal road into Lahaina. The night blooming cereus were out, and beyond them was the ocean. I was happy there was a full moon, because there weren't many street lights back in those days. I had the windows rolled down on the Gray Mouse and hung one arm out. The air was intoxicating, putting me in a magical mood.

Looking for a parking spot in Lahaina wasn't easy. There were MPs and sailors walking everywhere, darting in and out between cars. I finally found a spot and parked. I walked along the seawall to the Pioneer Inn.

I spied Annie sitting at a table with a few empty glasses in front of her. There was a local band in the corner of the bar, and the place was jumping. I sauntered in, and from the way the sailors at the bar were checking me out, I knew I looked hot. I sat at the table, and before I said hi to Annie, a couple of sailors came over and offered to buy us drinks.

Annie said, "Sure, I'll have a vodka and soda, and Riana here will have a gin and tonic." The night was off to a crazy start.

I wasn't looking to meet anyone, just to have a night of flirty fun. All the guys were young, sweet, and aimed to please. They were happy to buy us whatever we wanted, and we were having a rip-roaring time.

Suddenly, a chair flew past our table. I thought, *What the hell?* I heard a ruckus and two big guys walked out from behind the bar, I guessed security, trying to break up the fight. Tables were overturned, and soon a general brawl broke out. The band took cover, running outside.

Annie grabbed my hand, "Let's get the hell out of here." We left our drinks, and as we ran out the door we heard whistles and saw a bunch of MPs run in.

"We made it out just in time," I said.

"Let's walk across the street to the Whale's Tail," Annie said.

We made our way to Front Street, passing sailors and MPs left and right, and up the stairs to the Whale's Tail for a nightcap. We were already tipsy from all those free drinks, but of course Annie wasn't finished. I usually left her at a bar when I'd had enough, but tonight was different. She was in a mood, and she began rambling on about her life and her husband.

"You know I'm Irish, right?"

Before I had a chance to answer, she said, "I'm Italian by injection—my husband, Tony. He was a bastard. He beat me and the kids. He molested one of my daughters, and she's in a mental hospital."

I didn't say anything and just let her talk.

"One of my sons had a disability. Tony beat him up so bad I thought he'd killed him. I started sleeping with a knife under my pillow, and I told him if he ever touched me or the kids again, I'd stab him to death."

I lay my hand on her arm, but I don't think she even noticed. She was in a zone.

"Tony slept with my twin sister. I don't talk to her anymore."

I thought, *Another Annie? A twin? Could that even be possible?*

"The fucker told me he only had sex with her because she reminded him of me."

Tim Kork walked in and put his arms around Annie. I was glad he showed up. "How're you ladies doing tonight? I checked just about every bar in town looking for you girls."

"Timmy," she whined, her eyes beginning to water.

"Now let's have none of that." He looked uncomfortable yet sympathetic. "Come on, Annie, I'll walk you home."

I nodded in approval and smiled. "Tim, my car is parked near here. I'll be fine."

Tim put his arm around Annie's shoulder, helped her off the barstool, and walked her out.

I sat there in a cloud of sadness. I didn't realize what was behind that fun-loving façade, and I began to tear up. I paid the tab, left a tip, and walked out.

~~~~~~

June is mango month in Lahaina, and the trees were full of them. Owners who had houses with mango trees in their yards left the fruits in cardboard boxes for passersby to take. There were mangos smashed on the sidewalks that had fallen from the trees, and crushed mangos in the streets from cars driving by. Walking toward the Crafty Mermaid, the sweet, rancid smell of the rotting mangos combined with the emissions from the sugar mill on the corner permeated the air. The loathsome odor followed me to work.

It was King Kamehameha Day. Hannah and Haku insisted I walk to Front Street to see the Pa'u Riders, saying it was an annual tradition. Horses and riders came from all the islands to "represent." I took my camera, headed out, and picked a good spot along the seawall to watch the parade.

It was a local event for sure. There were floats with students representing their schools, well-known local celebrities, and even Mayor Hannibal Tavares went by waving to the crowd from his convertible. I saw the horses coming in the distance. Groups of four or five horses and riders trotted slowly down Front Street, each group wearing the color of their island. The paniolos (Hawaiian cowboys) carried the banner from their island (Lanai, Molokai, Kauai, etc.). The women wore long silk royal robes, so long that they covered the horses' backs. They wore ornate, tropical, floral headpieces and lots of leis. Even the horses wore leis. I'd never seen anything like it. When the group representing Maui went by, everyone cheered, and the horses were trained to bow to the crowd.

PA'U RIDERS

Watching the parade, I flashed on the spectacles I would see as a child. I mentioned growing up in an Italian neighborhood in the Bronx. On various saints' days, the statue of that particular saint would be taken out of the church, carried on men's shoulders, and paraded through the streets. A procession of neighborhood residents would follow. Onlookers often threw money or would get close enough to the statue to kiss the saint's feet. People who were crippled or had disabilities were carried or pushed in wheelchairs. Those were solemn occasions. In contrast, the Pa'u parade was joyous.

～～～～

The pawn shop across the street was closing, so Hannah Klein convinced Annie to work in the Crafty Mermaid as a saleswoman. They were sure she'd be perfect for the store. I was happy about it.

We often socialized outside of work. One of our favorite things to do on a day the shop was closed was to drive to Wailuku and have lunch at La Familia Mexican Restaurant. Back in those days there were hot tubs in the courtyard behind the restaurant. We'd start out with frozen margaritas, chips and salsa, and a bowl of guacamole. When we finished our meal, they'd let us take our margaritas to the hot tubs in the back, and we'd hang out for hours. The first time we took Annie, I remember the water in the hot tub overflowed as she got in.

~~~~~~~

There was a new guy cruising around the hood. I remember seeing him talking to the harbor rats when I was hanging around with Peyton Parker at the Pioneer Inn. He was hard to miss, very good looking with dark curly hair and dark eyes. He resembled Omar Sharif, the actor. He had that triangular surfer's body: broad shoulders, muscular arms, narrow hips, and strong legs. He wore the same yellow board shorts every day, as if he'd just emerged from the waves. I asked a few of my neighbors about him, but no one seemed to know anything.

One evening I was sitting with the guys on their lanai drinking beer and watching the sunset when he appeared. He greeted one of the guys and glanced in my direction. He was really nice and very funny. At some point, he walked off.

"Any of you guys know anything about him?" I asked.

"That's Mango Mike," someone said. "He's always eating mangos."

"Mango breath," another guy said, laughing. "I swear, the guy probably drives all the way to Hana to find them when they're not in season on Lahaina side of the island."

Another guy said, "I think he said he was born in Alexandria."

They were all laughing, but I was interested in Mango Mike.

~~~~~~~

At the Crafty Mermaid the next day, I was standing at the counter talking to Annie. A group of women came into the shop and began fishing through the racks. Annie left me standing at the counter and began twirling around the shop, pulling out painted silk pareos and dangling them in front of the tourists. Annie was surprisingly fast on her feet for a woman her size. She made sure she showed them the most expensive items in the store. She sure knew how to sell. Two of the women were so pleased with the selection, they bought sarongs and pareos for themselves, and some to take home as gifts for family and friends on the mainland. I think Annie rang up over a thousand dollars on the register when tallying up the sale. After they left, I mentioned how skinny one of the women was, but that she probably looked great in a bathing suit.

"I'll bet a thick juicy pork chop would kill her!" Annie said, and we both had a good laugh.

~~~~~

That evening when I got home, I strolled over to my neighbor's lanai, knowing they'd be out there drinking and watching the sunset. Mango Mike was there. As I approached, Mike stood up to give me his seat. *Now this is nice,* I thought. I sat down and one of the guys handed me a cold beer I wasn't familiar with, Olympia.

Mango Mike started a conversation with me. After the sunset, I got up and said, "Thanks, guys," and walked slowly back to my studio hoping Mike would follow. But that didn't happen. Although, when I turned around, I noticed his eyes followed me.

I opened the sliding screen door on my back lanai, grabbed the hose, and watered my orchids. Ono was lying there on his back until he heard the water. He ran inside to the kitchen, knowing I would feed him when I was finished.

~~~~~

The next day was a Sunday, and I had the day off. I was making coffee when there was a knock at the door. It was Mango Mike, in those same yellow board shorts, holding mangos in his arms.

"For me?" I asked.

"For us," he answered. "I thought we'd have breakfast together."

"I have plenty of food in the house," I said.

"Show me what you've got, and I'll make us something."

I showed Mike what I had in the refrigerator, handed him the frying pan, and he went to work. I stood alongside him watching as he skillfully sautéed onions and potatoes. Then he scrambled some eggs and threw them in the pan.

I took two plates out of a cabinet, found silverware, and put two slices of Hawaiian sweet bread in the toaster. We sat at my table right inside the sliding screen door and ate while Ono sat under my chair. Mike walked back into the kitchen, sliced one of the mangos, and returned to the table.

"Dessert," he said.

"So, I have to tell you, the guys call you mango breath," I said with a chuckle.

"I don't let shit like that bother me. Mangos are good for you."

"I'm slightly allergic to them. I can eat the fruit if someone peels it for me."

"I can do that for you," he said. "But I never heard of anyone being allergic to mangos."

"Did you know that the mango tree is in the same family as Poison oak? And I'm very allergic to Poison oak. I got it pretty bad a few times, when I lived in California. It's the sap from the tree."

"Wow, I'm really learning some stuff today," Mike said.

"Eventually, a doctor told me to take vials of something called 'Immune oak,' before the Poison oak season hit. It was so dry in California that the oils actually flew around in the air."

"Adriana, that's crazy," he said, shaking his head.

"Native Americans ate miner's lettuce that grew along a stream near Poison oak bushes. That way they were getting small doses of the poison and would be immune."

"You're a wealth of information, Adriana. Hey, let's walk down to the beach."

I put the breakfast dishes in the sink, got into my bathing suit, and grabbed some towels. We walked down the road to the ocean. We had fun frolicking in the water and lying on the sand enjoying the sun. Mike kept me laughing all day long. That night he stayed at my place. We had sex on the kitchen floor. I can't remember how that came about, but I remember staring at the mangos on the counter while the Bee Gees new song, "Stayin' Alive," played on the radio.

I began sleeping with Mango Mike on a regular basis. There was nothing heavy between us, but I liked him a lot. I knew it was monkey business, but he filled my summer with fun and companionship. It had been more than a month since Demo left for Europe, and I had yet to receive a phone call from him. I didn't tell Annie about Mike, not because I thought she'd judge me, but because she and Demo were close friends. I figured I'd best keep Mango Mike to myself for the time being. I also wondered why sex with Mike was so much more intense than it was with Demo.

Annie and I went on a shopping trip to Honolulu. Mike assured me he'd stop by my studio and feed Ono while I was gone. We went to Honolulu a few times a year to get a dose of city life, Hawaiian style. We took the small Royal Hawaiian plane at Airport Beach. When I got to the little airport, I went straight up to the Windsock Bar, figuring Annie would be sitting there talking to High School Harry and sipping a bloody Mary. I walked up the spiral staircase and there she was. I sat next to her and ordered a Mary. I listened to them trade stories about streaking the Corner Bar in Lahaina, and Annie winning the wet T-shirt contest in Kaanapali back in the day. When we heard the plane engine start, we walked down the staircase with mostly empty bags, knowing we'd be doing some serious shopping.

I loved feeling the vibration as the prop plane took off. We sat right behind the pilot, and during whale season he'd take us directly over a pod of whales for a close encounter. However it was the summer, and the whales were in Alaska. He did fly the plane very close to the cliffs of Molokai, so we could see the rugged coastline with waterfalls.

As soon as the plane landed on Oahu, Annie turned to me and pointed her finger in my face. "Now remember the rule. I don't know you, and you don't know me. Got it?"

"I know," I said swiping my finger across my closed lips.

"Now let's get a drink," she said.

We walked into one of the Honolulu airport bars. That was the routine, and there was no sense arguing with Annie. I knew she meant to engage in some serious monkey business.

～～～～

We took a taxi from the airport to the Ala Moana Hotel. I rarely rented a car in Honolulu, since most favorite things in our orbit were in walking distance. Besides, we drank so much in those days that driving was out of the question. The hotel had a ramp on the second floor that went straight to Liberty House Department Store (now a Macy's). At that time Ala Moana was the largest outdoor shopping center in the world, with a number of restaurants and bars. Hawaii is the crossroads of the Pacific between the US Mainland and the Orient. Anything you could ever want could be found in Honolulu on the Island of Oahu. There was a pop-up bar on the second floor of Liberty House in the ladies department, and since we always split up to shop, we'd meet there for a glass of champagne midday to talk about what we'd purchased so far. Riding up the escalator in Liberty House, you were serenaded by the piano player on the main floor. It was all so elegant and wonderful.

Our hotel room had two queen beds, and when we were finished shopping for the day, we enjoyed laying our purchases out and playing show and tell. Then we'd carefully pack round one in our suitcases. We took showers and watched the nightly news, until Annie became restless.

"Let's get going," she said.

Walking out the door, Annie ran into someone she knew in the hallway, which was a common occurrence. Taxis were lined up outside the front lobby, and one of the bellman signaled a taxi for us. I slipped him some cash.

"Where to, ladies?" the cabbie asked as we got in.

"The Tahitian Lanai," Annie said, squeezing my hand.

~~~~~~

The Tahitian Lanai was packed with old retired veterans, probably regulars, mostly servicemen and servicewomen who remained in Hawaii after the Second World War, since the Pearl Harbor days. Honolulu has a large military presence because of the base. There was a piano player who had a glass tip jar filled with cash. People shouted out their favorite songs, and he'd play them. I noticed he never looked at the crowd, or anyone in particular. I mentioned it to Annie. She whispered, "He's blind."

We had a few drinks as the night wore on. We'd arrived late because we went to dinner first. I noticed the place never emptied out. At the end of his last set, everyone stood up, held hands, swayed from side to side, and sang "Aloha Oe" ("Farewell to Thee"). It was very emotional and powerful. I admit I was totally overcome, tears rolling down my cheeks, and I wasn't the only one.

We took a taxi back to the hotel and walked through the lobby.

"Let's go to the discotheque at the top of the hotel," Annie said.

"Not me, I'm ready for bed."

"Well, I'm just getting started," she said.

She left me standing alone in the lobby and walked to the elevators that went to the top floor.

For a woman in her late fifties, she had a lot more energy than I did. Then again, I always had the impression that Annie was making up for lost time. I don't remember when she got back to the room, but she was asleep in bed when I woke up the next morning.

~~~~~~~

We ran into a friend of Annie's the next day while roaming around Ward Center. Chip Newton seemed like a really nice guy, and I got the feeling she was trying to match me up with him. Even though he was an attractive guy, I didn't feel a romantic connection. We had lunch together. Annie and Chip did a lot of drinking and talking about their escapades in Las Vegas, and I drank iced teas. I had to check myself before speaking, because "Fig Newton" was always on the tip of my tongue. He was tall, good looking, and tan, with strawberry blond hair, and his eyebrows were so light they were almost invisible. He was really sweet, but I knew nothing was going to happen between us. I left them having happy hour drinks at a bar on the third floor of the shopping center. I could foresee being between two wild and crazy people that night.

Sure enough, Annie made reservations for us to have dinner with Chip Newton at an Italian restaurant that was famous for their authentic tableside Caesar salad. Chip showed up at our hotel room and threw himself on my bed. He smiled up at me as if anticipating something was going to happen there later on. I was just going along for the ride at that point. We had a really nice dinner, and yes, the Caesar salad was epic, which I ordered with grilled shrimp on top. We went to a popular bar and had drinks, and then to another bar. It seemed like they knew where every bar on Oahu was. I was ready for bed, but Annie and Chip had something else on their minds.

"Let's go to the Monkey Bar," Annie said.

"It's in Pearl City, the Pearl City Tavern," Chip said, noticing my puzzled expression.

"Now?" I asked. "Isn't it late to be going all the way to Pearl City?"

Out of that bar we went, into another taxi, the three of us squeezed into the backseat. Chip was all over me like jelly on peanut butter. If there was one thing I couldn't stand, it was a sloppy drunk. We must have driven for half an hour or more until we finally reached the Pearl City Tavern. It looked like a nice place, but was in a very out-of-the-way section of Pearl City. Chip paid the cab driver while I helped Annie out of the backseat. I figured out why they called her Fat Annie as I pried her loose from her reclining position.

Inside the tavern there were only a few stragglers at the bar. The place was closed. Chip and Annie were disappointed, but I was happy. At that point, I just wanted to lay down somewhere and go to sleep. It all seemed like a wild goose chase to me. They put up such a stink with the manager that he pulled a chord opening a curtain behind the bar. To my amazement there was a bunch of monkeys behind a glass partition that went the whole length of the bar. I stared at them as they went bonkers, swinging on tree trunks and screeching. I imagined they were pissed off at being woken up. The manager let us have one drink since we drove all the way from Waikiki.

When we got back to the hotel, I left Chip and Annie in the lobby. They were on their way up to the disco, and I was going up to the room. I was aware that the next day was our last day in Honolulu, and I wanted to finish my shopping. I prayed she wouldn't bring Chip back to the room.

I was woken a couple of hours later by Chip lying next to me on the bed. Annie got into her bed laughing and was soon snoring. I ignored Chip, and eventually he gave up and moved to the carpeted floor, falling asleep in a drunken stupor.

The next morning, Chip treated us to breakfast at Michelle's. It was outside of Waikiki but well worth the drive. When you walked into this fancy restaurant on the ocean, you felt as if you were in Hollywood during its heyday, and expected to see movie stars sitting at the tables. White tablecloths, silver utensils and sugar bowls, and small café lights on each table, in case you were having a romantic dinner. They served the best eggs benedict in Honolulu. And when you asked for more coffee, there were no fill-ups; they brought a fresh pot of coffee and a new cup. We had a wonderful breakfast and then went back to Ala Moana for some last-minute shopping before packing up and heading to the airport.

Boarding the small plane to go home, I was so exhausted I fell asleep as soon as I felt the engine's vibration. I didn't even look out the window as we flew away from the island of Oahu.

I woke up when we landed in Kaanapali. I left Annie walking up to the Windsock Bar at Airport Beach and took a taxi home. Looking back, I think that was the craziest shopping trip I'd ever been on.

~~~~~~

My friend Suki Rosmond came for a visit that summer. It was so good to spend time with her. I told her all about Dominick French, and how everything seemed to come together from the first week I arrived on the island. She was a little confused about Mango Mike, but I told her not to judge. She got a big kick out of Annie, and we all went to the Waterworks a few times.

"You said your mother is coming soon. What do you think she'll make of Annie Hughes?"

"I've been wondering about that myself," I answered.

"How long will Demo be gone?"

"Three long months."

"What will you tell him about Mike?"

"I'm not going to tell him anything. Why would I do something stupid like that? What do you think he's doing in Europe?"

I took Suki to Demo's house. She roared with laughter at the camel in the living room.

"Look, it has a place to put nickels in to make it move up and down." She giggled, getting on.

Suki was staying in a small bed and breakfast in Lahaina, across the street from the Crafty Mermaid, in the same building where the pawn shop used to be. She had her Realtor friend, Kenny, with her. I hung out with them in town, but every time I looked at Kenny, my mind bounced back and forth between his Silver Bullet and the Grand Central Sauna. I got queasy at the thought of him banging me to the beat of the music. I walked across the street when I was finished with work. I climbed the stairs to their room and knocked on the door until Suki answered.

"Kenny's sitting outside on the lanai," she said.

I walked out to greet him. "Hi there."

"Hey, you," he said as he took hold of me around the waist and pulled me on his lap.

I gave him a friendly kiss on the cheek, seeing my image in his mirrored Aviator sunglasses. We took turns taking photos of each other and finished off a bottle of champagne they had in the room.

It was so good to spend time with my Virgo sister from the old commune days, and I was thankful we were still friends. She and I walked to Front Street and went shopping. It's funny how, over the years, wherever we each lived, we seemed to pick up as if no time had passed between us.

~~~~~~

Love and Loathing in the islands   **147**

In a few days my friends were gone and things returned to normal. I met Annie at the Waterworks for a drink. Neither one of us could face the Mission Bar when Demo wasn't there.

When I arrived at the bar, Annie was already four sheets to the wind. I sat next to her at the bar, but she didn't notice me. A tourist she'd met was buying her drinks. They were involved in a deep conversation, too deep for me. I wasn't aware that Annie read palms! The bartender set a gin and tonic in front of me, being familiar with my drink by now. When I lifted the glass, Annie finally noticed me.

"Riana," she said, throwing her arms around me. "You know that I know your name is Adriana, but I just like to call you Riana."

"I know," I said, smiling. "I don't mind. I kinda like it."

"You know you're my best friend, and I love you like a daughter."

"I know, Annie, and I love you too. I'm afraid my mother will be jealous of you," I said.

"Oh, your mother will be happy that I took you under my wing and showed you the ropes."

That's what I'm afraid of, I thought. "You're probably right," I said.

The tourist who was buying Annie all the drinks in return for getting his palm read, met a floosy that was sitting at the other end of the bar. When I looked up, he had moved to the barstool next to her. Annie was so far in the zone, she didn't even notice.

"You know, I ran away from home when I was fourteen," she said. "I was adopted, you see. My foster parents didn't even tell me I had a twin sister, that we'd been separated at birth. I found that out years later. They weren't very nice to me either. I had a hard life, Riana. I lived on the streets for a while, and I got abused. It was a way to make money."

"Annie, really? I'm sorry you had it so rough," I said with a frown.

"Then I met Tony, my bastard husband. He was so good looking, and he was nice to me at the beginning. Well, I was just a stupid kid. I got pregnant, so we got married. I was only fifteen."

"There had to be some good in him. After all, you stayed with him."

"Well, after five kids, there was nothing else I felt I could do about it."

"You have five children?" I asked in amazement (she never talked about them).

"All caesarians, they were."

I hugged Annie. "Come on, I'll walk you home."

I helped her off the barstool. I looked at the bartender, who pointed to the tourist with the floosy, and said, "It's all taken care of."

I smiled back at him and left extra cash on the bar.

We walked across the street together, my arm around her shoulder. Even though she was old enough to be my mother, I tried to envelop her with a feeling of safety. The two of us walked up the stairs to her apartment.

Annie fumbled through her purse for the keys. "Can you stay with me tonight, Riana? I don't want to be alone."

"Yeah, no problem. I'll sleep on the floor."

She didn't even make fried eggs or drink milk that night. She lay down, and I covered her with the cotton blanket at the foot of her bed.

I sat next to her and touched her arm. "Annie, you're safe now. You know that, don't you?"

She opened her eyes briefly and said, "Yes, I'm safe now."

I waited until she fell asleep. I got off the bed and sat on the porch for a while. I cried a little to think of the life she'd had. I looked at the moon shining brightly over the ocean, creating that jagged line as if it were a Gauguin painting. I was thankful I came from a home that may have been dysfunctional at times, but it was a home of love and safety. I often wondered if my mother had stayed with my father all those years for my welfare, although it was my father who told me he stayed with my mother for me. I threw myself on Annie's floor and dozed off, dreaming of a fan and my own bed.

NINE

MANGO BREATH

A woman has to live her life, or live to repent not having lived it.

—D. H. Lawrence

I was cleaning my condo in anticipation of my mother's visit. I hadn't heard from Mango Breath for a few days and wondered where he'd disappeared to. I wasn't in love, but I'd gotten used to having him around. True, he was a horny guy, but he was also sweet, kind, and caring.

No sooner than I was thinking of him, he appeared outside the sliding screen of my back lanai. Ono the cat was standing next to him, and both were peering in at me. I was in my robe making the morning coffee in the kitchen.

"I have some mangos for you," he said.

I smirked as I walked across the room and let them both in. He set the mangos down on the kitchen counter, as well as a box of hot-cross buns.

"I stopped at the robberette on my way here," he said.

Back then there were no supermarkets that far north in Napili, and you had to drive all the way to Lahaina to buy groceries. There was a tiny store at the end of our road we all called the "robberette" because the prices they charged for the few essential items they carried was highway robbery.

Mike put his hands under my robe, caressing my breasts. "Can't call my baby sugar, 'cause sugar never was so sweet," he said in a soft, sexy voice.

"I didn't know you liked Muddy Waters. And where have you been?" I asked.

"I went to Hana for a few days."

"Well, I have to admit I missed you," I said reluctantly.

"Did you miss this?" he said, taking my hand and moving it down to his member.

I giggled a little at how hard it was.

"I thought about you the whole time I was in Hana," Mike said.

I didn't have a chance to answer. He slipped his yellow board shorts down and stepped out of them. He sprang into action, and I wasn't resisting. He walked me into the living room, lay on the carpet, and pulled me on top of him.

"The curtains are open," I said.

Mike jumped up and closed the curtains. Ono looked at him as if to say, "She hasn't even fed me yet!"

He looked down at me, hesitated, and said, "Open your legs."

He went down on me, his tongue darting around, giving me great pleasure. Mike sure knew how to please a woman. Then he got on top of me and we had intercourse. I tried to muffle my moans and grunts, hoping my neighbors wouldn't hear. Sex with Mango Mike was great.

The cat stared at us when we were finished. Mike laughed at Ono, then his expression changed. He took the silver-etched band he always wore on his ring finger and placed it on mine.

"I want to give this to you," he said, putting his arm around me.

"I'll always treasure it," I said.

We lay there for a while, until hunger overcame whatever it was we were feeling. Mike stood up and slipped his board shorts back on and walked into the kitchen.

Ono slinked over to me for pets, I guess feeling neglected.

"What's for breakfast?" I asked. "And don't say mangos."

Mike opened the refrigerator and looked around. "I'll make us Portuguese sausage and eggs."

I lay there feeling satisfied watching Mike cook breakfast in the kitchen. I wondered why sex was never this intense with Demo, who I figured I was really in love with. *Maybe there are different kinds of love,* I thought.

"My mother's coming next week, so we're gonna have to tone this down," I said.

"Oh, we'll find a way," Mike said. "We should take your mother to Iao Valley."

"Yeah, I think she'd really like that."

I wondered about the few days Mike spent in Hana, and why he didn't tell me he was going. He was a mysterious guy, and I had the feeling I wasn't the only woman he was playing around with. But like I said, I wasn't in love, just in lust, and there definitely was a difference. For a moment I felt sad because I remembered what it was like when I felt both with one man. Was finding that with one person as common as everyone made it out to be? Or did life present us with difficult choices?

From my journal:

I have to question the man's motives, if there are any. It may be a simple case of my being hot for him, and he being hot for me. One might assume there is a trail of horseshit along the beaten path he travels. My concern seems only temporary. As I sit at my table watching the sunset with Ono on my lap, I delight in the beauty and fragrance of my orchids. I glance at the mangos sitting on the kitchen counter and smile. For now I am content with the memories of true love and Xanadu, and look forward to another sunrise in paradise.

Star Green came for a visit in July. My Pisces sister and I went way back to our communal days, living and traveling together. Pisces is the last sign in the zodiac, and even though we were both water signs, we had our differences. I dragged her to the Crafty Mermaid, Demo's house, the Waterworks, and the Missionaries Hotel, although without Dominick French, the Mission Bar was dead.

My birthday was a big event. We all went to Nimble's Bar and Restaurant. Annie was in top form with her sarcastic and racy rhetoric. Haku Neilson was there with her new boyfriend, the sea captain. She spent most of the evening sitting on his lap, staring into his blue eyes. He was strikingly good looking, tall, blond, and stately. She told us the story of how she swam out to the boat he was working on. He gazed back at her, beaming. Hannah Klein was there with a lamenting tale about how her husband shaved off his beard, and she discovered he had no chin. She wasn't sure if she was in love with him anymore, and we all had a good laugh. We drank and ate a lot. A birthday cake mysteriously appeared with thirty-one candles. I made a wish and blew them out. It was the first time in years that I celebrated a birthday in such a big way, and it was a joyful experience. Suki Rosmond and Star Green visited quite a bit during my first few years on Maui. The three musketeers were still connected.

～～～～

My mother, Vita, came to stay with me for the whole month of August. We slept together in my queen-sized bed against the wall of my studio. It was so nice to have her with me. I bought a plumeria lei at Nagasako's Variety Store in Lahaina on my way to the airport. I was so excited driving over the Pali.

How she got to Maui is another story.

When I reached the airport, however, her flight had never arrived. I stood there like a dummy wondering what in the world could have possibly happened. I went to the airline's counter and found a crowd asking questions. I finally was able to speak to an attendant, who informed me that the plane my mother was on from New York was delayed. When it reached Honolulu on the island of Oahu, the last commuter flight of the day to Maui had already taken off.

"Don't worry, your mother is in a hotel in Honolulu, at our expense. I am sure she will call you later this evening."

I left the airport disappointed and concerned, since it was the first time my mother had flown on a plane. I drove home over the Pali with the fragrant lei sealed in a plastic bag sitting on the passenger seat instead of my mother.

That evening she called me from her hotel room. She was exhausted and rightfully frustrated.

"I could almost see the other island, your island, and I was so close. The airline made me take my suitcases with me. I had to drag your guitar all over the airport."

"Mom, I'm so sorry that happened to you."

"I was kicking that guitar case of yours, inch by inch, toward the sliding exit doors."

"Can you get a flight to Maui tomorrow?" I asked, to change the mood.

"They have me on a nine o'clock flight tomorrow morning. I tried to get them to give me a seat on the small plane to Kaanapali on the Royal Hawaiian Airline you mentioned, but they said that those flights were all booked."

"Even Kapalua Airport?" I asked. "It's an interisland commuter airport only fifteen minutes from my house. Our mail and freight comes in there every day."

"No, they never even mentioned that airport."

"Mom, don't worry, I'll be there tomorrow morning to pick you up."

"I can't wait to see you," she said. "I love you."

"I love you too, Ma. Get a good night's sleep."

~~~~~~~

The next morning I took the plastic bag with the plumeria lei out of the refrigerator and headed on that long drive back to the big airport. I was hoping my mother was in a better mood. I knew it must have been quite an ordeal for her. I wondered why the hell I asked her to bring my guitar. I could have collected it the next time I was in New York. Of course, in reality, I wasn't sure when that would be. I was filled with excitement and a little nervousness on the drive.

My mother was standing outside the terminal with two suitcases and my guitar when I arrived. She looked annoyed but was in much better spirits. I put the lei around her neck and we hugged and kissed. I shoved the baggage, and my guitar case, in the backseat of the car.

"Ma, what's in this little suitcase? It's so heavy."

"That's all the cheeses, and I brought some Italian salami and pepperoni."

"Mom, we do have supermarkets here in Hawaii."

"Well, I wanted to bring all your favorites, the things you probably can't get here."

"I'm sure I'll love everything," I said.

Inwardly, I knew I really didn't eat like that anymore, but I heard my therapist, Joan, whispering in my ear to accept the good strokes my mother was giving me.

"Everyone was so nice to me," she said, getting into the passenger seat.

We drove off in the Gray Mouse, chatting on the long ride back to the west side of the island.

My mother oooddd and aahhhd the whole way. "It's like the Hawaiian Riviera," she said looking at the scenery as we drove over the Pali. Back in those days, there was so much open space, with fields of sugarcane and pineapple.

When we finally reached Lahaina, I took her to lunch at Kimo's, and we sat at a table right on the ocean. My mother was so impressed that the aggravation of her last twenty-four hours blew away on the trade winds. I ordered her coconut-crusted shrimp and a mai tai. I had a salad and an iced tea.

~~~~~~

Those first few days were wonderful. My mother fell in love with my cat, Ono. Mango Mike stayed away for the first couple of days to give us time to catch up and bond again. He showed up on the third morning with a basket of mangos and a fresh pikake lei, which he placed around her neck, kissing her on both cheeks.

"Aloha, Mom," Mike said.

My mother beamed from ear to ear.

"Did I miss breakfast?" Mike asked.

"No, but you can cook something for us," I answered.

"Adriana, he's a guest!"

"He's no guest here, Ma," I said, which caused my mother to take a closer look at him.

"You know who he looks like? That actor Omar Sharif!"

"Ma, please, you'll make his head swell." *And something else too,* I thought.

I toasted a few slices of Hawaiian sweet bread while Mike made breakfast. It reminded me of the Italian Panettone bread, but without the tiny candied fruit. My mother laughed at everything Mike said. Well, he was a funny guy. I have a photo of the two of them sitting on my bed with their heads together smiling up at the camera. I chose not to tell my mother about Dominick French just yet.

I let Mike drive the Gray Mouse, like a chauffeur, and I sat in the backseat with my mother. We took her to Iao Valley State Park. She loved the waterfalls, the tropical flora and fauna. We even saw a mongoose scamper into the brush. She stared at the swift-flowing Iao River. Mike told her about the history of the war between ancient Hawaiian tribes, and how the river had turned red with the blood of the warriors. She stared at him with a frown at the loathsome image of a river of blood. But I was sure she appreciated the history lesson. We took lots of photos, and I treasure the memory of that day.

When we arrived back at my condo, I hinted for Mike to leave. He seemed disappointed but did as I asked. I wanted to cook her dinner and spend some alone time with her.

~~~~~~

We sat at the table after dinner watching the sunset through the screen. Ono sat on the lanai, staring at the gulch, hearing bleating.

"What's that?" my mother asked. "It sounds like a baby crying."

"No, Ma, it's just the goats that live in the gulch."

"Goats?" She looked at me, surprised.

"Yes, I think they're wild goats, or maybe someone feeds them. I'm not sure."

"That reminds me of a story from my childhood," she said.

"When we were little kids and lived in Grandpa's house, he brought a lamb home and tied it to the fig tree in the backyard. We kids fell in love with the lamb and made a fuss over it. Then one day the lamb disappeared. It was around Eastertime. Grandpa told us it must have run away, and we all cried and cried. When Easter Sunday came, all ten of us sat down to dinner after church. We stared at the lamb, head and all, laid out on a large platter on the dining room table. We were all so upset, we began yelling and crying. Of course, no one would eat the lamb."

"Ma, I can just imagine how awful that was."

"I guess my father took the lamb to the butcher. That's how it was done in those days."

"When I was a little girl, I remember you plucking the feathers off a dead chicken you got from the Italian market on Arthur Avenue in the Bronx. It was years before I could eat chicken."

My mother laughed. "Life was sure different back then."

"I remember Grandpa putting sliced peaches in a tall glass of red wine."

"Oh yes. Your grandfather would let it sit for hours until the peaches soaked up all the wine." She had a sentimental expression on her face, as if missing her father in that moment.

Later that day I took her to the supermarket so she could buy all the foods she liked.

"I don't see Locatelli Romano," she said.

"Ma, this is an island. We have to wait for the barge to come from the mainland."

She looked at me as if she couldn't grasp what I was saying. She was used to getting whatever she wanted, any time she wanted it, in New York. "I don't know what you see in this one-horse town," she said. "I wanted to make us ravioli on Sunday. That's the one cheese I didn't think to bring."

"We can make it next week," I said, hoping Locatelli Romano would be on the next barge. "Let's bring everything home. I want to take you to the Yacht Club tonight. There's someone I want you to meet."

~~~~~~~

As I walked my mother down Front Street, I had concerns of how she'd react to Annie Hughes. They were so different, and there was the aspect of Annie being like a mother to me. This was a recurring theme in my life regarding my mother. We had a difficult time bonding and burying the hatchet over past issues from my childhood.

As we approached the unimpressive entrance to the Yacht Club, I saw my mother's expression change. I imagined she was expecting something grand, but in contrast, this yacht club was very casual.

"Is this it?" she asked, a surprised expression on her face.

"Yeah. Let's go inside." I reached in front of her to push open the swinging doors.

"It looks more like a saloon," she said, rolling her eyes.

It was Annie's Idea to meet at the Yacht Club, figuring it was a more respectable place. I saw the usual suspects sitting on their barstools and searched the crowd for Annie.

"Riana, over here, I saved two seats at the bar," Annie yelled out.

"Who's Riana?" my mother asked. I ignored her question for the moment.

"Annie, this is my mother, Vita," I said, putting my arm around my mother's shoulder.

"I'm Annie," she said, taking my mother's hand and smiling. "I've heard so much about you from your daughter."

That put a smile on my mother's face.

I directed my mother to sit on the barstool next to Annie so they could talk. I had the feeling sitting between them wasn't a good idea. They engaged in conversation until the bartender stood in front of us and asked what my mother wanted to drink. He handed Annie the logbook so she could sign us both in. She was a new member, and we liked going to a private club once in a while. I was nervous at just how my mother was going to react to the whole situation, but the whiskey sour she drank loosened her up. While watching the two interact, my mother seemed so refined and gracious compared to Annie, who was rough and tumble. But I loved Annie just the same. She had a big heart and everyone loved her.

Tim Kork showed up and stood behind Annie. He seemed to appear wherever Annie was. He ordered a drink and introduced himself. We all sat there talking and enjoying the night.

After watching the two interact for a while, my mother leaned over to whisper in my ear. "So how long has that been going on?"

The barroom banter was so loud that I was sure my mother's comments couldn't be overheard by Annie or Tim. "What are you talking about, Ma?"

"Annie and that younger guy, Tim."

"They're just friends," I said, a little surprised at what my mother was inferring. "They know each other from Las Vegas."

"Come on, Adriana, you're a big girl now. Can't you tell they're lovers?"

I glanced at Annie and Tim. Suddenly it was all so obvious. How in the world did I miss that? My mother, who I thought was clueless, picked up on it immediately. I realized I would never look at Tim Kork the same way. I knew my mother was right. Damn it, she was always right.

Tim was telling us about Annie's Restaurant. When they first arrived on Maui a few years back, he and Annie borrowed money and started a local storefront restaurant off the main drag. It served breakfast and lunch only, and was popular with the locals.

"Annie baked about ten or fifteen pies, and trays of biscuits, in her apartment every night. I'd deliver them to the restaurant each morning," Tim said.

I looked at Annie. "You never told me about that. I always assumed that sign, Annie's Restaurant, that's over the entrance to your porch was just a joke."

"There's so much you don't know about me," Annie said."

I couldn't help but think of the time a guy at the bar remarked, "If you hang out with Annie Hughes, everyone will think you're one of those girls." I was confused and annoyed.

"Annie's my friend, and I don't care what anyone thinks or says."

A memory shot through my brain like a bolt of lightning. The time Annie's friend from Los Angeles came to stay with her for a while. The day I got caught in the waves in front of that restaurant on Kaanapali beach.

When we got back to Annie's apartment that day she invited me to an event. "There's a big poker game tonight, and we're going. You can come if you want. You dress very provocatively and serve drinks. If the men win, they could tip you a few hundred dollars."

At the time it sounded a little creepy. I found the thought of a bunch of old, drunk, sweaty men pawing at me loathsome. True, I was new on Maui and needed money, but that seemed sordid.

"What if they lose, or what if they expect me to do other things?"

"You don't have to do anything you don't want to."

"No, that doesn't sound like something I'd be interested in," I told her.

I'd heard rumors about Annie being a madam at one time and tossed that aside as hearsay, but at the moment I was having second thoughts. Still, she was my friend.

On the drive back to my condo, my mother asked, "Why does she call you Riana?"

"Just a habit, something she called me from the day we met."

"Well, I don't like it. Your name is Adriana, and that's what she should call you."

"Ma, it's just an endearing term she uses. It's her affectionate name for me."

"Well, I guess there are worse things to be called," my mother said, twisting her lower lip.

~~~~~

I took my mother to work with me the following day. As we walked along Front Street, a number of passersby said hello to me.

My mother squeezed my hand and said, "Everyone seems to know you. I think I understand why you like it so much here."

She loved the Crafty Mermaid and hung out there all day talking to Annie at the counter. Hannah and Haku made a fuss over her, and my mother, Vita, relished the attention. She told them about the dress factory she had for twenty years, and how I learned to sew there as a little girl. I let my mother sew a few wraparound sarongs for me upstairs on one of the Berninas, and she marveled at the power and speed of the sewing machine. She felt right at home with the cutting table and rolls of fabric behind her. We all went for lunch together, and the revelations of the previous night disappeared in the celebratory atmosphere. The mai tai she drank helped a lot.

~~~~~~

Reggie Paulson and Leo Thomas came by my studio apartment. They were driving upcountry to Kula and asked if we'd like to come along. My mother's eyes brightened at the thought of an island excursion. She was somewhat familiar with the guys from New York. Reggie had been my supervisor for quite a while when I worked for the market research company in Manhattan.

We went for breakfast at Lahaina Broiler and then drove over the Pali to East Maui. Driving up Haleakala Highway, my mother commented that it was much cooler than where I lived.

"Well, it's cooler at the higher elevations than at sea level," I said.

I don't think she realized that there would be such a variance in the climate depending on where you were on the island.

"It even snows up here once in a while during the winter. When it rains at sea level, it could mean snow up here when the temperature drops below freezing."

My mother couldn't believe there could be snow on Maui.

Soon we drove past eucalyptus trees, and she marveled at the fragrance. I never knew eucalyptus came from trees," she said.

I directed my mother's attention to the anise growing along the side of the road.

She said, "Your father told me anise grows on Mount Etna in Sicily."

"I think it has something to do with the volcanic soil," I said.

We passed row upon row of cactus, which were filled with fruits.

"Stop the car!" Vita shouted. "Those look like prickly pears."

Reggie pulled the car off the road, took a pear off a cactus, and gave it to my mother.

"I love prickly pears, but I had no idea they grew on cactus," she said.

My mother was like a little kid in an amusement park for the first time. She was in total wonder at everything around her. We stopped in a field of pineapples to take pictures, and she was surprised that they grew so close to the ground, and from a solo plant.

"Mom, this isn't like a market in the Bronx, where everything is in a neat little box on a shelf."

"I see that now. It's all so wonderful," she said.

Whenever someone from the mainland came for a visit, I seemed to fall in love with the island all over again. My mother enjoying it? Well, that was icing on the cake.

We had lunch at Kula Lodge and then headed back down the volcano through the cowboy town of Makawao. We stopped in Paia, which was a bit of a hippie town, and there were hippies walking everywhere on the streets. I wondered if my mother was thinking about when I was a hippie, but she didn't comment. Leo suggested we stop in Charley's for a drink before getting back on the highway. My mother didn't want to, until she heard Willie Nelson was affiliated with the bar.

~~~~~~~

All in all, we had a fabulous day, and I believe my mother enjoyed it. She was exhausted when Reggie and Leo dropped us off in the hood. She wanted to take a nap, so I had her lie down on my bed and relax. No sooner than she made herself comfortable, she slipped into a deep sleep.

All I could think of was Mango Mike. He was probably feeling ignored, and I figured he'd be hanging out on my neighbor's lanai. I walked across the lawn and spotted him. He was wearing a blue plaid flannel shirt with his yellow board shorts.

As soon as he saw me, he walked over and held me around the waist. "I've missed you."

"Me too. I really want you right now."

"I live with a bunch of guys, and there's always someone around," he said

"My mother's taking a nap. Maybe we can sneak in and do it in the bathroom."

"Oooo, kinky," he said. "I like that."

"What's with the flannel shirt?"

"I was out in the water most of the day. I felt a little chilled when the sun went down."

I grabbed his hand and led him over the lawn toward my studio. Luckily the front door was ajar, so I pushed it open slightly. My mother was sound asleep. We tiptoed in and quietly walked to the bathroom. Once inside, I closed the door and locked it. We took our clothes off and dropped them on the floor. We embraced and kissed for a bit. I turned on the water and we stepped into the shower, which we figured would muffle any sounds. A sexual interlude, the perfect end to a wonderful day.

~~~~~~

Later on that evening, when my mom woke up, I was busy making dinner.

"It's so nice to have you cooking for me," she said.

"I'm making sautéed chicken and broccoli. Did you have a good rest?"

She turned over on her back and stared at the ceiling. "Yes, it was very restful. I did wake up once though. I heard water running and figured you were taking a shower."

"Yes, I needed a shower, and it felt so good. You can take one whenever you want."

My mother was in a quasi-awake state, and she continued to stare at the ceiling. "They finally caught the Son of Sam, the serial killer that terrorized New York for over a year. People were actually afraid to go out at night."

"Well, that's a relief," I said.

That night we stayed home and watched *The Rockford Files*, a new detective series. My mother also mentioned that she liked *Three's Company*. I'd never seen it before, but I watched it with her because I wanted her to feel at home.

"You know I'm going to miss you. I wish I could stay longer, but I don't like leaving your father alone. He's really getting up there in years."

I took her hand and said, "I'll be coming for the holidays, and that's not too far away."

She smiled at me and put her hands together as if praying it would happen.

~~~~~~

It was the middle of the night when the telephone rang, jarring us awake.

"Hello," I said.

"It's Sydney Greenstreet," the gravelly voice on the other end of the line said.

There was dead silence on my end of the line.

"I'm calling you from the lobby of a hotel in Singapore. I'm sitting on a couch with a tropical fabric pattern, and the gardenias made me think of you. You should have come with me, you'd have loved it," he said.

I sat up in bed, a chill running through me, but still, I wasn't sorry I fucked Mike.

"Demo, when are you coming home?"

"I'll be home real soon, a week, maybe two. I miss you and can't wait to see you."

"Well, you'll miss my mother. She's leaving in a few days."

"I'll be taking you with me next time, I promise," he said.

For a moment I believed him. He sounded like he'd been drinking a lot. I could tell by the way he was rambling from one subject to another. I tried to pull up his face in my memory, but for some reason I couldn't, and it frustrated me.

"Wait until you see your house," I said.

"Yeah, I told Annie she had full reign as to whatever she wanted to do with it."

"I ran into your mom and dad at your house a while back. They're both fine."

"I have to get off, but I'll be seeing you real soon. Love ya," he said, and the line went dead.

"Who was that calling in the middle of the night," my mother asked.

"That was my boyfriend, Dominick French," I said, reluctantly.

"Uh huh, so what's that all about with Mike and his mangos?"

"I don't know. I'm a little confused."

"Be careful, Adriana. You're swimming in murky water and playing games."

I told my mother the story of how I was in love with Demo, but he went to Europe for the whole summer and left me behind. How I felt that every time we were getting really close, he pumped the brakes. How he was a talented and popular musician and was a friend of Annie's. I mentioned that he liked to play a hot and cold cat-and-mouse game with me.

"Adriana, your father always told you that it's more important that a man loves you than you love him."

"That makes no sense to me at all."

"It's a man's world, and they can be cruel when they know you love them unconditionally."

"I'd have to love someone very deeply to want to marry him."

"Now this Mike seems to really like you," she said.

"I never really thought about him in a serious way."

"So you want to go after someone who drops you like a hot potato when it suits him?"

"I'll see how I feel when he gets home."

That's how I ended the uncomfortable conversation.

~~~~~~

Annie, my mother, and I spent a day at Airport Beach in Kaanapali. My mother didn't have a bathing suit, so Annie rigged up a scarf to cover my mother's large breasts over her black brazier. Since she was wearing a black girdle in the form of shorts, we convinced her that it would look like a bathing suit.

My mother said, "I haven't been in the ocean in twenty years!"

All the more reason, I thought.

Annie coaxed Vita reluctantly into the water, and I watch them bobbing in the ocean, my mother squealing with delight. Afterward they lay on the sand, drying off like two beached whales.

I overheard my mother tell Annie about how she would swim way out to the barges between the Bronx and City Island when she was young. "I was quite the long-distance swimmer."

THE TWO MOMS

My mom was nearing the end of her vacation on Maui, and I couldn't let her leave without experiencing Hana.

"What's Hana?" she asked.

"It's what the real Hawaii is all about," I said. A phrase I snagged from Hank Cooper's playlist.

"Where is it?"

"The drive there will be part of the experience," I answered.

Why the hell I thought dragging my mother on that long road to Hana, with all the bridges and switchbacks was a good idea, I'll never know.

After breakfast my mother and I made our way to east Maui toward Hana. The trip started out okay, but when we passed the turnoff to Haleakala Highway, I began to wonder if it was a mistake. I failed to mention that it was a three-and-a-half-hour drive, and that once we got there, we'd be turning around and driving back.

My mother began squirming around in the passenger seat. She asked, "Are we there yet?" Just like a bored child would ask on a long road trip.

We stopped a few times to stretch our legs and take photos of waterfalls, but that didn't seem to help. A little further along the road, my mother spotted a shrine set in the side of a mountain. It was a statue of the Virgin Mary with flower leis wrapped around her neck.

Mom said, "Stop the car. I want to get out." She examined the shrine with interest, made the sign of the cross, and kissed her fingers as if blowing the kiss up to heaven. It seemed to calm her.

"You know, I just love your church in Lahaina," she said.

"Maria Lanakila Church?"

"Yes, it's so beautiful. And I felt so peaceful sitting inside."

"I understand it was designed after a church in Rome."

"I will never forget sitting in the pew looking out the window and seeing a tree filled with mangos. I thought that was so unique."

"Yes, isn't that something? You sure can't forget you're in the tropics, not even in church."

"And I loved the Tongan choir at mass. That was really something," she said.

"Remember when I told you to touch the hand of Father Damien's mosaic?"

"Yes, you told me it was a tradition for people to place their hand on his."

After we rested for a while in the town of Hana, we began the long drive home. She wasn't impressed with Black Sands Beach.

Looking at the palm trees, she remarked, "Seen one tree, you've seen them all."

I shook my head but didn't answer.

Somewhere along the drive back, my mother began to feel sick. She complained of a headache. Then she said her mouth ached and she was nauseous. Soon she couldn't stand the pain. She told me that the last time she saw her dentist, he mentioned that she might need a root canal, but that it could wait until she got back from her trip.

Luckily the drive home was shorter, with no stops, and we were back in the hood in no time.

"Don't mention the road to Hana to me ever again," she said.

I gave my mother a cotton ball soaked in whiskey to put on her tooth. I called my dentist the next morning and got her an emergency appointment for a root canal. We relaxed in the condo the next day, until my mother felt better. Mike hung out with us, feeding my mother mangos and keeping her laughing.

We took my mom for a last ride up north through the pineapple fields. She wandered around in the red dirt examining all the prickly fruits closely. "I want to take one home," she said.

Mike snapped off a tiny one, "It's just the beginning of a pineapple, so maybe Agriculture will let you take it on the plane as a decorative pineapple."

We watched the sun set over Molokai across the channel, and the sky was turning beautiful shades of red and purple.

Mike put his arm around me and played with his silver ring on my finger. My mother gave me a look that said, "See? This guy cares for you."

~~~~~~~~

It was a teary goodbye with my mom at the airport, but I would be going to New York for the Holidays, which softened our parting.

Driving back over the Pali, the Bee Gees song "More Than a Woman" was playing on the radio. I knew my mother was probably right about everything; she always was. I hoped I wasn't falling back into old habits of the past.

When I arrived back at my studio, I felt a little sad. Mike was waiting there for me.

He stood up and put his arm around me. "You missing your mom already?"

"A little," I answered.

I saw my guitar standing beside the bed, the guitar that my mother kicked all over Honolulu Airport. I picked it up, sat on the bed, and began to feel the strings.

"Play something," Mike said.

I strummed around for a while testing some chords and checking the tuning. Mike lay on the bed, propped himself up on an elbow, and leaned against the wall. He watched me with interest.

I asked, "You like Bob Dylan?"

"Yeah, sure, who doesn't?"

"My mother, for one," I answered. "Every time I'd play his music when I was younger and lived at home, my mother would yell, 'For God's sake, take that guy off!'"

I decided on "Farewell Angelina." I strummed the tune and sang the lyrics.

"That's nice," he said, stroking my leg.

"It's one of the first songs I learned to play on the guitar," I said.

"I always thought that was a Joan Baez song."

"Yes, I think she made it famous, but Bob Dylan wrote it. You do know that they were an item?"

"Yeah, I heard that somewhere. Keep playing, I like it," he said.

Mike lay his head on my legs and gazed up at me. I felt content and at peace. I played a few more tunes and then propped my guitar up against the wall beside the bed. I looked toward the window, and it was already dark outside. I got up and closed the curtains, when a sudden rain came down.

I lay down next to Mike.

"I want to make love to you tonight, not just have sex. You know what I mean," Mike said.

He turned off the light and hugged me. I wasn't feeling the same emotion about him, but I did feel a closeness and affection. It was a beautiful end to another day in paradise.

From my journal:

Time passes and I am comfortable here. My heart can be full, but I keep it at a certain level. Should I be on my way to Xanadu, or will I settle for paradise? Maybe paradise is a state of mind. To be able to walk to the ocean every day, and to feel the trade winds whistle past my ears, is enough for me. An evening rain on the palm trees thrills me. But other feelings emerge in me, and I fear that eventually, even the peace of paradise won't be enough.

Adriana Bardolino

TEN

GIRL ON FIRE

From my journal:

Men flock around me like moths to a flame, but I am in love with only one. Is it for him that I have tossed off other lovers? Is it the pursuit of art, beauty, music, or all those things? Is true love fantasy or reality? Are two people born for each other, or is it random luck? Do we pursue it, live in it, or turn our backs on it for other things? If my wings get singed, am I the one to blame?

D ominick French was back in town and playing at the Missionaries Hotel. I didn't make an appearance at the piano bar right away, so as not to seem too eager.

I was working upstairs on the Bernina at the Crafty Mermaid when I heard a familiar gravelly voice downstairs. I looked over the railing, and Demo was standing at the counter talking to Annie.

"Look who's back in town!" I yelled.

Demo looked up and smiled. "Yeah it's me. I'm taking you to lunch. I have a lot to tell you."

"I'll come downstairs, just give me a minute," I said, attempting to quell my excitement.

"We'll go to Kimo's," he shouted as I was walking down the steps.

Demo loved that place because it was right on the ocean. He knew everyone, and more importantly, everyone knew him. He hugged me and gave me a peck on the cheek.

"Come on, you can do better than that," Annie said.

Demo searched for my lips and planted a soft, loving kiss on them.

"That's better," Annie said.

We walked along the seawall, Demo holding my hand.

"I was in so many different countries, and everyone loved my music," he said.

All about him, I thought. He didn't seem interested in what I did, or how my mother's visit went. I wanted to blurt out, *I had a fun summer too, and months of great sex with a really hot guy who resembles Omar Sharif!* But I kept my mouth shut.

We walked into Kimo's and were escorted to a table right at the edge of the water. The waitress handed us menus while making a fuss over him. It was a beautiful, sunny day, and the salty sea air was refreshing. We ordered iced teas and mahi burgers while Demo jabbered away about his vacation. His good mood was infectious though, and I soon succumbed to it.

"Did you see what Annie did with my house?"

"Your parents were speechless when they walked into the living room," I said.

"The camel," he said, widening his blue eyes.

"Your living room is like a scene out of Arabian nights," I said, through spurts of laughter.

Suddenly, I felt a twinge of sexual desire for Mango Mike, who exuded Arabian mystery.

The waitress delivered our food, and we ate. During our few moments of silence, I stared at the musical notes tattooed up the inside of his arm as he lifted the mahi burger to his mouth. When our eyes met, the laughter began again. I felt uplifted and good with him. He was quirky, and we had a similar sense of humor.

He reached for my hand across the table. "I want you to come with me next time. I missed you so much while I was away. I had no one to talk to. I missed us."

He had a serious expression on his face as he stroked my hand.

I felt that old feeling, and as I stared into his eyes, I was falling in love all over again. Like I've said before, it's not so much how you feel about someone, but how they make you feel about yourself. He made me feel essential to his life and well-being. He told me he had big things planned for us as he walked me back to the Crafty Mermaid.

"Come down to the Mission tonight," he said, leaving me at the entrance to the shop.

"Okay, I'll be there later," I said.

Annie waddled out from behind the counter and asked, "So how was lunch? Did he tell you he loved what I did with his house?"

"Yes, he loves the house," I answered, holding back the laughter bubbling in my throat.

"Are we going to the Mission tonight? I know I want to go."

"I wouldn't miss it for the world," I answered.

~~~~~~~

When I got home from work I fed Ono and avoided happy hour drinks on my neighbor's lanai. I wasn't ready to deal with Mango Mike and figured he'd be hanging out there. My life seemed confusing enough as it was, and I didn't want to add any more into the mix.

I took a shower and picked out a slinky, lavender pant set I'd made at work. I had purchased a few strands of deep purple orchids from Nagasako's Variety Store that week. I arranged the orchids on either side of my face and pinned them to my long, dark hair. I drove the Gray Mouse into Lahaina, filled with excitement. Annie told me she'd be at the Mission early to secure us a table near the piano.

Walking in, I caught sight of Demo standing at the bar talking to the bartender. He stared at me as if he'd seen a mirage. He grabbed his drink, walked over, and escorted me to the table where Annie was already seated.

Everyone turned to looked at me as if to say, "Who the hell is she?" I felt significant, and what was more important, I felt I was special to Demo.

He pulled my chair out, saying, "For you, Cleopatra."

Annie called the waitress over and ordered me a Tanqueray and tonic.

"With a lime," I shouted as she was walking away.

When Demo's break was over he sat down at the piano and played my favorite song, "Exactly like You." He turned, smiled, and winked at me. I was on top of the world.

It was a fun night at the Mission Bar, and Demo was playing at the top of his game. At one point he tossed off his shoes and worked the piano pedals with his bare feet. He'd stomp his feet on the floor and the crowd would get worked into a frenzy. He sat with us during his breaks and was very attentive. Our interaction seemed to pick up where it left off before he went away for the summer.

A woman, I think a tourist, was so overcome by one of his blues songs that she jumped up and threw her arms around him while he was playing. Annie got up, as she often did, and pulled the woman off his back. Demo glanced at me to see my reaction, but I remained calm, cool, and collected. He shook his head and laughed.

Before his last set, he came to our table and asked me to wait for him. He wanted to go out on the town when he was finished at the Mission. I figured, what the heck, it's our first night back together, so why not go bar hopping to celebrate? I didn't care, as long as I was with him.

When his last set was over, Annie left and the place emptied out. I patiently waited for him at the table. He came over, took my hand, and we walked out into the street past his Corvette. Demo liked listening to other musicians in town. He enjoyed the comradery. Occasionally, they'd ask him to sit in and play a tune. He did the same when one of his musician friends walked into the Mission Bar.

We eventually ended up at Le Toots. Everything else in town was closed. If it was crowded, we'd climb right through the window that opened to the street. By now we were both very drunk, and driving home was out of the question.

We dragged ourselves up the stairs to Annie's apartment, banged on her door, and begged her to let us sleep on her floor. She opened the door and let us in, but we could tell she was pissed off. She tried to fall asleep as we giggled and fooled around for the next hour or so. It wasn't the romantic night I had envisioned, but we had fun, and that first night broke the ice of a long three-month separation.

~~~~~~

The next night I stayed away from the Mission Bar. I figured I'd let Demo take the lead. I spent the evening with Annie at the Waterworks and went home around ten that night. All was quiet in the hood when I got back from Lahaina. Luckily, Mike hadn't been around while I was home.

I took a shower, fed Ono, and got into bed. I was inebriated, so I fell asleep right away. The phone rang, waking me from a dead sleep. It was Demo. He was drunk, and rambling about a meatloaf Annie left in his refrigerator. I lay there with my eyes closed listening to him. Then I heard heavy rain outside beating on my lanai, and the sound put me back to sleep.

A ruckus outside woke me up again, and I realized the phone receiver was next to my arm on the bed. The line was buzzing, but there was no one on the other end. I tried to listen to what was going on outside, when I recognized Demo's voice. There was a loud knock at the door.

"Who's there?"

"Open the door, it's Sydney Greenstreet."

I opened the front door and there was Demo, standing in the pouring rain with a pan of meatloaf. I was slightly in shock but began to laugh. He could be slightly crazy and eccentric at times.

"I think I knocked on just about every door, until someone told me this was your door."

"Demo, you're soaked through. Hurry, come inside," I said, closing the door.

I ran to the bathroom for a towel. "Give me that meatloaf," I said.

"Well you didn't show up at the Mission tonight, and I was planning to share this meatloaf with you," he said like a little boy, his voice hoarse from singing.

I set the meatloaf on the kitchen counter. "Demo, I do love you, you crazy thing!"

"I wanted to be with you tonight." He had a lost expression on his face. "Why did you have to have such beautiful lips?" he asked, rubbing his finger along my mouth.

I sat on the bed next to him. He sat there very still as I dried his hair with the towel. He rested his hand on my leg while I slipped his wet shirt off and threw it on the floor. He stood up and slipped his jeans off, then his underwear, and walked out of them. He stumbled onto the bed and lay down. I lay beside him. He turned on his side and kissed me very softly. He pulled away and ran his finger across my lips, smiling. He caressed my breasts, and his hands wandered all over my body. Soon we were making love. I had the strangest feeling of euphoria. I just wasn't sure if he felt the same thing. I lay my head on his chest, rubbing my hand along the inside of his tattooed arm. Soon I fell asleep.

From my journal:

Antony and Cleopatra return to Rome amid a glorious reception. They are carried along a path of fountains gushing into mosaic-tiled pools. Cleopatra descends a golden staircase with thousands of steps out of a dream. We kissed lightning, sparked thunder, and shivered in each other's arms. The wind blew cherry blossoms over us, while rain drove fertility into the ground. Sheltered in a Roman temple we made love, and when the sun reappeared, the earth glistened with lushness and beauty.

The next day Demo had an appointment with his dentist in Wailuku. I had the day off, so he asked me to tag along. I noticed his shirt was still damp as we got into his Corvette.

"You'll catch a death of cold driving in an open car with that wet shirt on," I said.

We stopped at his house so he could change his clothes. I laughed as soon as I walked into the living room and caught sight of the carousel-sized, coin-operated camel sitting in the corner of the living room.

"I know," he shouted from his bedroom, laughing. He emerged holding something. "I brought something back for you from the Orient."

I stared at him trying to see what it was. He handed me a jewelry box of dark cherry wood. It had inlaid mother of pearl Chinese designs and a gold latch. The other item was a black satin pouch embroidered with roosters and feathers. I inspected them with affectionate interest.

"Demo, I love them."

"I thought of you when I saw the jewelry box, and the silk purse fits your hippie side," he said.

"I'll treasure them always," I said, kissing him on the lips.

The drive over the Pali in his convertible was lovely, and the Bee Gee's song "How Deep Is Your Love" played on the radio. It was such a beautiful day. Surfers were lined up on the ocean in groups, sitting on their boards waiting for a decent set of waves.

"Some friends are getting married on the island of Kauai, and they asked me to play at the ceremony. I'm bringing you with me."

"When is the wedding?" I asked.

"Not this weekend, but the one after it."

"Demo that will be so much fun."

~~~~~~

That afternoon, we hung out at his house. Demo cooked a concoction in a sauté pan with odds and ends from his refrigerator. We sat at the high wooden counter in his kitchen and ate lunch. Then we sat in the straw chairs on the porch and watched the ocean for a while. It was a lazy afternoon. He took my hand and walked me to his bedroom. A salty breeze from the ocean followed us in.

We sat on his bed, and Demo unbuttoned my blouse, caressing my arm. "Your skin is so soft."

I felt little chills when he touched me.

I stood up. "No, don't go," he said, catching hold of my arm.

I'm just going to the bathroom. I'll be right back."

"Did I ever tell you what a great ass you have?" He watched me walk out of the room.

He was lying in bed nude when I returned. He lifted the cover, signaling me to get in. I felt so natural with him, and his quirkiness allowed me to be a little crazy too.

"I feel so good when I'm with you," I said.

"It makes all the difference in the world when you feel this way about someone, doesn't it?"

"Yes," I whispered. "All the difference in the world."

He leaned over and kissed me. I felt him tremble a little. I loved the smell of his hair, even after a night of playing the piano, when it was all wet and sweaty. I think I fell in love with him before we were ever intimate. I could barely look at his face without feeling overwhelmed, like a teenager's crush on a popular musician or movie star. It was an ethereal type of love, not so much a carnal love. I wondered if that was going to be enough for me in the end.

It was getting dark outside, and I knew it was almost time for him to leave for work.

"The ocean is really loud," I said.

"Forget about the ocean."

He got on top of me, and we made love. It wasn't ever hardcore sex but was tender and exciting all at the same time. That's the way it was with Dominick French.

I watched him get ready for work, putting on a clean aloha shirt and jeans.

"If you're not in the mood for the Mission tonight, you could hang out here."

I imagined wanting me to be there when he got home. *Are we playing house?* I wondered.

"I think I'll go home. I have to feed the cat, and I want to paint my toenails, and do girly stuff."

I was sitting on his couch watching him walk from room to room, making sure he wasn't forgetting anything. Then he came over, gave me a kiss on the lips, and walked out the front door. He soon returned.

"Adriana, you need new tires on the Mouse. Are you going to just drive that car into the ground, or wait until the wheels fall off?" He shook his head, laughing, as he turned around and headed back out. I heard the familiar sound of the screen door slam. I'd remember that sound for many years to come.

I hung out for a while after he left and then went to examine the tires on my car. *Maybe he's right. I'd better get the tires checked out soon.* I got in the Gray Mouse and drove home.

<hr>

As soon as I was at my front door, Mango Mike appeared out of nowhere.

"Finally! I've been looking for you for days. You're never around anymore."

I took his hand and told him to come inside. I was playing with words in my head so I would say the right thing.

He put his arms around me, but he felt me resist his embrace, so he pulled away and looked into my eyes. "What's up? You met somebody else?"

"It's a little more complicated."

"I'm not a stupid man."

I hesitated. "I had a boyfriend before I met you. He was gone for a while. He's back on the island now, and I think I'm in love with him."

"Wow, subtle—like an eviction notice," he said, as if I'd kicked him in the stomach.

"I didn't think you were serious about me, that I was the only girl you were hanging with."

"Maybe so, but I really like you a lot," he said. "We can still fool around, can't we?"

"I don't think that's a good idea," I said. "I really like you a lot, but I'm not in love."

He took my hand and played with the silver band on my finger he'd given me. "Keep the ring. I never really gave you anything, so I want you to have it to remember me by."

"Mike, how could I ever forget you?"

"He's a lucky guy, the rat bastard. I saw you with a guy at the harbor once. Is that the guy?"

I had forgotten I ran into him when I was hanging with Peyton Parker at the Pioneer Inn.

"That was long ago," I said. "No, that was someone else, a guy I knew from the mainland."

"You sure have a lot of guys after you."

"Well, you know what they say, women can be fickle when it comes to men."

Mango Mike kissed me gently on the cheek and walked out the door. I felt terrible, but I knew it was better to just rip off the Band-Aid with the truth.

Ono sat there staring at the door as if Mike just went to get something and would walk back in at any moment. When he didn't, Ono looked up at me.

"I know you're hungry," I said.

I opened a can of cat food and put some in his dish. I petted the top of his head and felt him purring. I was sad all of a sudden. I thought of how sweet and kind Mike was to my mother, and how thoughtful he always was to me. Then there was the great sex. I was comfortable with him, but perhaps it was more like friendship with benefits. Suddenly I felt unsure of myself, of my choice. Old fears of love being snatched away from me were surfacing. My friend Casey Cutler used to say, "No matter how many times you pack your bags, you take yourself with you wherever you go." Then I reasoned with myself and knew the truth was that I wasn't in love with

Mike, I was in love with Demo. Whatever my choice brought me, I would have to live with it.

〜〜〜〜

That Friday, Haku took me to her house to paint sarongs. The racks at the Crafty Mermaid were low on hand-painted garments. We both enjoyed the routine.

"Adriana, I'm so happy now, and I have you to thank for it."

"You mean your sea captain?" I asked.

"Yeah, I'm crazy about him, and I think he feels the same way about me. I was so unhappy with my old boyfriend for such a long time. I'd forgotten what that special feeling was like."

"I just gave you encouragement to take the leap in the direction you wanted to go."

"How is it going with Demo? He seems to be very attentive to you lately."

"It used to be hot and cold. We'd get to a certain point, and then I'd feel him pulling away."

"Maybe he's afraid of commitment."

"Things seem good now, and I'm getting the message that he wants to take our relationship to the next level." I wondered if I was the one with the commitment issues.

We drank wine and painted all day, but I didn't want to discuss my insecurities with her, how they still nagged me to some extent. The painted garments had been lying out in the sun in her backyard drying for most of the afternoon. When they were completely dry, we gathered the garments and carried them back to the Crafty Mermaid. We walked in with our arms full.

"Thank God, because I just sold the last hand-painted sarong," Annie said.

Haku was busy tagging them and hanging them on the racks in the store.

"Not to change the subject," Annie said. "But my sons are coming for a visit next month. Let's go to the Yacht Club and I'll tell you all about them."

〜〜〜〜

Annie and I walked to the Yacht Club after work. As soon as we sat down, the bartender set our usual drinks in front of us without even asking. I told her I needed to get health insurance, because the girls at the store didn't cover me.

"You have to have insurance," she said. "Now, if you were to become a member of the club, you can get on their group insurance."

"I'll look into it. You never know when something is going to happen to you," I said.

"So my two sons are coming, and I'm a little uncertain about it."

"What do you mean?"

"Well, after my bastard husband, Tony, died, my kids began treating me like I was a child. They watched everything I did, where I went, and who I was meeting. It was as if they were the parents, and I was the child."

"Really!"

"I was still a young woman in my early fifties when Tony died. I had a good friend in Vegas who was moving to Maui. I didn't say anything to my kids until I bought the plane ticket. You should have been there for that scene!"

"You came here with Tim Kork, right?" I asked.

"No, it was a much younger guy. The romance didn't last long, but at least it got me to Maui."

"Well, I'll back you up regarding your sons if you need it."

I left Annie sitting at the bar, wondering what her sons were like.

~~~~~~

The following weekend, Demo and I flew to the island of Kauai for the wedding. We took a Royal Hawaiian prop plane out of the small airport in Kaanapali. We stopped at the Windsock Bar for a bloody Mary before boarding. I was ready for an adventure being I had never been to that island. As the small plane approached Kauai, I saw steep cliffs with endless waterfalls. During the flight, Demo mentioned that the rainiest spot in the world was on the island of Kauai. He had all the accommodations arranged at a small bed and breakfast. We walked around town, did some sightseeing, and had lunch at an outside café. Our room had a great bathtub with a view overlooking a canyon. Demo loved baths, though I preferred showers, but of course I always appeased him.

In the tub, we discussed the day's events, and how beautiful it was on Kauai.

"I brought a nice dress to wear at the wedding tomorrow."

"Not white, I hope," Demo said.

"Now why the hell would I wear a white dress to a wedding?"

"You like being the center of attention."

"Oh, you're one to talk," I said, laughing.

"The bride and groom are friends of mine, and they want to take us to dinner tonight."

"That sounds really nice. Maybe I should have you pick something out for me to wear!"

Demo smirked at my comment, and by now my hands were pruning in the water.

"I'm getting out of the tub," I said.

I sat on the couch in the next room while he continued to soak, jabbering away.

That night we dressed very casually and met the bride and groom at a restaurant in one of the hotels. The dinner was fabulous, and the atmosphere was dreamy. While Demo was having a conversation with the groom, I turned to the prospective bride.

"Are you ready for tomorrow?" I asked.

"Can't wait," she answered.

There was a jazz trio playing while we ate. It was a nice evening, but when we got back to the B&B, Demo seemed edgy.

"What's up?" I asked.

"Nothing really. Just hoping you don't feel neglected while I'm busy tomorrow."

"Don't worry about me, I'll be schmoozing with the guests."

"That's what I'm afraid of," he said.

~~~~~~

The day of the wedding arrived, and we were both excited. I suppose Demo more than me, since he was providing the music for the ceremony. We arrived at the venue, and the first thing he did was check out the piano.

I looked around for someone to hang out with. Servers were passing trays with pu pus and glasses of champagne. I immediately reached for a flute and downed a glass.

Demo shot a disproving glance in my direction, but I just laughed it off.

He walked over to me and said, "Don't get crazy, and remember, I'm the entertainment."

I looked at him with an annoyed expression.

A waiter walked past me with a tray of champagne, and I quickly nabbed another flute of the bubbly as an answer to Demo's stupid comment. Guests were arriving, and the groom asked Demo to play some tunes on the piano. Suddenly I found myself hoping he was familiar with the wedding march, when I knew it would be required of him. Then I figured he wouldn't have accepted the gig if he didn't know the song. The festive atmosphere went on for quite a while, and so did the champagne.

When the bride arrived, we all looked for seats. She went straight up to the piano, hugged Demo, and thanked him for being part of her wedding. I was close enough to hear everything she was saying. I heard her tell Demo to play their favorite song after the ceremony, and to take any guest requests that might come along.

There were benches along the walls on all sides of the room with large candles on ledges for a romantic affect. I was so into Demo's playing that I zoned out of everything around me. The bride came over to me and gave me a gardenia to wear in my hair. She handed me yet another glass of champagne while thanking me for participating in her wedding.

"It's all so beautiful, and I wish you all the luck and happiness in the world," I said.

She squeezed my hand. "Thank you, Adriana. I'm happy you're here to share it with us."

A Hawaiian *kahuna* (holy man) showed up to perform the ceremony. He began with a blessing and a speech about the sacred joining of two people. The words were beautiful. People wore layer upon layer of leis, and the aroma of the flowers was overwhelming. The men in the wedding party wore maile leaf leis, the women's heads adorned with haku leis.

Demo played the wedding march, and we all stood up. I was feeling a little unsteady, so I leaned back against the wall for support. The ceremony began, and I closely observed every word and moment. I glanced at Demo to see how he was doing, and he had the strangest expression on his face. He was playing the piano, but his eyes were very wide and staring in my direction. I imagined he was overcome with emotion like I was. There was the strong odor of smoke, but I was somewhere in the twilight zone.

Suddenly, the woman next to me began beating the back of my head with her hands. "Your hair is on fire!" she yelled.

Everyone turned to look at me, including the bride and groom. Unbeknownst to me, I had leaned back into a lit candle, and it set my hair on fire. Luckily she was able to smack the flames out, and all that was left was a little smoke rising off the back of my head.

~~~~~~~

When the ceremony was over, I ran to the bathroom. Luckily, there was only a minor burn to my hair and none on my scalp. When I walked out of the bathroom, Demo was waiting for me.

"You had to do it," he said.

"Do what?" I asked. I didn't know what he was talking about.

"You had to hog all the attention."

"It was an accident," I said, raising my voice.

"Always have to be the center of attention."

I walked away from him, angry and annoyed, knowing he thought I would do such a thing on purpose. As I sobered up, I felt embarrassment. People were pointing at me, so I ran outside crying. The total joy of the day was turning into a pile of shit, and it was all my fault. I looked for a place on the grounds and sat on a bench next to a fountain. The grounds around the venue were like an enchanted garden, with sculpted trees and bushes of tropical flowers. I was comforted by the peaceful scenery.

The bride walked over and sat next to me. "You weren't hurt, were you?"

"The back of my hair was singed," I answered.

"Don't worry about anything. It was really sort of funny, and people were laughing."

"I'm embarrassed. And worst of all, I embarrassed Demo. He's angry with me."

"Don't worry about him. I'll talk to Demo." The bride walked away, and I saw Demo walking toward me.

He stopped to speak with her. I couldn't hear what they were saying, but I did see his expression change. She hugged him and walked back to the venue. Demo sat next to me on the bench. We sat there silently for a bit.

"I made such a fool of myself. I'm sorry I embarrassed you. I don't even know if I could walk back in there."

"Adriana, it was nothing really. I laughed about it after seeing the smoke."

"Demo, the way you looked at me."

"I was trying to get your attention to the flames, but you were oblivious."

"I feel like an idiot. I guess I drank too much."

"Riana," he said in a teasing, affectionate tone (knowing full well it was what Annie always called me), "Let's go back inside. We're not going to miss it all. It's what we came here for. The bride and groom really like you and think so much of you."

"Really? That makes me feel better."

Demo took my hand, and we walked back inside together. No one in the room made a fuss or stared at me, and I thought maybe I made a bigger deal out of it than it actually was.

"When we get home, you know that I'm never going to let you live this down," he said with a smirk.

On the flight back to Maui, I went over the details of the whole weekend in my head. I felt that despite everything, it was a fabulous trip—well, except for the candle lighting the back of my hair on fire. Every time Demo looked at me, I could tell that he had a hard time holding back laughter.

He had asked Annie to keep an eye on his house while he was gone. Also, Demo had a dog he rescued off the street, and she was to feed him as well. He was a large dog, a mutt, that Demo named Kona. He just wandered in one night without a collar, and Demo started feeding him. Kona soon became part of the household.

Demo parked in his driveway next to Annie's station wagon. "You're staying here tonight."

"Okay," I said. "One of my neighbors is feeding Ono while I'm gone."

The house smelled wonderful. We found Annie in the kitchen cooking supper. She loved to do things like that for him. They were good friends, and I was happy about that. The three of us ate dinner together while Kona lay at Demo's feet waiting for scraps. Annie asked about our trip to Kauai.

Demo went into a laughing fit, and Annie had a hard time deciphering his words. "She was a girl on fire," he blurted out, the words all jumbled up.

"I set my hair on fire," I said.

"Jesus, Riana, what the hell? Only you'd get into a situation like that," she said.

"No, Annie, we had a really good time," Demo said, taking my hand and caressing it.

"The wedding was beautiful, but I got punchy from the smell of all the flowers."

"You mean from the champagne," Demo said, teasing me.

Annie got up, washed the dishes in the sink, and walked out the front door. "G'night."

"I'll see you at work tomorrow," I called out as the screen door slammed.

Demo sat on the couch, and I settled in next to him. He eventually got up and fished through stacks of LPs on the floor. When he came across the right one, the one he was in the mood for, he carefully put it on the record player. It was usually a really old, obscure blues album. It reminded him of his teenage years growing up in New Orleans. At least that was how he explained it to me. He made us a couple of drinks, and we hung out until it was time for bed. I noticed little wrapped chocolate balls dangling from the lampshade on the end table next to me. They were left over from a fine box of chocolates someone brought him as a gift for Easter. I was surprised that Annie missed them while cleaning his house like an Irish tornado.

Suddenly I noticed the wrapper move. "It's moving," I said.

"What are you talking about?" Demo asked.

"There, I just saw the wrapper move again."

Demo reached over me and touched the tiny lavender foil ball, very gently, with his finger.

"The ants are eating the chocolate and leaving the wrapper," he said, laughing hysterically.

"That's just the craziest thing," I said, laughing right along with him.

Demo took my hand and rubbed it affectionately. "Let's go to bed, fire girl."

ELEVEN

BARKING DOGS

He who learns but does not think is lost! He who
thinks but does not learn is in great danger.

—Confucius

t was the fall of 1978 when Annie's two sons, Sonny and Tony Jr. (who
everyone just called Junior) arrived. They were like a comedy duo and
reminded me of those cartoon characters, Heckle and Jeckle. They had
heavy New York accents and were as funny as all get-out. They had a silly
routine they performed when they stopped by the Crafty Mermaid to see
Annie. I guess they had to have a sense of humor growing up in a family as
dysfunctional as theirs. Somehow, though, I got the impression they had
mob connections, so I maintained my distance. There were family dinners
in Annie's tiny studio apartment where she made all their favorite Italian
dishes. I didn't see them shower their mother with any gifts or praise.
Sonny announced that he was planning on moving to Maui from Brooklyn
and bringing his new wife with him. I didn't have a good feeling about it
and figured he was running away from something. Junior was living in
Vegas and had no plans to go anywhere else. I voiced none of my concerns
to Annie because she seemed so happy.

Dominick French played a benefit concert on a boat out of Lahaina
Harbor. It was quite a scene watching them lift a piano onto the deck. It
was a crazy day out on the water. Just about everyone I knew was on the
cruise, which turned into a booze cruise. Demo paid little attention to me,

so I hung out at the rail with Annie, waiting for a whale to spout or flash its tail. It was surreal watching Demo bang on the piano keys, while the boat rocked back and forth, tossing everything and everyone from one side of the boat to the other. All except the piano, which was tied to the rafters. The whales put on a great show, Annie sang a few tunes, and that's how the day went. When the boat docked, I quickly headed for the ramp to get off.

"Adriana, we're all going to Kimo's," I heard Demo shout as I was walking down the plank.

I wanted to make believe I didn't hear him, but I turned, waved, and said, "I'll see you there."

~~~~~~

Loretta Perino called me to say that she had rented a great three-bedroom house in Lahaina on Nanu Street, behind the sugar mill. She asked if I was interested in moving in with her and took me to see the house. Of course, I loved it. There was a converted garage apartment around back, with a private entrance. A Hawaiian girl named Lani lived there. Haku, who had broken up with her longtime boyfriend and was dating the sea captain, moved in with us as well. A large yard wrapped around the house with banana plants and bushes of *lilikoi* (passion fruit). The entrance was to the kitchen through a large carport that could hold up to four cars, and there was plenty of parking on the street. The front interior of the house was one large space: the kitchen-dining room-living room, which we separated with a couch. I took the master bedroom with a private bath at the end of a long hallway. One of the best features for me was that I would be able to walk to work. I left Ono the cat in the hood. It was his territory. He was there before I moved in, and I knew others would feed him. But I'd miss him terribly.

We had been living on Nanu Street for over a month when some issues came to light. No one warned us about the centipedes that lived in the cane fields and plagued the house during rainy season, when everything that lived outdoors headed indoors. They would find their way into the house and scare the hell out of us. These loathsome insects could be as large as a mouse, six to eight inches in length. They had stingers, and if they stung you, you could get swelling and a fever. You had to examine your clothing before wearing, and your bedding before lying down. I stepped into the shower once, and as soon as I turned the water on, a large centipede leaped out of the drain. Then there were the scorpions that hid in stacks of wood in the yard. And lest I forget, the cane spiders, which were as large as a fist and lurked in corners below the ceiling.

The redeeming grace about that place was that there were neighbors' yards filled with gardenia bushes. In fact the name of the street, Nanu, means gardenia in Hawaiian. During gardenia season, we'd walk around the neighborhood with scissors, clipping flowers off the neighbors' bushes. We'd arranged the gardenias in glass jars throughout the rooms, which gave the house a divine aroma.

I began working at the Crafty Mermaid on Sundays. A group of us would meet at the Travel Lodge for breakfast, which had the best pancakes in town, and an endless cup of coffee. This weekly delight went on for a very long time, and counteracted the fact that Annie and I had to open the store on Sundays.

Demo had a drummer now who played with him at the Missionaries Hotel on a regular basis. He was a local Hawaiian/Filipino/Chinese guy named Nathan. He was fairly nice looking, average height, dark, short, curly hair, and rough features. He was a mysterious type who kept to himself. I happened to mention to Nathan how New York drivers had statues of saints on the dashboards of their cars. He laughed like hell, and so did I, until he showed up at our new house on Nanu Street with a rather large statue of St. Anthony. I tried displaying it in different areas of the house, but I couldn't sleep at night. Something about the statue's eyes. I called my mother in the Bronx, complaining. She suggested I find a nice place to put it in the yard, maybe under a tree. I looked around the yard and thought I'd found the perfect spot for it. Still, I tossed and turned all night.

The next time I spoke to her, she said, "Adriana, you just can't get rid of St. Anthony. Bring the statue to the church and leave it there."

I walked to Maria Lanakila Church and left the statue near the altar. I said a prayer to St. Anthony, explaining that it was nothing personal. I placed my hand over the mosaic hand of Father Damien, blessed myself with holy water, and left. That night I finally had a good night's sleep.

Demo and I were sitting on his porch drinking beer when Nathan walked up the steps. Demo told him to grab a cold beer, so he went to the kitchen and soon returned with a Primo. He stood against the wooden railing since there were only two straw chairs on the porch.

"I've been thinking of checking out the island of Niihau," Nathan said.

"I never heard of that island," I said.

"You have to be Hawaiian, part Hawaiian, or be invited to visit the island."

"Wow, I didn't know any of this; tell me more."

"The Robinson family, who own the island, wanted traditional Hawaii to remain somewhere in this island chain. They grow their own food, and they hunt and fish. Generators supply power, and they rely on neighbor islands for some products."

"Do they only speak Hawaiian?"

"They speak Hawaiian, but I heard English squeezed through somehow."

"Nathan, this is fascinating. If you go to Niihau, please come back and report to us."

"They're famous for distinctive shell necklaces. I'd bring one back, but they're very expensive."

~~~~~~~

That night I showed up at the Mission Bar and sat at a table as close to the piano as I could. Annie was busy showing her sons off and introducing them around town. Demo didn't see me walk in because my table was behind him, but Nathan nodded at me from the drums. I ordered a drink and was grooving to the music.

A really attractive guy walked in and stood against the bar, watching Demo at the piano. I thought, *Damn he's hot,* observing him with a lingering interest. Suddenly I felt guilty with Demo just a few feet away and turned toward the piano. I noticed Demo checking the guy out with the same intense interest. I thought, *That's odd,* but figured I was just imagining it.

When Demo took a break, he went straight to the bar and stood next to the stranger. He caught sight of me after a while but ignored me. Nathan came and sat at the table with me, and we chatted until their break was over. Demo walked back to the piano, never saying as much as a hello to me. I walked out during their next set.

I had a hard time falling asleep that night. I played the night's scenario over and over in my head. What did it mean? Why was Demo looking at him like that? Why did he totally ignore me? I had a funny feeling about it but attempted to block it out of my mind. It was a feeling of déjà vu. I'd been there before with my long-time gay friend and former lover, Adam Hirschfeld.

I went to work the next day, and as the day wore on, the events of the previous night evaporated in the heat of the afternoon.

~~~~~~

Demo's dog, Kona, had a habit of wandering into town on his own. He'd often get a call from a restaurant or bar saying, "Demo, come pick up Kona, he's here at the bar." If Kona spotted Annie's station wagon in town stopped at a light or a stop sign, he'd jump through the rear window into the backseat, expecting her to drive him home, which she often did.

We were sitting on Demo's porch.

Nathan was cooking us something in the kitchen. He yelled, "I'm sure you've never tasted anything this good!"

We laughed and wondered what he was up to.

Demo said, "Nathan goes hunting with his brother, and he brought the meat over himself."

The odor from the kitchen was pungent and didn't smell familiar, so I was skeptical. To me, most hunted meats were too gamey or just tasted like chicken.

Nathan walked out with two plates. "You're going to love this," he said, handing them to us.

"It's some sort of stew," I said, tasting a forkful.

"I doesn't taste like anything I've had before," Demo said. "What is this?"

Nathan walked out to the porch with a plate and was eating with gusto. "Dog," he said.

Kona lifted his head, made a strange noise, and ran off the porch to the backyard. Demo and I spit out what was in our mouths. I felt sick to my stomach and wanted to kill Nathan, who was snickering. Demo was mad, but since he and Nathan were such good friends and played music together, he was cautious as to what he was going to say.

"Man, you should have told us," Demo said.

"Sorry, friend, but I knew if I told you, you wouldn't try it."

"I could have lived the rest of my life not knowing what dog tasted like," I said.

Nathan took our plates, which were barely touched, and went back into the house. He cleaned up the kitchen and eventually reappeared.

"I'll see you at the Mission later," he said. He walked down the steps and got into his car without glancing back at us.

The two of us were speechless.

Demo stood up and said, "I'll go find Kona."

I was nauseated just at the thought of what we'd just eaten. Demo came back with Kona, holding him by the collar.

"I hope he can't smell it on me," he said.

"How can I forget this? I understand an animal is an animal, but this is revolting!"

"I feel the same way. I didn't want to insult him, but he should have told us before we ate it."

"Demo, I think he knows how we felt. Did you see the expression on his face when he left?"

"Let's try not to make more of this than it is," Demo said.

"And for God's sake, don't tell Annie. She'll never speak to Nathan again," I said.

Kona heard a dog bark, his ears perked up, and he ran through the yard back to the shed. Suddenly a pack of dogs walked past the house, barking.

Demo looked at me and asked, "Do you think they know?"

I stared at the dogs and then at him. Soon we were both laughing.

~~~~~~

Sonny and Junior (Heckle and Jeckle) were still in town, and I joined them at the Waterworks for drinks. They kept us laughing nonstop. Annie beamed with pride at having her sons there with her, and old grievances were washed away with vodka.

I went alone to the Mission on another night. I walked up the steps of the hotel and through the lobby, waving at everyone. When I arrived at the piano bar in the back, the place was packed. There weren't any seats near the piano, so I sat in the back and ordered a Tanqueray and tonic. I looked up and saw not only Nathan on drums, but a new guy playing saxophone. Demo said nothing to me about another musician, so I assumed he had a friend in town. When they took a break, they all came to my table and sat down.

Demo said, "Adriana, I didn't see you come in. This is a saxophonist I met in Europe last summer, Liam. Liam, this is Adriana."

Liam extended his hand and said, "It's nice to meet you."

I thought, *He didn't say, "Liam, this is my girlfriend, Adriana."*

They all sat down, and we had a pleasant conversation. No one mentioned eating dog.

When their break was over, the three of them walked to the stage area together. They conversed, I supposed discussing what songs they wanted to play in the next set. I also got the feeling that there was something more than friendship between Demo and Liam. Then I thought maybe I was just imagining it. I expected to hear my song at any moment. Sure enough, they played "Exactly Like You," but after Demo played the intro on the piano, he sang the words directly to the saxophonist. I felt my face flush. I stayed for most of the set but left before the end.

From my journal:

> My love life is like the lyrics of an old Billie Holiday song. I find people hard to forget. Was I meant to be alone singing the blues? "Am I Blue"? You're my Sydney Greenstreet. I have a romantic image of us gliding across a room to my favorite song. You in your pumpkin suit, and me in a skimpy white dress with gardenias in my hair. The other night at the Mission you sang my song to the saxophone player. My mistake! "Don't Blame Me" for falling in love with you.

I tossed and turned all night. How could I have been so stupid? It was all there in front of me, so why didn't I see it. I thought, *Maybe it's true what they say, love is blind?* All those times I wondered why sex with Demo was not like sex with Mango Mike or a host of other guys I'd been with. I thought, *That's why he didn't take me to Europe.* I saw the whole image I had of our relationship crumble.

I didn't sleep at all, so when it began to get light, I got up to make the coffee. Loretta was standing at the stove cooking her favorite breakfast, egg in a frame. She cut a hole in the center of a slice of toast, set it in a frying pan with butter, and dropped an egg in the center.

Haku walked into the kitchen just as Loretta was flipping it over in the pan. Haku took a mug out of the cupboard, filled it with coffee, and sat at the table with me.

"What's up?" she asked.

"I couldn't fall asleep last night, and now I feel like shit."

She looked at me as if she knew I was holding something back, but didn't pry.

Demo called me at work that afternoon, asking me where I'd disappeared to the night before. I told him I had to work the next day. I'm sure he knew that was an excuse, because work never stopped me from having a good time. "I'm off tonight. Come over. I'm making New Orleans-style gumbo."

~~~~~~

Demo was sitting in one of the straw chairs on the porch when I arrived at his house.

"Here comes Cleopatra," Demo said, watching me walk up the porch steps. Kona was sitting at his feet.

I sat in the other chair, and he took my hand and caressed it. There was a deafening silence, except for the sound of the waves breaking on the shore.

"Something smells good," I said.

"It's the gumbo."

He got up, and I followed him into the kitchen. We sat at the tall table eating gumbo, and laughed about the crazy things that happened during that week.

"Did your friend, the saxophonist, go back to Europe?"

Demo stared at me but didn't answer.

"What's going on?" I asked. "I'm not stupid."

Demo took my hand across the table and caressed it. He was working up an answer. "Adriana, you know I'm in love with you. You're my Cleopatra, the girl of my dreams."

"I thought I did, but now I'm not so sure."

"There's a problem," he said, moving his free hand down to his crotch. "These turn me on too."

I waited for a while before answering. "I guess I figured that out on my own."

"Do you still love me?" he asked, his face softening.

"Of course I do. Love isn't a faucet you can turn on and off."

"I don't do it all the time," he said. "Maybe we can try an experiment."

"What kind of an experiment?"

"What if we try a threesome? I'll even let you pick the guy."

"I don't know, Demo. Really, I was never into that."

"Weren't you a hippie? I figured you'd dig that sort of thing," he said.

"I don't want to lose what we have, so let me think on it," I said, ignoring his snide comment.

I slept at Demo's house that night, but we didn't have sex. That was not uncommon. As I said, sex wasn't a big thing in our relationship. I fell asleep in his arms listening to the waves and the soft rustle of the palm trees. I felt safe, loved, and strangely secure with him.

In the morning I woke up, and Demo was resting on one elbow watching me. He smiled when I opened my eyes.

"I'm really horny," he said.

"Me too."

We embraced, kissed and made love. Afterward, he got up and made coffee.

"I can't stay. I have to go home, shower, and change for work," I said.

Demo followed me. "I'll call you later," he said, as the screen door slammed behind me.

~~~~~~

Famous musicians who passed through town on vacation, or were doing a concert on Maui, ended up at Dominick French's house. I sat on his couch listening to quite a few famous people play his piano. I won't name names, but it was always thrilling. They'd often show up at the Missionaries Hotel, and play a few tunes with Demo. I thought of Annie, and how she always told me that he was my claim to fame. But when you're in love with someone, you can overlook important things. In the middle of it all, at that time, none of those things seemed to matter.

One night, it was quiet at the Mission Bar, and there were only a few people in the whole place. Demo told me it was like playing in his living room. He was used to a crowd whooping and hollering. An attractive guy walked in and was giving me the eye. I thought, *Here's my chance.*

Demo caught sight of him and glanced at me. I nodded. People came and went, but set after set, the cute guy stayed. He noticed me looking at him and eventually walked over and asked if he could buy me a drink. That's how it began. When Demo took a break, he invited the guy back to his place after closing time to listen to his rare record collection. The guy thought it was a great idea, especially when he knew I would be there.

The three of us walked up the porch steps and into Demo's house. I was very nervous and wondered why I was doing something that went against my sensibilities. I suppose it was to please Demo, not myself. We were all drunk, and Demo began to go through his albums, like a disk jockey, and pick out the ones he wanted us to hear. The situation was friendly and somewhat comfortable. I can't remember exactly how the three of us ended up in bed together, but we did. It was nothing like I'd expected. They didn't seem to have any interest in each other, so they took turns screwing me. It was weird and unsatisfying, both sexually and emotionally. It meant nothing to me.

After the guy left, Demo and I lay in bed together. It took me a while to fall asleep. I wasn't embarrassed, well not until I ran into the guy walking down Front Street the next day. We said hello, as if nothing had happened between us the previous night. I suppose nothing really meaningful did.

~~~~~~

At the Crafty Mermaid, Hannah, Haku, and I discussed how to promote the one-of-a-kind clothing we made in the store. Haku wanted to put a brochure together. I had a hard time concentrating because of my hangover and the weird events from the previous night. She wanted to take photos of all of us wearing the clothing from the store. I thought it was a great idea. We photographed each other wearing matching tie-dyed Danskin and sarong sets, and Annie wearing tropical shifts and muumuus for the larger women. Later that evening I mentioned it to Demo. He suggested we come by his house on the weekend, and he volunteered to do a whole photo shoot. Haku and I picked out some new designs we had in the store, and we drove to Demo's house that weekend. His porch, the yard, and the ocean were the perfect backdrops for the photoshoot.

PHOTO SHOOT

It was almost the end of October, and Annie's sons had flown back to the mainland, so we returned to our usual routine. It was close to Thanksgiving, and we began discussing plans for the holiday. Demo mentioned to me and Annie that he wanted to have Thanksgiving at his house, and we both agreed.

After work that day, Annie and I went to the Yacht Club to have a drink. I had become a member of the club, so Annie didn't have to sign me in anymore. After that we walked to her apartment; she wanted to show me her new curtains. We were standing in the kitchen area when a myna bird landed on the railing of her porch. The bird hopped off the railing and began edging its way into her studio. Annie freaked out, running after it with a broom.

"Annie, what are you doing? It's just a bird."

"No, it's my bastard husband. He said he'd never leave me alone. I know it's him."

I stared at her, dumbfounded. The bird flew around the apartment avoiding the broom. I opened the front door and it escaped. She began to cry, so I put my arms around her.

"Annie, Tony's in his grave. You don't have to be afraid of him; he can't hurt you anymore."

"My sons reminded me of what he always said, that even after death, he'd never let me go."

"Why the hell would they dredge all that stuff up?"

"I was happy to see them, but I'm glad they went home," she said.

"Yes, family can be a mixed blessing. Speaking of family, I was planning on visiting my parents for the holidays, but now I want to spend the holidays on Maui with Demo."

"Riana, there's so much going on in town right now, we haven't even gotten through Halloween. This just isn't the time to leave the island."

<center>~~~~~~</center>

There were some big events sponsored by the Yacht Club that I enjoyed. One of them was the annual fishing tournament, and the other was the Vic Maui Races. Approximately every other year a sizeable amount of sailboats race from Victoria, British Columbia, to Maui, Hawaii. That year Annie volunteered us to be on a committee to sponsor one of the boats. We were responsible for keeping track of the boat's progress out in the open ocean, and had to be ready to greet the boat when it arrived in Lahaina harbor. The journey could take up to fourteen days or more, depending on weather and ocean conditions.

In the meantime, I went down to the harbor at daybreak to watch the boats set off for the first day of the fishing tournament. There must have been at least a hundred boats sitting in the harbor, waiting for the start signal. Everyone watched and waited, until a loud gunshot could be heard, and the boats took off from the harbor, out to the open sea. It was an awesome sight.

After work, I made my way back to the harbor to watch the boats filter back in. Bleachers had been set up for spectators at the weigh-in station. The boats could be seen motoring back into the harbor with various colored flags flying, the color indicating what kind of fish they caught. The winners in each category was the highest weight for that type of fish, the largest marlin, mahi-mahi, snapper, and others. The overall winner was the largest fish caught over the three-day competition. It was all so exciting, and there was plenty of fresh fish around for days. Annie and I checked in daily at the Yacht Club to see how the boat we sponsored was progressing across the Pacific.

The phone woke me up at two in the morning, interrupting a dream about Mango Mike. It took me a moment to figure out where I was.

Annie said, "Hurry, get dressed. Our boat is about an hour from the harbor."

The previous day we were notified that the boat was near Maui, so we bought leis and a bottle of champagne for the crew.

I got dressed and drove the Gray Mouse to the harbor to meet Annie. We waited patiently for the first sign of the boat. We chatted with the harbor rats on the dock, catching up on harbor news. The harbormaster blew a horn as the sailboat approached the dock. The crew looked like they'd been through a war when we walked up to the craft as it was tying up on the dock. They all had smiles, knowing they made it across the Pacific. They knew they weren't the first boat to arrive, so there would be no trophy or cheers. I'd hoped the champagne and leis would soften the blow.

Annie said, "Now where can we get a drink at this time?"

"I'm going back to bed," I said, walking back to my car.

When I got home, a stray cat was behind the door in the carport. I knew he was a male because he had the biggest balls I'd ever seen on a cat. He walked right into the kitchen when I opened the door and made himself at home. We named him Ball Buster, Buster for short. He was a little unkempt, slightly ratty, but very affectionate. He loved the way we girls fawned over him. He got plenty of food and loving from us, but he never lost his tough-guy status. He was a good mouser too, and we certainly had enough loathsome creepy crawling critters to deal with on Nanu Street. Buster kept them all in line, and in turn, we showered him with love and cat treats.

~~~~~

Star Green showed up from San Francisco wanting to experience Halloween on Maui. She stayed with me at the house on Nanu Street. One of the first things we did was go out on a booze cruise. When the boat docked back in the harbor, we decided to have more drinks at the Pioneer Inn, as if we hadn't drank enough on the cruise. The place was packed and there were no empty tables, but luckily I spotted some friends who motioned for us to sit with them. We ordered drinks, and everything was going well until one of my friends asked Star where she was visiting from.

"Peru," she answered. "I'm from Peru."

I felt the color drain from my face. She sat there and continued to make up stories about herself and her life, as if she wasn't happy with the one she had. When we left the Pioneer Inn, I let her have it.

"Star, what the hell was that all about?"

"I was just having a little innocent fun," she said.

"With my friends?"

"I don't understand why you're making such a big deal out of it."

"Why would you lie and make up stories?"

"Stop it!" she yelled.

I was so annoyed, I dropped her off on Nanu Street and told her I was spending the night at Demo's. She sat on my bed watching me look for a change of clothes to take with me.

"When are you coming back?" she asked.

"Tomorrow."

I was fuming getting into the Gray Mouse, but as I drove away, I thought that perhaps I'd overreacted to a simple prank. Then I recounted the morning she showed up at Dominick French's house looking for me. He and I were asleep. Star stood in the yard outside his bedroom window, whining about how she didn't feel well, and hinting that she was being neglected. I had to get out of bed and deal with her. Maybe I had misplaced anger about that incident. Star always told me that I neglected my friends.

I parked next to Annie's station wagon when I got to Demo's house. Kona was wagging his tail as I walked up the porch steps. Annie was standing at the stove, and Demo was sitting at the table next to a bottle of tequila.

"I'm off tonight and some friends are coming over," he said. I eyed the tequila and poured myself a shot. Demo held out a small dish of limes. I took one, sunk my teeth in, licked the salt he'd sprinkled on my index finger, and we did a shot together.

"Too late for us to take a bath. Besides, Annie is here," he said.

"I don't care what you two do," Annie said, uncomfortably shaking her head.

By the time everyone got there, the three of us were slap-silly drunk. Demo sat at the piano and played some crazy stuff. Annie stood at the sink washing dishes. It was a really hot night, and I noticed she'd taken the top of her dress down, and her bra off, exposing two very large breasts. No one paid her any attention, and the festivities went on.

The party was winding down and people were leaving. Demo sat at the piano and began playing sentimental songs. Suddenly he began to cry.

"Demo, what's the matter?" I asked, slurring.

He told me a story about a woman in New Orleans he was in love with, that he thought of her all the time, sitting at her piano, her baby on her lap. It was almost as if he was in a trance, purposely trying to hurt me, and I wasn't liking it.

Annie came out of the kitchen. "Don't pay him any attention. He's just drunk and rambling." She threw herself on the bed in the extra bedroom and passed out.

When it got dark outside, a derelict wandered in off the street. He was a dirty, loathsome character, and he changed the whole mood of the night. I thought, *Demo never locks his front door, so this is what happens.* At first the guy seemed nice enough, until he wasn't. Soon he became combative and nasty and began threatening us. It all turned bad so fast, and with us being so drunk, we were frozen and felt vulnerable.

The guy must have woken Annie with his shouting. She came flying out of the bedroom like a witch on a broom, grabbed the guy by his shirt collar, and pushed him out the door, yelling, "Get the hell out, bastard, and don't come back!"

Then she calmly said, "It's time for me to go," waddled out the screen door, and drove off.

Demo and I laughed as that crazy night came to an end. No sooner than Annie had left, a pack of dogs passed the house barking, collars jingling.

Demo said, "I'm telling you, they know."

~~~~~~

We were planning a big Halloween night on the town. Annie, Star, and I would start at the Yacht Club, which had a private party. Then we would all meet and end the night at the Missionaries Hotel. I was wearing a red Chinese brocade sleeveless top over black satin pants. Demo told me he was wearing his pumpkin suit and straw hat. There was such a lead-up to the night, I was hoping it wouldn't turn out to be anticlimactic. You know how that can easily happen—when you hype something so much, a letdown is almost inevitable.

All of us women congregated in the house on Nanu Street to help each other get into costume. It was a really hot night, and we were sweating bullets putting our makeup and costumes on. Haku fixed my long hair up with decorative chopsticks and jewels. Loretta lent me her wooden sandals with the red velvet straps. We planned to meet up at the Mission Bar later that evening.

Star and I walked through the swinging doors of the Yacht Club and the place was filled to capacity. A guy standing outside was counting the people entering. Once it hit a certain number, you had to wait for people to leave in order to get in. We spotted Annie sitting at the bar and worked our way over to her. The bartender had a hard time keeping up with the drink orders, and we were happy to get drinks at all. We stayed for one drink, then headed back out to Front Street, which was filled with masses of people, most in costume. I frowned upon tourists who showed up with beach chairs and sat along the seawall, just to observe a freak show. It always rubbed me the wrong way. I felt if you're not going to get into costume and participate, stay home.

We waded through crowds and walked a few blocks to the Missionaries Hotel. Annie was stopped a few times. Everyone wanted to photograph her. She wore a cornflower-blue bustier, a slip skirt, blue feathers in her hair, long fake diamond earrings, and a lot of makeup. She looked like a fat saloon madam from the 1800s in the old west.

We walked up the steps of the hotel, past all the employees whose mouths were agape, and into the piano bar. I spotted Loretta immediately. She wore an Arabian princess costume in pale blue, looking like the character Jeannie, on that TV show *I Dream of Jeannie*. The guy sitting next to her wasn't in costume, but they seemed to be connected. They had secured a large table near the piano.

Demo lit up like a firecracker when he caught sight of us. I heard my song, and I was in a special place in heaven. He called Annie up to sing a few tunes, and the place went wild.

I remember that whole night vividly, every detail. It's funny the way some things disappear from our memories and others linger forever.

Demo finished his last set, and at closing time he insisted on going bar hopping. The two of us walked along Front Street, which was still packed, although the crowds had thinned out after midnight. We walked up the steps of the Blue Max, Demo in that crazy pumpkin suit holding my hand. He was my Sydney Greenstreet for sure that night. Of course Demo knew the owners and the musicians, and I have to admit that I felt proud to be with him. Looking back, I know Annie was right about his being my claim to fame, but at the time I was blind to it.

After the Blue Max we headed to Le Toots for one more drink and to see who could possibly be there. Annie was there dancing with some young thing.

"You want my key?" she shouted over the loud music.

I was planning on a romantic night back at Demo's house, but before I had a chance to answer, he shouted back, "Yeah," and took her key.

We walked out of Le Toots, past some very drunk people in costume, and as we approached Annie's apartment, a pack of dogs followed us, barking.

"Hurry," I said, rushing up the stairs to Annie's apartment, the jingle of the dogs' collars fading.

It was hotter than hell up there. We went out on her porch and looked down at the revelers walking in the street. People waved up at us, and some stopped to talk. We were pretty drunk, and I figured it was smart for us not to drive home. Demo took his jacket off, and I took my Chinese brocade top off. We lay on Annie's floor, staring at the ceiling.

"This is a crappy place, but I love it because it reminds me of New Orleans," he said.

I rolled on my side and put my arm over his chest. He pulled me toward him and kissed me on the lips. It was a soft, loving kiss. We were expecting to hear Annie's footsteps coming up the stairs at any moment. I couldn't help but feel it was Demo's plan to avoid intimacy. I soon fell asleep listening to Demo breathing, his curly wet ringlets touching my shoulder.

We'd been asleep for a while when the front door swung open, and a blast of somewhat cooler air swept the room. Annie stumbled in totally drunk. I squeezed Demo's hand and whispered for him to be quiet. She walked to the refrigerator, opened it, and took a long gulp out of the milk container. On her way to the stove, she tripped over something and muttered a curse we couldn't quite make out.

Annie fumbled around in the bottom compartment of the stove and got a frying pan out. "Fuck," she said loudly, waddling back to the refrigerator, and took two eggs out of the carton.

Demo squeezed my arm so hard to stop himself from laughing that I almost shouted. She put butter in the heated pan, broke the eggs, and threw the shells in the sink. We stifled our laughter as we heard the sizzling sounds coming from the pan. She took a dish out of the cabinet and slid the fried eggs on to the plate. We made believe we were asleep as she nearly tripped over us on the floor.

"These two fuckers are here again," she said, walking out to the porch with her dish.

It was all I could do not to bust out laughing.

Annie narrowly missed us again as she stumbled back to drop the dish into the sink. She stripped her clothes off and threw herself nude on the bed. Before long she was snoring.

~~~~~

Demo arranged for us to go out on a friend's boat. It was a lovely day on the ocean. The sun was glorious, and the sea air filled my lungs with freedom. On our way back to the harbor, the boat's owner confessed that he accidentally dropped the boat's keys in the ocean, and he'd be unable to dock the boat in the harbor. There was a big kerfuffle as to how we would get back to shore. They decided that Demo and the captain would take the boat's dinghy to the dock, and the deckhand and I would motor to the inlet in front of Demo's house, anchor the boat there, and wait for instructions.

I watched as Demo and the captain disappeared in the ocean toward the dock on that little dinghy. They seemed to have a plan to resolve the situation that made no sense to me. We motored to the area right off the beach in front of Demo's house, and the deckhand dropped the anchor. We sat on the boat deck waiting for a couple of hours. The deckhand received a call on the boat's radio from the captain, telling him the boat had to remain anchored there overnight. I was stymied as to how in the world I would get to shore. I could see the shore and Demo's house, but it was a long ways away. I heard a bullhorn, Demo's bullhorn. He was yelling at me to swim to shore.

The deckhand said, "You can do it."

"I can't swim that far," I said.

"There's a surfboard on the boat. You can lie on that, and kick your legs. I'll swim beside you."

After a vision of sharks tearing at my legs, my desire to be on dry land won out, and the task began to seem doable.

"I'm a little afraid, but I think I can do it," I said.

"Good," he said. "The owner wants me to stay with the boat, so I'll have to swim right back."

He jumped in the water with the surfboard and coaxed me in. I jumped in and got on the surfboard. I lay down as if I were swimming, and kicked my legs vigorously to ward off any sharks that might be in the area, and we headed for shore. As we got closer, I noticed a crowd forming.

Demo was on shore shouting words of encouragement through his bullhorn. "Adriana, it only looks far away."

I wanted to kill him. He certainly knew how to turn a tenuous situation into a spectacle.

"You can do it!" he blared through the bullhorn.

When we finally made it to shore, I stood up in the shallow water, looked back and saw how far away the boat was, and felt proud of myself.

The deckhand jumped on the surfboard and swam back to the boat.

Demo put his arm around me and said, "See, I knew you could do it."

The crowd that had gathered on shore broke out in applause.

He wrapped a towel around my shoulders and walked me to the house.

Nathan was sitting on the porch petting Kona and snickering as we walked up the steps.

"You'd better stop laughing," I said, giving him stink eye. By now I was shivering, but my mind was occupied with how to get rid of that bullhorn.

"I'm drawing you a hot bath," Demo said.

"I'll cook us something," Nathan said, and we all walked through the screen door.

"No thanks, Nathan," I said.

Kona looked up at Demo with affection, and Demo tugged on his ear.

I heard Demo say, "Make sure none of your dog friends are hanging around the kitchen!"

TWELVE

HOOKED ON YOU

Before I knew the poets, I was as a man lacking in one of the senses. In my solitary walks at night I used to feel a strange uneasiness; I used to wonder why I could not sleep; why I should find such pleasure gazing upon the stars that I could not tear myself from their presence. Why my heart should suddenly beat with joy upon seeing certain colors, or grow sad, even to tears on hearing certain sounds. At times I was so alarmed on comparing my continual agitation with the indifference of other men of my class that I even began to imagine that I was mad. But I soon consoled myself with the reflection that such madness was sweet, and I would rather have ceased to exist than be cured of it.

—*George Sand,* **Mauprat**

Ginger Pie Turner came to live with us on Nanu Street. She was a tall, pretty, wholesome type with a mass of strawberry blonde hair, an hourglass figure, and phenomenal boobs. Lani moved out of the garage apartment in the back of the house, and Loretta Perino took that space. Ginger Pie took Loretta's old room.

I remember meeting Ginger Pie for the first time. She said, "Hi, I'm Ginger Pie Turner, but everyone just calls me Pie."

We connected right away. We had a natural affinity for each other. We laughed at the same things and had easygoing natures. My intuition told me we'd become close friends.

It was an early morning during Thanksgiving week, and we were all sitting around the kitchen table with our coffee. Even though I planned to spend the holiday with Demo and Annie, I knew we would be making a turkey at the house. We were discussing an awful story we'd seen on TV the previous night about Jonestown.

"Those crazy cult followers, all killing themselves," Pie said.

"Yeah, what a pack of loonies," I said.

Loretta chimed in. "How do people get into a mind-set where they're willing to commit mass suicide, because Jim Jones told them to?"

"Total madness," Pie said.

"What the hell is in the water in Guyana?" I asked.

"I think he directed his followers to all drink poison," Loretta answered.

"The authorities found all his followers dead in their beds," Haku said.

"I think some escaped, but I'm not sure," I said.

"So let's just make a big turkey, and we'll have it to munch on all week," Pie said.

We all nodded in agreement.

We often congregated around the kitchen table at any hour of the day or night to discuss things. We made sure our plans were in sync and that no one felt left out or was alone on a holiday.

"I have to take a shower and get ready for work," I said, getting up.

~~~~~

I was filling a thermos with water and ice cubes to take to work with me when I heard a scream. Pie came running into the kitchen holding her jeans in one hand and opening drawers with the other. I saw her grab a big knife.

"What in the world is going on?" I asked.

"A centipede was in the leg of my jeans, and it stung me," she said, shaking.

I screamed, backing away from her.

"I'll kill it with this knife," she said.

Pie shook her jeans vigorously until the centipede fell out, wriggling onto the floor. She chopped it in half with the knife, and we looked on in horror as the two pieces of the vile creature ran in separate directions. I grabbed one of my cork wedges from behind the front door and hammered one half a number of times, until it stopped moving. Pie kept chopping at the other half until it was dead.

"Your leg is swelling up like you were attacked by a swarm of killer bees," I said.

"It really hurts, but I'll be okay."

"We haven't seen one of those in a while, but it is the rainy season," I said.

"Yeah, just one of the things we have to live with here."

"Are we still going to Sheila's Junkatique on Saturday?" I asked.

"A damn centipede bite won't keep me from the Junkatique."

"I'm on my way to work. If you need me, just call the store," I said, walking out the front door.

~~~~~~

I enjoyed my day at work and walked home in a good mood. The carport was empty, and the house was quiet for a change. I grabbed the mail on the kitchen table and flipped through it. There was a forwarded letter from an old boyfriend, Blake Middleton, back in Marin. He wasn't living with Casey Cutler anymore. They'd had a huge fight, and Blake moved out. I was happy we remained friends over the years. I wasn't sure if he knew that his mother sent me a Christmas card every year, with a detailed letter informing me about the goings-on in his life.

The phone rang. It was Demo. "Are you coming to the Mission tonight?"

"Yeah, I'll be there," I said.

"We need to talk about Thanksgiving, because Annie's driving me crazy."

"Don't worry. Listen, whatever she's planning, try to remember it's your house!"

That evening I made myself something to eat, fed the Ball Buster, took a shower, and tried on a dress I took home from the store, a new wraparound design Haku came up with.

"It looks great on you," she said.

I put some flowers in my hair and walked to the Missionaries Hotel. The air was balmy, and the night sky was clear and filled with stars. It was only a twenty-minute walk from the house, but wearing cork wedges was a big mistake.

I walked up the steps of the hotel, through the lobby, and into the piano bar. It wasn't that crowded, but I knew a few people. Still, I sat alone at a table near the piano.

Demo saw me come in and played my song. One of the waitresses brought me a gin and tonic. I patiently waited for Demo to finish his set while I rubbed my aching feet.

When Demo took a break, he went straight to the bar, got another drink, and sat down with me. "It's my own liquor," he said. "I don't know if I ever told you that."

"Your own liquor?"

"Yeah, I buy the tequila by the case and keep it behind the bar."

"Aren't you the clever one?"

"Let's talk about Annie. She's taken over everything, and it's frustrating me."

"I know how she can be. But you know she means well."

"Yeah, but I want certain foods on Thanksgiving, and she has her mind set on other stuff."

"Tell me what you want. I'll make it at home and bring it."

"Really? You'd do that?"

"Come on, you know I will. I feel the same way you do. There are specific foods I like for Thanksgiving, and I have to have them."

Demo reached in his pocket and gave me his house key. "I'll be home early," he said getting up.

I watched him walk back to the piano amid applause. He sat down, turned, and winked at me. I listened to a few tunes, finished my drink, and walked out of the Mission. I had to walk home, get my car, and drive to his house. My feet were killing me, and I knew I was going to feel it the next day. What made me think it was a good idea to walk all those blocks in high-heel wedges?

As soon as I was in the carport, I took off my shoes and threw them in the pile with all the other shoes (Hawaiian custom). I figured it would be a while before I could wear them again. I put on flip-flops and drove to Demo's house.

~~~~~

I walked up the porch steps and saw Kona sleeping on one of the straw chairs. I thought, *Some watchdog!* As soon as he saw it was me, he began wagging his tail.

I unlocked the door and went inside. When I switched the lights on, I noticed the place was a mess. I put a nickel in the camel and rode around for a few minutes, laughing, as the Arabian curtains rippled in the breeze coming off the ocean. When I had my fill of Arabia, I looked for a pad and pencil, sat on the couch, and made a list of all the foods I considered traditional for Thanksgiving. About an hour later Demo walked in, lay on the couch, and put his head in my lap.

I rattled off my list. "Candied sweet potatoes, broccoli or string bean casserole, mashed potatoes, lots of gravy, cranberry sauce. I prefer the jellied canned cranberry. Did I leave anything out?"

"No, but Annie wants to make boiled potatoes and canned string beans," Demo said.

"Demo, first of all you're inviting a bunch of people. Make it a pot luck."

"That's a good idea. I'll buy the turkey and Annie can roast it in the oven here."

"Yes, let her cook whatever she wants. You can send everyone home with doggie bags, no pun intended. I'll make candied sweet potatoes."

We heard a dog's collar jingle outside.

"I'm sure they know," he said, frowning.

"I certainly hope not," I said, laughing.

"I think we have a plan for Thursday, and I feel much better now." Demo took my hand. "Let's go to bed."

I wondered why no records tonight but was happy to be off my crying feet. After we had sex, I played with the back of his hair. He completed me in some strange way I didn't comprehend. My love was a sweet madness I didn't want to be cured of. I was hooked on him like a drug. I nuzzled my face against his neck. He put his tattooed arm around me and I fell into a contented sleep.

From my journal:

I lay there silently listening to the ocean. I'm in love all right, the delicious but dangerous kind where you lose yourself. My love's like an addiction, sweet and exciting, yet threatening. Like flowers with thorns crushed against my body until my heart hurts. He accepts me for who I am, and I feel safe with him. I fell asleep in his arms. My heart has wings when I'm with him.

The next day was a Friday. Haku and I got in the habit of setting up a folding table in the yard so we could continue our Friday tradition of painting clothing for the store. She had some coke, which I hadn't done in a while. I took a bottle of rose out of the fridge. I switched on the radio as she opened the wine. The Bee Gees' song, "How Deep is Your Love" was playing again on the radio, and I had a flashback of the previous night. I grabbed an aqua tie-dyed silk pareo and dipped my watercolor brush in the bright red paint. I painted a row of anthuriums across the bottom border. The silk absorbed the paint quickly. Haku took a snort with the tiny straw, watching me intently.

"That's beautiful, Adriana," she said, handing me the mirror.

"Thanks," I said, turning my attention to the white lines of powder. I smiled, snorted up a couple of lines, and took a sip of wine.

"I'm so glad we're still doing this. I need to keep my creative juices flowing. When I don't paint or draw for a while, I feel dormant. It's a need in me," I said.

TIE-DYED SILK PAREO WITH ANTHURIUMS

Walking into the house after work the following day, I found another forwarded letter, from Daisy Holmes, on the kitchen table. *I've got to give everyone my new address,* I thought.

I began reading about her new home in the Alaskan outback. She and her boyfriend were living in a remote area, accessible only by canoe or small prop plane. I stopped reading and said, "She's pregnant!" That was great news. My own timeclock was ticking, and I wondered if I'd ever have a child.

Thanksgiving went off without a hitch. Demo's house was packed with his friends and musician buddies. Pie and Haku came by for a while. Kona seemed to like the festivities and circulated among the crowd getting pets and belly rubs. Demo kept telling people not to give him scraps, but no one paid attention.

That evening, after the crowd left, and even though Annie and I were inebriated, we cleaned up the kitchen.

"Thanks for the candied sweet potatoes," Demo whispered, his breath tickling my ear.

In the living room, he sat at the piano barefoot and played bluesy tunes. I sat on the piano bench beside him, with my legs swung to the opposite side. I felt a calmness wash over my body, sort of a release. Then I felt a whoosh and stood up when I realized my pants were wet.

Demo's blue eyes widened. "You've got blood on the seat of your white pants."

"I guess I got my period."

Demo shook his head, laughing. "I saw my girl, Flo," he incorporated in the song he was singing.

I wondered where Annie was. I hadn't seen her leave. I went to the bathroom, took my pants off, and soaked them in the sink. I wrapped a sarong around me and went looking for her.

"Demo, Annie's up on the roof," I shouted.

"What?" he said, getting up from the piano and following me to the ladder that led to the roof.

Demo climbed to the top and found Annie staring at the stars. He stood on the ladder next to her, and for a while they were up there together staring off into space. I wasn't in the mood to deal with these two loony stargazers. I went straight into Demo's bedroom, slipped the sarong off, and threw it on the floor. I got in bed and went to sleep.

~~~~~~

After Thanksgiving, Haku decided to move in with her boyfriend, the sea captain. She didn't live with us very long, but did I mention how hot the sea captain was? We needed another person to share the rent. Ginger Pie Turner worked at the Bay Club in Kapalua and was friends with one of the other waitresses, a Hawaiian girl named Malia. She brought Malia by the house to meet Loretta and me, and though really young, we felt she'd be a great addition. Along with Malia, we had to put up with her boyfriend at the house on a regular basis. We often were faced with a strange guy sitting at the kitchen table on the odd morning, a normal occurrence living with a bunch of single women.

On Saturday, Ginger Pie and I both had the day off, so we drove to Wailuku to rummage around the secondhand stores. I found a teddy bear and a Chinese doll with long black braids at the Junkatique. We managed to find what we thought were treasures that day. When we were shopped out, we stopped in La Familia Mexican Restaurant for lunch. We were drinking margaritas, eating chips and salsa, and discussing Roman Polanski, the producer who had fled France when he was caught with a thirteen-year-old girl.

Out of the corner of my eye I caught sight of Mango Mike. He was sitting with a bunch of guys in a booth at the other end of the restaurant. He spotted me and walked to our table. I noticed that he'd finally bought a new pair of board shorts, orange with palm trees and surfboards, although he was wearing the same blue plaid flannel shirt he always wore.

He slid into the booth and sat next to me. "Hi babe," he said with a smile.

"Mike, this is my friend Ginger Pie Turner."

He looked at her, smiled and said, "Hey, howzit?"

"What have you been up to?" I asked.

"I moved to Hana recently. I'm in town visiting friends and stocking up on groceries at Ooka's"

"You look good," I said.

"Well, my original offer still stands," he said, smirking.

"I'll think about it," I said.

"My friends and I have been sitting here for a while and they're ready to leave, but I just wanted to say hi. You still look good, Adriana. You know I'm around if you need me." He kissed me on the cheek and said, "Love ya, babe."

I watched him get up and leave the restaurant with his friends. I couldn't help flashing on steamy nights with Omar in the hood, and even felt a twinge of missing Ono the cat. *We certainly had some great sex,* I thought. I sat there in a sort of daze.

"Adriana, who was that?" Pie asked.

"That was Mango Breath."

She laughed but had a confused look on her face.

"We hung out together for a while when I lived in Napili Hui, in the hood. The guy was obsessed with mangos. Actually, his name is Mike."

"He looks like that actor, I can't remember his name. You know who I mean, the guy who was in *Doctor Zhivago*."

"Omar Sharif," I said.

"Yeah," that's who I was thinking of. He's so handsome."

I wanted to say, *And he was dynamite in bed, too,* but I keep that to myself. We finished our margaritas and drove back to the west side.

~~~~~~

We pulled into the carport on Nanu Street and noticed a bunch of unfamiliar cars. Malia's boyfriend, Toby, was a *haole* (Caucasian) guy, much older than she was, and totally crazy about her. Pie always said he was pussywhipped. A bunch of guys we didn't know were sitting in the living room. A fresh Christmas tree stood in a bucket of water in the corner.

"Where did that come from?" I asked.

Malia smiled and said, "Toby bought it for us."

I was a little flabbergasted but was happy to have a real Christmas tree.

Pie and I walked to my bedroom. I set the little teddy bear and the Chinese doll I found at the Junkatique on top of my dresser with their legs dangling down.

"He'll do anything for that girl," Pie said. "He's like a lovesick puppy."

"He seems so much older than her, it's a little creepy," I said.

"Not so much his age but the way he stalks her," she said.

"Yes, I find him creepy. But hey, we got a real Christmas tree out of it."

"Yeah, well now we have to buy lights and find decorations. I wish we would have known this while we were rummaging around the secondhand shops today."

"Why do I get the feeling that Toby is a married man?"

"Oh, I don't think he's married." (Pie always thought the best of people).

We bought lights for the Christmas tree, and Annie gave us some ornaments she had in boxes stacked on her porch. She didn't put a tree up anymore. We made a night of it on Nanu Street. I made my mother's eggnog, and we put out some pu pus (appetizers) on the kitchen table.

Demo wandered in behind Malia's creepy, but thoughtful, boyfriend, Toby. Loretta made a pan of lasagna. We had a fun night decorating the Christmas tree. Demo and I walked down the hallway to my room.

He laughed when he saw the teddy bear and the Chinese doll sitting on my dresser. "I know I'm sick, but I have to do it," he said, laughing.

He lay the Chinese doll on her back on the dresser and positioned the teddy bear between her legs. It was comical, and I left it that way. I displayed them right next to the Chinese Jewelry box Demo brought me back from Singapore. I threw my arms around his neck and kissed him.

DOLL AND BEAR

Dominick French played at the Mission Bar on Christmas Eve. I stayed for a while but left after the first set. The place was packed, but Annie wasn't there, and I didn't know anyone. There was a bunch of women throwing themselves all over Demo, and I didn't want to get jealous or make him uncomfortable. I wasn't in the mood to spend the whole evening wondering if the last dance would be for me.

When I got home, Malia told me that my friend Adam Hirschfeld called from New York. I had jotted down my phone number on the last letter I wrote to him. We did write to each other from time to time. We gossiped about people we both knew, and with what was going on in our lives.

"What did Adam say?" I asked.

"He said to call him tomorrow. He mentioned that he was coming to Hawaii in January."

I thought, *This is the month of letters and long-distance phone calls.*

~~~~~~~~

The phone woke me at one in the morning.

It was Demo. "Why did you leave so early?"

"I was tired, and I wanted you to feel free to get as crazy as you wanted with your fans."

"Adriana, its Christmas Eve! You have to come over," he said, his voice hoarse from singing.

I got dressed and drove to his house. I had done this on numerous occasions. I found Demo drunk, playing records, and in a crazy mood. He kept putting different discs on the record player.

"You've got to hear this one."

"Demo, is this what you wanted me to come here for?"

Demo didn't answer but swiped his finger across his lips, as if to shush me. He kept up the manic routine, which I was familiar with. I began to drink heavily, hoping I'd pass out on the couch. Lying there, my mind wandered to a terrible thing I did when I was living with my parents. It was right before I left for California on that crazy cross-country trek with the O'Brien sisters.

I had yelled at my father, who had been chastising me about my life choices. "What have *you* done with *your* life," I yelled at him. It was one of those ugly scenes you regret for the rest of your life.

My father began to cry and eventually left the room. My mother shot me an angry, disappointed look. He retreated to their bedroom and didn't come out for the rest of the night.

Demo sat at the piano playing a sad song, and I burst into tears. At first he ignored me and continued playing. When I seemed to go into a spasm of sobs, he got up from the piano and sat on the couch with his hand on my leg, I suppose intending to calm me.

I was writhing around like a woman possessed, blubbering through tears. "I want my father, I want my father!"

He stared at me but didn't stop me. He let me cry it out, waiting for the spasm to end. Eventually the sobs became whimpers, and suddenly they stopped. I lay there still in a kind of trance.

A stranger walked in the front door. Demo seemed to know him. The guy sat on the floor as if he'd been there before, and he refused to acknowledge me. I had a feeling that Demo met him at the Mission Bar and invited him back to the house. The stranger never left, and Demo made no comments or movements that hinted at going to bed or sleep anytime soon. I sat up and wondered why I was there. I was too drunk to drive, so I called the house.

Pie answered the phone and was surprised to hear my voice. "I didn't even know you weren't here asleep in your bed," she said.

"Please, Pie, I think I've had too many drinks to drive. Can you come and get me?"

"I'm on my way."

She knew the routine, as it wasn't the first time Pie rescued me in the middle of the night from Demo's house.

~~~~~~

I called my friend Adam Hirschfeld the next day and told him he was welcome to stay with us, that we had a couch that doubled as a single bed in the living room. I told him I had a boyfriend and confided in him about some of the details of our relationship.

"Adriana, you went through some of that with me, remember? How is this going to end?"

I didn't have an answer for him. I told Adam we'd talk about it when he was on the island.

Meanwhile, Pie drove me to Demo's house to get my car. It was early in the morning, so I knew Demo would still be asleep. I didn't stop in, just jumped into the Gray Mouse and drove off in a huff.

Later that day, Christmas Day, Demo came by Nanu Street with his tail between his legs. "I was really drunk last night."

"You woke me up out of a dead sleep, and for what?"

"I know how crazy I can get. I have to stop drinking for a while."

I stared at him. "When is that going to happen?"

"Adriana, it's Christmas Day. I want you with me."

"I'm not in the mood for shenanigans."

"No shenanigans, just Annie Hughes," Demo said, laughing.

"What do you mean?"

"Annie is at my house cooking right now. I'm having a bunch of people over, and I want you there. It won't be Christmas without you."

"I was planning on hanging with the girls today, they're alone." (I was lying, of course. I'd cancelled my trip to New York to spend the holidays with him.)

"Bring them along. Oh those lips," he said, running his finger along my mouth.

"I promise, I'll be there," I said, smiling.

Demo rubbed my hand and gazed at me lovingly. I was relieved the holiday had been salvaged.

"I'm expecting you later Riana," he said, teasing me. He kissed me affectionately and walked out the front door.

I took a shower and looked through my closet to find the perfect outfit. I waited a few hours before driving to his house. I walked in a little late, and everyone was already there.

Demo gave me a big kiss on the lips. He whispered, "You always have to make an entrance."

Annie was in the kitchen, cooking and serving. Demo sat me down on the couch next to him and put his arm around me. I'll never forget the look he gave me when our eyes met. I was back on top of the heap, as Annie would say. I slept over that night and thought the year would end on a high note.

New Year's Eve was a big event at the Missionaries Hotel, and I knew Demo would be playing at the piano bar. Annie volunteered me to sew him a gold lamé jacket for the event. I wanted to kill her.

"Annie, I haven't done any tailoring since I was in fashion college."

"You'll figure it out," she said.

"You should have asked me before you promised Demo!"

"Riana, the jacket doesn't have to be perfect."

"You just don't understand what's involved."

Annie had no idea how difficult tailoring was. It was a craft in itself. There were precise corners that had to be sewn, folded inside out, and stitched down. Since Demo was already excited about it, I felt roped into the situation. I didn't want to disappoint him.

I left work that day and thought about the task at hand, walking all the way home. I dwelled on the fact that I got nothing from Demo for Christmas. Was it the fact that I didn't receive a gift that was bothering me? Or was I expecting a ring, or something substantial? True, he never let me pay for anything, and had taken me on trips, but this was different. His thoughtlessness irked me. Perhaps it was a case of my having great expectations.

~~~~~~

That following week a nuclear submarine, called the USS *Hawkbill*, was in Lahaina Harbor. The Navy had an open house and was taking a hundred civilians on board from Lahaina, Maui, to Honolulu, Oahu. Demo made arrangements for Annie and me to go. He seemed to be making amends for Christmas Eve. Demo vowed to cut down on his drinking, but I remained skeptical. It was the holidays, and emotions were running high, so I let that last manic episode slide. We got on a Zodiac from the dock and motored out to the submarine. The salty sea air sprayed our faces as the Zodiac slapped the waves.

The sub looked huge as the tiny Zodiac pulled alongside. The scene of Annie waddling her way up that skinny ladder and then down into the hatch was hysterical. A few sailors had to push her up the ladder by her ass and then squeeze her down the narrow hatch. Demo and I were laughing uncontrollably, waiting our turn.

"Shut up, fuckers!" Annie yelled at us, to the surprise and dismay of the sailors, who were just trying to help her.

It was a crazy day. Gordon Lightfoot played an impromptu concert in the torpedo room. I guessed he was on the island for a vacation. A siren went off, and I heard, "Dive, dive, dive," over the intercom. It was the strangest sensation going down, but once the submarine was under the surface of the ocean there was a feeling of suspension. They had a lunch prepared for everyone, but all I remember was the chocolate and vanilla sheet cake for dessert.

We civilians were given a tour of the submarine. I was shocked at the tiny compartments the sailors slept in. They never revealed the depth we were at, I imagined for military security purposes. I was amazed at how the submarine converted seawater into drinking water. When the submarine reached Honolulu, it surfaced. The ride up from the depth of the ocean felt like a plane taking off. We stood in the control room as they docked in Honolulu. Annie decided to stay in Honolulu for a day of shopping, but Demo and I flew right back to Maui.

<center>~~~~~~</center>

On New Year's Eve everything came to a head. We had a table at the Mission Bar with Annie, Pie, and all my girlfriends to ring in 1979. Demo wore the gold lamé jacket I made him, and Annie covered his straw hat with the fabric left over from the jacket. Unfortunately, I got twisted drunk and made an ass of myself. I guess all my insecurities surfaced as I watched women climbing all over him, overcome by the bluesy piano and his funky style. He didn't pay much attention to me that night. Perhaps to him it was a job. I'll never know. I was frustrated and embarrassed in front of my friends.

Annie leaned over, pinched my arm hard, and said, "Don't pay attention to those girls, he's going home with you dumb ass."

But I wasn't having it. I was fed up with it all. I got up, causing a big scene, and stormed out of the Mission Bar.

"Riana!" she yelled after me.

As soon as I hit the cool night air I wanted to throw up.

Pie walked outside after me and put her arm around my shoulder. "Let's go home."

There were a few taxis parked in front of the Missionaries Hotel. She motioned for one. The cabbie got out and opened the door for us. I recognized him. He was a regular, always wore shorts, flip-flops, an aloha shirt, and a plumeria behind one ear. The tourists loved him, especially the women.

I didn't say a word on the ride home while the cabbie blabbed away. I felt numb all over. Pie just stared at me and stroked my hand. She probably was trying to avoid a big explosion that she figured was coming. When we arrived home, she paid the cabbie.

"Thanks ladies, and Happy New Year," he shouted, as he drove away.

I kicked off my shoes, followed her in, and busted out crying.

"Adriana, what?" she asked.

"My friend Adam was right. Why didn't I see this? Why did I let myself fall in love with him?"

"Adriana, we can't help who we fall in love with."

"He didn't even buy me a stinking gift for Christmas."

"Demo seems to love you very much; he shares his life with you. Isn't that enough?"

"I made that damn lamé jacket for him. Do you know how hard that was?"

"I get that, but on a night like tonight, he belongs to everyone. It's his job."

I knew everything Pie was saying made sense, but nothing seemed to quell my disappointment, and the gin was exacerbating my emotions.

"I'm going to bed and try to forget tonight," I said.

I was walking to my room, when I turned around. "Pie, thanks for coming to rescue me from Demo's house on Christmas Eve."

"You know you can depend on me, always," she said.

I got undressed, washed my face, and got into bed nude. It was a hot night, and the chirping of the geckos sounded louder than usual. Dusty Springfield was singing "I Only Want to Be with You" in my head. I soon fell asleep after another bout of senseless tears.

~~~~~~

After the holidays, things with Demo returned to a familiar pattern, but the seeds of discontent were already sown. I was needing more art in my life and decided to buy a canvas and some acrylic paints. I was well aware of my pattern of ignoring my art when I was in a relationship. I didn't do this consciously, it just took that course. I didn't want to fall back into that pattern. Music is a different form of art, and I certainly dated a lot of musicians. The weekly routine of painting garments with Haku helped somewhat, but I guess it wasn't enough.

From my journal:

I've always found it easy to love musicians. Music grabs the soul. It lifts the spirit and causes the heart to fly. It's just right there, although an intangible thing. I can remember how it felt when I sang. Things I could never express in words, or paint on a canvas, poured out of my mouth in musical notes. Good sounds chill me to the bone, steal my spirit, and give my mind away to images and fantasies.

I didn't hear from Demo for a few days. I'd guessed he was pissed off at me for making a scene and walking out of the Mission Bar on New Year's Eve. It was crazy, but no matter what Demo did, where he went, or what he said, I found that I couldn't live without him. He was entwined in my Maui life from the very beginning. As long as we were together, I didn't care about anything else. He had some sort of crazy hold on me, and my emotions were like a ship riding up and down on the waves in the ocean, and he was at the helm.

I stared at the blank white canvas for a moment and then began to paint. I painted a man and woman standing nude in a tropical paradise. The general feel of the painting was Gauguinesque. It took a little more than a week to complete. When it was finished, I studied it. I noted that the man's eyes were closed, but the woman's eyes were wide open. The man stood very still, stiff, and aloof, while the woman seemed relaxed, engaged, and smiling. I didn't even realize it at the time, but years later it came to me. It was actually Hank Cooper and me in his backyard in Kahului when I had been on Maui for a month's vacation, before I even lived on the island.

"Each painting has its own way of evolving. ... When the painting is finished, the subject reveals itself."

—William Baziotes, American painter

I was upstairs sewing at the Crafty Mermaid when I heard Annie laughing and talking on the phone at the counter downstairs. I heard her mention my name and a short conversation about me. I went downstairs to ask if someone was asking for me.

"It was Demo, but he just wanted to know if you were here."

"Why didn't you tell me the phone call was for me?"

"He asked me not to."

I climbed back up the stairs annoyed, sat down at the Bernina, and finished a dress I was sewing. I had the radio on and that song "Baby Don't Get Hooked on Me" by Mac Davis was playing. *How apropos*, I thought.

Not too long after that I heard Demo's voice downstairs, and then footsteps walking up. Soon he was standing at the top of the stairs staring at me. I was in a bathing suit and sarong. I turned around and smiled at him.

"The seamstress at work," he said, teasing me. "I'm not here to talk about New Year's."

"I feel stupid. I let my emotions run away with me."

"You always want to be the center of my attention, even on a night like that," he said.

"I'm sorry. I only wanted to be with you."

"Why don't you come to my house after work? I'm not playing tonight."

"Okay, about five-ish?"

Demo smiled, turned, and walked down the stairs mumbling, "See you later."

I drove the Gray Mouse to Demo's house after work and parked in his driveway next to Nathan's car. They were sitting on the porch taking turns petting Kona, who had a satisfied expression on his face. As soon as I began walking up the wooden steps, Nathan got up to let me sit down.

"I gotta go anyway," Nathan said.

I had the feeling they were discussing me before I arrived, and that Demo wanted to talk to me alone. Nathan ran down the steps to his car, shooting us the shaka sign with his right hand, a "hang loose" gesture used often by surfers.

"Bye," I said, watching him get into his car.

I sat next to Demo in silence for a bit. The sun was still out, and the sea air was pleasant as I stared at the ocean.

"Nathan was telling me about the island of Koolawe, that the US government used it for bombing practice. Nothing grows there anymore," Demo said.

"I never heard of that island."

"The Hawaiians want all that to stop and to bring the island back to life."

"Yeah, well that will take years. The soil is already poisoned."

"So what the hell was that all about on New Year's Eve?" Demo asked.

"Probably jealousy." I mentioned nothing about not receiving a gift for Christmas.

"But you knew you'd be coming home with me, right?"

"I guess I wasn't sure. I never know what you're going to do."

"Let's try to move on as if that didn't happen," Demo said.

"I've been meaning to tell you. A friend of mine is coming for a visit this month," I said.

"Do I know her?"

"It's a guy, Adam Hirschfeld. He's a longtime friend and was once my lover."

Demo turned his face back in my direction. "Is he someone I should worry about?"

"He's gay," I answered.

~~~~~~~

Adam Hirschfeld arrived at the end of January, and it was so good to spend time with him again. I took him to all the popular tourist haunts, my favorite restaurants, and dragged him to Wailuku with me and Ginger Pie to rummage around the secondhand shops. We had lots of laughs together.

"So when am I going to meet the famous Dominick French, your boyfriend?" he asked.

I wasn't sure how to approach the issue. I decided to treat his visit like I would any of my other visitors. I'd take him to the Missionaries Hotel one night, which was an initiation into my world.

A few people stared at Adam and me as we walked through the hotel lobby, and the bartender stared as we searched for a table near the piano in the Mission Bar. I suppose they thought I had a new boyfriend. Demo smiled and quickly played my song to greet me, probably relieved that we finally showed up. Adam and I had drinks and enjoyed the music. When Demo took a break he came to our table with his drink. He sat down, gave me a sloppy kiss on the cheek, as if marking his territory: *she's mine.* He stared at Adam and held out his tattooed arm to shake Adam's hand. We talked until his break was over. Adam and I left before the end of the next set. We had plans to go on an early morning whale watch. Demo's eyes followed us with a concerned expression as we walked out.

The whale watch was exciting. There were plenty of pods out there with breaches, tail flips, fin slaps, and huge spouts. That evening I took Adam on a candlelight tour of the Baldwin house. Dwight Baldwin was a doctor who was one of the first missionaries to build a house and live on Maui with his family. The house sits right near Lahaina Harbor across from the Pioneer Inn. Seeing all the primitive doctor's instruments, and the sparseness of the rooms with rigid furniture, I wondered how anyone survived illness or daily life back in those days. There were trellises of grapes outside the house, which I saw as a remnant of civilization they brought with them to the island. Adam loved the tour.

Demo called me to say he was invited to a wedding in the west Maui Mountains and wanted me to go with him.

"My friend Adam is still in town," I said.

"Bring him along. I'm sure he'd like to get a taste of the real local flavor."

"Yes, I imagine he'll love it."

"Just come by my house on Saturday, around noon, and we'll drive together," Demo said.

"Sounds like a plan. See you then," I said, hanging up.

~~~~~~

Adam and I showed up at Demo's house at noon on Saturday. Demo was dressed like Sydney Greenstreet, sporting white linen pants, a white silk shirt, and his straw hat. I wore a white gauze wrap skirt I made at work, and a colorful, flimsy, tie-up blouse with no bra. I picked some white plumerias off the tree in Demo's yard, fastening them to my hair. I have a great photo of Demo and me, which Adam took that afternoon. We headed out in Demo's Corvette, Adam's curly blond hair blowing wildly as he sat scrunched in the backseat. We laughed all the way up into the mountains but became silent as we descended into a magical valley where the wedding was to take place.

The wedding was anything but traditional, and I remember belly dancers. One took her scarf off and waved it in front of Demo. He gazed at me with a crazy look on his face. Demo sat on a chair in the corner by a window, while Adam and I stood around the champagne table. I happened to look in Demo's direction and saw the same belly dancer climb through the window. She stood in front of him and began gyrating. She took off her silky magenta scarf and waved it past his face a few times, then wrapped it around his neck. Adam and I watched from a distance as she did her thing. She removed her scarf from around his neck and eventually, but reluctantly, shimmied away. After the three of us got over a fit of laughter, Demo ran into a friend who was lurking around the food table. Demo suggested we all continue the party at his house.

We drove to Demo's house in two cars. I had a feeling I knew what was on Demo's mind and wondered if I should clue Adam in. I chose to just let things unfold organically. I mentioned that Adam was a chef, and that he would make us a nice dinner, which he did with whatever he found in Demo's refrigerator.

After dinner, Demo put us all through his disk jockey routine. His friend left, and the three of us continued to drink until it was time to go to bed. I took Adam's hand in mine cautiously. We went into Demo's bedroom and took off our clothes. I knew Demo was in no way Adam's type, but I figured I'd just let things happen, and they did.

In the morning we woke up at roughly the same time. No one said anything as the three of us stared at the ceiling until Adam remarked, "Are the waves always this loud?"

Demo didn't answer. He rolled over and made love to me while Adam watched, occasionally playing with my hair and touching my exposed breast.

When we were finished, Demo smiled, got up, and said, "I'll go make us breakfast."

As soon as he was gone, Adam got on top of me and we had sex. They were both men I loved and had a sexual attraction for.

Demo appeared in the doorway of the bedroom. "What's going on in here?"

Adam slid off and lay next to me.

"What do you mean by that? You know exactly what's going on here," Adam said.

"Can't trust you two alone for a minute," Demo said, in a jealous tone.

"She seems to be where all the action is," Adam said.

Demo left the room in a huff, but soon returned. "So what kind of toast do you want?"

"Whole wheat," Adam answered.

~~~~~

Before Adam Hirschfeld left the island, we had a candid talk.

"You know he's a rogue. You always pick these self-centered piggy guys," Adam said.

I didn't know how to answer him. I tried to think of all the boyfriends I had during our long friendship. I always thought they were all so different from each other.

"I picked you once, Adam," I said teasingly.

"That was in another lifetime."

"Maybe so. I suppose I do tend to compromise myself, and not just with men."

"We'll always be friends no matter what, or who," he said, rubbing my fingers.

We hugged.

"Same goes for me," I said.

I felt sad driving Adam to the airport. I wasn't sure when I'd see him again.

"I had a fantastic time, and you were part of it. I'll remember Maui always."

I watched Adam walk away at the gate. I waved and blew a kiss. "*Maui no ka oi!*" (Maui is the best) I shouted after him.

He walked across the runway and up the stairs to the plane. Before he disappeared inside, he turned and waved.

I stood there until I saw the plane disappear into the clouds, as I had done so many times with so many others I'd loved.

THIRTEEN

POOR BUTTERFLY

From my journal:

Random thoughts of a lifetime of schemes, seemingly different yet somehow the same. Falling in and out of love with masters of distance. Dreams of promises never fulfilled. Fleeting feelings of the moment, which I learned to put away in a picture book of unsolved mysteries. Countless tales of beautiful fantasy and reality I jotted down in a journal, never recognizing the difference between them. A sage once said that the key to a happy life is indifference. Well, I never pretended to be a sage.

I received a four-page letter from my father, Andre. It was filled with advice and news of what was happening in their lives. It was my parents' forty-second anniversary. He had just retired and admitted just how much he missed his barber shop, even writing that he often dreamed about it.

"I still cut some of my old customers' hair in their homes, and on Saturdays I work in someone else's barber shop," he wrote.

My father mentioned that he planned on doing some traveling now that he had the time … but not to visit me, of course, because he would never fly. His youngest brother, Red, was visiting New York, and my father was toying with the idea of driving back to Florida with him. His advice to me about Demo was, "Don't get jealous; he should be jealous of you. It's more important that the man goes after the woman. A man should always love more."

I took a break from Demo. I was still miffed about the holidays, and things with him seemed to be on the downslide. He flew to another island for a gig, and I didn't go with him. I met a guy, a tourist, at one of the bars in town. I had no idea what his story back on the mainland was, nor did I care. It was an exciting and somewhat self-affirming few days. Perhaps subconsciously I was getting back at Demo. We engaged in romantic dinners with wine at an out-of-the-way eatery in town. Then there was the sex, which we did a lot of, as if wanting to make the most of our short time together.

From my journal:

It's nice to be made love to over and over again, not dwelling on the past or future. I ran into him this morning in town with his friends. I stood motionless as we all talked. He spoke in tones of casual conversation, while I had flashes of us kissing passionately and having sex. I want more, but he leaves tomorrow. I'm not in love or attached, but I look forward to tonight.

Dominick French had a blues singer with him now, Bessie Waters. She was foreign, had a great voice, and I liked her a lot. She lived on Maui but touted having a Dutch passport. She boasted of being a world traveler and told me she'd lived in Barcelona, Morocco, and the Canary Islands. Annie Hughes always made fun of the way she lifted one leg every time she hit a high note, as if it helped her get the wind out of her lungs. Some nights, after the Mission Bar closed, we'd invariably end up at Le Toots for a nightcap, but lately I was going straight home before the end of Demo's last set.

The phone rang at one in the morning, waking me up.

It was Demo. "I'm calling you from the phone in Le Toots. Come meet me."

"How will I find you? It's always so dark and crowded in there."

"Oh, you'll see me right off," he answered.

"We're having so much fun, and you're missing it all," I heard Bessie yell in the background.

Like a total ass, I dragged myself out of bed, got dressed, and drove down to Le Toots. Like I said, he was an addiction.

When I got there, I looked through the window that opened onto the street, because the entrance was packed. There in the corner was Demo in a Viking helmet, Bessie Waters sitting beside him. He smiled at me and waved.

I climbed through the window and clawed my way through the crowd. I slumped into a chair next to him at their table and noticed that they were both pretty drunk. Having just been woken up I was a little groggy.

He put his arm around me as if announcing that I was his girl.

"Where the hell did you get that helmet?" I asked.

"I was hoping you'd come home with me tonight, but you disappeared during my last set."

"You didn't answer my question," I said.

Demo called the waitress over. "A gin and tonic for my baby."

"And one more for the road," I sang, suddenly coming alive (the "Demo drug" kicking in).

The music was really loud, but we managed to have a conversation, though none of it made any sense. I was actually beginning to enjoy myself. A couple of guys asked me to dance but turned around when they saw Demo reach over and put his arm around my shoulder.

"Let's go home," Demo said.

The three of us made our way through the crowd on the dance floor and through more people who were trying to get in the front door. Every place else in town was closed, but Le Toots would be hopping until the wee hours of the morning. Once out in the night air I breathed a sigh of relief. In those early days, you were able to smoke in bars, and Le Toots had been dense with smoke.

Demo held my hand and yelled, "Good night!" to Bessie as we walked down Front Street.

Bessie shouted, "Demo, I know you still have some life left in you."

Demo stopped in his tracks, turned, and looked at me for approval.

"I wanna go home," I said, expecting him to leave with me.

"Adriana, let's go back inside. Bessie's right, the night's still young."

I was livid. I wasn't going back in there, I was going home. I stared at Demo, took his arm off my shoulder, and began walking away.

"Now, Riana," he called after me, as if I were a naughty child.

I kept walking, leaving the two of them standing in front of Le Toots.

Demo often used his being drunk as an excuse to do outrageous and thoughtless things.

~~~~~~~

We already had a trip planned to another island. He was playing a gig on the big Island known as Hawaii Island. It was a beautiful, fancy affair, and it went off without any mishaps. I was careful not to set my hair on fire. We stayed in a really nice hotel, and the only flames were from the candles around the Jacuzzi tub in the bathroom. Things between Demo and me went back to a somewhat normal status. He was a funny guy who kept me laughing, until my laughter turned into tears. It is said that laughter is the joy of the soul, and the happiness it brings is boundless. No one ever speaks of the flipside.

My love affair with Demo was total madness, like a carnival ride, but I was holding on until the end. Even though our sex life was lacking, I was hooked on him like he was a drug I needed to function. I overlooked his faults and forgave his cruelty. There were times when he seemed to go out of his way to make me feel shitty. He liked to bait me, talking love to me one day and on another day would remark that he wished he was in love. Like giving a little girl a lollypop and then snatching it away after she'd already licked it. My emotions were getting jerked around, and it was draining. I was like a butterfly going through a barn fire.

~~~~~~~

It was spring 1979, and I was going back to New York to spend a month with my family over Easter. I was hoping that being separated from Demo would give me some clarity on our relationship.

Demo lamented, "A whole month? What will I do without you, who will I talk to?"

I didn't answer but tilted my head to the side, frowning.

The week before I left, Annie and I spent almost every night at the Mission Bar listening to Demo play and sing. I was recording each moment in my mind to recount while I was away. I slept at his house a few times during that week as well. The sound of the ocean, making love, and falling asleep in his arms. It had to last and eventually be weighed. I knew I was addicted to him, and an addiction can be sweet while under the influence. But I knew I wasn't happy anymore. I wanted a complete love.

Pie and I were sitting at the kitchen table drinking our morning coffee.

"I'll drive you to the airport tomorrow," Pie said.

"That would make leaving so much easier," I said.

"He'll miss you, make no mistake. Besides, you'll be spending time with your family."

"I know, but I hate to leave Maui. You know how I feel about the island," I said.

"I'll be missing you too. We're like two peas in a pod."

Looking at Pie's face, I had the feeling that it would all work out okay. "I want to tell you how much it meant to me, I mean all those times you came to rescue me from Demo's house in the middle of the night."

"Oh shush. You know I'm there for you. It's what friends do."

I'd become very close to Ginger Pie Turner. We had a strong connection I didn't share with the other women. Loretta and I had a history, but Pie and I were riding the same wave. I wanted us to be friends forever. I knew she'd be there when I got home, and it gave me comfort.

The day she drove me to Kahului Airport, we talked about all the things we would do when I returned. Driving over the Pali I was overcome with a feeling of dread. I was missing Maui and I hadn't even left yet.

She dropped me off at the outside ticket agent. I hated waiting on line. For five bucks I could give the outside attendant my information, and he'd do everything for me. He checked me in, loaded my bag after customs, and gave me a boarding pass. I hugged Pie and waved goodbye as I walked to the gate. When the plane took off I looked down, feeling as if I was leaving life itself behind. Maui was part of me now, like blood in my veins. I looked at Haleakala, the cane fields, and row upon row of pineapple below us. Everything got smaller until it all disappeared when we flew into the clouds.

～～～

My parents picked me up at LaGuardia Airport in their gold Oldsmobile with the statue of the Virgin Mary on the dashboard. I had a momentary lapse of giddiness thinking of the large St. Anthony statue that Nathan had given me. We all hugged and cried a little. I put my suitcase in the trunk, and we drove along parkways with familiar air streaming in the window. Funny how each place has a distinct odor.

The cats were happy to see me. The three of them raced around the apartment bouncing off walls and stopping to sniff my suitcase. My mother made one of my favorite meals, Italian sausage and potatoes roasted in the oven. We drank wine and talked a lot that first night. I reveled in the familiarity of it all, and the love I felt for them. I was overcome with the knowledge that it was a place I could always return to and be welcomed. My parents were getting up there in years, and I felt time dwindling. I was so happy I'd made the trip and vowed to return every year.

~~~~~~~

My habit when I was back in New York was to take the train downtown and wander around the city by myself. New York City is a feast for the senses, both good and bad. So of course after a weekend of rest in the Bronx, on Monday I took the subway into Manhattan. I started out in Greenwich Village, my old stomping grounds. Then I walked a few miles uptown to Central Park and hung out on one of the park benches to observe all the passersby. It was a day of noticing new trends in fashion and remembering old times. Spring is a time when New Yorkers gleefully emerge from their cold winter hibernation, feeling their way along sunny sidewalks.

From my journal:

The normally dirty streets of New York City somehow seemed clean today. People running to and fro, pushing racks of clothing through the garment district, and popping in and out of delicatessens with lunch bags. They finally emerge from their stuffy heated apartments into the pleasant spring air. Lifeless concrete everywhere with occasional statues of important people. Walking through Port Authority I saw an old woman sitting alone on a bench. She looked as if she'd slept on the streets all winter. The closeness of the air inside, and the state of her madness, was too much for her. I stood there for a while watching paramedics lift her onto a gurney and wheel her out of the building. I wanted to cry. I wondered if she ever experienced the mountains and streams of the country. I wished she could have spent her last days in fresh air, walking on green grass, but I knew it was not where they were taking her.

I visited my aunts and uncles, even if it was just for cake and coffee. I realized how much I missed them all. My cousin Jenny was older now, in her twenties, with a boyfriend of her own. I didn't know much about her because she was among the youngest of my cousins. She invited me to go bar hopping with her on Long Island. We went from bar to bar doing shots of tequila with soda chasers.

"I remember going to Queens dancing when I was a teenager," I said.

Jenny downed a shot of tequila, took out a pack of Virginia Slims, and lit one.

"Jenny," I said, surprised. "I didn't know you smoked."

"I don't smoke in front of my parents, so they don't know."

Yeah right! I thought. I remembered her mother, my aunt Camille, telling me that my uncle Pietro smoked in the bathroom with the window opened and assumed she didn't know about it.

"Jenny, you know I had a terrible experience at a bar in Queens when I was in high school."

She looked at my face with intense anticipation. "I'm all ears."

"It's a crazy story. A friend fixed me up with a Russian guy named Gerry, who turned out to be a psycho. We went on a double date, and the four of us drove to Queens. The guy was barking at a dog in a car outside a diner, where we'd stopped for a bite. I should have left then!"

"He sounds like a nut job," Jenny said.

I nodded and continued. "At the bar in Queens, he got totally trashed. He threw a drink at me when I told him I was taking a cab home. My friend had given me cash, but Gerry wouldn't hear of it and insisted on taking me home. I still can't figure out what made me get back in his car. The car was going about a hundred miles an hour on the freeway. I had my heart in my mouth. The other couple in the backseat were afraid of him too and sat frozen, not uttering a word. Gerry said the car needed gas, so he eased off an exit. But instead of pulling up to the pumps at the gas station, he was backing up to the entrance to a motel. I thought, *I'm a virgin, and I'm not giving myself up to this maniac.* I opened the car door and tumbled out while it was still moving. He tried to run me down. I ran into the gas station where I saw a mechanic working on a car. I asked for the phone.

While I was calling 911, Gerry appeared behind me, threatening to smash the phone through my skull. For some stupid reason, perhaps immediate fear of my life, I got back in the car. I was shaking like a leaf, but soon I became defiant and refused to let him terrify me. We drove for a long time in silence, my heart beating out of my chest."

"Jesus Christ, Adriana!"

"Believe me, I could have used Jesus Christ that night. I suppose he was watching over me."

I continued. "I could tell by the scenery outside the car window that we were back in the Bronx. Gerry slowed down and parked the car near a swamp. I thought, *This is it. I'm going to be raped and murdered.* To my relief, he just had to pee. He got back in the driver's seat and drove along the back roads to my neighborhood.

"He parked in front of my apartment house, grabbed my hand, and said, 'I've never met a woman like you before. You've got some balls to stand up to me. I want to see you again.' I pulled my hand back from his grip and jumped out of the car, leaving the door wide open. 'Not if you were the last man on earth!' I yelled back, and ran into the building."

"I leaned on the buzzer in the vestibule until my father came down the stairs in his pajamas. Gerry saw my father, pulled the car door shut, and drove off. My dad hugged me with a relieved expression on his face. He didn't ask questions, just put his arm around me and walked me upstairs."

Jenny stared at me. "God, you were so lucky. Just think of what could have happened to you."

"I know, but I wonder how many other women weren't so lucky."

Jenny and I continued drinking and trading stories until the loud music began to get on our nerves. Well, we'd also had enough tequila by then.

"Let's get together again before you go back to Hawaii," she said.

"I look forward to that, Jenny."

We did another shot of tequila and walked out to Donna Summer's new song, "Hot Stuff."

~~~~~~~~

My cousin Jeremy, my uncle Red's son, called our house from the thruway. He was a big rig trucker. He'd often stop by to see my parents when his haul took him through the Bronx on the I-95. He knew I was in town and wanted to see me. We got a big kick out of watching him park that truck, which took up half a city block. My mother made coffee while we talked in the dining room. He was married with a few kids already. Jeremy and I reminisced about how we double dated when we were teenagers, and all the trouble we got into.

"Jeremy, whatever happened to Jude Walker, that English friend of yours I dated for a while?"

"He doesn't live that far from Grandma's house in Bensonhurst," Jeremy answered.

"He always reminded me of a young Anthony Quinn, with his dark hair and eyes."

"We're still friends," Jeremy said. "We even go to Coney Island once in a while."

"Really? The next time you see Jude, please say hello for me."

I flashed on the night I was giving Jude Walker a blow job in the dark on the grass in Pelham Bay Park. We were both teenagers. We never had intercourse, but we did everything else. I'd heard a rustling in the bushes behind us. I looked up and noticed a man's legs and saw two piercing eyes. I whispered in Jude's ear, "When I count to three, get up and run. There's a man watching us." I snickered at the memory but realized the story wasn't appropriate in present company.

<hr>

My mother and I looked forward to Sunday nights, when we were glued to the television watching *Mystery* on PBS's Masterpiece Theater. I still think of those days when I hear the Masterpiece Hour theme song. We'd sit on the couch together and sometimes talk about that particular episode. Occasionally, we'd laugh or cry, depending on the storyline. That show was one of the things my mother and I actually bonded with. I had the feeling that she spoke with her sisters before I arrived, to make sure that my cousins took me places so I would feel at home again. However, by that point in my life, Hawaii had become my home.

My cousin Rory, one of Jenny's older brothers, invited me out for a sail on his boat, which was docked on City Island. We drove over the little bridge that connects the Bronx to City Island. This tiny strip of land which juts out into the Long Island Sound, is filled with seafood restaurants, quaint houses, art studios, and cafés. My mother had a friend whose house resembled an Italian villa right on the sound. I loved going there.

Rory and I stopped in the Black Whale café for a cappuccino and pastries. I thought of my trips to City Island as a teenager with my boyfriend, Ronny Donnelly. He introduced me to oysters. I remember trying to swallow one, gagging, and spitting it out. When we got to the dock, Rory told me he named his boat the Pinocchio because it was made of wood. We had a relaxing day out on the water. The weather was unusually mild and sunny for spring on the East Coast. We glided back to shore as the sun was setting.

PENCIL SKETCH OF THE PINOCCHIO

"Let's hang out at my apartment," Rory said, docking the boat.

"Okay, and anyway, I haven't seen your place yet."

"It's not far from where your parents live," he said.

We walked into the vestibule of his apartment house, which overlooked the I-95, with a snippet of Pelham Bay Park visible. I remember hearing the steady flow of traffic from his apartment, which was pretty high up in the building. Sitting in the corner of his living room was my father's barber chair, which gave me a start.

"Your father gave me one of the barber chairs when he retired and closed his shop."

"I'm so glad you have it, Rory. There are a lot of memories in that chair."

Rory opened a bottle of red wine, and we sat on the floor around the coffee table catching up about our lives. Rory was a dead ringer for his dad, Pietro. We laughed about all the times I slept at their house when we were kids. How they once took me to midnight Mass when we spent Christmas at my aunt Camille's. On that same Christmas Eve, my cousins took me to a grotto on the church grounds. All I remember about it was seeing the statue of martyred St. Lucy lying on a slab holding a plate with her eyeballs, which had been plucked out. I had nightmares about that for weeks. We laughed about the time we had Christmas at Aunt Porciella's and Gia's father, Faustino, drank nearly a whole gallon of red Gallo wine and wanted to jump out of the third-floor window. Faustino was a construction worker and as strong as a bull. It took three of my uncles to hold him back.

〰〰〰

I called my friend Adam Hirschfeld and told him I was in New York for a month. He mentioned he was coming to the city for a few days. A week later he called me from an apartment in the East Village where he was staying. He mentioned that Big Mama Thornton was appearing at a small club in town, and that we should go to the concert.

We met in the Village and had something to eat at a popular falafel place on the Lower East Side, and then headed to the club. I loved Willie May Thornton's gruff singing style of rhythm and blues and had always wanted to see her in person. It was a very small club, so we were close to the stage. It all started out great with her singing a few blues songs but deteriorated into chaos when she chased the drummer off the stage and sat at the drums, banging away. She seemed to be under the influence of something. The concert ended when she got up, walked off the stage, and didn't return.

I said, "At least we got to hear one of the songs she wrote, 'Ball and Chain,' before she faded."

Adam and I were disappointed about the abrupt end to the concert. We walked to the Ninth Circle in the West Village for a beer. We did not discuss Dominick French, or that crazy threesome we had back on Maui when Adam visited.

It was always good to connect with Adam. He was meeting a friend for a late dinner, so we hugged and kissed goodbye. I headed to the Eighth Street subway station, and Adam walked in the opposite direction.

~~~~~~

My father, Andre's, routine on Sundays was to walk to the park and sit on the rocks by the Pelham Bay Lagoon. It was a fabulously sunny day, and I went with him. When we reached the shore, my father rested his cane against the rocks and sat. I left him there to walk along the beach. There was litter all over the sand, and the lagoon looked polluted. I combed the sand looking for seashells and noticed a rag covered in black tar. When I gazed across the lagoon I saw oil slick on the surface from a wreckage not far offshore. Children played on the beach that was filled with debris. I was reminded of how pristine the water and the beaches in Hawaii were. I had a pang of missing Maui.

On our way back through the park we ran into my uncle Pietro. He was playing cards with a group of men on one of the stone tables.

Pietro stood up and hugged me. "Good to see you again, Adriana. Are you here to stay?"

"No, I'm here on vacation. Uncle Pietro, remember when we had family barbeques here?"

"Oh yeah. Me and your other uncles would drive here in the middle of the night on a Saturday and sleep on the picnic tables to secure a large area for our Sunday three-family picnics."

"Yeah, those were the days," I said, smiling at the precious memory.

My father interrupted. "Adriana, your mother is cooking, and she's waiting for us."

My father and I said our goodbyes to the men. Sunday dinner was a big thing in those days.

I spent one of my last few days in New York roaming around Manhattan, rummaging in the secondhand stores for treasures. I checked out the art supply stores to stock up on paints and brushes. The enormous selection of art supplies was unparalleled. I planned to pack everything up and mail a couple of boxes back to Hawaii. It began to rain. Not a heavy rain, just a mist that blanketed the city streets as I wandered around.

From my journal:

The city is wet but strangely pleasant. Stylish men and
fine women cruising everywhere. There's always a feeling
of radicalism here. Even though its residents are from so
many different cultures, there's a feeling of togetherness.
Nobody dares back down from a fight. It's what made
me strong. My mind rests here in familiarity, yet it fills
my heart with turbulence. It excites me and revolts me.
Time, the all-encompassing concept. Time marches on,
but New York is still inside me.

My cousin Jenny called to tell me that Eubie Blake was playing at a
club in Greenwich Village. I knew he was a very old man and a master of
ragtime on the piano. I didn't want to miss the opportunity to see him in
person while he was still around. My vacation was winding down, and I
wanted to make the most of my last week in New York.

Jenny picked me up and we drove into the city. The club was a converted
restaurant. Eubie Blake was a treasure. As he played, I had 1920s images of
black and white women shaking the fringe on their flapper dresses. I saw
marcel waves, crystal-studded headpieces, dark-red lipstick, and Dominick
French's smile.

We talked on the car ride back to the Bronx, knowing it would be a long
time until we'd see each other again. Jenny dropped me off in front of my
parents' apartment house. We hugged in the chilly night air. She waved at
me as she got back in her car and drove away.

I thought about the concept of home. What is it? Is home with your
family, close friends, a lover, the place you were born, or the place you are
most at peace?

A few days before I was to leave, I mailed two boxes of art supplies
and clothing back to Hawaii. The last two nights I spent with my parents
enjoying their company. It was always difficult to leave them, but there was
comfort in the fact that I would return each year. On the way to LaGuardia
Airport I stared at the Virgin Mary on the dashboard.

From my journal:

The importance of blood relations is realized. A lifetime
of intricacies in every moment. There exists an unspoken

natural bond, devoid of change with the passage of time. For those who understand the meaning of family, roots, beginnings, familiarity, endless interest, and nurturing. A constant knowledge that we are not alone in the world. The ability to always return.

The plane ride back to Hawaii was a blur. Thoughts of the family and friends I was leaving behind, and anticipation of the family and friends I would be with very soon filled my head. I often wondered how people who traveled for a living dealt with that dichotomy. It probably explains how some traveling salesmen found it easy to establish a family or love interest in each city. I never found the process easy over the years, and looking back, I certainly understand my confusion.

As the plane circled the airport, my feelings were mixed between excitement and relief.

I spotted Ginger Pie Turner at the baggage claim at Kahului Airport. We broke out in smiles as we walked toward each other. She put a fragrant plumeria lei around my neck, and I was home. The Maui air caressed me and I breathed it in deeply.

"How was your trip?"

"It was wonderful to spend time with my family, and I got to do all the New York things I love."

"Well, nothing's changed here on the rock," she said, tilting her head to the side.

"Have you seen Demo?"

"I ran into him in town the other day, but I haven't been to the Mission since you left. He asked when you were coming home."

"I'll keep my distance for a few days," I said.

"Then he'll wonder why you stayed away."

"I don't want to seem eager."

"Men take advantage when you show your hand," Pie said.

"I've never been good at breasting my cards," I said, and we both laughed.

~~~~~~

Annie Hughes was working the counter at the Crafty Mermaid on my first day back at work. She clued me in on all the things that happened while

I was gone without making me feel like I'd missed it all. I told her how my mom raved about the great time she had on Maui, and how much she enjoyed spending time with her. Annie was happy to hear it.

We decided to go to the Missionaries Hotel on Friday night.

"Demo missed you," she said.

I smiled but didn't answer. I'd made up my mind that I needed more than what I had with Dominick French.

Pie and I took a walk around the neighborhood that Friday evening with scissors. We clipped a bunch of gardenias and carried them home. Their aroma was phenomenal. I put one gardenia in my hair for the evening and the rest in jars for the house.

When it got dark, we drove to the Missionaries Hotel. Pie was telling me how much she missed me while I was gone. I knew exactly how she felt; I felt the same way.

We found Annie sitting with a couple of guys in the Mission Bar at a table next to the piano. She'd saved two seats for us. Demo began playing "Exactly Like You" without even turning around. I figured Annie must have signaled him in some way that I'd shown up.

Annie introduced us to the two guys sitting at the table. She said, "I picked them up at the bar in Kimo's."

Ginger Pie and I rolled our eyes. The guys asked us what we wanted to drink, and before we knew it, the drinks were sitting in front of us.

When Demo took a break, he didn't even come to our table to say hello. I felt let down and wondered if it would be a night I would be ignored. I got up from the table, annoyed, tore the gardenia from my hair, tossed it in his tip jar, and walked out with Pie.

Demo came after me and tugged at my arm. "Wait for me; this is my last set."

I walked back inside with him.

The two guys at our table sitting with Annie stared at me, wondering what that was all about. I didn't mention Demo being my boyfriend. "I know him very well," I said as I sat back down at the table.

The two guys traded suspicious glances while gulping their drinks.

When the music was over for the night, Annie left for Le Toots with the two guys.

Demo walked over and sat on the empty chair next to mine. "I want to hear all about your trip to New York. Let's go to my house."

Pie stood up, smiled at me, said goodnight to Demo, and walked out of the bar.

I drove my own car to Demo's house. I had to work the next day and would have to drive back home in the morning, to shower and change for work.

〜〜〜〜

Demo was already home when I arrived, sitting on the couch in his living room.

"Where's Kona?" I asked.

"He wasn't around when I got home, but I'm sure he's okay."

I walked straight to the kitchen to get a glass of water.

"Best ass in town?" Demo said, smiling as I walked past him.

I sat next to him on the couch and told him about my trip, my parents, their cats, and some of the things I did while I was in New York. I touched my sheer green and white striped blouse and told him that I found it in a secondhand store in Greenwich Village.

"You're a regular Secondhand Rose. Remind me to sing that song for you the next time you're at the Mission," he said, shaking his head and snickering.

I felt a little shy. It had been more than a month since we slept together, which I imagined was coming. We were silent for a while.

"I saw Adam while I was New York," I said to break the ice. Then I thought, *That probably wasn't the best thing to say.*

"Really?" he said, but didn't ask me for any details.

"We went to see Big Mama Thornton in Manhattan." I told him how she sat at the drums and played and then walked off the stage and never returned.

Suddenly there was a car horn. Demo got up and went to the porch to see who it was.

I followed him.

"Kona jumped in the back window when I stopped in front of the Broiler," Annie said.

"Thanks for bringing him home," Demo said.

We walked back into the house, and I delighted in the familiar sound of the screen door slamming. Demo fed Kona in the kitchen, and all seemed right with the world.

He ran his finger across my mouth and said, "Oh how I've missed those lips," and kissed me.

We walked to his bedroom together, and I felt the salty breeze from the ocean drift in the windows. We got undressed and climbed into bed. I closed my eyes and listened to the waves as what I had anticipated was about to happen.

In those days, there was a movie theater in Kaanapali. We went to see *Alien* on Demo's next night off. It was a bit terrifying, even though I knew it was just a movie. I remember burying my face in his chest when that alien offspring tore its way out of the man's body.

We stopped for a drink at a restaurant in one of the hotels on Kaanapali Beach, and then drove back to his place. We were playing house again, and I was hanging out with him on his nights off. He talked about going to Europe in the summer again, which made me queasy.

"Oh you're coming with me this time, I promise," he said.

I believed him and began to get excited and plan what clothes I was going to pack. While he was talking, I looked around the house that Annie had so meticulously cleaned, organized, and decorated, and noticed it was deteriorating into junk status again. The only remnant from her refurbishment was the coin-operated carnival camel sitting in the corner of the living room.

It was the end of May, and I had thoughts of starting my own hand-painted clothing business. The ladies of the Crafty Mermaid said they'd sell my designs in the shop. Anything hand painted flew off the racks. This gave me artistic motivation, and I figured it would be a creative way to make extra money. I thought, *I'll get serious about this when Demo and I get back from Europe.* I would start small with hand-painted T-shirts and cover-ups. I would have to find a wholesale outlet for white T-shirts. I figured I could even tie-dye them, which was still popular, and add a tropical flower or palm tree here or there. It was definitely a thought process at that moment in time.

~~~~~~

My birthday was in the first week of July. Annie, Pie, Loretta, and I planned a night out on the town ending up at the Mission Bar. We went out to dinner together. I had stacks of leis around my neck, and gifts to open. Everywhere we went, people were buying me birthday drinks, so by the time we arrived at the Mission Bar I was pretty twisted and anticipating a joyous end to the evening. We ordered drinks and my mood was festive. I waited to hear my song, but that never happened.

Demo called Annie up to the piano to sing as I sat there in a daze at being ignored. She sang a few of her favorite torch songs, "Poor Butterfly" by John Lionel Golden being one. She liked taking the microphone around to each table to sing to individual people. She must have noticed the downhearted expression on my face, because she stood in front of me and sang the lyrics directly to me.

As the night wore on I sat there shocked, numb, and angry, but mostly hurt. The lyrics to "Poor Butterfly" played over and over in my head. Pie and Loretta were pissed off at Demo's slight on my special day and walked out. I stayed until the bitter end with Annie. Perhaps I thought he'd cozy up to me at the end of the night, like he often did. I even attempted to talk to him, but he put his finger to his lips and shushed me. When Demo finished his last set, he got up from the piano and walked right past me and out of the Missionaries Hotel without a word.

Annie and I got up and walked outside the hotel and saw that his Corvette was already gone. I tore the leis off my neck, threw them on the ground, and began to bawl.

Annie put her arm around my shoulder and said, "Come on, Riana, you're coming home with me tonight."

We walked along the seawall, and even though the moon was beautiful and the surf was loud, I took no joy in either. I was crushed. *Why would he do such a cruel thing to me?* I couldn't figure it out. *What had I done wrong?*

I walked up the staircase to Annie's apartment in a daze. Once inside I couldn't hold back the deluge and broke down crying uncontrollably.

Annie held me in her arms and tried to comfort me. "You're in love with him, but he's not in love with you."

"He enjoys being cruel," I blithered through tears. "Cruel!"

I remember Annie holding me, rocking back and forth, singing "Poor Butterfly" while I cried.

From my journal:

A lei of carnations, a trail of drinks, and gifts from friends and strangers, but nothing from you. Not a glance in my direction, not even my favorite song. You enjoy being cruel. You brushed me off like dust on an old wooden table. All I wanted was to lie peacefully in your arms and fall asleep to the sound of the waves. I am no more than dust. My thirty-second birthday.

I functioned like a zombie for the next week. Work filled my days, and I was thankful for that. In the evenings I hung around at home with the girls. I returned none of Demo's phone calls. I figured out what that whole birthday fiasco was all about. He was going to Europe and he wasn't taking me. It was all too much for me to bear. I didn't know what I really meant to him. He wanted me, but he wanted his freedom. Maybe Annie was right. I was in love with him, but he wasn't in love with me! I couldn't erase her words from my brain.

On Saturday, Ginger Pie suggested we go to Sheila's Junkatique in Wailuku and spend the day rummaging around. "We'll bring our bathing suits and stop for a swim on our way back," she said.

Pie tried her best to cheer me up that day. She gave me the women's pep talk regarding men and relationships. Everything she said made sense, but none of it helped my state of mind. I thought that maybe when Demo left for Europe I'd have an easier time putting it all behind me. We had fun at the Junkatique and sat in a café on Market Street drinking chai tea and eating scones. Sweets always had a way of making me feel better. On the way home we stopped along the side of the road and parked at the beach. Even in the midst of all the beauty around me, I was still down in the dumps.

We got into our bathing suits and waded out into the ocean. It was remarkable how the elements were able to lift my spirits, even if only momentarily.

~~~~~

Dominick French left for Europe that summer. We reconnected after my birthday, but things were never the same. His leaving for Europe without me again, and the events over the past few months, changed my mind-set. I remember sitting on his couch with Bessie Waters on the day he left. He walked out the door with his suitcase, and I heard that screen door slam for the last time. I began to sob like someone who saw her puppy get run over by a car.

Bessie held me and let me cry. "He'll be back," she said softly.

But my crying wasn't for him, it was for love lost. I let myself be hurt, humiliated, and treated badly. That relationship was over! I put my love and faith in someone who couldn't return it, and everyone knows that unrequited love's a bore.

From my journal:

When everything beautiful turns ugly, and kisses once frosted with gold feel like dirty ice, I have to wonder what it all meant. There's a light in the darkness, and someone is listening who understands you, and you're no longer alone. Then it all changes and your every word drifts up into the clouds, unheard. You try to hold on to them, but the words slip through your fingers. I gaze at a jewelry box from China, and an antique silk purse embroidered with roosters and feathers. A queasy feeling in the pit of my stomach reeks of fear and loneliness that even paradise can't cure. Fresh flowers are replaced with crushed, dry petals, and the smell makes me sick. I miss you. I am lost. I laugh, I cry. I am angry at life and the loss of love.

FOURTEEN
TWO PEAS IN A POD

From my journal:

I have a vision of a time when women were goddesses
that existed in a heaven on earth, much like the ancient
worlds of strong maidens and equal men. How wonderful
it must have been to love a man as an equal, to occupy
oneself with the beauty and abundance of the earth. To
walk calmly and proudly, just as any other animal on its
way through life from beginning to end.

G inger Pie Turner suggested a trip to Honolulu for a few days to cheer
me up. "It will take your mind off Demo," she said.

I was definitely hanging out in the doom and gloom corner of life.
We shared a room at the Ala Moana Hotel and made use of the ramp on
the second floor that went straight to Liberty House. We arrived early in
the morning, too early to check into our hotel room, but were able to leave
our bags with the bellman for a few dollars. We had breakfast in the mall
and separated to shop our favorite stores. I wondered what it was about
shopping that lifted a woman's spirits. It certainly lifted mine.

We rented a car the next day and drove to the North Shore to watch
the surfers ride the big waves. The North Shore of Oahu is famous for huge
waves. It's where worldwide surfing competitions are held.

We parked on the side of the road and walked to the beach with our
cameras. There were locals and tourists alike lining the shore watching
the wave riders. It was quite a thrill. There was a contest named after

Duke Kahanamoku, also known in Hawaii as the father of surfing. He was famous when longboards were popular in the early 1900s. I'd seen old photographs of him with other surfers, standing on the beach with their longboards. They were known as the original Beach Boys of Waikiki.

"You know, Pie, the Duke won three Olympic gold medals in swimming for the USA in 1912, in Sweden. Hawaii was still a kingdom at the time."

Pie looked at me for further explanation.

"Hawaii wasn't a state yet."

We took lots of photos on that trip, which I still have. The fog of gloom seemed to lift from around my head with each passing day.

On the way back from the North Shore of Oahu, we stopped at a botanical garden. There were paths you could walk along through a variety of Hawaii's flora. It was such a magical place to get lost in for an hour or so, amid exotic trees and flowers. We passed the replica of a primitive hut with a history plaque about ancient Hawaii.

We ended up back at the shopping center later that day and got drunk at one of the bars. Looking back, drinking seemed to take the place of drugs. That night we hit the discotheque on the top floor of the hotel, and I wondered why I never went up there on all those shopping trips with Annie Hughes. We danced and drank until the wee hours of the morning. Ginger Pie and I never had a fight or disagreement. We were like two peas in a pod, as she often said.

On our last day in Honolulu, we explored Chinatown, with orange glazed ducks hanging in storefront windows and unfamiliar, odd-shaped vegetables in baskets outside on the street. We had lunch at our favorite restaurant, Hong Lo, and then stumbled upon a Chinese clothing import store. Ginger Pie bought a yellow satin brocade blouse with black frogs down the front. I found a long Chinese mandarin dress in ice blue, with deep slits up each side. I couldn't resist a short black silk robe with a red dragon embroidered on the back, so I bought that too. We played dress up and show and tell when we got back to the hotel room. Before taking the plane back to Maui, we had pu pus and drinks at one of the restaurants in the Honolulu airport.

~~~~~

I had a day off and was at home in a very creative mood. I had gone to the public library and signed out a book on Gauguin. I fished through the pages of his paintings and read some of the text on his concept regarding art. Sometimes I liked to do that before I set my brush to a blank canvas.

I read, "Work freely and madly, and you will make progress. A great emotion can be transmitted immediately, and look for its simplest form." His words always inspired me, and the colors he used set my mind on fire with all sorts of images.

As I was working on the painting the telephone rang. It was my cousin Terry in New York, my Aunt Camille's youngest son. He was a doctor serving as an intern in a prominent hospital in New York City.

The ocean needs to be more aqua, I thought, staring at the painting as I listened to him on the phone.

"I'm coming for a visit," Terry said.

"Our roommate Malia will be on the mainland, so you could stay in her room," I said.

Someone always seemed to be visiting, moving out, moving in, or moving back to the mainland. Hawaii could be very transient. It's not an easy place to live when you consider its remoteness on the planet. Not everyone is prepared for life on a small island. You have to get used to being without some of your favorite things, losing friends, and missing people.

After hanging up with Terry, I went back to painting. I was listening to the radio when I heard the song "Dust in the Wind" by Kansas. Suddenly I was drawn back to a place of sadness and loss, thinking of Demo. I wondered where he was in Europe and if he ever even thought of me. I was angry with myself for hanging on to his promise of taking me to Europe with him. When it came to love, I tended to hang on to people's words more than their actions. As time went by, his words got watered down, and his actions never followed through. I had a momentary lapse of missing him. Picking up the paintbrush again, he slipped from my mind.

I decided to consult the I Ching for its wisdom going forward. The trigram I received after tossing the three Chinese coins was "inner truth."

From the *I Ching: The Chinese Book of Changes*:

"Trigram #61, Inner Truth: from the line nine at the top in the image: The cock is dependable. It crows at dawn. But it cannot itself fly to heaven. It just crows. A man may count on mere words to awaken faith. This may succeed now and then, but if persisted in, it will have bad consequences."

There was a sliding window that separated my bedroom from Loretta's garage studio apartment. She kept it covered with an Indonesian bedspread on her side. I had the Native American blanket I purchased in Santa Fe covering my side. I was trying to fall asleep one night and having a pleasant flashback of Navajo Tommy when I heard Loretta arguing with someone. I figured she dragged some guy home from the restaurant she worked in.

"I won't kill an innocent creature. It's only a centipede!" I heard the guy say.

That really pissed Loretta off, and she went ballistic, yelling, "Kill it, kill it!"

I stared at the can of bug spray on my dresser, wondering, *Should I do it?* I leaped up, grabbed the can, pulled aside the blanket, opened the window, and shoved the can through. Everything went silent, and all that could be heard was the hiss of the bug spray.

The guy began to freak out, yelling, "What are you doing?"

I heard Loretta say, "Time for you to go home, and take that disgusting insect with you."

After the guy left, we had a good laugh about it.

"Loretta, you can keep the bug spray," I said, closing the window.

I lay down and stared at the blanket. *Now where was I with Navajo Tommy?*

Speaking about that strategic window, it got me out of a scary situation once. I got drunk at the Yacht Club and dragged a tennis pro home. He was a really hot guy with a great physique. We had dinner at the club and he was very charming, disguising himself as a gentleman. We were enjoying each other's company when the numerous gin and tonics I downed clouded my judgement. He later morphed into a cad, and sex wasn't enough for him. He was out of control and began tossing me around and bouncing himself off the walls of my bedroom.

Loretta was woken up by the racket and stuck her head through the window, yelling, "What's going on in there?"

Thank God she did. The guy quickly gathered up his clothes, and ran for the front door.

Ginger Pie and I went to a Bob Marley music event on the other side of the island. It combined reggae music with ballet and modern dance. Cultural events such as these didn't come to Maui often enough in those days. Bob Marley was super, and the whole experience was like living art. On the drive home I was filled with artistic inspiration.

Toward the end of the week, Annie and I went to the Waterworks for drinks. We sat at the bar avoiding the elephant in the room, Dominick French. I knew how fond she was of him, and I knew she loved me like a daughter, so I didn't want to get into that sandbox with her. I was trying to avoid it turning into a pit of snakes, but alas, it couldn't be avoided.

"Have you heard from Demo since he left?"

"No, I haven't. But I wasn't expecting a call from him after the way we left it off."

"Demo can be selfish, and he likes his space," Annie said.

"He strung me along again, promising to take me to Europe with him."

"Riana, love doesn't have to be perfect. Give the guy a chance."

"There are so many things you don't know, too much to tell."

"Think about what you're throwing overboard."

"I've already walked the plank a few times over the past two years."

"Relationships take time and patience," Annie insisted.

People don't change, and nobody learns anything, I thought.

"I don't foresee things changing," I said, taking another sip of my drink.

I sat there hoping she wasn't taking his side in all this; after all, she had encouraged me all along. I knew I still had feelings for him, but that didn't mean I wanted the relationship anymore.

"Whatever happens, we'll always be friends," Annie said.

I lifted my glass and faced her. She did the same, and we clanked our drinks together.

~~~~~~

The next time Ginger Pie and I had a day off together, we went to Iao Valley State Park. We wanted to go swimming in the Iao River and check out what flora was in bloom. We headed out in the Gray Mouse with our cameras and bathing suits. The state park was filled with tourists, but we knew a path that would take us to a secluded area. I heard the waterfall in the distance as we walked along the path. The trail opened to a valley with a rocky pool fed by a waterfall. I imagined I was in the Garden of Eden. There were bushes of pink shell ginger drooping down like grapes on a vine, and red torch ginger with little yellow spikes. The aroma was heavenly.

We stripped down and didn't bother with our bathing suits, since no one was around. The water was heavenly as it bubbled and rushed around us.

"Like two peas in a pod we are," Pie said.

"I feel like Isis at the dawn of civilization," I said, splashing her.

IAO VALLEY

We floated on our backs for a while, silently taking in the beauty. I especially enjoyed the sound of rushing water from the fall, and I saw little fish below the surface. After spending half an hour or so swimming around nude in the rocky pool, we climbed up on the rocks.

"I forgot to take towels when we left the house," Pie said.

"No need, let's just lie here in the sun."

I listened to the chattering myna birds, who somehow found our secret hideaway. When we had our fill, we got dressed and walked back to the main area of the park.

"Can you drive home, Pie?"

"Sure," she said. "Tell me what you know about the goddess Isis."

"Well, she was considered the universal mother to the Egyptians. I know that Isis was goddess of the moon, affecting health, marriage, and fertility," I said drowsily from the passenger seat.

"Didn't she have some kind of power?"

"She was considered a healer, supposedly could cast spells and resurrect the dead."

"That's a lot of power," Pie said, laughing.

Soon I dozed off into a pleasant sleep as we drove over the Pali.

~~~~~~

Ginger Pie's family came to Maui for a visit. They stayed at a hotel in Kaanapali. Pie wanted to treat them to all the popular tourist attractions. Her family invited me to tag along on their excursions. The luau was fantastic; it always impressed. There were free leis and mai tais for everyone. They marveled at the pig being dug out of the ground that later was the kalua pork on their plates. I didn't tell them that it wasn't the same pig that just came out of the *imu* (pit). It would have ruined their experience.

Even though it wasn't whale season, we decided to take her family on a sunset cruise. A day out on the ocean is always rejuvenating, and the view of Lahaina with the West Maui Mountains as a backdrop is always impressive. As the sun set, I became aware of a couple at the bow of the boat. They were enjoying the view and the sea air. The trades always picked up at sunset, probably something to do with gravity as the sun dips below the horizon. Their togetherness made me feel loneliness, yet I was glued to their image.

From my journal:

I saw a man and woman at the bow of the boat, their blond hair tangled together in the trade winds like butterscotch in a Botticelli painting. They were clutching each other in a warm embrace. One could tell they were in the magical throes of their relationship, when everything has a glow. As they laughed and drank profusely, I wondered, sadly, if what they were feeling that day would fade. But on that day, what they were experiencing was profound and beautiful. Will I ever feel that way again?

Pie's mother rented a cabin at Wainapanapa State Park in Hana. The ride along that winding road was long and full of tropical photo-ops. We stopped at the iconic Hasegawa's General Store for local snacks. We investigated just about every waterfall, and walked into the bamboo forest. Pie's mom had to pee really badly while we were driving, so we pulled over to the side of the road when the traffic stopped. She squatted in the grass and peed. Suddenly a tour bus appeared out of nowhere and caught her midstream, and we all had a good laugh.

The cabin had bunkbeds and all the necessities, including a stove, so we cooked our own meals. We saw a couple of those loathsome centipedes wriggling outside in the grass, but vowed to not let them ruin the weekend. Pie and her sister took a hike in the surrounding mountains and returned to the cabin with magic mushrooms. I watched them eat the mushrooms, very daintily, with peanut butter. I did not participate. I wasn't in a psychedelic state of mind. It was obvious to me that Pie was ecstatic to be with her family, and I knew she'd miss them when they went home.

Pie seemed a little strange after her family went back to the mainland. She had a close connection with her siblings. It must have given her a feeling of being blanketed with love and security. Being an only child, I didn't have that. I did feel something similar with the members of the commune, well, with the people I was closest to. At first I didn't dwell on it, but I did see a definite change in her.

～～～～～

The Preservation Hall Dixieland Jazz Band came to Maui. I had seen them when I passed through New Orleans with the O'Brien sisters. I thought it was a weird twist of fate that they were in the islands while Dominick French was somewhere floating around the jazz clubs in Europe.

Pie and I went to the concert, which was at the tennis stadium in Kaanapali. It was a large venue, so it wasn't anything like seeing them, as I did, in a small club on Bourbon Street. All through the concert I had intense flashes of Demo. I felt his presence, almost as if he was there with me. There was a dance floor set up in front of the stage. I looked up and saw Buddy and Betty French gliding along the dance floor, and emotion overwhelmed me. At the end of the concert, the band had everyone on their feet, encouraging us all to dance. People actually formed a conga line, like you'd see at a wedding reception. The line weaved in and out of the seats, past the stage, and up the aisles. It was quite a grand finale. I went home missing Demo that night. Thinking back, I was always missing him.

~~~~~

That summer, the Gray Mouse was acting up. *Could I possibly take anything else going wrong?* I thought. Loretta told me about the Quonset hut at the cannery in Lahaina. (A small shopping mall with a Safeway, a CVS, and other shops occupy that area now.)

Loretta said, "There's a bunch of mechanics there. That's where I always take my car."

I drove down to the cannery and looked for the repair shop. There were a bunch of guys standing around talking. They watched me get out of my car with intense interest. They looked at me and then looked at each other. I imagine they were jockeying for position as to who was going to deal with me.

One of them, a tall guy with straggly, dirty blond hair under a Mopar cap walked over to me. "Something wrong with your Datsun?"

"Yeah, it just feels like its running rough."

I heard the other guys snickering in the background.

"We can check it out, but it will cost ya," the guy said, with a smirky smile.

"I wasn't expecting anything for free," I answered.

An older man walked out of the back of the shop, and from his demeanor I got the impression he was the owner or manager. His name tag read Ron. "What seems to be the problem with the car?"

I repeated the statement about it running rough.

Without any comment, and a stony expression on his face, he walked around and lifted the hood. "When was the last time you had this car serviced?"

"I can't remember," I said, feeling dumb.

"You'll have to leave the car with us so we can check everything out."

"That's all right. I can walk to work from here," I said.

I was in foreign territory as I followed him to the office. I had absolutely no knowledge of car engines and felt totally out of control. He had me sign a work order, gave me a copy, and held his hand out for my car key, never once cracking a smile.

I walked out of the Quonset hut hoping the bill wouldn't be exorbitant. Women always feel like they're being taken for a ride when they walk into a car repair shop without a man. It's just a fact of life. The guys were still watching me with interest as I walked out.

It was like a scene out of a Hunter S. Thompson novel:

> There is no way to explain the terror I felt when I finally lunged up to the clerk and began babbling. All of my well-rehearsed lines fell apart under that woman's stoney glare. "Hi there," I said. My name is....ah, Raoul Duke......I have my attorney with me....We brought this Red Shark all the way from the strip and now it's time for desert, right? ....The woman never blinked. *Fear and Loathing in Las Vegas*

I didn't hear anything back from Ron at the repair shop all day, so I had Hannah drive me to the cannery after work. The mechanics saw me get out of her car and watched me walk into the shop. The same blond guy approached me. I took a closer look at him this time. He had a large scar down the right side of his face, but was very handsome, and for me, the scar only added to his attractiveness.

"Your car needed a tune-up really bad. I changed the oil and tidied things up under the hood."

"Is this going to be expensive?" I asked.

"You'll have to talk to Ron about that," he said. "Why don't you go to the office? He's in there."

I thanked him, smiled, and walked to the office. Ron was sitting at the desk fumbling through papers. The smell of grease and motor oil was overwhelming.

He looked up. "Oh, hey, you're the one with the gray Datsun 510."

"Yes, one of your mechanics told me what he did to the car."

"That's Derick," he said, handing me an invoice.

I looked it over quickly. After all, what the hell did I know about a car? This was the first time I had an issue with the Gray Mouse since I bought it from Daisy Holmes.

I handed him the cash, and Ron finally cracked a smiled. "I hope you'll bring your car here for regular tune-ups and services."

"Oh, I will," I said, walking out of the office.

I glided past the mechanics working on cars.

Derick smiled at me. "Hope I'll see you again."

I smiled back as I got into my car and drove off. All that evening I couldn't get Derick out of my mind. The way he looked, the way he smiled at me, even the memory of the smell of the grease gave me a thrill. *I'm not dead after all*, I thought.

There was a chili cook-off at the Yacht Club, and I was meeting Annie there. I found her sitting at the bar with Tim, Bully, and a few of the regulars. There were no seats, so I stood behind them. Tim ordered me a drink while Annie was busy telling me about whose chili won the competition. The Gray Mouse was fixed, my spirits were up, and I was feeling good just to be among friends.

~~~~~~

The following week I was on my way into Nagasako's Variety Store to get lightbulbs when I heard someone yell, "Hey!" I turned around and saw an unfamiliar pickup truck with black primer.

I walked closer to the truck and recognized Derick, the mechanic who worked on my car.

"It's me, Derick, from the cannery," he said.

"Yes, I see that," I said, noticing his expressive and melty hazel eyes.

"There's dancing Saturday night upstairs at the Shack House. You know that place?"

"Not really," I said, concentrating on his sun-bleached dirty-blond hair.

"It's in the back, upstairs, right next to that twenty-four-hour Denny's."

"Oh, I know where that is."

"Why don't we go? It'll be fun, I promise," he said, staring at me intently.

"Okay," I said, smiling at him.

"Meet me there about nine o'clock."

"Sounds like a plan. I'll see you on Saturday night," I said, as I heard his foot release the clutch.

Derick drove away in the black pickup. The guy sitting next to him never uttered a word. I walked into Nagasako's in a good mood. I ran into Bessie Waters, Demo's singer, in the light section. We talked for a while, but I didn't ask about Demo. I kept picturing her lifting her leg when she'd hit a high note, but I managed to keep a straight face. She told me she was singing upstairs at the Whale's Tail on Front Street. The whole time I stood there talking to her, I had flashes of Derick—his face, hair, eyes, body, the whole package.

"Have you heard from Demo?" she asked.

"No, but I wasn't expecting to."

"You know how he is, he'll just appear back on the island when you least expect it," she said.

Bessie had a boyfriend. I think he was from Canada. There are a lot of Canadians living in Hawaii, Canucks they're called. Her boyfriend was mild-mannered compared to Bessie, who was a bigmouth, and she seemed to enjoy bossing him around. She was tall and very attractive, with a thin but solid form. I had an image in my mind of a mythical Amazon warrior woman, and she fit the bill. She was always nice to me, except when I thought she was inciting Demo against me. I couldn't blame it on her, since he was always a willing participant. I promised Bessie I'd check her show out at the Whale's Tail as I walked toward the cashier.

~~~~~~

When Saturday night arrived, I was a little nervous walking up the staircase of the Shack House. The place was popping with people dancing, Disco strobe lights flashing, and loud music. I was just catching the tail end of the disco era, having missed most of it during my hippie years. I saw a few people I knew right off the bat. I cruised the crowd to see if Derick was there. I caught sight of him waving at me and made my way to where he stood. He was with another guy I recognized from the cannery. They were leaning against a wall as I made my way through the crowd.

"This is my friend Carter," Derick said as I reached them.

Carter smiled at me.

"Hi, I'm Adriana."

"Everyone calls me Cotton," Carter said when the music stopped.

"Can I get you a drink?" Derick asked.

"Yeah, I'll have a Tanqueray and tonic."

When Derick went to the bar, Cotton said, "I know your roommate Loretta. I've worked on her car a few times." *Loretta must have mentioned me to him,* I thought.

"Loretta told me about the repair shop at the cannery," I said, to keep the conversation going.

I wondered if she had dated him and said nothing to me.

When Derick came back with my drink, the three of us stood around and talked for a while. I heard the Knack's song "My Sharona" and began bobbing in place. Derick took my hand and led me to the dance floor. The disco ball was spinning, colored spots bouncing off the walls. He had a loose, quirky way of dancing. It was freeform and a little awkward, but I liked it. I let loose and gyrated around the dance floor. I saw Derick light up with laughter. His friend Cotton was shaking his head and smiling as he watched us from the sidelines. We stayed on the dance floor for a few more songs. Derick exuded machismo in a subtle and sweet way. I don't remember ever dancing with Dominick French, except in my dreams.

When we parted at the end of the night, Derick didn't try to kiss me, although I'm sure it was on his mind, as it was on mine. We both agreed to do it again soon. I told him where I worked, and we exchanged phone numbers.

"By the way, my name is Derick Ellis. I already know your name from the invoice you signed, Ms. Bardolino," he said, grinning.

We walked out of the club into the night air, which was still warm. It was summer in Lahaina.

Sunday morning I dragged myself out of bed to make the coffee. I knew I had to open the Crafty Mermaid, and Loretta and I were meeting Annie at the Travel Lodge for breakfast.

"I heard you come in really late last night," Loretta said, walking into the kitchen.

"Yeah, I went dancing at the Shack House with the mechanic who fixed my car."

"I've had a couple of go arounds with Carter, one of the mechanics," she said.

"You mean the guy they call Cotton? He's cute, Loretta. They're both really hot."

"We should double date sometime," she said.

"Let's get going. Annie will be pissed off if she has to sit there in a booth by herself."

After work that day I strolled along the seawall in Lahaina before going home. I thought of how much I loved Maui. The island was part of me now, and I didn't want to live anywhere else. I walked along enjoying the fresh salty smell of the sea air and feeling the gentle trades. I realized for the first time since Demo left that I felt no anger or disappointment. I finally stopped feeling sorry for myself. A feeling of peace washed over me. It was only a month ago that I was buried in a deep ditch of despair, as if the joy had been sucked out of my life. I was happy for the time we had together and hoped in some way I'd given him joy. I just didn't see our relationship going anywhere in the future. I couldn't blame him. I went in with my eyes wide open. Even after all that happened, I still had love for him. I knew that once you loved someone, you'd always love them in a way. I was old enough now to know that love exists within a certain time frame, and I was glad I was there for that ride. You think you hold happiness, love, and beauty in your hands, but it can easily slip through.

From **reCreation**: *Some Notes on What's What and What You Might Be Able to Do about What's What* by Marc Estrin:

Don't rely on words. Words are the absolute in horseshit. Rely on *doing*. Go all the way every time. Accept contradictions; that's what life is all about. Have a good time. Wildness is the state of complete awareness. That's why we need it. Knowing that nothing need be done is where we begin from.

My cousin Terry, the doctor, arrived on the island. He was rewarding himself with a vacation in Hawaii for finishing medical school. He stayed in Malia's room, who was out of town. He rented a car, because I was very busy with work at the time. He'd be visiting most of the tourist sites on his own.

We all sat around the kitchen table listening to him tell us about his flight to Hawaii. He told us the stewardesses were giving out macadamia nuts very sparsely, as if they were laced with gold. During the plane's final descent into Hawaii, a cart was wheeled through the aisle with a replica of a volcano billowing smoke, from which they spooned mai tais into plastic glasses and served passengers. We all laughed at his experience. We went to breakfast at one of the hotels in Kaanapali. He loved the ocean and the gentle trade winds. We had some fun evenings on Nanu Street during his stay. We heard all about his drive to Hana, sunrise above the clouds of Haleakala, and a visit to a Maui coffee plantation. I wasn't even aware there was coffee grown on Maui. He told me secretly that he had a crush on one of my roommates but wouldn't tell me which one. I took him to the Yacht Club. He got a big kick out of Annie Hughes, whom he referred to as a tough old bird.

———————

I was driving to the supermarket along Wainee Street when I noticed that the brakes were failing on the Gray Mouse. They were working, but I had to press my foot down really hard to get the car to stop. *Oh, God, another bill,* I thought. I turned the car around and drove straight to the cannery. The mechanics were all working on cars when I pulled up.

Derick caught sight of me, got out from under a hood, and walked right over to me. "What's wrong with the car?"

"I think my brakes are going," I said.

"Leave the car here and I'll check it out. Go see Ron in the office."

I walked to the office past the other mechanics, who were giving me the eye. Suddenly, I heard Mae West's words in my ear, "It's better to be looked over than overlooked." I turned around and Derick's eyes were following me. He smiled when our eyes met.

I told Ron I thought I needed a brake job.

"There's a lot of red volcanic dust here, so your brakes may just need to be cleaned," he said.

That would be good news. I got the feeling that these guys were honest. I handed Ron my car key and left the office.

Derick asked, "Leaving your car here again?"

I made a face that said yes, as if I was annoyed at the prospect of another repair bill.

Ron called me at work that afternoon and told me that they had quite a few jobs lined up for that day, but if I could leave it overnight, they'd have it ready for me by the end of the next day. I told him I lived close to work and could walk home, so that would be fine. I was almost sad that I wouldn't get to see Derick again that day. God I was hot for him.

I walked home along the side streets after work, and that loathsome overpowering odor of sweet rancid rotting mangos permeated the air. Mango season was in full swing, but for me they were like poison. They were smashed all over the streets and sidewalks. I did take a few from a box that someone left on a rock wall in front of their yard. I figured Loretta, Pie, and my cousin Terry would enjoy them. I noticed a few cars in the carport as I walked up Nanu Street.

"Good thing you rented a car, Terry. Mine is back in the shop," I said, walking into the kitchen.

"What's wrong now?" Pie asked.

"The brakes felt funny, so I left it at the cannery. They were busy, so I had to leave the car."

"I can drive us anywhere," Terry said.

"I thought we'd all go for a nice dinner at Kimo's tonight," I said.

"Yeah, let's go to Kimo's," a chorus of voices agreed.

I didn't hear from Ron the next day, so my cousin Terry drove me to the cannery after work. Derick wasn't around, so I went directly to the office.

Ron was a little surprised to see me. "I didn't hear anything from you all day, so I just decided to pick my car up after work," I said.

Ron got up and looked for my car key on the wall with all the other keys but couldn't find it. He told me to have a seat while he went to see if the guys were still working on it. He was gone for quite a while and returned with a puzzled look on his face.

"Your car isn't in the lot. I've looked around, I've asked the guys, but no one knows where it is."

I had the feeling he knew more than he was saying.

Derick Ellis was walking toward the office.

Ron opened the door "Where the hell is the Datsun 510?"

"Ron, I didn't want to say, but I think a couple of guys took it someplace," Derick said.

"Took it someplace! What the hell does that mean?"

Derick seemed to be covering for the other guys. "They didn't think she was coming to pick up the car until tomorrow."

Ron was pissed. "I'll fix their asses. I'm calling the cops and reporting the car stolen!"

Meanwhile, I was sitting on a chair in the office totally dumfounded, and embarrassed in front of my cousin. Derick gave me a look, as if to say everything was alright, that it was something that had happened before.

Ron filled out a police report when the cops showed up. He told me he'd contact me as soon as he knew something. Derick wanted to drive me home, so I asked Terry to meet me back at the house.

When we pulled into the carport, I felt conflicted. I liked Derick, but I was miffed about the situation. Not that I thought he had anything to do with it.

I climbed out of his truck and said, "Thanks for the ride."

"Adriana, I hope you won't hold any of this against me."

"Why would I? It's not your fault some guys took my car for a joy ride."

"I've been thinking about you since we went dancing."

"I've thought of you too," I said.

"Let's get together soon," Derick said.

"Yes, I'd like that."

It was a strange and awkward moment as Derick drove away. *How the hell could a car get stolen from a repair shop?* I wondered. It was all so weird.

Days went by with no call from the repair shop or the police. Annie Hughes was meeting Terry and me at the Lahaina Broiler for breakfast. In those days there was an empty field where outlet shops are now. I spotted a car that looked like mine, parked along an empty stretch of grass.

"Annie, take Terry inside. I think I see my car. Don't wait for me. Order breakfast."

I walked across the street to the open lot, and indeed it was my car. I circled it, inspecting it. I didn't notice any scratches or dents. The doors were locked, and I saw the key in the ignition. I walked back to the Lahaina Broiler and used their phone to call both the police and Ron at the cannery.

When the cops arrived, I was ranting. "How come I found my own car parked right here on Front Street in plain sight? I filled out a police report four days ago," I yelled.

The two cops looked at each other but said nothing. Unfortunately, I had to pay a locksmith to break into the car to get the key, but at least I had the Gray Mouse back safe and sound. Ron told me to forget about the bill, that my brakes just needed a good cleaning.

Terry drove himself to the airport, since he had to return the rental car anyway.

Our house seemed so quiet with everyone gone, and life returned to the mundane. Yes, even in paradise life can be mundane. But I wondered what the hell could possibly happen next.

I wandered into the kitchen to make the coffee and found Ginger Pie sitting at the table. I was a little surprised to see her there.

"Up so early? I thought you weren't working until this afternoon."

"I've had something on my mind for a while but didn't know how to bring it up."

I set my mug on the table and sat. I took her hand. "Pie, you can tell me anything."

"I'm moving back to California," she said, a sad look on her face.

My heart dropped a little. I didn't think it could drop any lower. "The mainland? Really?"

"Yeah. I've been thinking about it for a while. It's not that I don't love it here."

"Well what is it then? Is it that you miss your family?"

"I don't feel like there's a future here for me. I want to be a respiratory therapist!"

"I understand. It's just that we've been so close, and I'll miss you so much."

"I know," she said, her voice cracking. "We've been like two peas in a pod."

I took her hand again. "Pie, we'll always be friends. You can visit any time, and I'll visit you."

We both got a little teary. I had a lump in my throat and an ache in my heart. We stood and hugged each other. I walked to the counter and poured myself another cup. I sat back down at the table, and we were both silent for a while.

"I want to make something of myself, make my own money," Pie said.

"It's not easy here. I lucked out finding the Crafty Mermaid when I first landed on the island."

"I don't want to suck dick to have some guy take care of me."

"Who the hell wants to do that first thing in the morning?"

"At least give me a chance to have my Wheaties, for fuck's sake!" she said, laughing.

"The breakfast of champions," I blurted out between spurts of laughter.

We began on a down note and ended up laughing. That's the way it was with me and Pie.

Ginger Pie Turner left for the mainland. I was in a cloud that whole day. I bought her a lei at Nagasako's Variety Store, placed it around her neck, and kissed her on both cheeks. I savored every moment on the drive to the airport. We hugged goodbye at the gate, and my eyes were glued to her as she walked across the runway. I watched the plane take off until it disappeared in the clouds.

I drove home in a daze. I didn't listen to the radio, because I was afraid I'd hear a sentimental song and start bawling. I knew life would be different on Nanu Street from that day forward.

<center>~~~~~~</center>

I threw myself into my artwork, which always revived me. It gave me a reason to go on each day. Ah, the resilience of art in my life. I felt truly alone for the first time in years. It was Friday, and Haku and I were painting garments in the yard. I was sipping on white wine while painting a bird of paradise on a sarong when a familiar song played on the radio. I pulled my paintbrush up and stared off into space. I closed my eyes and listened to "After the Love Has Gone" by Earth, Wind & Fire, the group that was synonymous with my first few years in the islands. Their music was always happy and uplifting but somehow seemed sad that day.

Haku had the look of an *ulukau* (Hawaiian soothsayer). "Tell me what's wrong."

"I'm having a hard time right now. Demo's gone, and another close friend has left the island."

"You gave me advice once, so I'm going to give you some now."

"Do you think advice will help how I feel?"

"I'm sure there's a plan in the universe. Maybe not right now, but it will reveal itself in time."

"That's a nice image," I said. "It's just that Demo is so intertwined with my life experience on Maui. I was only here a few months when I met him. Nothing will be the same."

"I understand," she said sympathetically.

"It's such a small town. Everywhere I go, everything I do, even being with Annie reminds me of him. So many things we did together. I can't even walk past the Missionaries Hotel without my stomach dropping out."

"He'll be back eventually; you know that."

"I know, but that relationship is over for me. Too many disappointments and useless tears."

"You'll see how you feel when he's back in town," Haku said, filling my wine glass.

Later that evening Loretta and I sat on the couch discussing if we really needed another roommate. Since Ginger Pie Turner left, we were enjoying the dynamic of the house as it was.

We were watching the exploration of King Tut's tomb on TV. Egyptian statues were inlaid with gold and turquoise with black coral eyes. It was fascinating. A peek into the world of thousands of years ago. The Egyptians lived and breathed art. It was part of everyday life. In fact, I remember learning in a class I took, The History of Art and Civilization, that art was part of everyday life in ancient times. There weren't artists, because everyone was an artist and a musician. In the modern world, artists are people getting in touch with an inborn part of their nature. Artists were revered at times in history and at other times treated as social oddities.

~~~~~~

It was a beautiful sunny morning when I drove to work. I parked on a side street near the Crafty Mermaid. I told Haku and Hannah about the saga of my car being taken for a joy ride, and how I found it myself, despite filling out a police report. We all had a good laugh about it. All day at the sewing machine I flashed on Derick, hoping I would see him again. I knew he was embarrassed about what had happened with my car. I didn't hold him responsible in any way, but I imagined how he must have felt.

After work I lackadaisically walked to my car in a good mood. Two people were walking toward me. As they got closer, I recognized Derick Ellis. He had a beer in one hand and his other arm around a girl. He stopped in his tracks when he saw me.

"I heard you got your car back," he said awkwardly.

"Actually, I found the car myself."

"Well you know how the cops are … donuts and coffee," he said, laughing.

"Yeah. I have to get home," I said, not wanting to dawdle in front of them.

"I'll see you around," Derick said, as they passed me and kept walking.

Who was that girl? I wondered. It never even crossed my mind that Derick might have a girlfriend. Was she his girlfriend, or just a girl he picked up? The way she was checking me out, I figured she wasn't just a friend. Suddenly it was clear. I wanted the mechanic who worked on my car to work on me!

FIFTEEN

HOT BLOODED

Jail is a good place for meditation. You are forced by the loneliness
and estheticism of your environment deeper into yourself, and you
can recall, with graphic detail, feelings and experiences of days long
past. The outside world does not exist. Your universe is now two walls,
one steel door, and a set of bars. You feel like the animal in a zoo you
saw as a kid. Your dreams, fantasies, and memories are all you have.
And the forced asceticism brings out your soul most clearly. You
remember minute details and feelings. Your thinking has clarity to it.

—*Jerry Rubin,* **We Are Everywhere**, *written in the Cook County Jail*

D erick Ellis showed up at the Crafty Mermaid looking for me.
Hannah told him I was upstairs. He appeared a little shy as he
gazed at me working on the sewing machine.

"This place is cool. I didn't know what you actually did for a living. I
was expecting to find you in a jewelry shop that sold Tahitian pearls," he
said.

"Yeah, this is where I work. I also paint on the clothing."

"That's cool. So you're an artist too?"

"I guess so," I answered.

"I was wondering if you want to go dancing, or out for some drinks
this weekend."

"Yes, I would."

"Maybe we can double with Loretta and Cotton," he said.

"That sounds good to me, but I don't want to answer for Loretta."

"I'll tell Cotton to give her a call."

"I'm looking forward to it," I said.

"I'll call before the weekend," he said, turning around and walking down the stairs.

After he left, I sat at the sewing machine elated, feeling something like Jell-O in the pit of my stomach. Something unfamiliar and wonderful.

~~~~~~~

On Friday night the guys picked us up at the house. I heard them pull into the carport, followed by a sturdy knock on the door. I opened it and invited them in. These were definitely two hot and crazy guys looking to have some fun.

"This is a nice place you've got here," Cotton said. "New compared to the place I live in."

"All these houses behind the sugar mill have a similar floor plan," I said.

"Where's Loretta?" Cotton asked.

"She lives in the studio in the back."

"She usually stays at my place," he said. *That was information I wasn't expecting.*

Derick was very quiet. I felt a little awkward because all I was thinking about was kissing him and imagining the two of us having sex. I was hoping he wasn't picking up on it. Everything about Derick exuded testosterone in a deliciously subdued way. Cotton had a sensual "little boy" face. He was also tall and had a mop of curly blond hair.

Loretta walked through the kitchen door. "I hope you guys weren't waiting long," she said, kissing Cotton on the lips.

"My friend Bessie Waters is singing at the Whale's Tail. What if we check her out?" I asked.

"Whatever you want to do is okay with us," Derick said, looking at me. His stare gave me chills.

"Do you guys want to drink something here first?" Loretta asked.

"We can do that when we get back later," Cotton said.

The four of us got in Cotton's car. Loretta sat in the front passenger seat next to him, and I sat in the back with Derick. We chatted on the way to the bar.

Walking up the steps to the Whale's Tail, I heard Bessie Waters belting it out on the microphone. She saw us walk in and smiled at me. The four of us took seats near the piano. We ordered drinks and were talking when I caught sight of Annie Hughes. *Oh, God. This is going to be uncomfortable,* I thought.

Annie waddled over to our table and pulled up a chair. "Fancy meeting you here," she said.

The guys looked on, dumfounded.

"Well, Bessie invited me to check her out. It was a last-minute decision," I said.

"You didn't ask me to come along?" Annie said.

"It was a double date. I didn't think it would be appropriate."

"Is this your boyfriend?" Annie asked, looking at Derick, making me very uncomfortable.

"We're all friends," I answered.

"Uh huh!" Annie said, turning away from me, annoyed.

I felt my face turning red as Derick stared at me. Loretta and Cotton weren't saying anything. I was convinced Annie was pissed at me for a number of reasons, and Derick was probably confused. Luckily, Bessie took a break and walked to our table.

"Hey, so glad you could make it tonight."

Her interference in the situation lightened the mood, and we ordered another round of drinks.

Bessie sat with us, and I noticed her trading glances with Annie, as if I were doing something wrong. *Screw them,* I thought. They both were aware of what the last two years were like for me with Demo. I had cried on both their shoulders, but I wasn't crying anymore, and they weren't going to make me feel guilty. Derick wasn't my boyfriend, well, not yet, so I let everyone introduce themselves. The vodka and gin mellowed everyone out, and it turned into a fun night.

Annie leaned in, squeezed my arm, and whispered in my ear, "Your date has sex appeal. I can understand the attraction. You're like a daughter to me, and I want you to be happy."

"He worked on my car, and now I want him to work on me," I whispered back.

Annie laughed heartily, but I sensed disapproval.

~~~~~~

It was late when we got back to Nanu Street, but we invited the guys in anyway.

"There's wine in the refrigerator," Loretta said.

"Any beer?" Cotton asked.

Loretta took out two local Primo beers for the guys and a bottle of wine for us. We were sitting around the table when Cotton pulled a small pouch of weed out of his pocket.

"Thai," he touted.

Derick took papers out of his shirt pocket and tossed them to Cotton, who rolled a joint. Derick lit it up, took a drag, and passed it to me. We were smoking Thai sticks and drinking pink Chablis. It put me in a loose mood, and I was sure Loretta was feeling the same when our eyes met. She had already been intimate with Cotton, but I hadn't been with Derick. The moment of truth came when Loretta took Cotton to her studio apartment in the back.

Derick and I sat there motionless and uncomfortably silent.

"So what's going to happen next?" he asked. I didn't answer.

"You're not letting me go home, are you?" he asked.

"No, I want you to stay," I answered.

A half smile broke out on Derick's face. I guess he considered it a subject not to be trifled with. I walked him through the hallway to my bedroom. The first thing he noticed when I switched on the small lamp on top of the dresser was the Chinese doll with the teddy bear between her legs. He stared at it but didn't react. He stood in front of me, bent his head down, and kissed me. It was a nice kiss, not sloppy, no tongue. Then we sat on the bed and began to make out heavily. He was a good kisser, and I wasn't disappointed. We undressed each other and lay on my bed. Derick had a large tattoo of the sun on his hairless chest. I was adding things up in the plus column: tall, good looking, facial scar, smooth chest, tattoo … sex with Derick Ellis was intense, and something I needed. It had been a long day and a crazy night, so we fell off to sleep soon after. He woke me up during the night, and we did it again. I wondered if Derick was going to be a real love interest. At that point it was lust at first sight. The guy gave me butterflies and chills.

Sunday morning I knew I had to open the Crafty Mermaid with Annie, and she'd be waiting at the Travel Lodge. I swung my legs carefully over the side of the bed so as not to wake Derick, and trotted to the bathroom nude to take a shower. When I came out, Derick was lying in bed with his arms folded behind his head, his eyes open, smoking a cigarette. He stared at my nude body and smiled.

"No," I said. "I have to work today. I'm meeting a friend for breakfast and I'm already late."

"Are you sure?" Derick asked with a pouty but intense expression.

All I saw was the large sun tattoo across his chest. I swallowed hard and looked away.

"I wish I could stay and hang out at home today, but I can't," I said, quickly getting dressed.

"But we'll do this again?" he asked.

"Yes, we'll do this again," I answered, smiling at him as I ran out of the bedroom.

I walked into the Travel Lodge and spotted Annie right away. She was sitting with a cup of coffee and checking out the menu. Why, I don't know, because we always ordered the buttermilk pancakes. I usually asked for a cup of fresh blueberries on the side. She saw me come in and moved further into the center of the booth.

"Where's Loretta," she asked.

"She's still in bed. She had company last night."

"I don't even remember going home last night," Annie said.

"You stayed at the Whale's Tail after we left?"

"Me and Bessie ended up at Le Toots," she said, with a crazy look on her face.

I was relieved that she didn't ask about my night. I wasn't ready to discuss Derick Ellis with her. We ordered our pancakes and talked about going to Wailuku on our next day off together.

When we finished our breakfast, Annie insisted we drive to the Crafty Mermaid in her old station wagon, even though the store was only a few blocks away.

"Let's go to the Mission tonight," Annie said. "I hear there's a dynamite piano player filling in for Dominick French."

I hesitated. "I don't know about that."

"We haven't been there since Demo's been gone. Don't you think it's about time?"

"Maybe. I guess I'll have to face it sooner or later."

"Good. It's like a second home to me," she said.

All day at work I was dreading the Missionaries Hotel. How would I feel? Was I really over Dominick French? I convinced myself that it had to be done. I needed to move forward without him, and this would be a good test.

When it was time to close the store, I walked downstairs.

Annie was tallying her sales receipts. "We had a good day. Hannah and Hoku will be ecstatic."

She looked at the expression on my face. "You're not getting cold feet, are you?"

"No, I'll be there," I answered, walking out of the store.

"See you there about eight o'clock," she called after me.

No one was home to talk to when I got back to the house. I walked straight to my bedroom to see how Derick left it. He actually made the bed. *That's a good sign,* I thought. It was hot and sweaty upstairs under the roof of the shop, and I'd spent the day at the sewing machine. I took a shower, had something to eat, and got dressed.

I decided to walk to the hotel, which was only a few blocks away. I knew I would need a few drinks to get through the night. I didn't like to drink and drive. As soon as I approached the block of the Missionaries Hotel, my stomach sank. Memories tumbled around me. It was almost too much to bear. Then I got hold of myself, and when I arrived at the entrance, I calmly walked up the steps, through the lobby, and past everyone who knew me. They all stopped and stared. I didn't make eye contact, just kept walking to the Mission Bar in the back. I could hear a piano. The sound of the piano keys were the same, but the style was different. I searched the room for Annie and saw her sitting with Tim Kork. I walked over and sat with them.

"You haven't been here in a while," Tim said, ordering me a gin and tonic.

"No, first time since Demo left," I said.

"This guy is pretty good, but nothing like Demo," Annie said.

"That's for sure," I said.

The crowd felt the same way. There were no whoops or hollers going on, just respectful applause. I sat there like a dummy all night. Without Dominick French, there was no magic to the place. I realized that when he returned from Europe, I would have to face the Mission in a new way. It would be difficult, but Lahaina is a small town, and you just couldn't avoid these situations. I knew Demo would be back when I least expected it, and I needed to prepare myself. I sat uninterested and motionless through another set, sipping my gin and tonic.

I was sure Annie and Tim were going bar hopping, and I wanted to go to sleep. "I'm going home," I said, standing up.

I bent over and kissed Annie on the cheek, and she seemed surprised. I think she wondered why, that maybe I had done something she wouldn't approve of. It was a rough night, but I was glad she got me to face my fear.

I walked home like a ghost floating somewhere between the past and the future, feeling nothing. When I got home, everyone's car was in the carport, even the Gray Mouse. The house was quiet, everyone asleep. The ball buster was sitting in the kitchen like a little statue waiting to be fed. I put some food in his dish, gave him some well-deserved pets, and then walked to my bedroom.

From my journal:

Olive me, why not take olive me? I remember you singing that song to me, "All of Me," with that little twist of the tongue. Everyone would laugh. I wanted all of you, but now I have none of you. We had a pattern. We'd get close, I'd be happy. Then I'd feel rejected or jealous, get angry and retreat. The hurt and anger would wear off, and with the first loving or kind word I'd go back for more. I was no longer in control of myself. The game couldn't go on forever. I had to make it stop.

That following Saturday night, Derick and I went dancing at the Shack House. I wasn't going to pry about the girl I'd seen him with the day I passed them on the street, but the thought dangled in my mind. We were sitting at a table having drinks, and after I downed a few I had the courage to ask.

"So the other day you were walking with a girl, you had your arm around her. How come you're not here with her?"

"Wow that was a while back. It was nothing. Let's just say a friend with benefits."

"The way she checked me out, I got the impression you were more than her friend."

"Like I said, she really meant nothing to me. Not like what you're suggesting."

"I don't mean to pry, just was curious."

"I like you more than a friend with benefits," Derick said.

As soon as he said that, I wanted to pull back and take it slow. The aspect of polarity was kicking in. I fooled myself into thinking my aim was to just get information out of him. The truth is, I was jealous. For some reason I didn't want to admit that I had feelings for him. When the song "Hot Blooded" by Foreigner blared through the sound system, Derick coaxed me out of my chair and on to the dance floor. I danced with wild abandon as I watched his quirky movements, and I felt sexy because of the way he was watching me. As the night rolled on, I couldn't wait to get him home. When a slow dance came on he held me tight, and I loved every moment.

I noticed a friend of Annie's on the dance floor. We smiled at each other in acknowledgement. I wondered if she would tell Annie she saw me at the Shack House dancing with a guy. I wondered why it was even an issue for me.

When we'd had enough of the smoke-filled air and strobe lights of the Shack House, we walked next door to Denny's, which was opened 24/7. We didn't drink coffee, but we had a full breakfast with eggs, pancakes, and bacon. We talked about how we came to the island, and about our families. I knew there was something more than physical between Derick and me. He was a little rough around the edges, but on the other side of the coin, he was really sweet. He was telling me about working on a farm when he was a kid.

"Cows will follow you around just like dogs," Derick said.

"Really?"

"Yeah, and they're often given names by their owners."

"That's something I didn't know."

We did a lot of talking and laughing until something else was on our minds.

"Let's go back to my place," I said.

Derick tossed his straggly blond hair to the side and got up. He held his hand out for mine, and I felt something major as we strolled out into the night air. Even with my stacked wedges on, he was taller than me. He helped me into his truck, which was high off the ground, too high for me to climb into on my own. He lifted me up, and I turned and kissed him on the lips. He wasn't expecting it, and a smile grew as he pulled his face away from mine. He walked around to the driver's side and hopped in.

The carport was full when we arrived, so he parked his truck on the street. It was about two in the morning, so I imagined everyone was snug in their beds, like the three little bears. We walked straight to my bedroom, and I shut the door.

"Where's the light?"

"I don't want the light on," I said.

"Okay, tiger," he said, chuckling.

I got undressed and lay on the bed. Derick took his clothes off and tossed them on the floor. He lay next to me and began kissing me with lots of tongue. He touched me all over until I moved his hands to my breasts. He played with my nipples with his fingers and then sucked on them. I felt he was hard, so I took my hand and played around with it. He put his fingers inside me and moved them around until I was at the brink. I began to moan and he got on top of me and thrust it in. Oh, God, it was so good. There were a lot of sound effects, but he held his hand over my mouth. Afterward, he rolled off me and we both laughed a little.

"That was real good," Derick said.

My mind was hearing that Foreigner song "Hot Blooded." I rubbed my hand along his chest in the dark, picturing his sun tattoo. I got up and switched the lamp on.

That's the craziest thing, the doll and the bear," he said.

"I found them at Sheila's Junkatique in Wailuku. A friend positioned them that way, with the bear between her legs." (I didn't mention the friend was Dominick French.)

Derick laughed. "That's just crazy."

I sat back down on the bed leaning against the wall, and Derick sat up next to me.

"I really like that tattoo. Where'd you get it?"

He reached for his pack of Salems on the night stand, lit a cigarette and took a drag. He hesitated, then said, "I did it myself."

"Did it yourself?" I asked, a little confused.

"In jail. I did it myself while I was in jail. I was in for two years."

"Derick, what happened? What did you do?"

"You see this scar on my face? Some guy did this to me with a chain. I needed more than two hundred stitches. I beat him senseless, almost killed him."

"Derick," I said, caressing his shoulder. I kissed him softly on the lips. I was feeling his pain.

He took me in his arms and hugged me. It took me a while to process what he told me. We held each other. I thought maybe he was expecting me to say something else.

"I figured I'd tell you about jail right at the get go," he said.

"I'm glad you told me, but I don't feel any differently about you, now that I know."

"I'm staying with you tonight, right?" he asked, his expression melting.

"Yes, I want you to stay."

Derick bent down and kissed me. He stomped out his cigarette in the ashtray. He slumped over and teased my nipples with his tongue. I knew I was in for round two, and I was ready for it.

<p style="text-align:center">~~~~~~~</p>

Malia moved out, and we were introduced to a new roommate, Shirley from Washington State, through a friend. She was a little wild, but we loved her. Loretta and I were dating best friends and were moving to the sunny side of life. I heard through the grapevine that Dominick French was back in town. I avoided the Missionaries Hotel like the plague. Annie told me he was asking for me, but she told him nothing about my being involved with someone. She said she was leaving that up to me.

I was working on the Bernina upstairs at the Crafty Mermaid when I heard a distinct gravelly voice downstairs. I felt my stomach flip, and I tried to gather myself.

Annie yelled up the stairs, "Riana, Demo is here to see you."

I peered over the banister and smiled down at him. "I'll be right down."

Demo watched me with interest as I walked down the stairs.

"I'm taking you to lunch," he said.

"Where are we going, Kimo's?"

"Where else?" he said, smiling back at me in a jovial mood.

"It's slow today. You can take a lunch," Annie said.

Demo entwined his arm in mine as we strolled along Front Street. I suppose he imagined we were picking up where we left off before he went to Europe. He had been gone for a long time. It was already late September.

We didn't say much as we made our way to the restaurant, save for a few greetings from people we knew on the street. We walked into Kimo's and a waitress seated us at a table on the water. The sun was bright, and the air was salty and fresh. We ordered Caesar salads and bloody Marys.

Demo took my hand and caressed it. "Everything is going to be different from now on," he said.

I stared at him, unmoved.

He went on when he saw I wasn't reacting to his words. "I know I could be a jerk, and I'm selfish at times, but I promise, it's all going to be different.

I waited before responding. I took a long swig of my bloody Mary to gain courage. "Oh it's going to be different alright. I've met someone else."

He stared at me, but there was no reaction except surprise. "Who? What do you mean? When did this happen?"

"I met a guy this summer. I really like him, and I want to see where it goes."

"Come on, you don't mean that. You're screwing with me, right?"

"No, I mean it," I said.

He took my hand again. "Adriana, you know I'm in love with you."

"Love shouldn't hurt like that," I said.

Demo was flabbergasted. He didn't know what to say or how to react. "Check," he shouted at the waitress, who was walking to another table.

We finished our drinks in silence. He threw some cash on the table, and we got up and walked out of the restaurant.

"You don't have to walk me back to work. I'll stop by the Mission one night soon," I said.

I turned and walked away from him. I felt his eyes follow me down the street, but I wouldn't turn around. My stomach was all torn up, and I wanted to cry for both of us.

I walked into the Crafty Mermaid, and as soon as I saw Annie's face, I began sobbing. She put her arms around me and held me. "Are you sure you're doing the right thing, Riana?" she asked.

"I don't know. I don't know," I blurted through tears.

"Maybe it meant something. Maybe not, in the long run, no explanation, no mix of words or music or memories can touch that sense of knowing that you were there and alive in that corner of time and the world. Whatever it meant."

—Hunter S. Thompson, *Fear and Loathing in Las Vegas.*

I wasn't sticking around for the holidays that year. I bought a plane ticket, planning to spend Thanksgiving and Christmas in New York with my family. I was going to stop in California on the way back to see Ginger Pie Turner. I told Derick I'd be back to spend New Year's Eve with him.

I began to see more of Derick, and it felt like a normal relationship, if there is such a thing. The big test was a night at the Missionaries Hotel, in the back room piano bar. I had to do it before Halloween, because we'd be bar hopping. I had an honest talk with Derick. I told him that I'd had a love affair with the piano player at the Mission Bar for two years but that it was over. I didn't give him too many details. Derick knew I was older than him, and he said he understood that I had a past.

We showed up at the Missionaries Hotel on a Saturday night. Annie said she'd get a table. Loretta and Cotton came with us. The four of us strolled through the lobby and into the Mission Bar. I felt tense but confident.

Demo was on a break, sitting alone at a table. He watched us get seated. I wondered where Annie was. Demo looked sad and dejected, attempting to stare straight ahead and not look at me. My heart dropped a little.

Derick put his arm around me, and glared at Demo. Suddenly I realized this was a bad idea.

Annie waddled in breathlessly and sat down. "I stayed longer than anticipated at the Yacht Club. Demo looks pathetic," she said.

I leaned in and whispered in her ear, "Revenge is sweet."

She looked at me with disappointment, and what seemed like anger. "Don't be that way. Is that why you're here, Riana? It could come back and bite you in the ass."

I took another sip of my gin and tonic, trying not to look in Demo's direction.

Demo stood up, walked to the piano, set his drink on top, and sat down. He didn't play my song, but I wasn't expecting him to. He played a few tunes, but then, all of a sudden he began singing a song about a cottage in the country, and "We'll have a B-A-B-B-Y," as he turned and stared at me.

Derick was up on his feet in an instant. I thought there was going to be a slug fest. I didn't know whether to laugh or cry.

I tugged on Derick's pants and said, "Sit down. Damn it, sit down. It's just a song."

Derick sat down, but the atmosphere was electrically charged as Demo kept up his cruel repertoire of love songs directed at me.

"Annie, I think we should go before there's a fight."

"Yes, maybe if the place was packed, it wouldn't have been so obvious to everyone that you were here with someone else. Demo acts like he doesn't care, but it seems like he's having a hard time digesting it all," she said.

The four of us left and went to another bar and had a few drinks. Then the guys drove us home.

Derick and I walked straight to my room, but I could tell he wasn't in a good mood. He had been quiet while we were drinking at the second bar. I lay on the bed, but Derick sat up against the wall. He reached for the pack of Salems in his shirt pocket and lit a cigarette. I felt a sermon coming.

"That guy's not over you," Derick said.

"He was drunk, probably used to me being there for him like a muse, or he was in the mood."

"He was trying to make a chump out of me. I'll knock his fucking block off," Derick said.

"You're making more of this than it is. It's just part of his routine, to engage with the audience."

"Do you think I was born yesterday?" Derick said. "Maybe you're not over him either."

"Stop this. I can't help what the guy says or does. You're acting like I set you up or something."

"I'd better leave. I'm not in a good mood," he said, stomping his cigarette out in the ashtray.

"Do whatever you want!" Now I was pissed off too.

Derick got up off the bed and stormed out of the bedroom. A few moments later I heard Cotton's car peel out of the carport. I guess Loretta would have to drive Cotton home in the morning. I lay there in a daze but was happy to be alone. I got undressed, took a shower, and crawled into bed. *These men are going to be the death of me.*

I switched the fan on and pointed it right at me. I lay there nude with my feet on the pillow and my head at the foot of the bed. I was staring at the Native American blanket hanging behind my bed. I thought of Navajo Tommy and yearned for uncomplicated sex with a guy I was just hot for. This love business was overrated. It took me a long time to fall asleep. I twisted and turned myself into a state of rumpled sheets and awful thoughts. I felt like I was living in a Hunter S. Thompson script. I began to look forward to my trip to New York and some time off the rock (Maui). I finally fell asleep.

The telephone woke me.

It was Demo, drunk and rambling. "Are you alone? Or are you with Scaramouche?"

I didn't answer. I knew he was hurt and was enjoying being cruel, so I just let him ramble on. I didn't say much as he did most of the talking.

"I hope this isn't going to be a habit, calling me in the middle of the night, because those days are over," I said, interrupting his midnight ramble.

"If you're alone, you can come over," he said.

"I have to work tomorrow. I'm going back to sleep." I hung up while he was still talking.

I lay there for a while, then took the phone off the hook to avoid any more phone calls.

~~~~~~

Early the next morning I wandered into the kitchen to make coffee. Loretta's car was gone. I figured she gave Carter, aka Cotton, a ride home. The coffee smelled good as I stood there at the counter waiting for the brew to finish. I took a cup from the cabinet and filled it with rocket fuel. I sat at the kitchen table and stared off into space, still reeling from the past night's events.

I heard Loretta's car pull into the carport. Soon she was in the kitchen sitting at the table with a cup of coffee. "Crazy night," she said.

"Derick and I had a fight and he stormed off last night. Then Demo woke me up from a dead sleep wanting to chat at three in the morning. I feel like a used dishrag."

"That's nothing compared to the story I heard from Cotton last night," Loretta said.

"What? I don't think I can take anything else in a twenty-four-hour period."

"Oh, it has nothing to do with you or Derick."

"Then what, Loretta?"

"Cotton got pretty drunk last night, and when we got home we did the usual—talked, had sex—but he opened up about his childhood."

"Did he have a troubled one?"

"His father left when he was a small child, and his mother struggled to take care of both of them. They developed a tight, interdependent bond, which is understandable in that situation. But when he got older it developed into something more."

"Loretta, what are you saying?"

"His mother began using him for sex. He told me it really fucked him up mentally."

"That's so sick and screwed up," I said.

"He hates his mother with a passion, won't even see her or talk to her anymore."

"Wow, Loretta, that story is hard to take in. It makes me feel dirty all over."

I got up from the table and put my mug in the sink. I was rocked by the story, but I had to get to work. I took a shower and got dressed in as little as possible, knowing I'd be working upstairs under that hot roof.

Loretta was still sitting at the kitchen table with a pensive look on her face.

"I'm off to work, but I'll be thinking of that story all day," I said, walking out the front door.

I worked for the next few days, almost happy to be preoccupied. I went to the Waterworks with Annie after work one night, and we had a great time with a couple of tourists. They bought us drinks all night and took us to a nice restaurant for dinner.

I thought of something my mother would say every time I got involved with someone romantically, "Adriana, you tried that. Don't you think you're better off on your own?"

Then I remembered my therapist, Joan, saying, "Adriana, you have to let someone love you."

I looked forward to getting off the island for a while. I needed to weigh things, think about what the hell I was doing. Did I really want to get involved with Derick in a deeper way? The sex was really good, and I was feeling intense about him, but he was a bit of a hothead. There could be no cool heads with hot blood. Besides, as much as I didn't want the relationship with Demo anymore, I wondered if I could still love him subconsciously. Getting involved with someone on the rebound from another love affair could have disastrous consequences. I had to think about it more rationally. Then again, when is love ever rational?

~~~~~~~

Derick showed up at my door one evening. I was cooking dinner.

I let him in and sat at the table. "So where's your sidekick?"

"Cotton's doing his own thing tonight."

"Sit," I said, pulling out a chair. "There's beer in the fridge if you want."

Derick got a beer. "Steinlager," he said approvingly.

"Yeah, well, New Zealand beer is more expensive, but I like it."

"I'm sorry about the other night. I got carried away."

"I totally understand, and I wasn't pissed off." (That was a fabrication.)

"This Friday night, wanna go dancing? We can stop in Denny's for breakfast after."

"That sounds like fun. We haven't been there for a couple of weeks."

I got up and went to the stove. Derick got up and stood behind me. He leaned over my shoulder and searched for my mouth. He ran his tongue along my lips and gave me a sloppy kiss, which sent shockwaves and throbs to the lower part of my body. We kissed for a while, but I didn't let on that I wanted more. I didn't want him to get the idea that temper tantrums were okay with me. I'd had enough of that to last me a lifetime.

He pulled away and smiled. "I'll pick you up at nine on Friday night," he said, walking out.

"I'll see you then," I called after him, already planning what I was going to wear.

DISCO FEVER

Derick picked me up on Friday night. Loretta thought we both looked so good, she took a photo before we got into Derick's truck. We walked into the Shack House, stood at a tall pop-up table, and ordered drinks. I found the music and strobe lights disarming. Derick looked hot, but then again, he always did. We talked over drinks as the night wore on. We went out on the dance floor when "Hot Blooded" blared through the sound system. We loosened up, shook it all out, and laughed a lot. Then a slow song came on, that song "Still" by the Commodores. Derick pulled me really close as we danced, rubbing ourselves on each other and touching our hands together. I felt a mixture of heat, butterflies, and a little fear. I was feeling emotional about him.

"Let's forget Denny's. You know what I want," Derick said.

I breathed in a little, feeling throbs down below. "Let's get out of here."

When we arrived on Nanu Street, Derick pulled his black truck into an empty carport.

"Looks like no one's home," I said.

We entered my bedroom and I shut the door.

He reached for the light. "No, don't turn it on," I said.

"Whatever you say, tiger." He liked calling me that, affectionately implying I was a wild thing.

He embraced me and we kissed for a while. He lay on the bed and guided me down. He pulled my skirt up past my waist and slowly pulled my lace panties down. He opened my legs and went down on me. While he was down there I had a quick flash of Navajo Tommy. I thought, *I have to get rid of that blanket.*

I pulled his head up by his hair and said, "Your turn now."

He moaned a little as I opened the zipper of his pants and took him in my mouth. Derick and I were a good match sexually, and I was thankful for that. But was I really in love? I wasn't sure. I didn't want to think about any of that. I was in the zone, and anticipating what was coming next.

~~~~~

Things were good with me and Derick Ellis. He drove me to the big airport when I left for New York. Driving over the Pali, we talked about all the things we were going to do when I got back to Maui. He dropped me off at the curbside check-in desk.

"I'm missing you already," he said.

"I'm sure I'll be thinking about you the whole time I'm in New York," I said.

He grabbed me close and kissed me. I pulled away, looking at his eyes. They were a deep golden shade of hazel, almost the same color as his hair. There was a wildness to them.

"I'll be back before you know it. Make a plan for New Year's Eve," I said in an uplifting tone.

"Be good," he called after me, watching me walk to the gate.

"How can I be bad if you're not with me?" I shouted back, strolling away.

SIXTEEN

BAD CASE OF LOVING YOU

I was filled with such a dangerous delicious intoxication that I could
have walked straight off the steps into the air, climbing on the
strength of my own drunkenness into the stars. And the intoxication,
as I knew even then, was the recklessness of infinite possibility.

—Doris Lessing, *The Golden Notebook*

My month-long vacation in New York was fantastic. It afforded me
the time to think things through and move forward. I stopped
in San Francisco to break up the long plane ride from Hawaii to
New York. I stayed with Star Green at her apartment in North Beach. Suki
Rosmond came to the city, and the three musketeers were back together
again. We spent a day roller skating in Golden Gate Park. I didn't linger
too long in the Twin Cities, but it was good to connect with my friends.

I spent Thanksgiving and Christmas with my family in New York and
visited old friends. I took my mother to Radio City Music Hall to see the
Rockettes' Christmas show. They're precision dancing reminded me of
the June Taylor Dancers on the old Jackie Gleason show. I met my cousin
Gia and her husband, Stu, at MOMA. After we viewed all the modern art
we'd seen before, we went to Greenwich Village for lunch. We walked past
Trude Heller's Discotheque, which they told me was fabulous in its heyday,
and I was sorry I missed it. I flashed on Derick Ellis and giggled a little
thinking of his quirky dance moves. I kept a winter coat at my parents'
apartment in the Bronx, but even with that on, the cold wind gusts went
right through me. I imagined my blood had thinned out after living in the

Adriana Bardolino

islands for almost three years. The inconvenience of shopping and having to remove hat, scarf, and coat, every time I entered a department store was something I didn't miss.

I took the train to Manhattan alone on one of my last few days in New York. I visited the northern entrance of Central Park. I wanted to see the Three Maidens Dancing Bronze. There was no water flowing from Untermeyer Fountain since it was winter. How different it all looked from the time I was there in spring with Adam Hirschfeld so many years past. I remembered the aroma of the wisteria as we strolled under the trellis. Even though it was winter, the three women were still dancing, as if attempting to conjure up spring. I thought of a movie I'd seen, called *Isadora*, about the life of Isadora Duncan, played very well by Vanessa Redgrave. Angela Isadora Duncan was an American dancer who was born in the late 1800s. She changed a form of ballet into modern dance. It wasn't just her freeform style of dancing, but she also changed the concept of the restrictive costumes of the day into flowing garments. She toured and lived in Europe and was popular in the 1920s. She was revolutionary.

From my journal:

If I could only dance as you danced. So free, so flowing with softness, your sheer garments only shading your nude body. If I'd only lived in the days of flowing dresses and flowered coiffures, waltzing around a dimly lit mirrored ballroom. Candles lighting the floor, revealing satin fabrics gliding everywhere, held by distinguished, handsome, young men with mustaches. Such a joy to the senses. Your life seemed beautiful yet sad, sensitivity its highlight. I myself danced nude in the woods once upon a time.

It was the first time I'd written anything in my journal in a long time, really not since my love affair with Dominick French went south. I was happy and felt that what I was experiencing, life itself, didn't need to be analyzed or recorded. Maybe subconsciously I feared someone finding my journals, reading them, and knowing every intimate part of me, my every thought. I was a woman and questioned if diaries were the silly ramblings of a young girl. I wondered if they should even be in my possession. Perhaps

I should leave them hidden in my parents' apartment, yet I kept them at the ready.

I stopped in Los Angeles on my way back to Maui to see Ginger Pie Turner and catch up with her life. I knew nothing about Southern California before Pie. She was living with her parents and studying to be a respiratory therapist. She dragged me to Disneyland, and we spent the day there roaming around. Before leaving LA I visited a friend of Annie's who lived in Hollywood. I met her when I first moved to Hawaii. She left Maui to marry a record producer. We laughed about the day I got caught in the waves on Kaanaplai Beach, and nearly lost the top of my bathing suit. Just a year or so after I'd visited her in Hollywood, Annie informed me that she died of a brain tumor. She was so young. I was happy I saw her that one last time. I realized I wasn't that young anymore, and I needed to make some serious decisions regarding my future.

Pie and I sat by the fireplace in her mom's house in our nightgowns, toasting our friendship with champagne, the New Year less than a week away.

~~~~~

I had arranged for Annie to pick me up at Kahului Airport upon my return to Maui, because I didn't know what was going on with Derick Ellis. As the plane was circling the airport, I saw Haleakala Crater looming in the distance. The pilot gave a speech about the Hawaiian Islands, and Maui in particular. A feeling of pride and love washed over me, and I actually got choked up and felt goose bumps. I realized how in love I was with Maui.

Annie was waiting for me at the gate with a plumeria lei. Their familiar aroma signaled to me that I was home.

On the car ride over the Pali in her old station wagon, going at a snail's pace, Annie brought me up to speed on what I'd missed while I was gone. Demo had moved an old girlfriend into his back room, which was actually a screened-in porch. It wouldn't be a place I'd want to stay. Annie said she was back on the island from California and needed a place to live. I didn't say much, but my stomach reacted a little.

"She's just a friend now, according to Demo," Annie said. "He told me she was a little screwed up because a refrigerator fell on her head when she was a kid."

Even though it wasn't funny, I found it comical and began to laugh, picturing a woman I didn't even know riding the coin-operated camel in his living room.

"Well, that sounds like someone who could tolerate Demo's midnight rambling disk jockey routine. I hope she knows what she's getting into," I said. I thought of the time Demo told me I could move in with him, if I stayed in that back room. What a sham that would have been.

"I went to the Mission a few times while you were gone, but not as much," Annie said.

"I have no idea what's going on with Derick."

"Just take things day by day," Annie said, as cars passed us.

"I don't think there's any other way."

"Demo knows I'm picking you up today."

"Did you tell him, or did he ask?"

"He asked me a few times when you were coming home."

She convinced me to stop at the Yacht Club and have a drink before I went home. Even though it had been a long flight, I agreed. It was still early, and I didn't want to disappoint her.

We walked through the swinging doors, and as soon as I was sitting on a barstool, I felt like I'd been there the previous night. Funny how that works. Before I knew it there were drinks lined up in front of me, more than I could handle. Annie made sure everyone at the bar knew I had just returned to the island from the madland (what islanders liked to call the US mainland). I quietly signaled the bartender that I didn't want to drink anymore. I began to slide extra drinks in his direction, and he'd make them disappear.

I finally convinced Annie to take me home, complaining that I was tired and needed to unpack and get settled. The girls of the Crafty Mermaid were expecting me back at work by the weekend. We had no tab, since the regulars were buying. I slipped the bartender extra cash, and we walked out.

When Annie dropped me off at home, the carport was empty. I was almost happy no one was around. I wanted to get settled. I set my suitcase down in my bedroom and went back to the kitchen to look through the stack of mail waiting for me on the table. There were a few bills, and a letter from Blake Middleton, which I would read later. Then I saw a familiar handwriting: it was my own. I picked it up. It was the Christmas card I'd sent to Daisy Holmes in Alaska. It had been returned to me stamped DECEASED. I knew I had her correct address because we often wrote letters to each other. At first it didn't register in my brain. I had no idea what time it was in Alaska, so I figured I'd deal with it first thing in the morning.

When Loretta came home she was happy to see me. We sat around the table and talked for a long time. I told her all about my trip, and she told me what she did over the holidays.

Loretta said, "Adriana, Derick can't wait to see you. Every time I'm with Cotton, Derick's always talking about you."

"That's good to know."

"I think he really likes you, Adriana."

"I really like him too, but should I get involved with someone seriously, so soon after Demo?"

"I get what you're saying, but he seems like such a nice guy."

"I'm not going to call him tonight. I just want to relax and get my bearings."

"I'm glad you're home. I don't have a history with the other girls like I have with you."

"How's Shirley working out?" I asked.

"She's a wild one. Out every night, and now she met a guy who's on leave from the navy."

I was getting sleepy, and the time difference was catching up with me. I left Loretta in the kitchen and shuffled to my bedroom, lay on the bed, and fell off to sleep.

～～～～

In the morning I went to the kitchen to make coffee, and a guy I didn't know was sitting at the table smoking a cigarette. His face was all scrunched up like an unmade bed.

"Hi, I'm Shirley's friend Dennis," he said.

Occasionally one of the girls would have a guy stay over for the night. I pulled my robe tightly around my body, because I'd slept in the nude. He had already made coffee, so I poured myself a cup and sat down.

"I'm Adriana," I said, smiling.

Luckily, Shirley walked in. I was beginning to feel awkward. She hugged him and kissed him, and I felt like an intruder in their love scene.

"Glad you're back," Shirley said.

"I'm glad to be home," I said.

"Did you see that letter that was returned to you?" she asked.

"Yes. I have to get in touch with her somehow, but she doesn't have a phone."

"Best way to find out is to call the post office where she gets her mail," Dennis said.

"I'll do that," I said. I grabbed the stack of mail and retreated to my bedroom.

I made a few calls, first to the main post office in Fairbanks, Alaska, which Daisy had mentioned a few times. They gave me the phone number of her local trading post. After a few tries I finally got someone on the phone.

"I'm trying to reach a friend of mine, Daisy Holmes. I've been sending her mail at this address for more than three years. Her letter came back to me stamped deceased!"

"Oh, I know Daisy Holmes," the man said. "I'm sorry to have to tell you this, ma'am, but she died in a small plane crash."

"Her baby?" I asked, shaking all over.

"Her little girl is fine; she's with Daisy's boyfriend. I'm really sorry, miss," he said.

"Thank you for telling me," I said, my voice trembling.

I hung up and began to cry. "Daisy, Daisy," I blubbered. I composed myself for a moment. I remembered the turquoise ring she had left in the glove compartment of the Gray Mouse. I hadn't worn it in a while.

I walked to the dresser, opened the Chinese jewelry box Demo brought me from Singapore, and searched for her ring. I found it and slipped it on my finger. "Daisy, I'll treasure this ring always," I said through a barrage of tears.

She was so young, much younger than me. Her life snuffed out just like that. She left a little girl without a mother. I was enveloped in sadness.

I knew I had to call Derick. After I composed myself I dialed his number.

Cotton answered. "Hey, you're back. How was your trip to the Big Apple?"

"Cold but lots of fun."

"Derick's not here," he said.

I didn't want to pry, so I said, "Tell him I'll call him later tonight."

"I will," he said.

After I hung up, I immediately wondered if he was with someone else. Why? Insecurity, I suppose. When I left for New York, we were just beginning a relationship.

I spent the day cleaning my room, unpacking, and doing laundry. Just the mundane aspect of doing chores gave me comfort. I heard nothing back from Derick, so I decided to make myself dinner.

Shirley was at the stove when I walked into the kitchen.

"I was just thinking about making something to eat," I said.

"No need. I'm making meatloaf, mashed potatoes, and string beans."

"That sounds so good, Shirley. I've had a terrible day."

"I heard you crying. I figured you'd need some comfort food. I didn't want to say, but I saw how that letter was stamped, and I figured your friend was dead."

"It's just so sad. She was so young. She'd just had a baby," I said, choking up.

"Life can be cruel. We never know when our time's up. Enjoy it now, that's my motto!"

"I have enjoyed mine so far. I don't think I've said *no* to too many things in life."

"So Dennis, I call him Den, is on leave from the navy. He's going back in soon," Shirley said.

"That's rough. What does the future look like for the two of you?"

"We're serious. I don't want to jump the gun, but he's talking marriage when he gets out."

"That's great, Shirley! I hope everything works out for you," I said, feeling somewhat off track.

I heard a truck pull into the carport. I knew that sound—Derick's truck.

He knocked on the door, opening it slowly. He smiled when he saw me. My heart jumped as soon as I saw his face. I felt a mixture of butterflies, lust, and fear. It was always like that with him.

"Cotton told me you were back. I was at work," he said.

We embraced and kissed.

"I've missed you," he said.

"I thought about you a lot while I was away."

"I have to get back to work. I have a big motor job I've been working on, but I had to see you."

The smell of the grease on Derick evoked sexual desire in me. I wanted to drag him back to my bedroom and fuck his brains out, but I played coy.

"I'll call you later and we'll make a plan," he said, rushing out the front door.

"Yeah, call me later," I shouted, watching his black truck back out of the carport.

My spirits lifted, and I knew everything was going to be all right.

~~~~~

Derick called later that evening and wanted to go out for drinks, but I told him to just come over so we could catch up.

I took a shower and put on a black, tropical print sundress I made at work before I left for vacation. I could hardly eat any dinner in anticipation of seeing him. I heard his truck pull up and tracked his footsteps to the front door.

He knocked, and I yelled out for him to come in. We immediately hugged and kissed. I went to the fridge, got two Steinlagers, and set them on the table. We sat and talked for a while. I could barely keep my mind on what was being said but managed a decent conversation for half an hour or so.

"Where is everyone?" Derick asked.

"Shirley, our new roommate, met a navy guy on leave, so I guess they're doing up the town, and Loretta is working at the restaurant, the late shift. I think she's closing the place."

"So are you saying we have the house to ourselves?"

I smiled at Derick and said, "Looks like it."

We stood up, walked to my bedroom, and shut the door.

"I've been thinking about this for more than a month," he said.

He slowly lifted my dress over my arms and tossed it on the floor. I stared at the tattoo on his chest as he took off his T-shirt. He unzipped his pants and I pulled them down.

"Don't lie down yet," I said. I slid his briefs down and played with his member while looking up at him.

"I can't take it," he said.

He pulled off my pale-blue satin panties, the ones with beige lace trim along the edges (I made sure I wore those), and tossed me on the bed. He got on top of me and pushed my legs opened with his. I wrapped my legs around his back and held on.

"Oh, God," he said, looking at me.

It was over pretty quick, but I knew round two was coming at some point.

In the morning, it was Derick's face Shirley had to contend with at the kitchen table. He was sitting there in his jeans with no shirt, smoking a Salem and waiting for me to make coffee. When her boyfriend, Dennis, woke up, he walked into the kitchen and stopped in his tracks when he saw another guy sitting at the table.

"Den, this is Adriana's guy, Derick," Shirley said. They said hi to each other and talked while we filled the mugs and brought them to the table.

It was a cozy scene. It was a long time since I woke up with a man next to me. It felt good, like I was part of the human race again. Derick stayed over that night as well, and subsequent nights to come. We were good together.

I noticed that Derick liked to wear a long-sleeved, red and white striped shirt around the house. He was sitting on the couch in the living room playing my guitar, and I felt the need to ask him about it.

"Derick, you always wear that same shirt when we're hanging out."

"It's my prison shirt. I guess there's something about it that keeps me calm."

"Like a security blanket?"

"Something like that."

I lay down and put my feet on his lap. "I love it when you play guitar. It gives me a funny feeling, like jelly in my stomach."

Derick stopped playing and grabbed my foot. He massaged it and played with my toes.

"That feels good," I said. "Keep doing it."

He slid his hand up my leg and under my dress. He stuck his fingers inside my panties and fingered me right there on the couch. I opened my legs so he could do it more easily. I saw his expression melt and he put down the guitar.

"Wanna go to my bedroom?"

"No one's here. Besides, I want to watch your face when you come," he said.

I began to breathe heavily and moan. I let him move his fingers around until I climaxed. He leaned over me and kissed me, alternating rubbing his lips along mine.

~~~~~

At the Crafty Mermaid, the ladies were happy I was back from vacation. It wasn't busy over Christmas, but January would begin the busy winter season in Hawaii. All the tourists would be coming in droves to get away from the cold weather.

"What are you doing for New Year's?" Hannah asked.

"Derick got us tickets to a party at the Sheraton. Loretta and Derick's best friend, Carter, are coming with us. Actually, a bunch of us will be celebrating together."

"That sounds like fun," Haku said. "So things are going well with Derick?"

"Yes, things are great. There's the occasional three in the morning phone call from Demo, but I've started taking the phone off the hook before we go to sleep. Derick gets so pissed off!"

"Well, I can understand that," Hannah said.

"I guess Demo misses me listening to his midnight rambles."

"Eventually, Demo will give up the ghost," Haku said. I wondered about that.

When I arrived home, I stopped at the mailbox, and there was a Christmas card from Blake Middleton's mother in with the letters and bills. She was complaining about his drinking and said that she continued to keep tabs on his music career. I was happy about that. I knew firsthand just how talented he was. She mentioned his having had a baby with a girl he was living with. For some unknown reason she kept me abreast of his life. Blake never revealed much in his letters.

~~~~~

On New Year's Eve, we all got dressed up ... well, dressed up for Maui. The Sheraton had joined two ballrooms and created a nightclub. We had all our friends at one long table. The drinks were flowing, the food was great, and the band was hot. We danced our way into 1980 to Robert Palmer's "Bad Case of Loving You." I was so happy that night. I felt my life was going in the right direction. I had a man who seemed to love me, a great job that I enjoyed going to each day, and wonderful friends. What more could I want?

We stumbled into the house. Shirley and Dennis retreated to her room, Loretta and Cotton went to her studio in the back, and Derick and I retired to my bedroom. We talked for a while, made love, and then fell asleep.

The phone woke us up at three o'clock. *Damn it, in my drunken state I forgot to take the phone off the hook.*

"Don't answer it," Derick said.

"Hello," I said.

I heard Derick breathe out, pissed off that he was woken up.

"I wore the gold lamé jacket you made for me last New Year's Eve. Remember?" Demo said.

Derick poked my arm, and I could tell he was annoyed.

"That was a long time ago," I said. "Demo, it's the middle of the night."

"Are you by yourself? You can come over if you want," he said.

"I'm not alone, and I'm hanging up, so go to sleep," I said.

"Oh, you must be lying next to Scaramouche," he said, laughing.

I slammed the phone down.

"What the hell did he want?" Derick asked.

"Just to wish me a happy New Year," I said, lying.

"At three fucking o'clock in the morning?"

I made no mention of Demo's snide comment about the scar on Derick's face. I knew Demo enjoyed being cruel, especially when he couldn't get his own way, like a spoiled child. He really pissed me off, and I promised to be more diligent about leaving the phone off the hook at night.

~~~~~~

We followed a local musician and singer, Willie Kalaiali'i. Willie K for short, since everyone had a hard time pronouncing his last name. He made the rounds playing in bars and clubs all over Maui. After dinner one night, the four of us went into Lahaina to see him. He was a skinny teenager with an afro who played a mean electric guitar. We all thought he was talented and unique, even back in those days. Who could have predicted that he would become a Hawaiian sensation in years to come, when he would embrace his Hawaiian roots and music? His voice was phenomenal, gave you chicken skin.

Things almost seemed to be going too well in my life. I felt the need to consult the I Ching for guidance going forward. Now that I was in my thirties, I saw the odd gray hair, which troubled me. I decided to use a red henna rinse, which I was told would turn the grays into red highlights. I waited until I was alone, mixed the concoction, and applied it to my hair. I got the book out and tossed the three Chinese coins six times, with the question of my immediate future in mind. These were some lines of wisdom I'd received.

From the **I Ching**:

Ta Yu/possession in great measure: The fire in heaven above shines far, and all things stand out in the light and become manifest.

The judgement: Possession in great measure. Supreme success. The two trigrams indicate that strength and clarity unite. Possession in great measure is determined by fate. Power is expressing itself in a graceful and controlled way.

The Image: The sun above, shedding light over everything on earth. Possession of this sort must be administered properly. The sun brings both evil and good into the light of day. Man must combat and curb the evil, and must favor and promote the good.

I set the *I Ching* back in my underwear drawer and put the coins away in my jewelry box. I sat on the bed contemplating the meaning of the trigram, and how the commentary would apply to my personal life. I was thankful for the joy in my life but was troubled by the statement about the sun bringing both good and evil into light. *What the hell could that mean?* I certainly wasn't going to dwell on it, but I knew something would reveal itself eventually. It always did.

I threw my relationship fears out the window and Derick Ellis moved in with me. I couldn't have been happier. Shirley's Dennis lived with us for a while but eventually went back in the navy to finish his enlistment obligation. She wanted to get married to this guy. Personally, I had reservations because she didn't know him that long, but who was I to judge?

Loretta decided she didn't want to live with two couples. She was letting Cotton move her to different places around the island with him. We still saw each other all the time since he and Derick were besties. We met a woman through Hannah Klein, Bridget, and she moved into the studio apartment at the back of the house when Loretta moved out. Nanu Street was like Siddhartha's River. It kept flowing and changing, but was still the same river.

<center>~~~~~~</center>

I came home from work and found Derick sitting on a beach chair in the yard. He was holding something and it looked alive. I stood there for a while staring at it and then at him with a questioning expression on my face. It was an adorable puppy.

"Want to pet him?"

"Derick, what did you do?" I asked, as I picked it up and cuddled it.

"We have to think of a good name for him," he said.

"Are you saying he's ours?" I asked, reluctantly.

"I saw his mother, she's a black lab. We're not sure who the father is." He laughed. "She was running around the repair shop with a pit bull and an Afghan."

"He's a brindle, but he doesn't have the body of a pit bull, and his tail is skinny," I said.

I handed him back to Derick, who petted and fawned over the puppy like it was a baby. I could sense Derick was definitely in nesting mode, and I immediately felt fear. My alone script was surfacing. It's funny how the subconscious works. Nagging issues are like pieces of wood you hold underwater. You can only hold them under for so long before they pop up to the surface.

"Come on. You afraid of a little puppy?"

"No, it's not that at all," I said.

"What harm can a little puppy do?" he asked, kissing it on the head.

I took the dog in my arms and sat on Derick's lap.

"You can even name him if you want," he said.

"Rebel," I said.

"Okay, tiger, Rebel it is."

Derick insisted the puppy sleep in the bathtub. I wondered how long that would last. The first night he whimpered, whined, and yelped. It was like having a newborn baby. That went on for a few nights, but before I knew it, the baby was sleeping in bed with us. Derick was so attached to this puppy that he took it everywhere. Rebel was an adorable little thing, and the way Derick fawned over him, I was a little jealous. The sex was still great, but the cuddling was with Rebel, not me.

~~~~~~

I was almost ecstatic when Star Green came for a visit. She stayed with us, and we did a lot of things together, which took my mind off Derick's love affair with Rebel. There was an old, classic, tall ship called the Esmeralda in Lahaina Harbor. It had a crew of Spanish sailors who were trained for sailing the ocean in an old-fashioned clipper ship. It was something impressive to look at with its sails at full mast. They had an open house on the ship with a luncheon and all the wine you could drink. Star, Shirley, and I, took a dinghy out to the ship, and were welcomed aboard by Spanish sailors. We had a fun day out on the ocean. We drank quite a bit, but even after a day of nonstop drinking, we decided a few drinks at the Pioneer Inn were in order.

Once we were back on the shore, we ran into some friends of mine on the dock. We all walked into the Pioneer Inn, got a table, and ordered drinks. We were having so much fun—well, until Star and I got into a silly argument about where we would be going that night. I had reservations about going to the Mission Bar because of Derick, and she insisted that he was being childish about the whole thing.

"Childish?" I asked.

"I know Derick's younger than you, but he needs to grow up."

"Star, that's easier said than done. I have to consider his feelings."

"So what are you going to do, avoid Dominick French at all costs, even if it means having less fun?" she said with slurred speech.

"I haven't worked it out in my head yet, but I will. I just don't wanna ruin Derick's night."

"You need to put your foot down with him."

"Relationships are about compromise," I said, feeling embarrassed in front of my friends.

"Whatever. I have to go to the bathroom," she said, getting up and walking away.

Suddenly I was stone-cold sober and angry at her. *She sure talks big for someone who isn't even in a relationship,* I thought. I'm not sure why it bothered me so much. Thinking back, Star often said something thoughtless, and I had the habit of appeasing her.

When she returned, she sat at the table and took my hand. "Let's not fight."

We stood up, said goodbye to my friends, and drove home. When we arrived back on Nanu Street, I went straight to my room.

She knocked on my bedroom door, opening it slowly. I was sitting on the bed, and she came in and sat beside me.

"I didn't mean to offend you in front of your friends," Star said.

"I just don't understand how your mind works at times."

"I know, I can get a little careless when I drink."

"Look, let's not dwell on this. I want you to have a fun vacation, and I don't want to fight."

"I promise I'll be more thoughtful in the future," Star said, her blue eyes pleading and melting my heart. I loved her so.

We hugged, and my annoyance with her evaporated in the afternoon heat.

Star stood up and said, "I'll make us something. Will Derick be eating supper?"

"I imagine so. He should be home from work pretty soon.

"He's really nice, Adriana, and he seems really into you."

"I know. It's just that he's such a guy's guy. Different than some of my other boyfriends."

"And you've had so many of those over the years," Star said, rolling her eyes.

"What's that supposed to mean?" I asked, annoyed again.

"You've lost your sense of humor," she said.

She turned on her heels and walked out, slamming the door.

Maybe she was right, and I was being a stick in the mud. I thought of the time she came with me to the free clinic in Haight-Ashbury in the early 1970s when I'd decided I was tired of birth control pills and wanted an IUD implanted. She held my hand in the doctor's office during the procedure and put up with my blubbering. We had a history, Star and I. Perhaps she was right, and I'd lost my sense of humor. She had only a few days left of her vacation, and I wanted her to have the best time, and to go home knowing we were still sisters.

I was upstairs at the crafty Mermaid when I heard a commotion downstairs. There was a bit of squealing and Annie's unmistakable cackle. I peeked over the railing, and Haku was talking a mile a minute, waving her arms about.

"What's going on down there?"

"I'm getting married," Haku said, smiling up at me.

"Oh my God! The mermaid is marrying the sea captain," I said.

I hurried down the stairs and hugged Haku. I looked in her eyes, which were watering.

"You helped me see what was right in front of me all the time," she said.

"Well, I don't want to take any credit," I said, with a serious expression. Then I laughed.

"We're getting married in Hana. We've rented out the whole Heavenly Hana Inn," she said.

"I hope we're invited," Annie asked.

"Of course, I want you girls there," Haku said.

I walked home after work with so much on my mind. I felt joy for Haku but uncertainty for myself. I was able to coax her along in realizing what she truly wanted to happen in her life. I needed someone to do that for me. I had hopes that my relationship with Derick Ellis would turn into something deeper and lasting. I thought of my friend Daisy Holmes, who had just died a very young woman during the height of her happiness at being a new mother. It was all snatched away from her in an instant. I imagined she wasn't prepared for it, and I wondered what the last thing on her mind was. I was overcome with emotion and was happy no one was around when I reached home. I opened the door and began to cry—for Daisy, for her baby, for me, for everyone who died too young or had love and happiness snatched away. I lay on my bed and stared at the ceiling. My body shuddered at the thought of death. Suddenly I stopped. I realized I was alive, and my life was pretty good. I was in love with someone who loved me back.

I got up, washed my face, and drove to the beach to watch the sunset. I knew the sun was sinking below the horizon, and I also knew it would be rising again the next day. In that moment, I was filled with acceptance, and paradise came back to me.

~~~~~~

It was a long drive to Hana, and we had Annie with us. Derick and I talked and listened to music along the switchbacks, bridges, and waterfalls. Annie slept most of the way. I knew we were close to Hana when we passed the church in Kipahulu on the peninsula where Charles Lindbergh is buried. We arrived at the Heavenly Hana Inn the night before the wedding. Haku's family came from Oahu, and all her friends were there.

On the day of the wedding, Derick wore all white with a yellow plumeria lei around his neck. I wore a red tropical dress and lots of yellow plumerias in my hair. Annie got chummy with the Hawaiian holy man who was there to perform the ceremony. She was trying to pick him up. Then again, nothing Annie did ever surprised me. I watched Haku get her long, dark hair made into a single braid with flowers entwined throughout. Larger flowers were arranged on top of her head to make a crown. She was as beautiful and radiant as a Hawaiian princess. The tall, blond, blue-eyed sea captain was stately in all white, with a red sash, and a maile leaf lei around his neck. The ceremony was beautiful, with Hawaiian chants and Christian vows.

That evening we put off thinking about the drive back to the west side of the island. Everyone took off their fancy garb after wedding photos and relaxed around the grounds of the inn. There was a local band playing and an array of homemade local food favorites to pick on. It was such an uplifting weekend in the most beautiful tropical setting. The Inn sat in the center of a grove of large trees, and not far from the venue was the ocean. Our room was attached to Annie's with shoji screens. I remember having sex to "You Shook Me All Night Long" by AC/DC and had to concentrate on tantric breathing without noise.

We left on Sunday after a Hawaiian brunch. The ride back to Lahaina was shorter, but Annie jabbered the whole way from the backseat. She didn't stop until we dropped her off at her apartment.

~~~~~~~

As soon as we walked in the front door, Derick picked up Rebel, making a big fuss, kissing and petting him. He fed him right away. I watched him, thinking, *He'd make a great dad.*

Shirley was sitting at the kitchen table, drinking Olympia beer and eating a plate of spaghetti.

"How was the wedding?" she asked. "I want to hear all about it."

"It was really beautiful. But that drive is a killer."

"Annie tried to chat up the Hawaiian holy man who performed the ceremony," Derick said.

"Figures," Shirley said, laughing. "You guys hungry?"

"Are you kidding? I think I'm more tired than hungry," I answered.

"Speak for yourself," Derick said.

"There's more spaghetti in the pot on the stove, and there's cheese in the fridge," Shirley said.

Derick took a plate out of the cabinet and scooped a big portion of spaghetti out of the pot. He sat at the table with Shirley, both of them eating heartily.

"You haven't made Italian in a while," Derick said, looking at me.

I stood behind him, leaned on his shoulder, took the fork out of his hand, and took a bite.

"It's good, Shirley," I said.

"So you're gonna eat mine?" Derick said, playfully annoyed.

"No, I just wanted a taste."

Derick pulled me on his lap and continued eating. "Anything on TV tonight?" he asked.

"*Dukes of Hazzard, Three's Company.*" Shirley read off a list from the *TV Guide.*

Derick finished off two plates of spaghetti. He got up from the table and walked into the living room. He turned the TV on and slumped into the bean bag chair.

Shirley and I hung out in the kitchen.

"Shirley, when I was growing up in the Bronx, my mother was close friends with the woman who lived in the next apartment. We shared a common wall in the kitchen, and my mother would knock on the wall, which was the signal for Faye to come over for coffee. She'd always bring a treat with her. Occasionally on a Sunday, my mother would bring Faye a plate of her wonderful Italian tomato sauce with meatballs, sausage, and Italian cheese. Faye would only eat it from one of our plates. They were Jewish, and kept a kosher home, so they couldn't mix dairy with meat or eat pork. But Faye had no problem eating pork, or the pasta with meat sauce and cheese, as long as it was on one of our plates. Faye said it was due to an old orthodox health law. I have to tell you, as a child it seemed ridiculous."

"No kidding," Shirley said.

"That makes no sense," Derick said, from the living room, shaking his head.

"People have different beliefs, although even now I find it defies common sense," I said.

Derick was watching *The Dukes of Hazzard*.

Shirley and I looked at each and rolled our eyes.

"That's the stupidest show I've ever seen," I said.

"We'll watch what you girls want when this is over," Derick said.

Rebel climbed into the bean bag chair next to Derick. I could see they were both content. Looking at them, I couldn't get that song "Bad Case of Loving You" out of my head. At that moment I knew I'd fallen in love with Derick Ellis. God, I had it bad.

Derick looked up at me. "Hey, tiger, can you put my dish in the sink?"

I cleared the dishes and silverware from the table and set them in the sink.

I walked over to the bean bag chair and stared down at Derick. "Is there room for me?"

"Always," Derick said, moving over to make room.

I cuddled up next to him, and he put his arm around me. I slid my arm across his chest, nuzzling my face in his neck.

Rebel licked my arm and poked me with his wet nose, as if to say, *Hey, I was here first.* I felt warm and syrupy all over. I fell asleep to Derick laughing at something stupid on *The Dukes of Hazzard*.

SEVENTEEN

BLUSH LIKE YOU MEAN IT

Too much of a good thing can be wonderful.

—Actress Mae West

I t was the spring of 1980, and the Gray Mouse was acting up again. Derick had worked on it a number of times, but problems persisted. "I think it's time you get a new car," he said.

"Get rid of the Gray Mouse?"

"I know you have memories in that car, but it's beginning to have too many problems."

"Just see what you can do to fix it for now. I'll start looking for another car."

"There's a cute little red Toyota at the shop. We fixed some minor stuff, and the car runs great. The owner already bought a new car. You should buy it," Derick said.

"I'll have to look at it."

"It's not a beauty contest. I'm telling you the car runs great."

"Still, I want to see it."

"Drive me to work this morning, and you can check it out."

When we got to the cannery, I circled the Red Toyota and thought it was cute enough.

"Let's take it for a spin," Derick said.

I drove, and Derick sat in the passenger seat. I liked the way it ran and how it felt.

"You've convinced me," I said, watching his blank expression turn to approval.

I went to the office and talked to Ron. He drew up a note of sale for the Gray Mouse, and a purchase document for the red Toyota. I signed the papers, we shook hands, and it was a done deal. I stared at the Gray Mouse, which gave me my first feeling of independence and mobility, and suddenly it felt as if I was abandoning a friend.

Derick was watching me. "It's a car. Cars don't have feelings."

I half smiled, because that was not what my gut was telling me. I ran my hand along the dent in the side door and over the hood. I opened the passenger door and looked inside. I gathered all my personal items from the glove compartment. I flashed on picking the Gray Mouse up at the dock, and finding Daisy Holmes's silver and turquoise ring. I teared up a little.

Derick hugged me. "Tiger, the car will be fine. Someone else will love it the way you did."

Even though he thought I was an idiot for being emotional about a car, he played along and helped me make the transition. I got into the driver's seat of the Toyota and started the engine.

"I'll see you at home later," I shouted as I drove away.

"You'll have to pick me up, lolo, my truck's at home," he yelled, shaking his head and laughing.

~~~~~~~

We had the coldest day on record in Lahaina. I think the temperature had dropped to forty-five degrees overnight. That was common for winter up on the crater in Kula, but not for spring at sea level in Lahaina. I remember wearing a sweater over my T-shirt and shorts. I had the day off, and Derick was at work. I was watering all the shrubs and plants in the yard, and Rebel was sniffing every leaf and peeing on every bush to mark his territory. He was growing into a beautiful dog.

I went inside and started a lentil soup for dinner. I puttered around the kitchen all morning, and in the afternoon I worked on a painting in the yard. Suddenly it came to my attention that I hadn't seen Rebel in a while. I searched around the house, knowing he had the habit of sleeping in different places. He wasn't in the house, so I looked for him in the yard. I realized he was missing and began to panic.

I grabbed Rebel's leash and began walking through the neighborhood looking for him. I called his name and searched for more than an hour, but there was no sign of him. I had to call Derick at work. I knew he was going to be upset. Of course as soon as I told him Rebel was missing, he freaked out and was back at the house in no time.

We both combed the neighborhood again, but no one saw him. It crossed my mind that he could have been run over, and maybe was lying somewhere dying, and my stomach lurched. I felt cold chills all over, and it wasn't from the cool weather that day.

"We should have had him fixed. Maybe he got into a fight with another male dog," I said.

"I'm not doing that to my dog," Derick said.

"I don't think it would be a bad thing."

"Forget it, I'm not doing that to him."

It was the wrong time to argue with Derick. I knew he was upset. We walked back to the house, and even the lentil soup and garlic toast didn't appease him.

"This is your fault," Derick said, looking at me. "He's not even full grown yet."

"I'm sorry, I wasn't paying attention," I said, and began to cry.

"I'm just frantic. I didn't mean to blame you," he said, hugging me.

"I feel awful," I said, not wanting to look at him.

"Maybe he'll just come home on his own," Derick said with a downhearted expression.

We ate dinner and watched TV. Derick kept checking the windows, hoping Rebel would appear in the yard or scratch at the front door. We walked around the neighborhood again before it got dark, knocking on neighbors' doors. No sign of Rebel. There was no sleeping that night.

In the morning we moped into the kitchen, and I made coffee while Derick sat at the table staring off into space. Derick had to leave for work, so I walked outside with him to his truck, which was parked on the street.

"Derick, I think I see Rebel!"

We looked up the street, and there was Rebel, limping toward the house. He approached us cautiously, as if he had done something bad and thought he was going to be punished.

"His leg is all fucked up," Derick said.

He picked Rebel up as if he were a baby and carried him into the house. Derick fed him and checked him over. He had scratches here and there, but his leg looked broken. It was obvious that he'd been in a fight.

"You go to work, I'll take Rebel to the veterinarian," I said.

Derick agreed, hugged me, and pet Rebel. He was almost in tears, but I knew he was relieved. Derick went to work, and I took Rebel to the vet.

When I picked Rebel up the next day, the vet said, "If he didn't have those bites and scratches, I'd think he was hit by a car. I had to reset his leg and clean his other wounds." Then he asked me if I wanted to make an appointment to have him neutered.

I told him I'd let him know, although convincing Derick was a dead issue. I spent the rest of the afternoon babying Rebel. I called the girls at the Crafty Mermaid and explained the situation. After Rebel's leg healed, Derick took Rebel to work with him every day.

~~~~~~

We went on a long hike into the West Maui Mountains with Derick's boss, Ron, in his old military jeep. That thing went through streams, over rocks—no terrain was a match for that vehicle. They brought hunting rifles along. I wasn't raised around guns—my father was a hairdresser and then a barber. Guns were foreign to me, and it certainly didn't match my sensibilities. The forest was full of strange trees and shrubs. My favorite was an African drum tree—that's what Ron said it was. He tapped the trunk of the tree, and indeed, it sounded like a hollow drum.

Ron said, "There are a lot of wild pigs up here."

We walked cautiously through the narrow path as many had done before us. It opened into a clearing and we ate the sandwiches we brought. We hadn't been walking too long in the forest again when a loud shot rang out. Suddenly, a beautiful owl dropped to the ground in front of me. I looked at Derick, who was holding the rifle.

"What the hell did you do that for?" I asked.

"I didn't know it was an owl," Derick answered.

He had shot grouse, chukars, and pigeons before, cleaned, cooked and ate them, but an owl! I walked over to the owl and picked it up. Its head lay limp over my palm.

"You killed a beautiful owl!" I said.

Derick looked at the owl, and Ron looked at me.

"I told you it was a mistake. I thought it was a pigeon or something. It all happened so fast."

"For God's sake, pay attention to what you're doing," I said angrily.

My heart sank as I left the dead owl on the ground and followed Derick and Ron along the path. I was aware Derick grew up in Washington State and went hunting with his family, but I wasn't raised like that. If I had to kill my food, I'd be a vegetarian. I suppose I knew intelligently that my reasoning was hypocritical since I ate meat, and someone else had to kill it. It never crossed my mind at the time that if you were raised on wild game, you might actually like it.

None of us spoke as we walked along the path out of the forest and back to the jeep. I had some thinking to do. Was it just the joy he felt in killing something? Or was it an honest mistake? I knew my mind would dwell on that loathsome act for weeks.

From the **Tao Te Ching:**

Humankind, when living, is soft and tender; when dead, they are hard and tough.
The ten thousand creatures and all plants and trees, while they live, are supple and soft, when they die, hard and stiff.
So it is said: What is hard and stiff belongs to death; the soft and tender belong to life. Therefore, the weapon that is too rigid will shatter.
The tree made of hardest wood will break.
Truly: the hard and mighty are easily overthrown; the soft and weak endure and rise up.

Derick met a couple who owned a management company. They were looking for a maintenance/handyman for their vacation rental properties, and his being a mechanic was a plus with their fleet of mopeds. He quit his job at the cannery and went to work for the management company.

Things were looking up. Everyone at the company was awesome, and they had lots of get-togethers, which Derick and I attended. It was always someone's birthday or someone having a baby, any excuse for a party. I sometimes felt I was among women who weren't in charge of their own lives. They seemed to leave the important decisions to the men.

We got home late one night after just such a function and went to sleep early. The phone rang in the middle of the night, and I picked up the receiver, gazing at the clock. It was after two in the morning. Dominick French still called me on a sporadic basis. Even all these years later, I still can't figure out why I picked up the phone. I suppose I rationalized it with the fact that my parents were getting up there in years, and I couldn't afford to miss an urgent phone call. In reality, what the hell could I possibly do from an island in the middle of the Pacific Ocean?

"Hang up," Derick said, annoyed that he'd been woken up again.

"Hello," I said.

Demo was drunk and rambling, but something funny he said made me bust out laughing.

Derick got up out of bed, got dressed, and stormed out of the bedroom. Soon I heard his truck peel out of the carport. *What the hell?* I thought.

"I'm hanging up."

"No, wait, I need to talk to you," Demo said.

"You've caused enough trouble already. Derick just left pissed off," I said.

"Scaramouche will get over it," Demo said, chuckling.

"You need to grow up," I said, slamming the phone down.

I got up and switched on the light on the dresser. Rebel was still lying on the floor at the foot of the bed. Derick didn't like him sleeping on the bed now that he wasn't a puppy anymore. I told him that the dog probably slept on our bed when we weren't home, and that he was being silly.

Rebel picked his head up and gazed at me with affection. I motioned him to climb up on the bed. He hesitated, so I said, "Daddy's not home."

He cautiously climbed on the bed and lay down next to me, resting his head on Derick's pillow.

"You're getting big," I said, petting him.

I figured Derick would come home when he came to his senses or was tired and hungry. It never crossed my mind that I was oblivious to his feelings. I fell asleep with my arm over Rebel's body, wondering if the dog felt like he was cheating on Derick.

It was still dark when I heard Derick's truck pull into the carport. Rebel lifted his head and listened. As soon as he heard the front door, he jumped off the bed and lay on the floor next to the dresser. I chuckled a little, thinking that the dog was smarter than Derick gave him credit for. I sensed Derick was standing in the doorway in the dark. I didn't flinch. He got undressed and got into bed. He spooned me from behind, and I took his arm and put it over my waist.

"I was just pissed off," Derick said.

"I saw that."

"It's just that I think you still love him."

"Not in the way you're thinking."

"How then? I don't understand why you let him call you, if you don't still have feelings for him."

"It's a different kind of feeling. There are memories. It's not the way I love you."

"I can't help feeling jealous. I think he's still in love with you."

"Maybe, maybe not. More likely he's just bored or lonely when he comes home alone every night, wanting to talk to a familiar voice. It wasn't really a carnal love, it was more ethereal."

Derick was silent. I wasn't sure he understood what I was trying to tell him. He seemed to be digesting my words.

"Making love with him was nothing like it is with you."

"Well, if there's one thing I'm good at!" he said in a teasing tone.

I felt my face flush in the dark.

"And I'm glad for that. I'm in love with only you, Derick," I said

Derick put his arms around me and hugged me tight. He kissed me passionately and moved his hands over my body. I pictured his fists, which were as big as ham hocks. He was a big guy, good looking and strong. I was tiny next to him and knew he could toss me around and hurt me if he wanted to. I wasn't afraid, I was turned on. I knew he was into me sexually, not just emotionally, and that gave me power, a different kind of power. I regarded sexual energy as a life force, the actual living pulse of life. We were good together. He moved on top of me and pushed my legs apart. As soon as he was inside me I began to moan, which made him thrust deeper and with determination. I climaxed, whimpering. Derick grunted with pleasure. Afterward, we lay there together, heart, mind, and body.

~~~~~~

Annie called me at work from the harbor, letting me know there was a party at the Pioneer Inn. I walked to the harbor after work, and the drinks were flowing. I ran into so many people I knew on the dock. I saw Dominick French walking toward me. He'd shaved his head, and looked so different.

"You look good, Adriana. Then again, you always reminded me of Cleopatra and Egypt."

"You shaved your head."

"My head slips off the pillow now," he said, laughing.

I laughed right along with him.

Annie walked over when she saw us. She laughed like hell when she saw Demo's bald head. "I need a drink," she said, walking back to the inn.

"Will you have a drink with me?" Demo asked.

"Why not?" I answered.

The two of us walked into the Pioneer Inn together, found a table, and sat down.

"What in the world made you shave your head?" I asked.

"I got drunk one night, and it just seemed like a good idea. I had to go to a barber afterward."

"I guess it looks okay. It will take some getting used to. You had such beautiful hair."

"The things we do," he said, not taking his eyes off me.

"I hope things are good with you," I said.

"Things are always good with me. You know I'm living the life of Riley," Demo said, grinning.

"Things are good with me too. I'm starting my own hand-painted clothing business."

"So how long do you think you'll stay with that guy?" He totally ignored my business comment.

"I'm happy, content, and unless that changes, why would I leave?"

"You can't have much in common with him."

"We have things in common."

"Annie says it's all about sex with you and him."

I stood up, feeling angry. For some stupid reason, I volunteered to sit down and be humiliated. "I'll see you around Demo," I said, walking away from him.

"Nathan is having a party, and he asked me to invite you," he yelled after me.

I kept walking, making believe I didn't hear him.

I looked for Annie, who I found sitting at a table with a group of people I didn't know. "I want to talk to you," I said, tapping her on the shoulder.

We walked outside onto the dock, and she could tell I was angry.

"You look mad, Riana."

"Why in the world would you tell Demo that I'm with Derick just for sex?"

"I didn't say it like that," she said, blushing with embarrassment at being caught.

"I love Derick. Maybe we have great sex, but that's a plus for me."

"You made sex be the deciding factor between Demo and Derick."

"Well, there's no contest there," I said. "Demo was cruel, and I didn't see that relationship going anywhere. He disappointed me, and he hurt me. You said it yourself, I was in love with him, but he wasn't in love with me."

"I know what I said, Riana, but I think Demo just needed more time."

"I'm not twenty anymore, I'm in my thirties. I don't want to play his game of hide and seek."

Annie put her arm around me. "Riana, please, let's not let this break our friendship."

"Never, but try to think of me. I know you and Demo are close friends, but don't take sides."

We hugged each other and walked back inside together, sat at a table and ordered drinks. Annie and I had a tight bond, and I wasn't going to let Demo, or anyone else come between us. Here, I'd thought I finally found the man of my dreams, and now she had me questioning my motives. *Screw Demo*, I thought. *I'm going to that party and bringing Derick with me.*

"So where's this party Nathan is having?" I asked Annie, ending our spat.

<hr>

Derick was home when I walked into the kitchen. He was feeding Rebel and had something on the stove for dinner. He gazed up at me with a funny look on his face.

Shirley walked into the kitchen with Dennis.

"This is a surprise," I said, shocked to see Dennis.

"Den is out of the navy," Shirley said.

"We're getting married," Dennis said.

"Wow, that's great news. I'm happy for the two of you."

"We're going to be married in that old church on Front Street. The one with the long staircase. It's right across from the ocean and has a nice lawn. We've secured a priest from Hana," Shirley said.

"That will be beautiful," I said.

"We want you and Derick to stand up for us, you know, be best man and maid of honor."

Great, I thought. *Always a bridesmaid, never a bride.*

"It would be an honor," I said, glancing at Derick.

"We can have a reception in the gazebo in the courtyard of the Pioneer Inn," Shirley said.

"I'll look into that," Dennis said, adding it to the list he was writing on a pad.

Derick was silent as he turned the ingredients on the stove. He sneaked a look at me and rolled his eyes. We both felt that she hardly knew this guy. He was in the navy most of the time they knew each other. Then again, there is such a thing as love at first sight. I'd been there myself and wasn't going to judge. I couldn't wait to tell Loretta.

I announced, "We're all invited to a party at Nathan's house!"

~~~~~~

It was a beautiful day in May when the four of us walked up the steps to Nathan's house. We knew lots of people there in the crowd. Demo was there with his shaved head, only he was wearing a cap, looking very European. All their musician buddies, who played with them on a regular basis, were standing around. I met Demo's old girlfriend, who seemed quite normal for someone who had a refrigerator fall on her head. Nathan was at the stove stirring something in a big pot, and I hoped it had nothing to do with any of our canine friends. I sat on the couch between Derick and Dennis while Shirley schmoozed with a few of the girls.

I was doing a good job of staying away from Demo, not wanting to trigger anything weird or macho in Derick. That didn't last long, because when Dennis got up, Demo sat next to me. I was between my new lover and my old lover. They began talking to each other as if I wasn't there.

I got up to get a plate of food so I could let them do their thing. I was standing with Shirley and a couple of the other women, talking about Mt. St. Helen, which had just erupted in Washington State.

Shirley said, "I was hoping to bring Den back there to meet my family, but the volcano blew that idea right out of the sky."

From the corner of my eye I saw Demo and Derick stand up. They were seriously talking about something, which made me uncomfortable.

Nathan threw a bunch of tied-up rope at them, and Derick caught it. Shirley took a photo of the two of them standing together, Derick with his arm around Demo's shoulder. The rope was dangling from Derick's large hands, as if he was planning on hanging Demo from the nearest plumeria tree. Derick was laughing, and Demo had a dumb grin on his face. I figured it was time to go home.

Derick was quiet on the ride home, but when we got back to Nanu Street he exploded.

"He's still in love with you," Derick said. "And I think you're still in love with him."

"What the hell did Demo say to you?"

"The guy calls you in the middle of the night, and you always answer the phone."

I had no argument there. "What do you want from me, Derick?"

"I want you to stop talking to him anytime."

"Lahaina is a small town. I'm not going to do that," I said.

"Really?" he said, his voice cracking.

Shirley and Dennis retreated to their bedroom, and we continued arguing.

"Derick, I don't like these ultimatums."

"I don't have to put up with this shit."

"I'm not going to stop talking to people because it makes you uncomfortable," I said.

"Well, I don't like it."

"Tough darts," I yelled, getting angry and frustrated.

Derick walked away from me in a huff, and I followed him to the bedroom. He began emptying his clothes from the closet and dresser, stuffing it all in his duffle bag. I realized that this wasn't just about the party, it had to have been brewing for a while.

He walked down the hallway without a word. I ran after him, tugging at his arm. "Derick, what are you doing?"

I was reliving those horrible episodes from my childhood, tugging on my father's shirt sleeve, crying, and begging him not to leave.

"Are you going to leave me every time we have a fight?"

He wouldn't answer as he stormed along the hallway.

"It's for the best," he said. "I'll be staying with Cotton."

He reached for Rebel's leash and whistled for the dog to follow him. I continued talking to him, but he had no words for me.

Rebel ran out the front door with Derick, and I watched his truck peel out of the carport. I was in a state of shock. What had I done? Maybe I had been insensitive to the situation all along, thinking only of myself. But he was acting as if he caught me in bed with Demo when he came home from work, or saw us making out in a doorway on Front Street. It was such overkill. I knew Derick was younger than me, and figured his youth was at play. I felt my whole world crashing around me.

I had a very uneasy sleep that night. I tossed and turned. I almost wished I still had the Native American blanket hanging behind my bed, to remind me of when life seemed less complicated. This love stuff was tearing me up. I thought I'd found true love, but he walked out on me. I tried to recreate his words, looking for anything reasonable to wrap my head around. I thought of a million things that could have been troubling Derick. In the days to come, I looked forward to work, which kept my mind occupied. I was shrouded in loneliness and sadness, teetering on depression.

〰〰〰

Dominick French showed up at the Crafty Mermaid, wanting to take me to lunch. I figured why not? I was being accused of something that wasn't true, so perhaps I would just play the part. We went to lunch at Kimo's. We talked and laughed like old times. He told me he was leaving for Europe in June.

When we left the restaurant he walked me back to the store. Derick's black truck passed us on Front Street, and he saw us together. To Demo's surprise, I grabbed his arm and nuzzled up to him. Perhaps I was playing a game. A smile broke out on Demo's face, as if he thought I was warming up to him again. I had a feeling Annie had something to do with Demo showing up at the store that day.

That evening I was in the kitchen, and I heard Derick's truck pull in the carport. He opened the front door, and Rebel ran in wagging his tail profusely as he lunged his snout in my lap.

"So you're back with Dominick French?" Derick asked.

"We had lunch at Kimo's, that's all. And how would you know about that?"

"It didn't look like that to me, I mean the way you were holding on to him."

"Are you spying on me?" I thought, *A little jealousy always works.*

"I was driving by and saw the two of you on Front Street. You didn't see me."

I played dumb. I stood up and put my arms around Derick's neck. "You really believe that?"

"Well, I don't know what to believe. You never even tried to contact me since I left."

"Your mind's made up that I don't love you. I can't convince you if that's what you believe."

"I don't want to believe that," Derick said.

I'm not going to beg you to come home, if that's what you're waiting for."

"Just tell me you love me," Derick said.

My heart melted, getting lost in his eyes. "Honey, I love you something fierce. I want you here with me," I said, blushing.

Derick bent down and kissed me hard on the lips. "I love you so much," he said.

We walked to the bedroom, and Rebel followed.

"No!" Derick said, closing the bedroom door, leaving Rebel in the hallway whining.

I was relieved in so many ways. I flashed on that Bob Dylan song "Tell Me That it Isn't True," and thought of Derick's expression when asking me if I'd gone back to Demo.

~~~~~~~

Shirley's wedding was coming up and we were the maid of honor and best man. Dennis and Shirley took care of the arrangements for the church and the use of the gazebo in the courtyard of the Pioneer Inn for the reception. I ordered all the flowers from Nagasako's Variety, which had two large refrigerators in the back of the store with an array of tropical florals and greenery. Annie and Loretta volunteered to decorate the church, and Loretta said she'd decorate the table in the gazebo.

I was sitting on the couch when Derick came home from work. I didn't hear his truck.

"What's that you're watching?" he asked.

It's a new news channel, CNN. I like the way they show the news from all over the world."

"Forget the news, I want to show you something." He coaxed me off the couch, leading me out to the carport.

"Where did you get this?" I asked.

"It's Ron's brand spanking new black Pontiac Firebird. It cost him about six thousand dollars."

"Wow, that's some car, but what are you doing with it?"

"I asked Ron if I could take you for a spin."

He opened the passenger door for me, and the interior had that new car smell. I got in, Derick started the engine, and we drove off. The Firebird drove like a dream, and I could see Derick felt like a king behind the wheel, his sun-bleached hair blowing in the breeze. I almost felt like we should have dressed for the occasion.

"I'm sure glad you and Ron are still friends," I said.

That night Derick and I went to bed early, and just sat up in bed talking. Rebel was lying on the floor at the foot of the bed making believe he was asleep so he wouldn't get tossed out. I flipped on the radio, and that song by the Pointer Sisters, "He's So Shy," was playing.

Derick leaned over and kissed me. "I don't think I've ever felt this way about a woman before."

Was he expecting me to say the same? That isn't something you can just conjure up. I had been in love before. "I love you too, Derick, very much," I said.

He moved his hands over my body with skill. Derick was anything but shy. Once he knew what turned me on, he stuck to those places on my body. Most men didn't understand that. They were like awkward soldiers walking through a minefield. Derick paid attention to that sort of thing.

~~~~~~

The wedding day arrived. I had painted a crimson rose on a blue and white tie-dyed pareo to wear for the occasion. Derick wore all white, as did the groom, with maile leaf leis around their necks hanging well below their waists. Shirley wore a pale yellow silk pareo, which I also made at the Crafty Mermaid. Derick and I wore straw hats. We all looked très chic in a tropical way.

The four of us left the house together and headed to the church. Annie and Loretta were already there decorating the pews with flowers. We took wedding photos on the steps of the church. Shirley kept asking if anyone had seen the priest yet. We hung around waiting and waiting. Annie and I sat in a pew while the guys stood outside on the lookout. More than an hour passed. The caretaker of the church walked in and told us that the priest was stuck in Hana and couldn't get to Lahaina.

"Are you telling me the priest is standing me up on my wedding day?" Shirley asked.

"I'm just the messenger, ma'am," the caretaker said.

He made a few phone calls, and within an hour, we had a stand-in priest.

We all took seats in the gazebo for the reception after the church ceremony. Derick opened the champagne and filled the glasses, and we toasted the bride and groom. I sat between Derick and Loretta. The food was alright, but the cake was incredible, a whipped marvel of sugary white tufts over a yellow sponge. It was all going beautifully until the heat of the afternoon began melting the white frosting. Everyone sat around fanning themselves as the afternoon heat overcame us. Lahaina can be sweltering in the summer. Annie announced she was heading to the Yacht Club, and Loretta said she was meeting Cotton. Dennis and Shirley headed to a hotel in Kaanapali, where they had a room for a few nights, *As if they hadn't already had the honeymoon,* I thought. Derick and I headed home.

It's so incredible the way she comes out with it, all this beautiful and sensitive detail. Describing character, food, feeling, scenery. Incredible! Like a confection which rose all sugar from the waves. To call it pudding and so relate it to rice and tapioca would be an insult. Meanwhile, the wine glasses had flushed yellow and flushed crimson, had been emptied and filled. And this by degrees was lit, halfway down the spine, which is the seat of the soul.

—*Virginia Woolf,* **A Room of One's Own**

Derick and I had the house to ourselves. Being addicted to romantic love, I feared the mundane. I'd heard somewhere that if you fall in love before the age of twenty-five, you will never forget the feeling and will search to repeat it for the rest of your life. Perhaps that's what happened to me. I wondered what was going through Derick's mind. We had participated in two weddings since we were together. I had mixed feelings. I saw myself as an independent woman, yet I wanted love and companionship. After therapy, I was well aware of my patterns, but they seemed to function subconsciously. Women are groomed from childhood to want marriage and children. If you deviate from that, you are treated like a pariah by society and considered not normal. As much as I loved Derick, and wanted a mate, I had commitment issues, and a fear of the loss of the "self."

My birthday was in July. Derick's boss at the management company arranged for us to stay at a beautiful house in a valley in Napili. Shirley's cousin, who was on Maui for the wedding, was staying with us. I told her she could stay in our room while Derick and I stayed at the house in Napili. I didn't want to take my mother's expensive jewelry with us, so I hid the jewelry pouch in one of the pillows and threw it on my bed with all the other pillows.

The house in Napili was set in a cliff on an ocean cove in the middle of a forest. It was an old house filled with Hawaiiana. All the rooms opened to the ocean, with wraparound porches suspended in the forest. Rebel loved the place and ran through the woods like a wild animal. Derick and I felt like we were on a honeymoon. Looking back, I think we made love in every room of the house.

I woke up early, as the sun was rising. The sky was a pale yellow waiting for the sun to appear. I could hear the ocean as I lay in bed. Derick wasn't around, so I got up and slipped my robe on; there was a chill in the air. I walked out onto the deck and gazed out through the forest to the ocean. It was pure heaven.

Suddenly I felt Derick behind me. He handed me a mug of coffee.

"That's a new service," I said sleepily.

"I know of a better service."

He picked me up and set me on top of the wide wooden railing, spread my legs, got on his knees, and put his head between my legs. I wondered what the point of the coffee was.

"Oh God," I whispered, blushing, and losing all sense of our surroundings.

Suddenly I was falling backward, and pictured myself on the ground in the forest below. "Derick I'm falling over the railing!"

He carried me into the bedroom and sat me on the bed.

He pulled his jeans and underwear down.

"You do it to me now," he said, standing in front of me.

I took him into my mouth and moved my tongue around, teasing him for a while. He pushed me down, got on top of me, and thrust it inside. We rocked back and forth amid sighs, groans, and heavy breathing. When we were finished, he rolled off me and brushed his fingers across one of my nipples. I twisted myself away because the pleasure was almost too much. He snickered and pulled his hand back.

"Can I drink my coffee now?"

He got off the bed smiling and walked out to the deck to retrieve the mug. Derick handed it to me with a satisfied smirk. He could always get me to blush, and that time I meant it.

We went for a hike in the surrounding woods, and then went for a swim in the ocean. The place was what Hawaii living is all about—well, if you had lots of money! I felt lucky to be able to spend a few days in that incredible house.

"Thank you for making my birthday special. It was such a surprise," I said.

"Hold on, tiger—we still have another day here."

We walked back up the path to the house. I was suspended in a kind of heaven. When we arrived back at the house, Derick's boss was standing in the kitchen with his wife.

"Mind if we join you for supper?"

Derick and I glanced at each other.

"It's just for a couple of hours," his boss said, laughing uncomfortably.

There was a large pizza and a bottle of red wine on the kitchen counter. I felt embarrassed at my reaction, and my face turned blush pink. I thanked them for helping to make my birthday so grand. Inwardly I felt slightly invaded, although I knew it would be a short visit and that I was being silly.

After that honeymoon weekend we spent at the house on the cove, we returned home. Shirley's cousin had made my bed and cleaned my room. I lay on the bed and reflected on the wonderful few days we spent in Napili. I rummaged through the pile of pillows for my mother's jewelry pouch. It was gone, and I immediately panicked.

"Derick," I yelled. He came into the bedroom, asking what was wrong.

"The jewelry is gone, my mother's sentimental jewelry."

"Hold on," he said. "Don't get your panties in a twist. I'm sure it's here somewhere."

He looked under the bed and pulled out the pillow with the jewelry pouch.

"It must have slid in back of the bed," I said.

"I told you there was nothing to worry about."

~~~~~~

Loretta and Cotton came by the house on Nanu Street.

"Hey, there's a rodeo in Makawao this weekend for the Fourth of July," Cotton said.

Dennis said, "I've never been to a rodeo before, so I want to go."

"We can drive up in two vehicles," Loretta said.

"Adriana and I will take my truck, and you four can go in Cotton's car," Derick said.

We all agreed, and we had a plan for the holiday weekend.

On the Fourth of July we piled into two vehicles and drove upcountry. The weather was warm and beautiful. It was so clear that the summit of Haleakala Crater could be seen peeking above the clouds. The rodeo was held in the Roske Rice Arena in Olinda. That arena is also used for polo matches during the season. We drove through Makawao, a cowboy town, and stopped for breakfast burritos at Polli's Mexican Restaurant. The guys drank Mexican beers, and the girls had margaritas. Polli's still is famous for their margaritas. As we were leaving Makawao, Shirley remarked about the hitching posts along Baldwin Avenue. I explained that in the old days, cowboys rode to town on horses and that I had seen some still do that once in a while.

The opening ceremony at the rodeo was thrilling and somewhat emotional. A cowgirl rode into the center ring carrying an American flag. After she took a few spins around the arena, a *paniolo* (Hawaiian cowboy) rode out with the flag of the old Hawaiian kingdom. They circled the ring in complete silence, their horses adorned with beautiful leis, their flags waving in the breeze. It gave me chicken skin. However, I didn't enjoy animals being used for entertainment and had to leave my seat during some of the competitions.

RODEO PANIOLO

I received a call from my longtime friend and communal brother, Ross Grant. He was visiting Maui with a new girlfriend, Laura. They were staying at a hotel in Kaanapali. They had a crazy good room on a high floor, with a panoramic view of the ocean and the neighboring islands. His girlfriend was a model. She was very pretty, with short, dark hair, fine features, and spoke with a slight southern accent. Ross had taken her on a trip around the world and told us that Hawaii was their last stop. They invited me and Derick for lunch at their hotel. Laura confessed that she loved to eat tomato and mayonnaise sandwiches on white bread, while the three of us were eating burgers. Ross promised to take us out for a sail the next day. I was happy that Ross and Derick hit it off, Ross being like a brother to me.

While out on the sailboat the next day, Ross told me he was impressed with the work I was doing at the Crafty Mermaid and liked the idea of my hand-painted clothing business.

"Think about coming to Florida. I've got some cash I want to put to work. I'll back you and Laura in a clothing store. I think it would do well in Miami," Ross said.

This was something I wasn't prepared for. The thought of leaving the island had never crossed my mind. At that point I was happy with my life on Maui and had no plans to leave. I thanked Ross for the offer but said that leaving Maui wasn't on my radar. I began to worry about what Derick was thinking. I had a very strong will, but Ross had a way of convincing people to do things. We had a great day out on the ocean, and the four of us enjoyed dinner and drinks together that evening at the hotel.

Ross Grant whispered in my ear, "Just think about my offer."

~~~~~~

It was the end of October 1980, and Halloween was a few days away. We had some great ideas for costumes. We figured we'd just cruise Front Street, and leave it to chance as to getting a table in one of the popular bars. Of course I wanted to go to the Missionaries Hotel but wasn't sure what Derick would think of that. In the past it had been disastrous and I didn't want to play with fire.

When All Hallows' Eve finally arrived, I wore the pale blue satin Mandarin dress with the slits up the sides, the one I bought in Chinatown on that trip to Honolulu with Ginger Pie Turner. Shirley painted my face in pan white and gave me very tiny red lips. My long hair looked fantastic done up with jewels. Derick wore a black mask and my oversized, gold, tie-dyed, crushed velvet coat with a wide sash. He looked like Zorro. We walked up and down Front Street, marveling at all the crazy costumes. We stopped in the Mission Bar to meet Annie for a drink. Demo behaved himself, and there were no suggestive innuendos or love songs aimed in my direction. We finished the night at an upstairs club where Willie K was playing. The whole night was magical.

ZORRO, HALLOWEEN 1980

Shirley and her new husband, Dennis, moved back to Washington State to begin a new life together, and another couple moved in with us on Nanu Street. They were newlyweds, Italians from New Jersey, Regina and Dante Rinaldi. They were a bit straight-laced, except for smoking pot. We were lucky to find two people to share the house with. We rarely had anything to do with Bridget, who was renting Loretta's old garage studio in the back. Regina liked to cook Italian food, which made me happy, and Dante loved working in the yard. In no time we had a bunch of bananas, which Derick chopped down with a machete and hung in the carport in front of the kitchen window. Even the lilikoi bushes were blooming, but other than juice, I really didn't know what else to do with passion fruit. The four of us spent a lot of time together in the coming months. Derick and Dante liked smoking pot, and it was always on the coffee table in the living room. The couple adopted a female pit bull at the Humane Society and named her Honey Girl (popular Hawaiian girl's name), so Rebel gained a friend. Derick and I were living like a married couple, but we weren't married. There was no more blushing about anything. We were all living the good life and looked forward to the holidays.

EIGHTEEN

HAIR MAKES THE MAN

Truth comes from one's life experiences, not through ideas
or books. The savages must civilize us. The uneducated must
teach us truth. The young must show us right and wrong.

—*Jerry Rubin,* **We Are Everywhere**

D erick and I had been together for more than a year, and even though
I was in love with him, I realized I was in love with something else,
Hawaii. Everyone else joked about wanting to "get off the rock," but
I was happy with my life on Maui. Derick was the outdoorsy type, and we
did a lot of camping and hiking. He liked to hunt and fish, and he loved
night diving, which afforded us plenty of fresh fish. He became friends
with another guy, Jackson, who loved the same things, and we often went
hiking together with Jackson and his girlfriend, Molly. I remember the guys
coming home with a wild pig they caught up in the West Maui Mountains.
I saw it dead on the back of Jackson's truck. I found the thought of it being
gutted and cleaned loathsome. Luckily they dressed the pig before they left
the mountain, although I pictured a bloody carcass hanging in the carport
instead of a bunch of bananas. They cooked the pig's chops one night. It
was so gamey, I could taste the hair on the pig's back.

"Not for me," I said, pushing my plate away.

Christmas was only weeks away. Derick and Dante drove up into the
mountains in Derick's old boss Ron's jeep, to find a Norfolk pine, the

traditional Hawaiian Christmas tree. The Cook pines have much less symmetrical branches. Both evergreens were brought to the islands by the missionaries, along with pigs, chickens, and much of the flora and fauna that inhabit the islands today. We decorated the tree, took photos, and settled in for nights of Christmas cheer. It was all very homey, and I was so very happy.

Jackson had two pit bulls, which were kept in a cage in his yard. They were not considered pets. They were trained to sniff out and take down wild pigs. Dante decided to take his dog, Honey Girl, and tag along on one of their hunting jaunts. Regina was overcome with emotion when Honey Girl, her baby, came home with a large gash on her side from the tusk of a pig. She was lucky to have survived the attack. They immediately took her to the veterinarian, and Honey Girl had to have stitches. Regina said that was the first and last time her dog was going hunting. Derick remarked that he'd stitched himself up a few times while out in the wilderness, and we all turned to stare at him.

Regina was a pretty girl with long, dirty-blonde hair, and was a bit stoic at times. She seemed very traditional and spoke slowly and definitively. Dante was short and good looking, with similar features and hair. The husband and wife team looked like siblings.

I was standing at the stove cooking spaghetti and meatballs when Derick came home from work. I was dipping Italian bread in the pot to taste the sauce. When I say Italian bread, it was nothing like the crusty Italian bread from a bakery in the Bronx. It was a soft and soggy imitation. Dipped in my tomato sauce, however, any bread tasted good.

"That smells killer," Derick said, wrapping his arms around me from behind, and kissing me on the lips. "Did you hear?"

"Hear what?"

"It was all over the radio today. John Lennon was shot and killed."

"What? Where did this happen?"

"He was walking out of his apartment building in New York City, and a crazed fan shot him."

"I worked all day and we didn't have the radio on," I said.

"Why would a fan do something like that," he asked.

"Who knows? People are nuts on the mainland, that's why islanders call it the madland."

Derick took something out of his pocket, and I imagined he had a halfie of cocaine. I thought, *Not when I just made this delicious Italian meal. I want to enjoy it, not lose my appetite.*

"Put the wooden spoon down, I want to show you something," he said.

He handed me a small jewelry box, and it was a bit of a shock. I popped the lid and saw a small, yet adequate, antique gold ring. It was in the shape of a bouquet of flowers with small chips of rubies (my birthstone) and diamonds set in golden florets. It was simply beautiful.

"Derick," I said.

He smiled proudly. "Merry Christmas, tiger."

A short poem I wrote:

> A ring of golden flowers my true love gave to me.
> Rubies at their heart, diamonds glistening like snowflakes.
> A token of love to shine through the changes of time.

The year 1981 arrived with a mere whimper, as nothing out of the ordinary happened. We all were living a mostly mundane existence: going to work, cooking dinners, and taking the dogs for runs on the beach. Derick and I were in a good place, even though Demo continued his three in the morning phone calls when we least expected them. Derick probably realized that in reality I was lying next to him, not Dominick French.

At the same time Derick and I were cruising along in togetherness, Dante and Regina seemed to be growing apart. I wasn't sure what was going on with them, because Regina wasn't the type to talk about herself or her relationship. I certainly didn't want to get involved with their problems when everything was going so well with me and Derick. Dante was very possessive of Regina, as if she were a prize he'd won at the state fair. He expected to be consulted regarding every decision she made, even the most ordinary daily choices. She seemed unaware that women won the right to vote and could do things without their husband's approval. I may not have been in the political counterculture anymore, but I maintained my beliefs regarding women's rights. Regina and I were very different as women. I wondered if my relationship with Derick would change if we got married. It was a sobering thought. Even back when I was a hippie, I remembered in that political arena, men enjoyed dominance and brainstorming, while women made the coffee.

Excerpt from **We Are Everywhere** by Jerry Rubin:

Movement men objectify women. In movement organizations there were all the women in one room doing the typing and there were all the men in the other room sitting around the table like some fancy board of directors making all the decisions. Housewives are political prisoners. What would the business executives do if their wives revolted? What would happen to business if secretaries rose up against their oppression? Amerikan advertising is built around the domestication of the female kitchen slave. Young girls are faced with the horrendous models that Madison Avenue produces.

That winter we went on a few camping trips. One weekend Jackson reserved Poli Poli Cabin in Kula up on Haleakala Crater. We brought the dogs with us, a cooler of food, and the guys took their guns. The cabin was very basic with a stove and bunkbeds. The forest was full of different groups of trees. There were all sorts of evergreens, groves of eucalyptus, and fruit and nut trees that did well at the higher elevations. The guys didn't bag anything that first day, but we did bring plenty of food with us, so we had a fun night around the campfire toasting franks and marshmallows.

On the second day, the guys left before dawn with all the dogs. Molly and I rose when it was light. I made the coffee, and she went outside to the cooler to get milk, butter, cheese, and bread.

"I know I packed cheddar," she said, walking back into the cabin.

"I packed American cheese and provolone," I said.

"Maybe I forgot, but I'm almost positive."

"Maybe the guys took it for a snack."

"What do you think we should do while the guys are gone?" Molly asked.

"I'd like to go back to the eucalyptus grove and take some photos."

After we ate breakfast, Molly and I went on a short hike to the eucalyptus grove. The wonderful medicinal scent of the trees was calming, and the birdsongs were distinctive in the quiet of the forest. When we got back to the cabin the guys were still not back.

"I wish we had a deck of cards," I said.

"They're somewhere in with my clothes, if I could just find them," Molly said, combing through her duffle bag.

"I hear the dogs."

"The guys must be back," Molly said with a smile.

As soon as the guys walked into the cabin, they wanted food.

"It's all in the cooler," I said.

Derick walked out to feed and water the dogs, who were breathing heavily and wagging their tails in anticipation.

Jackson fished through the cooler looking for stuff. "Where's the cheddar?" he shouted.

"We were wondering the same thing. Molly thought you took it for a snack," I yelled back.

Derick got a fire started since the stove didn't look so clean.

"I'm grilling burgers," he said. "I'll top them with American cheese."

That night we walked to a clearing so we could observe the stars. There were thousands above us in the sky. We even saw a couple of shooting stars. It was so beautiful up there in the woods, and pretty chilly after the sun went down. The temperature could drop into the thirties that far up on the crater. We bundled up with sweaters and jackets and sat on the ground around the campfire.

Jackson told us there were people who lived in the forest. They hunted and ate fruits and berries that were in season. I knew about ferns and how to cook them, and decided that I would look for fiddlehead ferns the next day. Derick and I cuddled up in the bunkbed that night just to keep warm.

On our last day there, the guys took the dogs again to see if they could find any wild game. Molly and I slept in. She got up when the sun was already bright and put the coffee on. I lay there hoping it would warm up before I got out of my sleeping bag.

Molly walked out to the cooler to get milk. She came back into the cabin exasperated. "There's no milk! Do you think the guys would've finished it?"

"They wouldn't do that," I said. "Would they?"

"This is really crazy!"

"Yes, totally weird and creepy."

The two of us walked out to the cooler and looked through the food.

"The hot dogs are gone, and I only see one package of chopped meat. We brought three. We only used one last night."

"I hope the guys left us a gun," Molly said.

Suddenly we noticed the shadow of a man run through the bushes behind the cabin.

"Let's go inside and lock ourselves in until the guys get back," she said.

"I don't feel safe. I wish you had that gun," I said.

"Like Jackson said last night, probably someone living up here saw an opportunity for food."

Molly and I were getting bored trapped inside the cabin. She never found the playing cards she'd packed away, so we talked. Molly was telling me about the guy she went out with before she met Jackson, and how he kept trying to get her to have sex with him and another woman.

"He was obsessed with threesomes," she said.

"Did he ever suggest another guy?" I asked.

"Never crossed his mind," she said, and we both laughed.

"I went out with a guitar player when I lived in San Francisco. He had the same idea."

"Do tell," Molly said relishing the conversation.

"Well … He had this old house in Marin, and his neighbor right across the street was the wife of a famous comedian. I won't name names. I think she was divorced or they were separated. My boyfriend, Blake Middleton, had a thing for her. She was much older than us, but she had a body to kill for. We hung out at her house once in a while. Like I said, they were neighbors and friends. Anyway, he hinted that we should all get in bed together. I didn't like it, but he coaxed me into it. Cocaine and booze had a lot to do with loosening me up in those days. So the three of us were lying in bed touching each other when her boyfriend came home. He was a gorgeous hunk of a man! The guy got undressed and jumped on the bed. Blake had a 'Come to Jesus' moment and wanted to go home. He didn't think it was such a good idea anymore."

"Just like a man," Molly said.

"Of course, he wanted to screw my brains out when we got back to his place."

"His manhood was challenged in some way," she said.

"Seemed like it."

"Are you still in touch with him?" Molly asked.

"I get a letter from him every once in a while. His mom always sends me a Christmas card."

We heard the dogs barking so we knew the guys were back. They were jiggling the door knob.

"Open up," Derick said.

The guys seemed dumfounded as to why we were hiding inside the cabin.

"Why the hell did you take all the guns?" Molly asked Jackson. "Some guy was lurking around the woods behind the cabin. He's been taking our food right out of the cooler."

"So that's why stuff was missing," Jackson said.

"We're going home today anyway," Derick said.

"Still, we were scared. If we had a gun we could've fired off a shot and scared him off," I said.

"Down, tiger," Derick said, amused at my comment.

"Nobody's shooting anybody," Jackson said, laughing. "The poor guy was probably hungry. I told you, there are people living up here in the woods."

While we were packing up, I thought about how I hadn't seen Annie in a while. I had the feeling she didn't like Derick. She told me she thought Derick liked to kill little animals.

I understood what she was saying, but I knew he just had a whole different attitude about hunting small game. I wasn't going to argue with Annie. Besides, Annie hated cats and told me she set poison out on her porch for them, which I thought was cruel. I still loved her very much; she was my Maui mom. I mostly saw her at work, and once a week or so we'd have a drink at one of the bars in town. But our carousing days were definitely over.

~~~~~~

Derick had a friend with a sailboat, so we took Dante and Regina out with us for a day. It had been quite a while since I'd spent time on the water. I soon was aware of the vastness of the ocean and the remoteness of where we lived. The water was a little rough that day, and as the boat took off at full sail, it fought the waves, soaking us with salty spray. I watched Derick work the sails with the captain. I remembered being out on the water with Peyton Parker and how insecure I felt. Watching Derick, I felt secure knowing he belonged to me. He was my man, and I felt a warm thrill run through me.

I thought of a lot of things out on the ocean that day. I thought of how I didn't even see the scar on his face anymore. It certainly didn't detract from his good looks. I could tell by the way other women looked at him. Derick noticed me watching him and snaked his way over to me on the bow. We were getting tossed around in the swells.

"What?" he asked.

"Nothing. Just that I love you," I said.

His expression melted, and a shy smile broke on his face. When the ocean calmed down, I lay on the deck, feeling transported to a calm and beautiful place.

SUSPENDED IN TIME

In April we went on a weekend camping trip with Derick's boss and his wife. A whole troupe of people tagged along. When we arrived in Hana, we camped on a cliff right at the edge of the ocean. I could see palm trees and cows grazing on the mountain behind us. There was no shelter on the cliff, and it was very windy. It wasn't a hunting trip, so I wondered why Derick brought a rifle.

The first night was glorious under the stars, with just the sound of the surf below. I brought my guitar and played a few tunes, and we sang songs. Until that night, Derick seemed to play my guitar more than I did. But on that night, I was just enjoying the stars and the roar of the waves as they broke on the beach below.

The next day was a Sunday. We made breakfast in an iron skillet over the fire. In the light of the morning I watched the whales off in the distance. By the month of April, they were on their way to Alaska, but the ones that lingered were very frisky. They either hadn't mated yet or hadn't had their calves yet.

I was involved with watching the whales playing and spouting, and the time ran away from me. I didn't notice Derick around the camp. I stood up, and my eyes searched the vista for his form. A shot rang out, and I saw Derick on the edge of the cliff holding his rifle. He quickly descended along the path that went down to the beach. My sensibilities were shocked for a moment, and I wondered what the hell he shot at. My stomach was in a knot. Other campers were staring over the cliff, and my heart sank. Derick emerged from the path carrying something. As he got closer to the camp I saw that it was a turtle.

"Are you out of your mind?" I said. "There are campers all over the place watching."

"We're eating turtle tonight," he said, very pleased with himself.

"Derick, I don't even think this is legal."

"Don't worry about it."

"You're crazy. We can get arrested," I said.

That night, while Derick proudly fried up some of the turtle meat in the iron skillet, a park ranger walked into our camp. We were all stiff and nervous.

The ranger said, "I had a complaint from some campers that they heard gunshots coming from this direction."

No one said anything as Derick kept flipping the turtle meat in the iron skillet.

"No one here has a gun, sir," one of the guys said.

The ranger walked over to Derick and looked in the skillet but said nothing.

"Thank you for your cooperation," he said.

We watched the ranger walk to the next campsite near the other end of the cliff. I felt relieved when he walked away, but I was troubled about Derick's actions. He didn't consider the consequences when he got it in his head to do something like that. I had heard somewhere that green sea turtles were on the endangered species list. I had no idea what kind of turtle that was, but I'd heard there was a $25,000 fine for killing one. Everyone in our camp was laughing at how the ranger didn't even realize that *honu* (turtle) was being cooked in the skillet. It plagued my mind, and after that experience, I was looking forward to going home.

The following evening at home, Derick cooked turtle soup and coaxed me to try it. It tasted like seawater, and I didn't like it a bit. Everyone else ate it heartily. One thing I was certain of. If I was ever shipwrecked on a deserted island or lost in the wilderness, I'd want Derick with me.

~~~~~~

It was slow at the Crafty Mermaid, and I was standing at the desk talking to Annie while a few tourists were combing through the racks.

"I heard there's a scary disease going around," Annie said.

"What kind of disease?" I asked.

"AIDS. Not sure what the letters stand for."

"How do you get it?"

"I hear it's transmitted sexually."

"Oh, I'm sure penicillin or antibiotics could take care of it."

"No, people are dying left and right from it, especially gays," Annie whispered.

"Well, they do like random sex with strangers, at least that's what my friend Adam told me."

"They're saying it's an epidemic," she whispered so customers couldn't hear.

"Oh, God," I said. *Thank God I did what I did when I did it,* I thought.

Promiscuity was no longer an option, and I was relieved that I was in a monogamous relationship. I was happy with Derick, for the most part. He did seem to have a wild and savage side I was not familiar with. I wanted our relationship to develop into something serious, and I looked for ways to keep the romance going. I knew how mundane daily routines and stagnation played games with my sensibilities.

~~~~~~

Derick came home from work with a bouquet of flowers. My first thought was, *What the hell did he do?*

He handed me the flowers, saying, "I was at Nagasako's and they smelled so good, I just had to get them for you." Perhaps it was Derick's way of attempting to keep romance alive.

I took the flowers and smelled them, the aroma of the pikake being the most noticeable. It had been years since a man gave me flowers, not since Bobbie Becker on Staten Island. I found a vase and put them in water.

"I'm making beef stew," I said.

"Sounds good. I'm so hungry. I didn't feel like eating much today."

"That's not like you."

"Yeah, well," he said, as he got the dishes out of the cabinet.

"I added rosemary this time. I thought I'd try a new spice in the stew."

"I like everything you cook," Derick said, heaping praise on me. "Where's Dante and Regina?"

"They went out to dinner and a movie."

"We have the house to ourselves?"

"We do," I said, smiling.

After dinner (Derick had two helpings), we watched TV. Rebel tried to get on the beanbag chair between us, but Derick nudged him off repeatedly. He loved lying between us.

"I think he's starting to feel closer to you," Derick said.

"You're imagining it," I said.

Derick lifted his arm and put it around my shoulder.

"You say that, but I can tell the way Rebel looks at you like a lovesick puppy."

It crossed my mind that Derick might be jealous of the dog liking me more than him.

He was laughing at something dumb on *Dukes of Hazzard*.

The show was finally over, and Derick turned the TV off. He moved his free hand to my breasts and rubbed them until he felt the nipples getting hard through my T-shirt, and I wasn't stopping him. I reached down and brushed my hand back and forth along his member through his jeans, until I felt him get hard. He leaned over and kissed me on the lips.

"Let's move to the bedroom," he said.

We got up, leaving Rebel in the living room, who now had full domain over the beanbag chair. We closed the door in case Regina and Dante came home unexpectedly.

Derick sat on the bed and looked up at me. "Come here, tiger."

He pulled my dress up and stared at the lower half of my body. *Damn, I wish I'd worn those light blue panties he likes, the ones with the beige lace trim*, I thought.

Derick took his index finger and ran it under the edge of my panties, as if he were studying a statue in a museum he wasn't supposed to touch, and I felt little throbs of desire!

I took off my clothes while he watched me. I liked watching his facial expression change when he wanted sex; it was melty and hot. I lay naked on the bed and opened my legs just a little. When he took his T-shirt off, I stared at the sun tattoo on his chest. I watched with pleasure as he took off his pants and underwear. The light was still on, but this time I wanted to watch him. He got on top of me and kissed me, his hair brushing my face.

"I love you," he said. "We're good together."

I didn't answer him. I'm not sure why. Maybe I wanted him to want me more than I wanted him. He lay next to me, sucked on the nipple closest to him, and played with the other one. I was getting really hot and reached down to his member. I teased and played with it with my tongue. I moved on top of him and guided it inside me.

"It's okay if you want to be in charge," he said, with a little chuckle.

After we finished, we lay there for a while. I wanted to say so many things but said nothing. I let him be the one to express his love.

He hugged and kissed me. "I have to tell you something."

My stomach began to ache, twist, and turn. "What did you do?"

"Nothing. I didn't do anything," Derick said.

"Then what is it?" I asked nervously.

"The company is sending me off island, to Hawaii for three months."

"What the hell is there over on the Big Island?"

"They have an oceanfront property on the Kona side of the island that needs some maintenance. It will be big bucks for us."

"Three whole months? That's such a long time."

"You can fly over on the weekends. We'll go see Kilauea Volcano, and Parker Ranch."

"Is this what the flowers were for?"

"Now you're talking crazy," he said. "It will be fun over there, something different."

"If it's your job, I guess we really don't have a choice, huh?"

"No, no choice. I have to go. We'll get off this rock for a while," Derick said, with a pleasure that made me uncomfortable.

~~~~~~~

After Dereck left for the Big Island, I threw myself into my hand-painted clothing business. I had ordered five dozen white cotton T-shirts from a warehouse in Atlanta, Georgia. They were the cheapest I could find. I had them shipped by barge, which took about five weeks to arrive on Maui. I'd set up the folding table in the yard and paint, sometimes until sunset. Some of the white T-shirts I would tie-dye first, and when they were dry, I'd paint a tropical flower over the design. I was having fun with it.

The women of the Crafty Mermaid were displaying my painted T-shirts on one whole wall in the shop, and Annie was pushing them on tourists, along with the other hand-painted clothing. It was becoming a lucrative endeavor. Annie and I resumed our drinking at various bars in town, but in truth, I didn't drink that much anymore. I switched my days off to the weekends when Derick would fly me over to the Big Island so we'd have time together. I settled into a nice routine.

TIE-DYED T-SHIRT WITH OLEANDER BLOSSOMS

It was the weekend, and I landed at the Kona airport on that side of the Big Island of Hawaii and looked for Derick. He always picked me up in the company truck. I thought I saw the truck in the distance and walked toward it. As I got closer, I saw a face beneath a wild mop of wavy blond hair smiling at me.

"What the hell did you do to your hair?"

"I got a bug up my ass to perm it. I just wanted something different."

"I'm not sure if I like it or not. You have so much hair, it's a little wild."

"Well, I'm a wild guy," he said smugly.

"I guess I'll get used to it. You really look like a Leo now. All you need is a lion tattoo on your back. You already have the sun on your chest," I said, teasing him.

We drove to the hotel where he was staying and working. He had a great room with a view. We got in our bathing suits and hit the pool. The water was cool and refreshing, and the weather was still temperate. I dreaded the coming summer in Lahaina. I think Lahaina means land of the endless sun, and the summer can be brutal, with the sun scorching everything. By the end of summer, the hills turn various shades of yellow and brown.

We watched the sunset from the lanai of his room. He put his arm around me as we watched the sun dip into the ocean.

"I think we should go to Kilauea Volcano tomorrow," Derick said.

"I've always wanted to go there, ever since I landed in the islands a few years ago."

"We'll have lunch at the lodge right there, and then we'll hike around the volcano."

"It will be something we won't ever forget," I said.

"That's tomorrow. Let's get down to business tonight," Derick said.

"What business?"

"You know what I mean." He tugged on my long, sheer, white linen shirt. I was glad I was wearing my light blue panties with the beige lace trim.

On Saturday we drove to Volcanoes National Park. We went straight to the lodge at Kilauea and looked at the map to get our bearings. I could see a lot of the lava formations right from the lodge. We set out on a hike over lava rocks along a guided path. The volcano was dormant at that time, so we were able to walk right inside the caldron. The ground was dry, but there were pockets of steam rising up here and there. We spent a couple of hours exploring the various lava tubes and formations, then hiked down to the ocean. The terrain gave you the feeling that you were walking on the surface of the moon, save for the ocean in the distance.

Derick beamed with pride at being able to impress me with it all.

On Sunday we drove to Parker Ranch and rode horses. I hadn't been on a horse in years, but like riding a bicycle, it quickly came back to me. The scenery was incredible. When one thinks of riding horses, one thinks of the Old West and an arid landscape. But in Hawaii, the backdrop is of tropical mountains, valleys, and waterfalls. King Kamehameha brought Portuguese and Mexicans to the islands to teach Hawaiian cowboys how to herd cattle and ride horses.

"You know, a hundred years ago they brought horses and cattle to Hawaii on boats, and swam the animals to shore," I said.

"You're kidding."

"No, that was the only way it could be done."

"I'll bet they lost a few horses and cows in the process," Derick said.

"Probably. You know Parker Ranch was once the largest ranch in the United States."

"You know a lot about Hawaii."

"I've been here a while now, and I'm interested in history."

Derick's wild hair was flipping with every gallop of his horse, and I was beginning to like it. I thought, *Hair really does make the man!*

After a day out riding in the mountains, we drove back to the hotel. I felt sad that I had to leave early Monday morning. We took a shower together, and I made us something to eat. Suddenly the sky opened up and we were inundated with torrential rain. I walked out on the lanai to watch it. I loved the rain. The torrent was so heavy that you couldn't see any forms outside the hotel room.

"We really need the rain," I said.

Derick walked over to me and put his arms around me from behind, "I'm going to miss you."

I turned to face him and said, "Me too, so much."

The rain was dumping on the island. We watched it for a while in a state of peace.

Derick took my hand and led me inside. He stared at my body through the sheer white shirt. "You're beautiful," he said, his expression rearranging. "I love you."

I thought of something my father always said, "The man should always love you more," so I didn't respond and give away the fact that I felt the same way about him. I was overcome with the magnificence of his body. Even his crazy hair set me tingling. I pulled the sheer white shirt over my head and let it fall to the floor. I heard him breathe in. He pulled me to him and kissed me hard on the lips.

"I love you, Derick," I said, softly running my fingers through his tangled, wavy hair.

He was hard against me. "Take your pants off," I said.

He unzipped his jeans and pushed them to the floor. He took his underwear off and threw me on the bed. I was trembling as he got on top of me. Once he was inside me I began to make noise, lots of noise. Derick kept going until I climaxed in waves of pleasure that took over my body, which brought Derick to his end. The torrential rain outside was very loud, and I hoped it drowned out the sound effects coming from our hotel room.

> "Beauty, however, is like a temple in which the profane see naught but the external magnificence. The divine mystery of the artist's thought reveals itself only to the profound sympathy, and the inspiration in each detail of the sublime work remains unseen by the eyes of the vulgar."

> —*Mauprat,* George Sand

The next morning Derick dropped me off at Kona Airport for my flight back to Maui. I watched him drive away in the company truck, his hair blowing wildly.

On the short plane ride home I thought of the great time we had, and recounted every detail in my mind. I knew I had other weekends to look forward to, but I felt something else: vulnerable. I didn't like feeling so deeply about someone, where he totally controlled my well-being. I was feeling out of control where my emotions were concerned. I feared that if he stopped loving me, I would be lost. I'd been through love affairs before and knew how dark things could get when a relationship ends. Then I looked out the window as we were landing and saw Haleakala. I was in too deep already, and there was no turning back.

That was how the spring progressed, working all week on Maui and most weekends on the Big Island with Derick. Three months passed quickly, and soon Derick was back home.

I received a phone call from my friend Ross Grant in Florida.

"I'm getting married," he said.

"Really?" I was a little shocked at the news.

"I want you and Derick to be at the wedding."

I was thinking, *Oh, God, another wedding.* "Of course we'll be there to help you celebrate."

"Marty Feinstein, Milo Wallace, and Big Al will be there, Suki too."

Big Al was a freakishly large guy, sweet as pecan pie, which he ate with lots of ice cream.

"Oh, it will be wonderful to see everyone again," I said.

"Laura and I already had the honeymoon," Ross said, laughing. "We want to take you and Derick on our trip to Quebec City, in Canada."

"Really, Ross? Canada? I've been to a few of the provinces, but never Quebec," I said.

"Don't worry about money; it's my treat," Ross said. Ross Grant had an abundance of cash, and he enjoyed spreading it around.

"We'll be there, Ross. Love you," I said, hanging up.

Derick and I finally had the money for a real vacation. I was excited about a trip off Maui to the mainland. I wanted my friends and family to meet Derick.

When Derick came home from work that day, I told him the news, and he was all for the trip. I sat at the kitchen table with him watching him roll a joint, as I often did.

Derick said, "After their honeymoon in Quebec, we can visit your parents in New York. I've never been to the East Coast. And on our way back to Maui, we can stop in Washington State to see my folks. I'll show you where I grew up."

"I'm so excited, Derick."

"We're going to have so much fun," he said, slowly eking out smoke from the joint.

"I'll have to tell the girls at the Crafty Mermaid that I need a month's vacation."

"Well, at least it's summer, the slow time of year," he said.

I began planning what clothes to bring and what to wear to the wedding.

~~~~~~

In June of 1981, Derick and I flew to Florida to attend Ross and Laura's wedding. The plane took off, and this time I wasn't alone. I had a real partner, and knew we would be returning to the islands. There was no feeling of dread upon leaving Maui. I held on to Derick's arm as the plane soared into the clouds, and everything below us disappeared.

NINETEEN

THE MADLAND

What all the ads and all the *whorescopes* seem to imply was that if you were narcissistic enough, if only you took proper care of your smells, your hair, your boobs, your eyelashes, your armpits, your crotch, your stars, your scars, and your choice of scotch in bars, you would meet a beautiful, powerful, potent and rich man who would satisfy every longing, fill every hole, and make your heart skip a beat, make you misty, and fly you to the moon, where you would live totally satisfied forever.

Erica Jong, **Fear of Flying**

Entering the madland after you've lived on a tiny island in the middle of the Pacific Ocean is always a bit of a shock. Ross Grant picked us up at Miami International Airport in a fancy car. "Start Me Up" by the Rolling Stones was playing on the car radio. We talked and laughed all the way to his place. Ross could be a funny guy when he wanted to be.

"What the hell did you do to your hair?" Ross asked.

"Just wanted a change," Derick answered.

"I like it," I said, squeezing Derick's hand.

"It's certainly wild and crazy," Ross said, laughing.

"Well, I'm a wild and crazy guy," Derick said.

"I think it makes him look like the true Leo he is," I said.

Ross and Laura lived in a high rise in a nice area of Miami right on the water. He bragged about his boat, which was docked not far from the condo, and promised to take us for a ride the next day. Ross enjoyed pinning medals on himself. I was used to his bloviated bravado but was worried that Derick would be taken in by him. His apartment was beautiful, very modern, with wraparound terraces accessible from every room. Derick and I had our own bedroom and bathroom. The apartment was so spacious that we all had plenty of privacy.

Laura was waiting for us with tomato and mayonnaise sandwiches on white bread, which were unexpectedly tasty after the long flight from Hawaii.

It was a few days until the wedding, so Ross showed us around Miami and took us out on his boat. I was immediately reminded of how flat, flat, flat Florida is. Not a hill or a mountain on the horizon. Gazing out in the distance on Biscayne Bay, I could see a sporadic community of wooden houses on stilts rising out of the water. People were living right offshore in these homes. Ross told us it was called Stiltsville.

Laura was getting everything ready for their friends and family to arrive for the wedding, so she stayed at the condo. I understood how most of that stuff was delegated to women and didn't feel slighted by her not joining us. We were having a blast in Miami.

The four of us sat around on the couch in the evenings watching TV and snorting lines of cocaine. There seemed to be an endless supply of that around, and it was something I enjoyed. There were spectacular sunsets visible from their corner living room, and we witnessed a good thunderstorm, which sounded like bowling balls rolling around in the sky. It was so strong it shook the building.

Laura and I went out for drinks while Derick went with Ross to his bachelor party. I figured there'd be strippers and who knows what else going on, but I tried not to dwell on it.

Laura seemed to not have a care in the world. She had snagged her man, and nothing was going to get in the way of that.

The guys staggered home in the wee hours of the morning. Derick collapsed on the bed with a crash in a drunken stupor. I hated a sloppy drunk. I made believe I was sound asleep. He eventually turned away from me, and I soon heard snoring.

The next morning after breakfast, I walked out onto the terrace and was gazing out over the water. Ross came out and stood beside me, putting his arm around me.

"That guy really loves you," Ross said. "I had girls there last night who'd do whatever you wanted them to do, but …"

And just then Derick walked out to the terrace. I stared at Ross and smiled.

"I couldn't even finish my business," Derick said, hugging me.

"I really don't want to hear anymore," I said.

Derick laughed sheepishly.

~~~~~~

Their wedding was on a private yacht, and the guest list was a trip down memory lane. The first familiar character I ran into on the yacht was Milo Wilson, who I hadn't seen since I was living in Brooklyn with him and Harvey Cooper (aka Hank). I didn't ask about Hank, and he didn't offer any information. Suki Rosmond was there with her new beau, probably wishing she was the one marrying Ross. Suki and I caught up while sitting on two of the deck chairs. Marty Feinstein was there with his friend Big Al, an obese but funny guy who hung around with us when we had that old Victorian on Staten Island in the early seventies. Marty and Al standing together looked like that old comedy team Laurel and Hardy.

I wore a purple print sundress with accordion pleats, no bra, high heels, and a large, pink rose in my long dark hair. Derick wore a brown corduroy jacket over a beige aloha shirt. He knew how to dress and could be a bit of a dandy at times. We were both really tan from the islands. The bride and groom both wore white. Laura wore a white straw hat and a frilly but tasteful white sundress. She looked très chic, as if she were at Churchill Downs for the Kentucky Derby. She reeked of Southern class and syrupy charm. Ross was in a stylish white suit with a black bowtie. He had the look of a swarthy European aristocrat, with his dark, overgrown curly hair and beard. They made a beautiful couple. The ceremony was lovely, the food was great, and we all had a good time.

~~~~~~

Ross Grant wasn't kidding when he said he was taking us on his honeymoon. A few days after the wedding the four of us boarded a plane to Quebec, Canada, first class, all expenses paid. Ross secured us rooms in a very modern hotel in Quebec City, within earshot of Le Chateau Frontenac. Of course I would have loved to stay in the castle, but Ross said it was fully booked.

We did go to the Frontenac for dinner one night. The dining room was like the great hall of an old castle. The chairs were upholstered with rich fabric, and the drapes looked like Tudor wall tapestries. As we ate dinner in the opulent surroundings, a woman played a harp just a few feet from our table. The four of us had a difficult time sipping our soup without giggling. It was all a bit much. Knowing Ross as well as I did, I had the feeling he was wining and dining us, but a motive escaped me.

Quebec City had a European vibe. I had flashbacks of the time I'd spent in Montreal, when I was a hippie traveling around the United States and Canada. We were surrounded by outside cafes, tree-lined streets, large boulevards, markets, and boardwalks. We went on a boat ride, and though it was cold, I had Derick to keep me warm. After dinner on our third day, we returned to our room at the hotel, exhausted. I let myself fall backward on the bed, totally spent from another manic day of sightseeing. My head was reeling at how good we were all getting along. Derick lay down next to me and was silent for a while.

"Maybe we should get married," he blurted out.

I was a little taken aback but kept my wits about me. I smiled a contented smile and said, "Maybe we should. Do you think we're ready?"

"As ready as I'll ever be," Derick said.

"I love you so much," I said, gently caressing his face, which melted like a candle.

Florida was pleasantly warm, but Canada was cold. Even our hotel room was chilly. We curled up together on the bed and held each other.

"I'm happy with you," he said. He peered at me with an intense expression on his face.

"You're my man, Derick," I said.

"I want to make love to you right now, can't seem to get enough of you," he said.

He stood up, took his jacket off, and carefully placed in on a chair in the corner of the room.

"Get undressed," he said.

After all the things he said, I was already hot for him. Despite the chilliness of the room, I took my clothes off and tossed them on the floor. He didn't take his eyes off of me for a moment. He looked like a wolf in one of those old cartoons, licking its chops while watching Little Red Riding Hood.

We got under the covers and fondled each other. He was fingering me as I played with and teased his dick until it got it really hard.

"I'm gonna come," I said. Derick got on top of me and thrust it in. He moved really slow and steady until I climaxed and then he let himself explode.

"They're expecting to meet us in the lobby for a drink in the bar downstairs," I said.

"Okay, but I'll be thinking about this while we're sitting at the bar."

I thought about Derick's words throughout the next day. Whatever we did, wherever we went, I was preoccupied with the marriage topic. Friends around me were getting married left and right, like all fifty states were running out of marriage licenses. As much as I loved Derick, I feared things could change once we officially belonged to each other. I didn't like anyone telling me what to do, and men tend to do that when you belong to them. I thought of a book I read a few years past. I conjured up the passage that left a mark on my brain.

> "Martha thought: Here is another person who is complete. Finished in his way like Stella is in hers. Whereas she herself was formless, graceless, and unpredictable, a mere lump of clay. She rejected even the mere sight of him and returned to her own preoccupations."
>
> —*A Proper Marriage*, Doris Lessing

Before we left Quebec, we had lunch in a sidewalk café. It was much warmer with the afternoon sun and I loved sitting outside.

"Ross, I want to thank you and Laura for sharing your honeymoon with us. It means a lot."

Ross smiled at me. "I wanted to share our happiness, and I'm glad you came with us."

Derick reached out and shook Ross's hand. They seemed to get along really well despite their different personalities. After the commune broke up, Ross always seemed to have some sort of a business scheme he wanted to involve me in. My instinct was telling me that he had money to launder.

"You're using your talent to make your bosses rich? You should work for yourself!" Ross said.

"I'm comfortable on Maui, and I like my job at the Crafty Mermaid," I answered.

"Well, I'm not going to give you money if you're in Hawaii. You have to come here to Miami." Derick didn't get involved in the conversation.

"I can set you and Laura up in a store on Miami Beach. You girls will make a killing."

As Ross was talking, I wondered what sort of talent Laura had. I liked her a lot, but really didn't know much about her.

"I'll think about it, Ross. Right now I'm on vacation, and I know how different a place can seem on vacation. Living in Florida might be a totally different story."

Ross shook his head, annoyed. "You have a working-class mentality."

Derick's expression changed, like he wanted to punch Ross, but I kicked him under the table.

"Derick can work with me," Ross said.

I didn't like the sound of that at all. I had an inkling of what capacity that would be. Ross liked to get other people to do his dirty work.

"Adriana and I will discuss it when we're back on Maui," Derick said, abruptly tabling the issue.

~~~~~~~

With the wedding festivities in Miami, and the honeymoon in Quebec over, Derick and I turned our attention to New York and visiting my family. Ross had rented a summer house in the Hamptons. He wanted to fly to New York, but he wanted to use his car there. We made an arrangement with Ross to drive his car to New York, which saved Derick and me the price of a plane ticket. We left Florida very early in the morning. There wasn't much to see at seventy miles an hour. Derick had a lead foot. We slept in a couple of motels on the way, and stopped at a warehouse with a big sign: FIREWORKS. Derick loaded up on fireworks to take back to Hawaii for the Fourth of July. The car windows were wide open, as we raced north on I-95 to "Black Betty" by Ram Jam.

The plan was to drop Ross's car off at their summer house. We drove down a dirt road and through a thicket of trees until we found the house right at the edge of a lake. We spent a few days with them in the Hamptons before heading to the Bronx. Ross and Laura were definitely living the high life. Derick was in heaven, fishing with Ross on the lake each day, while Laura and I went swimming. There's nothing quite like the East Coast in summer.

Ross and Laura drove us to the Bronx and dropped us off at my parents' apartment house on their way to see Ross's mother in Brooklyn.

~~~~~~

My mother and I were so excited to see each other. We hugged, kissed, and squealed with joy. While we were engaged in a tangle hold, Derick and my father were shaking hands.

"Come in, come in," my father said.

We all sat at the dining room table and talked for an hour or so.

My mother prepared supper, and the three cats ran excitedly all over the apartment. I helped my mother clear the table after dinner. We were alone in the kitchen, and I could tell she had something on her mind. She was washing the dishes and I was drying.

"Adriana, this is the second time you chose a guy with a marred face."

I stared at her. "I don't even notice Derick's scar anymore," I answered.

"Well, it doesn't detract from his good looks."

"We really love each other. We're thinking of getting married."

"Really? Have you met his family yet?"

"No, but we plan on stopping in Washington state on our way back to Hawaii."

I could hear Derick and my father talking and laughing in the dining room. I was troubled that my mother made an issue about the scar on Derick's face. She had a way of making me question my choices in men, although most of the time she was right. But I wasn't a teenager anymore. I had plenty of experience with different men, and I wasn't going to let her remark dissuade me.

When I sat back down at the table, Derick asked me what was wrong, sensing I was upset. I told him it was nothing. He massaged the back of my neck, making me feel secure, and it calmed me down.

"I thought we'd take a trip up to Cape Cod for a few days," my mother said.

"I'll drive you anywhere you want to go," Derick said.

After that comment, my mother immediately began warming up to him. Over the next few days I dragged Derick around to all my Bronx and Manhattan haunts. We took my parents out for a seafood dinner on Staten Island. I remember my father taking his false teeth out at the table and slipping them into his jacket pocket. I could see by the expression on my mother's face that she was mortified. She began muttering something in Italian. Derick was almost laughing, and just about to say something when I kicked him under the table. I had the feeling his leg was going to be black and blue by the time we left the East Coast.

We visited all my aunts and uncles, who loved Derick. We played cards and engaged in all sorts of family activities. I remember arriving at my Aunt Camille's apartment. Uncle Pietro met us downstairs and waved us over to the back of his car. He opened the trunk, which was filled with cartons of cigarettes and bottles of liquor. He told us Aunt Camille didn't have a clue, but I knew better.

~~~~~~

We drove to Cape Cod, Massachusetts, Derick at the wheel, at seventy and eighty miles an hour in my parents' gold Oldsmobile, the statue of the Virgin Mary shaking on the dashboard. I was glad she was paying attention. My parents had their hearts in their mouths the whole way.

"Do you want to kill us?" my father said.

Derick didn't flinch and kept the pedal to the metal. "It's the thruway," Derick said.

"We don't care if we get there an hour later, we just want to get there," my mother said.

"Ma, Derick's an excellent driver. He just drove from Florida to New York."

One thing about Derick, he was a no-nonsense guy. He didn't put up with any backtalk or backseat drivers. I was waiting for my father to say something else. Derick would have pulled over and told him to take the wheel. Then we all would have been up Schitt's Creek without a paddle. Derick could be stubborn when he wanted to be. Luckily, there were no more comments, just the few odd gasps. We made it to the Cape in five and a half hours flat, safe and sound.

My cousin Angela and her boyfriend, Ash, had a house in Truro. Her parents, my Aunt Mari and Uncle Giuseppe, were so happy to see my parents. They were busy catching up on family gossip.

Derick and Ash went outside to chop wood for a barbeque that first night.

The next day we walked around Provincetown, which never seemed to change. I loved that place in summer. There was something magical about it. The sea air and quaintness of the small downtown area along Commonwealth always put me in a fairy-tale mood. We hung out in one of the cafes sipping tropical drinks, which sparked thoughts of Hawaii. Derick always made sure he had his hand on the back of my neck, gently massaging it to reassure me. He must have instinctively known that I had some old negative issues with my parents.

It was a fun trip to the Cape, and the drive back was inconsequential. Derick drove, and we all fell asleep. Before we left the Bronx, my mom made a big dinner and invited the family over. My cousin Gia and her husband, Stu, were there with their little girl, who wasn't a baby anymore. My whole family seemed to like Derick, and that meant a lot to me. The only thing I remember about that day was the tailored leopard-print jumpsuit with the red trim I wore. Derick told me I looked like a movie star.

~~~~~~

We left my parents and the Bronx behind and flew from New York to Seattle, Washington. I was nervous about meeting Derick's family. He handled my family so well. Derick's mother was tall and solid like him. She had steel-blue eyes and short graying hair. I'd looked up his surname, which had Anglican, Welsh, Scottish and Irish roots. Derick's sister looked a lot like me. She was petite, with dark hair, and very pretty. She was married with two small children. Derick's mother was remarried, and I felt some tension between Derick, his mother, and stepfather. I imagined there was some bad blood over his having been in jail. His family did a lot of eating and a lot of laughing. We went on a hike in the forest near their house with his sister and one of her kids. Washington is a very rustic place. I found it clean, with pristine water ways and fresh air. Derick took me to meet his grandmother, who lived alone in a tiny apartment. I was impressed with her sharpness of mind, and was captivated by the stylish shoes she wore. They were shoes that a young girl would wear.

One thing I remember clearly was a breakfast one morning. The whole family sat around a large table in the dining room. They were trading jokes about the sunny side eggs on the platter, inferring they were like a woman's breasts. Derick's mother giggled shyly as if she was saying something taboo. She didn't impress me as the shy or timid type. Then there was a strange comment when his family was teasing Derick about some of the girls he'd dated in the past.

Looking at me his mother said, "Well, we can see he prefers dark meat." Everyone laughed, including Derick. I didn't understand the humor, other than my being Italian. I wasn't any darker than Derick's sister, I was just tan. I imagined my being Italian evoked dark skin. I laughed too, realizing it was a dumb and uninformed comment.

~~~~~

I was glad to get on a plane back to the islands. I'd had enough of the madland to last for a while. One thing I did realize was that wherever we went, Derick and I were a team. We stuck together and supported each other.

As the plane descended through the clouds, I saw a few of the Hawaiian Islands peeking out of the ocean, and a familiar sweet caramel feeling engulfed me. I choked up as the pilot talked about the cliffs of Molokai and Haleakala Crater. Soon I felt all the tension of the madland slip away. Back on the rock, some would say, but to me it was home.

Dante and Regina picked us up at Kahului Airport. On the ride home they gave us the rundown of what had gone on while we were away. Derick made sure Dante knew he bought fireworks at a factory on the East Coast for the Fourth of July. Rebel was so happy to see us, he jumped in Derick's arms, whined, and wagged his tail profusely, while Honey Girl wagged her tail too but seemed oblivious as to why. We didn't even unpack that night, we just had something to eat that Regina had cooked. The weather was hot—well, it was July, one of the hottest months in Hawaii. We took a shower together, flopped on the bed, and went to sleep.

I was so happy to get back into my routine, one that I was familiar with. I thought of Ross Grant's comment, that I had a working-class mentality. It irked me. Did I really just enjoy the simple life? True, I liked things uncomplicated. I remember asking Laura if she ever felt troubled or afraid regarding Ross's business dealings.

"It's a business like any other," she said.

Was she clueless, or was I naïve? Either way, Ross Grant was a great guy. He was always generous, treated me like a sister, and I truly appreciated him. I had the feeling that Derick was taken in by him, along with that posh lifestyle. I wasn't, which made me wonder if Ross's deduction about me was correct.

July passed like a car going eighty miles an hour. The only thing I remember was us going to the movies to see *Escape from New York* with Kurt Russell.

The third week of August was Derick's birthday. The guys rented a charter boat for the day. I had met the captain of the boat before. I knew him from the Yacht Club. Derick's best friend, Cotton, came along, but not Loretta. I wondered why but didn't ask. We went swimming in the ocean, barbequed on the deck, and ate birthday cake with a fork right out of the bakery box. Derick let me steer the boat for a while. I leaned back against him, closing my eyes. I had the most euphoric feeling. I was loved and protected, with his arms around me. It was a strangely freeing and peaceful feeling. We stayed out until sunset. The sky was epic, with a million shades of pink and red.

Regina and I sat on the deck watching the guys on the bow as we motored back to shore.

She said, "I saw on TV today that the first woman ever was appointed to the Supreme Court, Sandra Day O'Connor."

"Seems overdue to me," I said.

"But at least we're making progress."

"I couldn't agree more." It was the first time I heard Regina concerned about women's issues or politics in general.

I watched Derick at the wheel of the boat. Stevie Nicks was singing "Stop Draggin' My Heart Around" on the transistor radio. I was in a good place in my life. I was in love with a man who loved me. I had fallen in love with the island of Maui, which I felt lucky to call home. My art and work were synonymous. I thought, *What could possibly go wrong?*

<hr />

Toward the end of that summer, things were changing at the Crafty Mermaid. Annie told me that while I was gone, she'd witnessed some tension between the owners, Hannah Klein and Haku Neilson. Hannah's husband, the guy without a chin, began hanging around the shop more than usual. Annie told me she noticed the girls taking large sums of cash out of the till at the end of each day, telling her not to tally it in with the daily receipts. It was troubling, but I didn't dwell on it. I figured it was their business, and none of mine. But Annie didn't like it and thought something bad was going on.

I concentrated on my hand-painted clothing business. I took my painted T-shirts around to some of the other clothing stores on Front Street. I wanted to expand my reach. Being all these stores were in close proximity, I committed to using different styles and designs in different stores. I didn't want them competing with each other. I convinced two stores on Front Street to carry my tie-dyed and painted T-shirts on a consignment basis.

I continued painting T-shirts in the yard, whether Haku came by or not. I began going to the library and combing through books about Gauguin, and paying attention to his perspective on art. I found his words provocative and inspiring.

This is a passage I copied from one of the library reference books:

Gauguin: a "**Synthesis—Form and Color**":

Don't copy nature too much. Art is an abstraction. Derive this distraction from nature while dreaming before it, and think more of the creation which will result (than of the model). Painting should seek suggestion, not description, as does music. Too great a technical perfection robs the canvas of its power to stimulate the imagination. Does not promise evoke mystery, since our natures do not include the absolute? The artist has little conscious control over the essence of his work whose formulation has nothing to do with reason.

Derick and I went on a hiking trip in the West Maui Mountains with Dante and Regina. We stumbled across an old concrete foundation under cactus and overgrown shrubbery. It looked like a primitive dwelling someone inhabited and then abandoned. We walked cautiously past the cows grazing on the cliff, and toward the rocks where the blowhole was. Water shot up like a geyser whenever a large wave crashed against the face of the cliff. We drove further north to Slaughterhouse Beach and parked on the cliff. We walked down the path and stood there watching the guys surf below us. It got its name because it's where the Hawaiians slaughtered cattle in the old days, and threw the gutted carcasses over the cliff into the ocean. It became a popular surfing spot in West Maui because of the huge waves in winter.

We took Rebel and Honey Girl with us. They had a great time investigating every rock and bush they came across. We had a hard time stopping them from chasing sea birds and other little creatures.

Derick had been quiet all day. I could tell he had something on his mind. I wanted to wait until we got home to pry as to what was going on in his head. Dark clouds rolled in over the mountains, and it looked like rain was coming. We took some group photos sitting on rocks and standing at the edge of the cliff. We coaxed the dogs into the back of Dante's truck with us, and headed south to Lahaina.

Lahaina was still hot in contrast to up north, which always had a cool breeze whipping through the space between the mountains. You could drive fifteen or twenty minutes north of Lahaina and it could be fifteen degrees cooler.

I felt like eating something Italian, so I searched through the refrigerator and cabinets for something to cook. Derick went straight to the beanbag chair and turned on the TV. He was listening to the news. While the sauce was simmering on the stove, I squeezed in next to him and rubbed his arm.

"What's up? You've been quiet all day. I can tell something's on your mind," I asked.

Derick hesitated. "I've been thinking about Ross Grant's offer. Not just for you, but for me too."

I stared at the television, not wanting to make eye contact. "Tell me what you're thinking."

"He can set you and Laura up in a real business. He's right about you being talented."

"It's not the first time Ross wanted me to go into some sort of business venture with him."

"What stopped you? Don't you want to make more money, work for yourself?"

"I get the feeling he wants to clean his money, and it's not really about me or you."

"He doesn't seem like that kind of guy to me. How far can we get here on this island?"

"Couldn't you tell he was wining and dining us? Besides you, I've fallen in love with Hawaii."

"I get that, but we could always come back if things don't work out," he said.

"I don't know, Derick. That would be a big move. I'd have to think long and hard about leaving Maui. I've been happy here, happier than I've been anywhere. I feel like this is where I belong."

"Just give it some thought," he said.

I went back to the stove with an unsettled feeling. I didn't expect Derick to want to leave Hawaii. Living somewhere else never even crossed my mind. I knew I had to stop being afraid of change. I remembered how I loved change at one time in my life, but it was usually the result of some drastic thing that happened. In Hawaii everything seemed to be going so well for both of us. I did like Florida, but we were there on vacation for two weeks. Was that really enough time to know if it was a place where we wanted to live? I wasn't sure.

~~~~~~

We were having a really busy day at the Crafty Mermaid, and Haku was downstairs helping Annie with customers. A while later she was up the stairs standing over me at the Bernina. I had been sewing up some new bathing suits for the shop.

"Come on, I'll take you to lunch," Haku said.

"I'd love to get out of here for an hour or so," I said.

She didn't ask Annie to join us, so I knew she wanted to talk to me alone. We went to the Yacht Club, sat down, and ordered iced teas.

Haku called the waitress back. "I need alcohol, rum and coke for me."

"They have opakapaka on the menu today. I'm having the fish," I said.

After we finished our lunch, she said, "I think you should have a drink too."

I knew something was up, so I ordered a Tanqueray and tonic with a lime and waited to hear.

"So we've been having some disagreements about the business," Haku said.

"You and Hannah?"

"Yes, and money problems. We've both been taking money out of the Crafty Mermaid."

So Annie was right about something fishy going on in the shop I thought.

"I'm glad you told me Haku."

"The money we deducted from your paychecks for taxes this past year, we never sent to the IRS."

I squirmed in my seat. "Haku, you have to pay it. You deducted it from my checks."

"I will, I just don't know when."

"You know I keep track in a book and have all the paperwork, so you will have to pay it," I said.

"Don't worry, Hannah and I would never screw you over."

"I would hope not. I've been with the Crafty Mermaid for almost five years."

We walked back to the shop together, neither of us saying much. When we walked into the store, Annie was with a customer.

Haku went straight to the register and took cash out of the till. "I'm leaving early today, but I'll be back tomorrow morning."

"See you tomorrow," I called out as she walked out.

I couldn't wait to tell Annie about our conversation over lunch. She was flabbergasted, but then again she observed things that were happening in the store that weren't right.

Annie and I went to the Waterworks after we closed the store. I saw my world crumbling around me as I drank. Was I blind to reality? What was my future on Maui without the Crafty Mermaid? All these were questions I didn't want to think about. I figured if they hadn't paid my taxes, they probably hadn't paid their business taxes either.

I left Annie at the bar and walked to the harbor. I sat by the dock watching the boats loading and unloading. When I'd sobered up enough to drive, I walked back to my car. I wasn't going to say anything to Derick just yet. I planned on thinking seriously about Ross's offer first.

~~~~~

On Labor Day weekend we all went to a barbeque up north. Everyone we knew was there. Derick's best friend, Cotton, the ladies from the Crafty Mermaid with their husbands, the guys Derick worked with, even Dominick French made an appearance. It was a benefit for someone's little boy who was in the hospital fighting for his life. It was a lovely day to be at the beach with friends.

Suddenly a sadness overcame me. How could I ever leave this place? I'd let myself get so attached to the island, to the people, to who I'd become, I just couldn't see myself anywhere else. Old fears began to surface. What if

Derick and I leave the island and it all turns to shit? Maybe we'd be different in Florida. What if it killed what we had for each other? I'd heard the loss of a child could kill a marriage, because every time you looked at each other, you'd remember that loss and feel the pain. I didn't have a child, but I had fallen in love with a place, Hawaii. It was in my veins, part of my identity. If I was out of my element, I might be unhappy and blame Derick. I might become a different person, and he wouldn't love me anymore.

I was leaning against a large rock when Derick walked over.

"What's the matter?"

"Just some stuff on my mind," I said.

"You can talk to me."

"I want to work things out in my head before I talk to you about it."

Derick held me and rubbed my shoulder. I was sure he knew what it was about, but he was giving me the time I needed.

"Whenever you're ready," he said.

Cotton joined us with two plates. I looked down at the food he handed us, and it was all local style—kalua pork, macaroni salad, chow fun, and lomi lomi salmon, heaped up in four neat piles. I began to tear up, so I turned my face away from them. Cotton went back for his plate and asked Derick if he wanted another beer. Derick nodded. I was taking it all in as if it was my last day on earth. The Last Supper came to mind. Strange how I sensed a change coming. That day I was recording it all in my head. The comradery of our friends, the food, the ocean, the palm trees, the majestic mountains, and the way it was with me and Derick. We were living aloha.

Some guys showed up with guitars and a ukulele, and the music began. Overcome with the Hawaiian music, Haku jumped up and began dancing a hula, her long dark hair swinging, her hips swaying, and her arms telling a story. Everyone sang along; we all knew the words by heart. It was emotional and uplifting. I realized how lucky I was to be in such a place and to have these people as friends, each one of them beautiful and unique in their own way.

When it began to get dark, we left the barbeque, and a bunch of cars followed us back to Nanu Street. On the drive back to Lahaina I gazed at the West Maui Mountains, and a beautiful rainbow appeared. I figured it must have been raining way up there. My senses were reeling as I took in the beauty of Maui, my home.

RAINBOW OVER THE WEST MAUI MOUNTAINS, 1981

We continued the party at home that night. After everyone left, Derick and I shared the large beanbag chair in the living room, and Dante and Regina sat on the floor.

"What a great day," Regina said.

"It was just wonderful to see everyone come together for that little boy," I said.

"It seems like that's the way it is here," Dante said.

"It's the spirit of aloha," I said.

Derick put his arm around me. "And everyone got along, no fights!"

"Did you see the new bunch of bananas in the yard?" Dante asked.

Derick and I shook our heads.

Dante got up and searched for the flashlight in the junk drawer. He walked out into the yard, motioning us to follow. Even the dogs tagged along with curiosity. It was pitch dark outside, except for the light from the carport. We walked through the yard to the back of the house. Dante pointed the flashlight to a large bunch of apple bananas. There are so many varieties of bananas, but apple bananas are a hybrid from the Philippines that are popular in Hawaii. I was so used to them I couldn't even eat a regular banana anymore.

"How cool is that?" Derick said.

"They should be ready in a week or so," Dante said.

I looked up at the stars, as I often did. Derick pulled me toward him and kissed me softly on my lips. He closed his eyes. I kept mine open.

"It's finally cooled down a bit tonight," Derick said.

"It's definitely a relief after the heat of the day," Regina said.

"I have to get in the shower, I'm all sweaty," I said.

Derick raised his eyebrows, signaling he would be joining me. We walked back into the house, leaving Dante and Regina feeling up the stalk of bananas.

The water was tepid and welcoming as we stood under the showerhead. We embraced and kissed, the water rushing over us, our bodies together. We dried off and jumped in bed nude. The weather had been so warm that we often slept in the nude. I needed at least a sheet over me to fall asleep, but we weren't going to sleep just yet. We weren't tired; the exuberance of the day's events was still with us. By now we'd learned to navigate each other's bodies, but somehow that didn't kill the thrill. That night, after we made love, I lay there awake wondering if it could possibly remain that good for years on end. I hoped the feeling wouldn't fade with time. Thinking of other men in my past, I had to wonder about that. Derick was already snoring. I felt drowsiness overtake me and fell asleep.

~~~~~~

It was a day like most others at the Crafty Mermaid. Annie was busy downstairs changing displays and helping customers. I was upstairs listening to the radio, hemming sarongs on the Bernina. "Slow Hand" by the Pointer Sisters was playing, and I had a flash of the previous night. I felt a throbbing desire for Derick and longed to be at home with him. It was devilishly hot under the roof, and there wasn't even a slight breeze coming in the window. I pointed the fan directly at me and finished up the sewing. Annie wanted to go to the Yacht Club after work, but I'd had enough alcohol at the barbeque the day before.

I walked home after work. No one was there except Rebel and Honey Girl. Rebel sneaked off the beanbag chair, and Honey Girl jumped down off the couch when they saw me come in. *Oh, if Derick was only home to see this,* I thought, laughing.

"You guys want to go out?" I asked, looking at them. They wagged their tails at me with pleading eyes.

I got my folding table out and decided to paint some T-shirts. I wasn't in the mood to do tie-dye, and anyway, it was too late in the day to start that process. I got my paints out and put my brushes in a large jar of water.

I'd gotten into the habit of reading from books on Gauguin I'd gotten out of the public library before beginning to work. I'd flip through the pages of his paintings, paying special attention to the colors he used. Gauguin talked about how the tropical sun makes everything around it blaze. He mentioned the Tahitian Eve (Tahitian woman) as being very knowing in her naiveté, walking around naked without shame, and possessing animal beauty. He referred to Tahiti as an immense palace of nature.

The dogs got bored with checking out every leaf and smell in the yard. They lay under the folding table where it was shady.

I reached for a paintbrush in the jar of water and dabbed it in a sea green color, which I'd already mixed. I began to paint with joy, and all my worldly cares dissolved like the paint into the fabric. The afternoon flew by, and I didn't even look up until the sun began to wane, and I knew everyone would be coming home.

TWENTY

ALOHA OE

From my journal:

The sea must know the answer. It's the only thing that
remains endlessly alive. All else dies, but the sea lives
on and flows with the changing tides. Sometimes silent,
sometimes raging. I too am like the tide. I change with
the moon and am drawn to the shore for rest. I never
wanted to soar through the air, or sail on the wind, for
that's man's realm. I am of the earth. I make things grow,
and dig my feet in the sand. I am anchored to the earth,
woman's domain.

Art has always been there throughout my life. It might have been
dormant at times, but it was still there under the skin. Art was a
constant I could rely on when things in my life went awry. Ah, the
resilience of art! I was in a good place in my emotional life as well. Derick
and I had been together for almost two years and had weathered the storms
around us. We were getting engaged at some point in the near future. But
I was at a crossroads as to where we should live. The dilemma plagued my
daily thoughts. I feared a big change could ruin the delicious cocktail that
was our relationship.

My hand-painted clothing business was taking off, and I had just
ordered another five dozen T-shirts from the warehouse in Atlanta. Haku
convinced me to spend a Friday at her new house painting sarongs. We
always had fun, and it gave us a chance to talk about our personal lives. I

didn't pry about the status of the Crafty Mermaid; perhaps I didn't want to know. She had put a great studio together, with a lot of light, in a sunroom off the side of the house. She disappeared from the room, and I wondered where she'd gone to. She soon came back with a chilled bottle of white wine and two glasses. Our creative juices were flowing, and we began to paint.

"I'm so happy we decided to do this again," I said.

"I've missed our Friday routine," Haku said. "It's been so crazy at the store lately."

"Haku, I want you to know that whatever happens, this job has been the dream of a lifetime."

"Hannah and I are so happy you wandered into our shop that day five years ago."

"I had only been here a few days and couldn't believe my luck."

"Not luck; it was your fate, Adriana."

"Yes, I believe it was fate."

"You helped make the store so much of what it turned out to be," Haku said, smiling.

"I've been mulling the thought over in my mind about moving to Florida."

"Really, Adriana? What about Derick?"

"Oh, I'm not going anywhere without him."

"I guess this is as good a time as any to tell you … we're closing the Crafty Mermaid."

I stared at Haku. "I had a feeling it would happen. I've been preparing myself."

After that statement, even the Chardonnay wasn't lifting my spirits. I was beginning to see a path open before me. I wondered if I should tell Derick, or keep this information to myself.

When I got home, the house was empty, which was a relief, because I wanted to gather my thoughts. I went to the bedroom and fished through my underwear drawer for the I Ching. I knew I could rely on the words from its pages to gain wisdom and enlightenment. I got the three Chinese coins out of the jewelry box and sat on the floor. I tossed the coins six times to determine the hexagram that responded to my question. The question in my mind's eye of course was, *Should I leave Maui and move to Florida with Derick?*

From the *I Ching* (The Chinese Book of Changes). Hexagram 56, The Wanderer:

The Judgement: Strange lands and separation are the wanderer's lot.
 The meaning of the time of the wanderer is truly great.
 The Image: Caution in imposing penalties. Fire does not linger on the mountain but passes on rapidly.
 The wanderer rests in a shelter. He has not obtained his place. He obtains property and an ax but is not yet glad at heart.

After reading my response, I wasn't sure of its meaning in regard to my personal life. Was there a hidden meaning, or perhaps an omen of things to come? I would try to consult it again in a few days. Perhaps there were other things to help me make my decision. I was putting the book back in the drawer when I heard the front door. It was Derick home from work.

"Here you are," he said, walking into the bedroom.

"I was going through my drawers and tidying everything up. It's a mess."

Derick walked straight to the bathroom, took off his clothes and hopped in the shower. I wasn't in the mood for hanky-panky after reading the *I Ching*, or I would have joined him. I was in a spiritual state of mind. I sneaked out of the room and went to the kitchen to look through the refrigerator. I was hungry and wanted something substantial. I had picked on crackers and cheese all day long at work. Annie always told me to stick to crackers and avoid bread if I wanted to stay slim. Looking at her, I had to wonder if that really worked.

~~~~~~

I received a call from Suki Rosmond in California. She was opening a store in San Mateo called Whimsy. It was to be an eclectic shop full of whimsical oddities. She mentioned Betty Boop memorabilia, handcrafted jewelry, and clothing. I told her about my tie-dyed and hand-painted T-shirts, and she vowed to carry them in her store. She had a friend, Tamara, who had a shop called Barnaby's in a neighboring town, and told me she'd speak to her about carrying my T-shirts as well. I mentioned that I could order other items from the warehouse, like sweatshirts, since it was cooler in California. My business was growing, and it gave me confidence and a feeling of security. I realized I'd been setting the groundwork for an inevitable change all along.

Annie and I went to the Yacht Club for drinks after work. We tried to get together at least once a week. She was my Maui mom, and I knew she'd give me good advice. Once we took a few gulps of our drinks, I was ready to spill the beans and get her feedback.

"Annie, I've been meaning to tell you something but didn't quite know how."

"Are you having a sex problem? Is someone after you? You want to get back with Demo? I can read your palm!" She rattled possibilities off waiting to hear my response. "What is it?"

"None of those things," I said. "Haku told me they're closing the Crafty Mermaid."

"Well that doesn't surprise me. I told you there was something fishy going on in the store."

"Yes, well, that's not all. Derick and I have been tossing the idea around of moving to Florida."

"That swamp?" Annie said. "Riana, you won't like it there, not after Hawaii."

"I was there with Derick for two weeks for my friend Ross's wedding, and it was beautiful. Sun, ocean, palm trees, and sandy beaches as far as the eye could see."

"Well, you weren't there long enough for the mosquitos, alligators, and those giant flying roaches they like to call palmetto bugs," she said, wrinkling her nose.

"I know it won't be Hawaii, but I can't think of a place on the mainland that would be more similar to Hawaii. Besides, I'd be closer to my family."

"My bastard husband, Tony, took us there every year, during the worst time, in summer."

"Annie, Derick wants to go, and I don't want to lose him. We're thinking of getting married."

I was looking for sympathy and support.

"Well, Riana, now you've said the real reason. If you have a chance for true love, don't turn your back on it. If that is the reason you want to go, then do it."

"I haven't made up my mind yet, but I am leaning in that direction. Especially if the store closes. What else could I do here?"

"You can always get a job in a gift shop in one of the hotels or on Front Street. You know that I've been working part time in a jewelry store in the Hyatt for a while now."

"I have a good start to my own business, and Ross offered to front it," I said.

"Riana, talk is cheap. Don't go after what someone says."

"There's no way to know the future before it happens."

"Besides, I will miss you something terrible," Annie said, her voice cracking.

We hugged each other and I swiveled off the barstool leaving Annie sitting at the bar, as I had done many times before. She was in a drinking mood and would probably stay there for hours.

I walked along the seawall and gazed out over the ocean with a feeling of dread at leaving the island. My car was parked across the street from the Crafty Mermaid. I felt sadness looking at the store. It was such a big part of my life on Maui, but I had to think of *the* ifs in life. If, the little word with the big meaning. I wanted to get married and maybe have a baby. I loved Derick and he loved me. I flashed on my therapist, Joan's, words again, "Adriana, you have to let someone love you."

~~~~~

Rebel and Honey Girl greeted me as I walked through the front door. I gave them chewy bones and they sat contentedly on the kitchen floor chomping away. *Derick can walk them when he gets home,* I thought. Rebel wasn't fixed, and he could be hard to handle if we ran into another male dog.

I heard Dante's truck in the carport. I went to the refrigerator for a cold beer. I had recently bought a couple of Foster's lagers, a new Australian beer. I took one of the tall gold cans and popped the top. Dante and Regina decided to take the dogs to the beach for a run and a swim.

"We'll give them a bath when we get back," Regina said.

"Oh, they'll love the beach," I said.

After they left, I sat on the beanbag chair and lay back. All the cares of the day, the doubts and fears about the future drained away with each gulp of Foster's. I was almost asleep when I heard Derick's truck. Derick walked straight over to the chair and stared down at me. I smiled up at him.

"You're a sight for sore eyes," he said.

"If you want a cold beer, there's more in the fridge."

"Fuck the beer, you know what I want," Derick said with a devilish expression.

He squeezed onto the beanbag chair next to me and kissed me, lightly brushing his lips against mine. Derick could be very persuasive in the sex department, even if I wasn't in the mood.

He pulled away and said, "I didn't see the dogs around."

"Dante and Regina took them to the beach. They left a little while ago."

"So they'll be gone for a while?"

He began to tickle my nipples. He unhooked my bra and pulled my T-shirt up. "They're as hard as cherry pits," he said, playing with them.

Derick took my hand and moved it down to his member, wanting me to feel it was already hard. I tugged the zipper down and it popped out. I moved my hand up and down along the soft skin teasing him, and he breathed in. I wrapped my lips around it and licked back and forth. He stroked my back, and I could tell he didn't want me to stop. I took it in my mouth and did more, much more. I wanted to concentrate on him even though I wanted him to fuck me. I kept going until he was finished. I looked up at him, his face all melty and rearranged.

"I'll get you later," he said softly.

~~~~~~

When Dante and Regina came home, they kept the dogs out in the yard and gave them a bath with the hose. We kept the dog shampoo outside in the carport. I saw the dogs shake off the excess water and get dried off with towels.

"Leave them out there until they're almost dry," Derick called out through the louvers.

"But tie them up so they can't run off," I said.

I am not sure why we needed to lecture them, they cared as much about the dogs as we did. I guess it had to be reiterated from time to time. Human carelessness is what gets animals in trouble.

Regina baked a meatloaf with carrots and potatoes, and I made an Italian green bean salad with garlic, black pepper, lemon, and olive oil. For dessert we had the chocolate cake she baked the previous day. The four of us spent that evening together watching television and playing cards. The dogs lay together on the kitchen floor looking up every time someone got up to get another beer out of the refrigerator, checking for any treats coming their way.

When Dante and Regina turned in for the night, Derick took my hand and said, "I picked up a little present for us." He pulled a tiny plastic bag out of his back pocket filled with cocaine.

I didn't do it that often anymore, but when it was around, I enjoyed it. It definitely made sex more intense. I walked into the bedroom looking for the little mirror we kept on the dresser for just such occasions.

Derick followed me in. He poured the white powder out on the mirror, and I chopped it up with a razor blade into neat lines, while he stood behind me, his head resting on my shoulder, watching. We sat on the bed with the mirror between us and took turns snorting a few lines with a tiny straw.

The first thing that always happened was a desire to chatter away about random thoughts and feelings. Cocaine made you feel that anything was possible. Of course that was the drug, not real life.

"What about that chocolate cake?" Derick asked, looking up at me.

"Tasted like the chocolate cake a neighbor of ours made when I was a little girl."

I told him about the chocolate cake our neighbor Faye would bring as a treat when she came to our house for coffee. It wasn't too sweet, had no icing or nuts, but was pure chocolate heaven. Derick listened intently to my story as he stroked my hand. We talked about our future together, and Florida became more desirable by the minute. Derick made it sound like a move that would be good for us, that Maui was a dead end financially. We'd be closer to our families, we could get married and live happily ever after. It sounded so promising.

Then Derick took the mirror and set it on the nightstand. He stared at me. "Wherever we go, whatever we do, we'll have each other."

I reached out and touched his face. I knew he loved me very much. I was thirty five years old, not a girl anymore. I loved Derick and knew he loved me. *It could work,* my heart was telling me.

He guided me down on the bed, gently but firmly. He began kissing me, his hair rubbing my face. I grabbed his hair, a glorious tangle of wavy blond, and played with it. He began biting my neck and moving his hands down. He sat up and took off his shirt, and as I often did, I gazed at the sun tattoo on his chest and was reminded of the time he'd spent alone in a jail cell. He was physically everything I was attracted to in a man. I checked off all the attributes in my mind as he began to touch and fondle me under my T-shirt.

"Take your clothes off," he said.

"You first."

He stood up and pulled down his jeans and then his briefs. He reached over to switch off the lamp on the dresser.

"No, leave it on."

"Okay tiger," he said, with a chuckle.

He lay back down on the bed and watched me as I got undressed. *Oh, God I'm in for it tonight.*

~~~~~~~~

My friend Star Green showed up on Maui for Halloween. She enjoyed visiting during that time of the year. We had a big night planned. We were going to dress up and cruise Front Street to see all the costumes. Then we'd work our way through the crowded side streets to the Missionaries Hotel. It was a bit of a sticky situation because I knew Dominick French would be the entertainment in the Mission Bar. There had been issues with Derick in the past, so I was a little reluctant at first, but Star said it wouldn't be the same if we didn't go there. I knew she was right. Everyone who was anyone would be there. Derick had put up with Demo's occasional three o'clock in the morning phone calls, so I figured we were past the jealousy thing.

I helped Star paint her face white and made up her eyes per her instructions. She put on a white clown outfit to mimic Marcel Marceau. *A mime, that's perfect for her,* I thought. Derick sat patiently still at the kitchen table while I painted a blue mask around his eyes and tapped glitter around the edges with my pinky finger. He looked like the Lone Ranger when I was done. I decided to dress as a 1920s flapper. Star helped me put my hair up in a fake diamond tiara with feathers. I wore a flimsy dress and slung long, jet-black beads around my neck. All that was missing was a cigarette holder. We did shots of tequila before we left Nanu Street, and were ready for a crazy night in town.

The best costume I remember that year was an Asian woman with a slinky, tightfitting mandarin dress wearing high-heel pumps. She carried about seven shoeboxes tied to each arm. "Imelda Marcos!" I yelled out. We tried to get into a few of the bars on Front Street, but they were all packed, so we forged our way a few blocks up a side street to the Missionaries Hotel.

The place was packed as we walked through the lobby to the Mission Bar in the back. We were lucky enough to see a group get up to leave. We rushed over and took their table.

Derick ordered us drinks and whispered in my ear, "You look really hot." Then I heard Star laughing. "Oh my God, look at Annie."

I turned toward the piano, and Annie was standing at the microphone dressed like one of those fortune tellers in a glass ticket booth at the entrance to a wax museum. You know, the kind that you flip a coin in the slot and she slips you a card with your prediction. She had a gypsy scarf tied around her head, large, clunky, gold earrings, and her ruffled dress was a riot. She waited for Demo's intro and began singing the old Sophie Tucker song, "Some of These Days." The crowd went wild. We laughed like hell and clapped profusely when the song was finished.

Dominick French caught sight of me and winked from the piano. I wasn't sure if Derick noticed, but I nodded back. There would always be a string of warmth and attachment between us. I knew it, Demo knew it, and I'm sure Derick knew it. It crossed my mind that it was yet another justification for us to move to Florida. Even when you're not in love with someone anymore, a thread of emotion remains, as do the memories. Luckily, as time goes by, all we remember are the good times. The tears and pain fade, or else how could life possibly go on?

I noticed Derick downing drinks like they were water, and it worried me. Not just because I loathed a sloppy drunk, but because I felt something else brewing.

Star, Regina, and I went outside to take photographs on the street in front of the hotel with our friends. I left Derick sitting at the table with Dante.

When we returned to the table, Derick grabbed me and sat me down hard on the chair. He leaned over and made a spectacle of kissing me long and hard on the mouth, then turned and stared at Demo, as if to say, "She's mine now, so don't even try anything stupid."

Demo, in turn, sang that old song "Don't Blame Me" (for falling in love with you …) while staring at me. Oh, God, there was going to be an ugly scene. I could feel it.

Derick squirmed in his chair.

"Honey, stop, It's just a song," I said.

"I don't like the way he's looking at you," Derick said with slurred speech.

I tried to signal Demo to cut it out, but he kept it up with yet another old love song.

Derick stood up and his chair fell back. I tugged at his pants to get him to sit down.

"Stop it, or else we're leaving," I said. "Derick, don't ruin the night over a silly song."

Dante put Derick's chair upright just in time for Derick to slump back down in it. I felt the flush of embarrassment sweep over my face. Dominick French got his way, a kind of cruel revenge. He upset Derick and pissed me off. Why would he torture me like that, singing all those love songs he always sang to me when we were lovers? I wondered if I still had love for him. Demo always told me that gin changes the personality, and that night gin was certainly twisting my brain. Was Derick my true love, or a love on the rebound? In my inebriated state, I wasn't sure. Why the hell was I questioning myself?

To make things worse, Star whispered in my ear, "Demo still loves you. I can tell by the way he looks at you."

Luckily, Dante hadn't been drinking and drove us all home. Derick was totally trashed. I put his arm around my shoulder and walked him through the front door. He began to ramble about shit, and I wasn't liking it. Some people are happy and fun drunks, but Derick was a sloppy drunk who acted dumb and could get belligerent. I walked him to our bedroom and closed the door.

"Lie down on the bed," I said.

"I know you wanna fuck me," Derick said.

"Hardly," I mumbled under my breath. "Let me get your shirt off."

"Then we're gonna do it, right?"

"Not when you're like this," I said with an annoyed expression.

"What, are you my mother now?" he said angrily.

"I'm not even going to answer you."

"Yeah that's real nice, don't talk to me. But if Demo called, you'd talk to him."

"Forget about Demo. You let him get under your skin every time."

"I should a whipped that fucking guy's ass a long time ago," Derick said.

"Best thing for you is to sleep it off before we get into a fight."

"Okay, okay, okay, I'll be quiet," he said.

No sooner than he said that, he seemed to wander off into Never-Never Land. I was lucky he wasn't the violent type, but he was a big guy, and that threat was always there. I waited until he passed out on the bed to lie next to him. Suddenly I jumped up and took the phone off the hook. All I needed was a three o'clock phone call from Dominick French to finish the night off.

Derick began to snore, and the fumes from the alcohol permeated the bed. I was angry that these two men succeeded in ruining Halloween. I, on the other hand, sobered up immediately. It took me a long time to fall asleep with crazy thoughts marching through my skull.

~~~~~~

I found myself alone when I woke up the next morning, wondering where Derick was. Fear crept into my mind, remembering the last time this happened and he walked out on me. I got out of bed, put on my robe, and walked along the hallway to the kitchen. I found Derick sitting at the table smoking a Salem, looking very glum.

At least he'd had the sense to wash the painted blue mask off his face.

"Did you make coffee?" I asked.

"No, but I will if you want me to. I've only been up about ten minutes."

"I'll make the coffee," I said, walking over to the coffee maker on the counter.

"Sorry about last night," Derick said.

"We need to talk about it. You got sloppy drunk and embarrassed me."

"I wasn't that bad, was I? I really don't remember much about last night."

"You got belligerent and acted like an ass at the Mission Bar in front of all of our friends."

"It was Halloween, I had a lot to drink. Shit happens," Derick said in a cavalier tone.

"You've had drinks before, but you never acted like that."

"I said I was sorry. What more do you want me to say?"

I poured a cup of coffee and sat across from him. "I really don't know."

"I was having a good time, just got a little carried away."

"Derick, you don't get it. If you want to be a jerk when you're out with the guys, okay, but dragging me into a Hunter S. Thompson scene isn't my idea of a fun night out on the town."

"How many times do I have to say I'm sorry?" Derick said, abruptly getting up from the table. He grabbed Rebel's leash and said to the dog, "Come on, we're going for a walk."

He slammed the door on his way out. I sat there with my coffee, wondering if I'd been too hard on him. Maybe he was right and I was acting more like his mother than his girlfriend. Was this a taste of things to come? Is this what marriage would be like? Fighting over stupid things? I could only wonder. I couldn't even finish my coffee. I set the cup in the sink and went back to bed.

I fell into a sound sleep. I guess I needed it after the sleepless night I'd just had. I felt someone's presence and it woke me.

Derick was sitting on the corner of the bed, silently watching me. He seemed so peaceful. It gave me a warm, contented feeling to see him back to normal. I held out my hand, and Derick kissed it while staring at me.

"Adriana, I don't want us to be angry with each other."

I sat up and covered myself with the sheet. "Come to bed, Derick."

He took his clothes off and got in bed with me. I put my arms around him and we hugged.

"Let's just hang out here today," I said.

"You feel so right next to me," he said, hugging me even tighter.

He planted a soft, affectionate kiss on my cheek, and we fell back to sleep.

~~~~~~~

Star and I went to Kaanapali Beach and had lunch in one of the hotel cafes. I enjoyed playing tourist once in a while. I told her about our plans to move to Florida.

"Where will you live?"

"I don't know, I guess stay with Ross and Laura for a while. They have a huge apartment."

"Remember how Ross can be at times," she said.

"It will only be temporary. Until we find a place."

"Still, he can be a tough pill to swallow."

"Oh, I know how Ross can be, but he wants to fund me and Laura in a clothing business."

"Well that sounds good, but there will eventually be a price."

"With the Crafty Mermaid closing, I'll be able to collect unemployment for a while."

"At least you have Derick, and he seems to care for you a great deal."

"Yes, I have Derick, and it seems as if events on Maui are pointing us toward Florida."

"You can always come back to Maui if things don't pan out."

I stared at the purple orchid floating on the surface of my chi chi cocktail and took another sip.

Star's words hit home at exactly what I was wondering, what the price would be, because everything in life has a price. Derick didn't see any downside, like the eternal optimist he was. I contemplated the possible downside—well, I was a pessimist. My mind flew back to that awful move to California I made with Romeo in 1970. I didn't want to leave the commune, but I didn't want to lose him. I remembered how everything went to hell in a handbasket, and I ended up leaving Romeo and moving back to the commune in New York. Star had been on that trip with me. I certainly didn't want to repeat that disaster. Star was leaving the next day. I was sad to see her go, but we always managed to keep in touch. I could always count on her for honest, but sometimes brutal, feedback.

~~~~~~

The Crafty Mermaid was closing its doors. I worked the last few days and it was a very sad time. It was the center of my universe from the first week I moved to the island. I'd become close friends with the owners, especially Haku Neilson. They both had husbands to fall back on, whereas I was just at the beginning stages with Derick.

Ross Grant called us and told us to just bite the bullet and come to Florida. He reminded me of how spacious his apartment was, and that we could stay with him until we found an apartment. He wired us a few thousand dollars to tide us over, and I promised I'd pay him back. What the interest or ultimate price would be was anybody's guess. A big move like this could easily turn into a pile of shit if things didn't work out as expected. On the other hand, I had a solid partner now in Derick.

I consulted the I Ching again for its wisdom and direction. I took out the three Chinese coins and tossed them six times.

The *I Ching* Hexagram #52, Keeping Still, The Mountain:

The Judgement: The problem of achieving a quiet heart.
    Things cannot move continuously. One must make them stop.

Do not miss the right time as their course becomes bright and clear.
The Image: The superior man does not permit his thoughts to go beyond his situation.
The heart thinks constantly. This cannot be changed, but the movements of the heart should restrict themselves to the immediate situation.
Thinking beyond this point makes the heart sore.

I put the book back in my underwear drawer. The trigram hinted that I needed to heed the changes that were happening around me, and not to dismiss opportunities offered. It hinted that thinking too far into the future was a waste of time and emotion because it was an unknown. This is what I got out of my reading. It may have been how I interpreted the hexagram, but it was meant to draw deep thoughts and desires out of your subconscious. As a result, I felt confident and positive about making the move.

When Derick came home from work that day, I told him of my thoughts and feelings, but not about the *I Ching*. He always thought I was too dependent on what the book had to say. He knew I had been a hippie and lived on a commune, so he chalked it up to a leftover ethereal superstition. We discussed all the things that were necessary to get done before leaving. First thing was to speak to Dante and Regina. They would have to find someone to share the rent. We needed to pick a time frame. One month seemed doable. We wanted to be on the mainland for Thanksgiving, when Ross and Laura were having a big dinner and expecting us to be there. It was uncanny, because when we spoke to Regina later that evening, she told us that she and Dante were planning to move back to New Jersey. At the time, I saw it as another sign that we were on the right path.

～～～～～

I spent our last month on the island running around like a chicken without a head. I went to the unemployment office to file a claim. I figured when I got settled in Florida, I would put in for a transfer, saying I found more opportunities for my line of work in Miami. I spoke to the owners of the two stores in Lahaina that were selling my hand-painted T-shirts. I assured them that I would mail a box of T-shirts to them every month. Derick put his truck and my red Toyota up for sale. We had a garage sale on Nanu Street to get rid of furniture and all the things we couldn't take with us. I packed a box of kitchen and bathroom necessities, which was coming on the plane with us as extra baggage, along with the television. I didn't want to have to make any large purchases as soon as we found a place. I found a boarding kennel in Miami for Rebel, since Ross said there were no pets allowed in his building. I was so busy that I didn't have time to worry or feel anything but anticipation. I made lists and checked items off like a robot.

Derick's boss and coworkers at the management company were sad to see him go. They had a little get-together for us one weekend. It gave us a chance to say goodbye and reminisce about all the crazy camping trips we went on together.

Then I had to say goodbye to Annie. I left that for last because it would be the most difficult. We met at the Yacht Club for drinks. We talked about all of our crazy antics and all of the fun we'd had over the years.

She turned and said, "Riana, I'm going to miss you so much. I feel like my daughter is leaving, and I don't know if I'll ever see her again."

I began to cry. Annie put her arms around me, and I saw that she was crying too.

"You've been my best friend. How can I ever forget any of this? I will come back for visits, I'm sure of that. And you can visit us in Florida anytime," I said.

"We were partners in crime," she said, laughing through her tears.

"Remember the monkey bar in Honolulu with Chip Newton?" I blubbered.

"God we had fun," Annie said. "Now you're going to a new life with someone who loves you."

"Yes, and that is making this all palatable."

"Never turn your back on love or look a gift horse in the mouth. These are things the universe offers us, but it's up to us to accept them."

I never remembered Annie talking about the universe, but the thought crossed my mind that perhaps the universe was sending me a message through her.

"The Dalai Lama says, 'Love is the absence of judgement,'" I said.

"What's our connection, Riana? I felt it the first day you walked into the pawn shop where I worked. We share something special and I will treasure it always."

"I love you, Annie. You are the hardest one to leave."

"Now, if the Dalai Lama turns out to be right, and things don't work out, if Derick turns out to be a bastard like my husband, Tony, you remember, you always have a place here with me."

Annie and I hugged and kissed again. I left her sitting on a barstool and walked out through the swinging doors of the Yacht Club for what I figured was the last time. I said, "Aloha oe" (Farewell to thee) under my breath. My heart was in pieces, scattered all over the sidewalk on Front Street. I walked along the seawall and breathed in the salty air.

I thought, *Oh, God, I'm going to miss this place.* I cried some more as tourists walked past me, wondering what the hell was wrong with me. I thought of all the times I slept on Annie's floor drunk out of my mind. I thought of that tiny studio I rented in the hood. It was the first time I lived by myself. The sound of the screen door slamming shut on the porch of Dominick French's house. I felt as if I was leaving the place that rekindled my lust for life, and where I went through a rebirth in my art. At that moment, life seemed so complicated. Then I remembered meeting Derick in the Quonset hut at the cannery, the way he looked at me, and how I decided I wanted him to work on me, not just on my car. I began to laugh and thought of how wonderful my life was, and how lucky I'd been.

~~~~~

Our last days on Maui were filled with goodbyes to friends and cleaning up the house on Nanu Street. We ate as many apple bananas off that stalk in the yard as we could. We took the dogs to the beach and went swimming in the waves. Dante and Regina were staying until the last day of November. Derick and I had plane tickets to leave a few days before Thanksgiving. Derick made sure I felt secure, and would often hug me for no reason at all. I'd found someone wonderful.

On the day before we were to leave, I decided to take a walk by myself along the beach, where my Maui journey began. Our cars were sold, so I hitched a ride to Kaanapali Beach, just like I did when I first arrived on the island. It was very early in the morning and the beach was deserted. I took off my shoes and shuffled along the sand, feeling its tiny cool granules caress my feet. Maui had become my home. I gazed out over the ocean to the neighboring islands of Lanai and Molokai with longing. I wished we were just going to another island, not all the way to the mainland. I didn't want to leave Maui, but I'd made a serious life decision and was praying it was the right one. I was following my heart. All sorts of beautiful images of my Maui life ran across my mind, and suddenly I felt warm tears. *God how I love this place,* I thought.

I dried my eyes with the edge of my T-shirt and kept walking. As the sun rose higher in the sky, my mind went to a positive place, knowing I was going on an exciting journey. There would be two sets of footprints in the sand going forward. If things didn't turn out the way we anticipated, we could always return.

The plane took off from Kahului Airport in the late fall of 1981. We could hear Rebel barking in the baggage compartment below, and Derick and I chuckled. I remember looking at an inflight magazine because I couldn't bear the thought of watching Maui slip away under me.

When the plane disappeared in the clouds I was relieved. I lay my head on Derick's shoulder and closed my eyes. He took my hand and rubbed it gently. I felt some turbulence, held on to his arm, and immediately calmed down. Soon I fell into a pleasant sleep.

~~~~~~~

I could faintly hear the stewardess talking, which woke me. Derick was asleep beside me with his head resting against the tiny oval window. I was glad the shutter was open so I could get a glimpse of Florida from the air. I leaned over and woke him. We both peered out the window. All we could see was glistening aqua water, endless white beaches, and palm trees. We turned and smiled at each other filled with anticipation.

Ross Grant was waiting for us alone at baggage claim. Rebel was being held at the animal quarantine station in the Miami International Airport. I told Derick and Ross to get all our bags, boxes, and the television, and I'd fetch Rebel. Soon we were in Ross's car dropping Rebel off at the dog kennel.

"We'll be picking you up real soon," I said to the dog, who looked confused.

On the way to Ross's condo, the three of us sat in the front seat, Derick with his arm around my shoulder. I was between my sweetheart and my good friend. I looked out the window, and Miami was sunny and bright, with an endless expanse of water glistening on the horizon. The Tom Petty song "A Woman in Love" played on the radio. Before long I was singing along with the lyrics, filled with joy, happiness, and excitement about our future. We sped down I-95 into a new life, and I was carrying the "Aloha spirit" within me.

Printed in the United States
by Baker & Taylor Publisher Services